'Frida Stewart wrote toward the end of her life:

"The most significant moment in my life was the day the ambulance took me across the border into Spain."

Angela Jackson helps us understand why this was so. She has written a fine and valuable study that helps us gain a new understanding of what Spain meant in the lives of a generation of British women.'

Professor James K. Hopkins

'Impeccably researched and exquisitely written.'

'Sensitive and intelligent interpretation.'

'While never simplifying, Dr Jackson always remains accessible to the general reader.'

Professor Helen Graham

'Very readable and engaging.'

'Full of original insights.'

'Powerfully reveals the interaction between individual women, society and culture.'

Professor Penny Summerfield

'Beautifully illustrated.'

'A marvellous resource for future scholars.'

'Extremely moving and drives home the absolute centrality that Spain played in the lives of these women.'

Dr Tom Buchanan

British Women
and the
Spanish Civil War

British Women
and the
Spanish Civil War

Angela Jackson

The Clapton Press

First published in 2002 by Routledge in collaboration with the
Cañada Blanch Centre for Contemporary Spanish Studies.

Third edition published in 2020 by
The Clapton Press Ltd., 38 Thistlewaite Road, London, E5.

ISBN 978-1-913693-01-5

A CIP catalogue record for this book is
available from the British Library.

Design and artwork by Bernard Chandler,
Glastonbury, England. www.graffik.co.uk
Text set in ITC Cheltenham with Gill Sans titling.

Front cover photograph:
Leah Manning and Nan Green in Spain, 1938.

DEDICATION

For inspiration:
Frida and Patience and the many women
on which this study was founded.

For guidance:
Professor Geoffrey Crossick, unfailing in his
encouragement during the writing of this book.

For information:
The enthusiastic historians, librarians and
archivists who helped me in my research.

For support:
The friends who maintained a lively interest
in my work over so many years.

For faith and forbearance:
My husband and children who made it possible
for me to complete this task.

ANGELA JACKSON

BIOGRAPHICAL NOTE

ANGELA JACKSON's research for her doctoral thesis included many interviews with women who had been involved with the civil war in Spain. These formed the basis for *British Women and the Spanish Civil War* and for a novel, *Warm Earth*, which fictionalises some of the women she met and their true stories.

In 2001, after moving to the Priorat in Catalonia where she lived for fifteen years, Angela became a founder member and President of *No Jubilem la Memòria*, an association for the recovery of events and memories of the civil war in the region. Further books followed, exploring the interactions between local villagers and the International Brigaders who were stationed in the area for many weeks before the Battle of the Ebro.

The letters between civil war nurse Patience Darton and the International Brigader Robert Aaquist inspired Angela to write a full and moving biography of Patience entitled *'For us it was Heaven'*. More recently, with the publication of the memoirs of Frida Stewart who drove an ambulance to Spain during the civil war, Angela has at last been able to fulfil a project she shared with Frida in the months before her death in 1996. *Firing a Shot for Freedom* was written by Frida in the 1940s but includes an Afterword in which Angela explores the following fifty years of campaigning for causes and gives insights into her indomitable character.

Contents

LIST OF ILLUSTRATIONS

ACKNOWLEDGEMENTS

Valentine Ackland - poem *Instructions from England 1936*, Carcanet Press, Manchester.

Felicity Ashbee - 5.6 courtesy of Felicity Ashbee.

The Duchess of Atholl - 6.3 Marx Memorial Library, London.

Celia Baker - 2.12 courtesy of Hilary Baker.

Winifred Bates and Lillian Urmston - 4.9 Imperial War Museum, London.

Cora Blyth *(m. Portillo)* - 6.4 courtesy of Cora Blyth de Portillo.

Elsie Booth - 3.8 courtesy of Dianne Bradford.

Isabel Brown - 3.1 courtesy of May Hill.

Cave Hospital - 4.3 Imperial War Museum, London.

Cave of Santa Lucía - 7.1 courtesy of Francesc Masip.

Elizabeth Crump *(m. Thornycroft)* - 2.11 courtesy of Elizabeth Thornycroft.

Patience Darton *(m. Edney)* - 1.2 News International Syndication; 2.1 courtesy of Patience Edney; 6.7, Nigel Tanburn.

Florence Farmborough - 2.10 & 5.5 courtesy of Fiona Howell Williams.

Helen Grant - 4.10, Mistress and Fellows, Girton College, Cambridge.

Nan Green - 2.4 & 2.5 courtesy of Martin Green.

Phyllis Gwatkin Williams, 'The Blonde Amazon' - 5.2 Corbis Images, London.

Charlotte Haldane - 3.6 Imperial War Museum, London.

Margot Heinemann - 2.6 & 6.10; poems *Grieve in a New Way for New Losses* and *Ringstead Mill* courtesy of Jane Bernal.

Hospital Train - 4.2 Marx Memorial Library, London.

Rose Kerrigan - 3.7 courtesy of Jean Kerrigan.

Micky Lewis - 2.3 courtesy of Micky Lewis.

Kate Mangan - 4.10 courtesy of Charlotte Kurzke.

Leah Manning - 4.7 Marx Memorial Library, London.

Elsie Marshall - poem *The Ballad to Bert Fletcher* courtesy of Elsie Marshall.

Molly Murphy - 4.4 National Museum of Labour History, Manchester.

Penny Phelps *(m. Feiwel)* - 2.2 & 4.5 courtesy of Penny Feiwel.

Posters of a *miliciana* in Barcelona - 1.4 Hulton Archive, London.

Margaret Powell *(m. Lesser)* - 4.8, 6.5 & 6.8 courtesy of Sam Lesser.

Eleanor Rathbone - 2.13 Women's Library, London.

Priscilla Scott-Ellis - 4.6 courtesy of Carmen Foster.

Thora Silverthorne *(m. Craig)* - 4.1 courtesy of Nares Craig.

Frida Stewart *(m. Knight)* - 3.4, 3.5, 6.1 & 6.2 courtesy of Frida Knight; 1.1, 2.7: courtesy of Frances Knight.

Priscilla Thornycroft *(m. Siebert)* - 5.7 & 5.9 courtesy of Priscilla Siebert.
Sylvia Townsend Warner - 5.4 Sylvia Townsend Warner and Valentine
   Ackland Collection, Dorset County Museum, Dorchester;
   poem *Benicasim*, Carcanet Press, Manchester.
Ellen Wilkinson - 2.8 Topham Picturepoint, Edenbridge, Kent.

The author and publisher have made every effort to find copyright holders.
If you have further information regarding the copyright of material used
in this book, please contact the publisher.

ABBREVIATIONS

AIA	Artists International Association
BCC	Basque Children's Committee
BUF	British Union of Fascists
CNT-FAI	Confederación Nacional de Trabajo – Federación Anarquista Ibérica
CPGB	Communist Party of Great Britain
IBA	International Brigade Association
ILP	Independent Labour Party
LBC	Left Book Club
LCC	London County Council
NJC	National Joint Committee for Spanish Relief
POUM	Partido Obrero de Unificación Marxista
SMAC	Spanish Medical Aid Committee
TUC	Trades Union Congress
WILPF	Women's International League for Peace and Freedom
WSPU	Women's Social and Political Union
WWCAWF	Women's World Committee Against War and Fascism
YCL	Young Communist League

Author's Preface
to the 2020 Edition

ONE DAY IN 1994 I unknowingly stepped onto a path of research that was to last years. In a basement sitting room, Patience Edney, her chair close to the warmth of the Rayburn, began to tell me of her experiences as a nurse during the Spanish civil war. At the end of the day I took with me not only a video recording of the lengthy interview but also, ringing in my head, her vivid descriptions of events in the front-line hospitals. A few days later I visited Frida Knight to record the first of several interviews in which she told me about her journey to Spain driving an ambulance and the time she spent working in Murcia and Madrid. In her Cambridge house I drew back the heavy curtains - woven in the workshops of William Morris - to let in enough light to film this tiny, frail-looking woman, surrounded by overflowing bookcases and huge antique furniture. As her story unfolded, I became increasingly aware of the fact that physical stature certainly does not reflect the size of the spirit within. The stories of these two women, the first of many I interviewed on the subject of the civil war, were amongst those that had never reached a wider audience. Attempting to remedy this situation brought me into contact with many unforgettable characters, leading me to Spain and eventually to live in Catalonia, from 2001 to 2015, not far from the mountains where the Battle of the Ebro was fought.

Many changes have taken place relating to the remembrance of the civil war since *British Women and the Spanish Civil War* was first published in 2002. In Spain, the process of 'recovering the memory' of those years gained momentum.[1] I took part in this historical

---

1 See 'Afterword: Remembrance and the Reconstruction of History' in Angela Jackson, *Beyond the Battlefield: Testimony, Memory and Remembrance of a Cave Hospital in the Spanish Civil War*, (Warren & Pell Publishing, Pontypool, UK, 2005).

renaissance at grass-roots level through working with a local group, *No Jubilem La Memòria*.[2] After many years of silence under Franco's dictatorship, those who lost their lives fighting for the Republic were being given public recognition in a proliferation of plaques and memorials. In some cases, the remains of those who died as a result of Franco's policies of repression were disinterred from communal graves and identified through DNA testing. Heated historical debates surrounding the war were evident in the massive numbers of published books, newspaper articles and documentaries on the subject. Research at local level was thriving. Though there were few still alive who had lived through the war, their grandchildren and great-grandchildren continued to seek answers to the many questions that remained unanswered about their forebears.

In Britain too, there were differences in the approach taken towards remembrance of the role of the International Brigades.[3] 'The International Brigade Association', whose members were all veterans of the war, was replaced by 'The International Brigade Memorial Trust'. In this new group, membership was extended to include the veterans' families and friends, together with historians, students and others who share an interest in increasing the awareness of the Brigaders' involvement in the war.[4] New publications on different aspects of the conflict have added to the already extensive bibliography on the subject and other unpublished texts have come to light.[5]

The arguments put forward in the first edition of *British Women and the Spanish Civil War* reflected my determination to focus not only on the women who shared an interest in party-politics equal to that of men, but also to give weight to the testimonies of the many women who were not *actively* involved in factional party-political struggles. The extent of their involvement remains an issue for debate.[6] At times there has been a failure to recognise the defining difference between those who had a positive commitment to a particular political party and the many others who were caught in the crossfire between

---

2   See www.nojubilemlamemoria.cat
3   Volunteers from over fifty countries joined the International Brigades to fight in Spain, supporting the legally elected Republican government against right-wing rebels led by General Francisco Franco.
4   See www.international-brigades.org.uk
5   For example, Nicholas Coni, *Medicine and Warfare: Spain, 1936-39*, (Routledge/Cañada Blanch Studies on Contemporary Spain, London 2008), and other books mentioned below.
6   See Tom Buchanan, 'The Masked Advance: Politics, intrigue and British medical aid for the Spanish Republic in *The Impact of the Spanish Civil War on Britain: War, Loss and Memory* (Sussex Academic Press, Brighton & Portland, 2007).

warring factions. The women whose writings on the civil war first entered the public domain were more likely to have been members of political parties. However, there were numerous others whose voices were not heard for years, not until the advent of oral history projects and the beginnings of research into the wider impact of the war. This latter group brought a very different perspective to the subject, making it necessary to redress the balance between those who had left written testimonies and those whose voices had remained for so long in obscurity. The interviews I carried out, together with the dozens that had been recorded by other historians, led to the conclusion that for a high proportion of women, party politics played only a minimal role in the perception of the key issues surrounding the war in Spain. An analysis of the defining differences between 'the political' in general terms, and 'party politics' became essential to the understanding of women's attitudes.[7] New material that has come to light since this book was first published has supported, rather than undermined, these original conclusions.[8]

The existence of such a varied depth and range of political commitment is part of the richness offered to the historian of the Spanish civil war. Through drawing on the experiences of women, a greater degree of balance can be achieved in the understanding of what war really means. It is certainly not just a matter of men 'going off' to fight. In the case of the Spanish civil war, many British women were involved in different ways as a result of personal choice. However, amongst the families of the volunteers, there were some who were unwillingly affected. In his 1987 article 'Say Nothing and Leave in the Middle of the Night', Hywel Francis wrote of the need to study war starting from the premise that 'there is nothing *manly* about such human dramas'. He warns against reducing our history to a 'series of glorious episodes which have little to do with the past' by omitting not only 'the men's so-called less manly or *macho* responses' but also the personal and family traumas, emotions and sacrifices.[9]

There is still much research to be done about the ways in which the war affected ordinary people, especially in Spain itself. The writing of this book led me to further research in Catalonia and the publication

---

7 See Chapters 2 & 7.
8 See for example additional material on Mary Bingham de Urquidi, Eileen Blair and Kate Mangan.
9 Hywel Francis, 'Say Nothing and Leave in the Middle of the Night': The Spanish Civil War Revisited', *History Workshop Journal,* 1991; 32: 69-76.

of two further history books that explore the different perspectives of soldiers and civilians; the men, women and children who lived through the war without achieving fame as soldiers or politicians.[10] The remarkable people I met during the course of this research have also been the inspiration for a novel, *Warm Earth*, and a full-length biography of Patience Darton, *'For us it was Heaven'*.[11]

British Women and the Spanish Civil War was written with the aim of contributing to the overall understanding of the war. Women's histories are at the heart of this book and the women themselves are its heart, frequently bringing with them a strongly practical, rather than a primarily idealistic, perspective.

Angela Jackson
2020

---

10 *Beyond the Battlefield: Testimony, Memory and Remembrance of a Cave Hospital in the Spanish Civil War* and *At the Margins of Mayhem: Prologue and Epilogue to the Last Great Battle of the Spanish Civil War* have been published by Warren & Pell Publishing, Pontypool, UK, in 2005 and 2007 respectively, and in Catalan as *Més allà del camp de batalla: Testimoni, memòria i record d'una cova hospital en la Guerra Civil espanyola* and *Els brigadistes entre nosaltres: Pròleg i epíleg a l'última gran batalla de la Guerra Civil espanyola* by Cossetània Edicions, Valls, in 2004 and 2008 respectively.

11 *Warm Earth*, (Pegasus Elliot Mackenzie Publishers, Cambridge, 2007). *'For us it was Heaven': The Passion Grief and Fortitude of Patience Darton from the Spanish Civil War to Mao's China* (Sussex Academic Press, Brighton/Cañada Blanch Centre for Contemporary Spanish Studies, London, 2012). Published in Spanish as *Para nosotros era el cielo. Pasión, dolor y fortaleza de Patience Darton: de la guerra civil española a la China de Mao* (Ediciones San Juan de Dios, Barcelona, 2012).

CHAPTER ONE

Introduction

THE CROWD ROARED. We stood at the top of a long steep ramp leading down into the stadium. Eager hands grasped the wheelchairs of some of the International Brigaders to guide their descent into the arena. We had entered through dim passages like footballers arriving for a cup final, but not one of the Brigaders could have been prepared for the warmth of the reception when they emerged into the light of the Sports Palace in Madrid, where a concert had been prepared in their honour. We were in Spain for the week of events commemorating the sixtieth anniversary of the Spanish Civil War. Already the occasion was touched with sadness for me because I had hoped to be there with the woman who had been the initial inspiration for this research, Frida Stewart.[1] She had wanted to return because the Spanish war had been of crucial significance in her life, a catalyst for her political beliefs. She had died a month before, and I had been asked to scatter some of her ashes on Spanish soil.

For Patience Darton who had been a nurse in the Brigades during the war, this first return to Spain since 1938 represented even more than the reprise of an early formative experience. The man she loved, a German International Brigader, had been killed in the battle of the Ebro. She had only recently begun to speak of this, and on the night of the concert, hearing the songs she had learned so long ago and being cheered so fervently by the people of Madrid, she was glad she had gone back. The next day and night I was with Patience and her son in the city hospital, holding her hand as she slipped deeper into uncon-

---

1 To maintain consistency, the women in this study are usually referred to by the surnames they had at the time of the war. In the profiles and where necessary in the notes, subsequent married names or previous surnames are also given, for example, Frida Stewart (m. Knight) or Patience Edney (née Darton).

sciousness and finally death. I had gone to Spain to understand the significance of this historic return but also discovered that the weight of symbolism can rest heavily on the heart. The grief felt by those who had known her was not diminished by a recognition of the allegorical implications of her death, a shared awareness of subtext that was also reflected in the language of newspaper reports on her death, *Morir en Madrid*, 'To Die in Madrid', the title of one of the most famous documentaries made on the Spanish war and now a headline for her obituary. Sixty years before, the Brigaders had been prepared to die for a cause in which they believed and now the circle was closed by their return to accept the tribute offered in gratitude by the Spanish people, and by the presence of death once again.

1.1 Frida Stewart in her later years.

This study attempts to understand why this Spanish war became such an important part of the life experiences of so many British women, not only for those who went to Spain, but also for the thousands of women in Britain who became actively involved with the war in a variety of ways.[2] Why had they been so concerned about a conflict in a foreign country? What active forms had their concerns

---

2   This research only includes women from Britain, not those from elsewhere in the British Empire. Studies on women from Australia for example, include a book by Judith Keene based on the diaries of Agnes Hodgson, *Last Mile to Huesca: An Australian Nurse in the Spanish Civil War* (New South Wales University Press, 1988).

1.2 The photograph of Patience Darton used by *El Periódico*,
9 November 1996, in 'Morir en Madrid: La enfermera más querida
del batallón británico fallece en su regreso a España.'

taken, and how had their lives been coloured by this particular memory of the past?[3]

The numerous books written on the Spanish Civil War have covered aspects such as the peculiarly Spanish nature of the causes of the war, the political, military and social history of the war itself, and the international implications of the conflict.[4] The war began in July 1936 as a result of a failed uprising of the right against the Republican Government, a 'Popular Front' coalition, elected earlier in the year.[5] The rising was initially defeated by the people in many of the major cities, including Madrid and Barcelona, but when General Franco succeeded in bringing the Army of Africa across the Straits of Gibraltar

---

3 The intention of this study was not to examine the attitude of British women in general to the Spanish war by including a representative sample from the public at large. The research focus is on women and the issues that are related to involvement, not to its absence.

4 Examples can be found in the bibliography, and in a bibliographical essay by Paul Preston in *A Concise History of the Spanish Civil War* (Fontana Press, London,1996) pp. 229-245. In particular, two earlier studies should not be overlooked, Gerald Brenan, *The Spanish Labyrinth* (Cambridge University Press, 1990, first published 1943) and an oral history, Ronald Fraser, *Blood of Spain: The Experience of Civil War 1936-1939* (Penguin, Harmondsworth, England, 1981, first published by Allen Lane, 1979).

5 The Second Republic had been established in 1931. The programme of reforms begun in the first two years was halted when the right won the elections of 1933. The victory of the left-wing coalition in February 1936, although narrow in terms of votes, resulted in a substantial majority of seats in the Cortes.

into Spain, the failing coup was converted into a war of attrition which lasted until the end of March, 1939.

Brief mention should be made here of some aspects of the conflict that are particularly relevant to this study. Before the Second Republic had been established in 1931, a reactionary climate had prevailed in Spain. The far-reaching reform programme that was then begun was much too radical for some, but too moderate for those impatient for change. One such area of reform related to the role of women in society. The aim of the Government to educate women, albeit perhaps in order to ensure that they would pass on Republican values to their children, was fiercely opposed by those who were committed to a more typically fascist traditional ideal of woman as the 'angel of the hearth', subservient to fathers, husbands and brothers.[6]

1.3 *Miliciana* posters in Barcelona.

---

6   See Helen Graham, 'The Failure of Democratic Modernity 1931-39', *Spanish Cultural Studies Reader: The Struggle for Modernity* (Oxford University Press, 1995).

1.4 *Miliciana* in Madrid.

During the first few months of the war, these fundamental differences of attitude were reflected in the contrast between the symbolic
ideological representations of women. Whilst Franco resisted the
forces of 'anti-Spain' with the preserved arm of St. Teresa of Ávila by
his side, and with a wealth of religious iconography of the Virgin and
female saints, the struggle of the people in the Republic to resist fascism
was embodied in the images of women and girls with guns, fighting
beside the men.[7] This spontaneous participation of women during the
first few days helped to prevent the immediate success of the military
rising. In some areas, they subsequently joined the men at the front
as the battle lines were drawn. For this short period, when diverse
militia groups formed the main focus for organised resistance

---

7   For more on the female iconography of the war see Frances Lannon, 'Women and Images
    of Women in the Spanish Civil War' *Transactions of the Royal Historical Society* 1991 pp.
    213-228, and Caroline Brothers, *War and Photography: A Cultural History* (Routledge,
    London, 1997) pp. 76-98. Photographs and posters depicting *milicianas* can be found in
    Las mujeres en la guerra civil a book produced by the Ministerio de Cultura in conjunction
    with an exhibition of that name in Salamanca in 1989.

against the insurgent troops, the *miliciana* became an icon of the fight against fascism. The challenge that the image of these few women represented to the traditional gender stereotype could not have been greater. Often dressed in *monos*, all-in-one workmen's overalls, and shouldering weapons, they appeared in press photographs and on posters, leading men to battle. By September however, the slogans had changed to 'Men to the War Fronts, Women to the Homefront'.[8] Their previously welcomed military efforts were now denigrated, and although some *milicianas* objected to being recalled, little public protest was made on their behalf.[9]

Meanwhile, in what came to be known as 'Nationalist' Spain, women who supported Franco were not initiating any such challenge to the notion of their subordination to men. Nevertheless, war did bring about a shift towards a more public role for women, even though their mobilisation remained within the strict parameters of National-Catholicism. Pilar Primo de Rivera, leader of the women's section of the Spanish Fascist Party, repeatedly stated that women should confine themselves to the domestic sphere, proclaiming at a victory rally for Franco in May 1939 that 'The only mission assigned to women in the nation's great task, is the home.' It is clearly apparent that there is an inherent paradox in finding a woman who was fulfilling a high profile role in a political movement, delivering these words at a huge public rally.[10] Furthermore, the traditional image of female domesticity she promoted contrasted with the reality of thousands of young women in 'Social Aid' travelling round on open lorries distributing food behind the front lines in the newly 'liberated' zones, far from the home environment. But for women who had eagerly embraced the prospect of equality in education and work that had been offered by the Republic, Franco's victorious advance heralded a period of harsh restrictions and abruptly extinguished their brief glimpse of wider horizons. For thousands of women who had opposed him, defeat brought execution, imprisonment or years of exile.[11]

In Britain, the response to the war reflected many facets of the political concerns of the mid thirties, crystallising the issues at stake.

8   As in Britain during the First and Second World Wars, women in the Republic undertook work in transport and in heavy industry, as for example, in the manufacture of much needed arms.

9   See Mary Nash, *Defying Male Civilization: Women in the Spanish Civil War* (Arden Press, Colorado, 1995) pp. 110-116.

10 Lannon, 'Women and Images of Women in the Spanish Civil War', p. 225.

11 See Shirley Mangini, *Memories of Resistance: Women's Voices from the Spanish Civil War* (Yale Univesity Press, New Haven & London, 1995).

The National Government, a largely Conservative coalition which came to power in 1931, was providing the degree of stability desired by a substantial section of the population. A policy of appeasement was being maintained towards Mussolini and Hitler. To avoid a possible confrontation over Spain, in August 1936, Britain supported the imposition of a 'Non-intervention' agreement which discounted the right of the Spanish Government to buy arms under international law.[12] The British Government continued its policy of inaction even when faced by massive Italian and German intervention in Spain, maintaining what came to be regarded as a policy of 'peace at any price' with the dictators. Were they reflecting the attitude of the majority in Britain towards Spain by doing so? Randolph Churchill bluntly assessed the majority viewpoint in Britain as one of indifference, saying 'A few excitable Catholics and ardent socialists think that this war matters, but for the general public it's just a lot of bloody dagoes killing each other'[13] But his judgement is not supported by several opinion polls. In January 1937, for example, when people were asked if they favoured recognition of Franco's Junta as a legal Spanish Government, only 6% of those questioned expressed no opinion, and of the remainder, 86% were against the proposal.[14]

British people became involved with the war in Spain at many levels, but the strongest active expression of support for the Republic was manifested through participation in the International Brigades. Even before the Comintern began the recruitment for the Brigades, volunteers had begun to arrive in Spain from all over the world, some already refugees after fighting nazism and fascism in their own countries. Around 2,400 volunteers for the Brigades were British, perhaps half of whom were Communist Party members. Contrary to earlier popular myths, writers and intellectuals were not in the majority, nor were they predominantly unemployed men trying to escape from the

---

12 Non-intervention and the further reasons for its implementation are examined by Gerald Howson in *Arms for Spain: The Untold Story of the Spanish Civil War* (John Murray, London, 1998) Chapters 6 & 16.

13 Randolph Churchill to Arnold Lunn, *Spanish Rehearsal* (London, 1937) p. 43. Quoted in Tom Buchanan, '"A Far Away Country of Which We Know Nothing"?: Perceptions of Spain and its Civil War in Britain 1931-39' *Twentieth Century British History* vol.4, no.1, 1993, p. 23.

14 The poll of February 1938 asked the somewhat biased question, 'Are you in favour of direct retaliation against Franco's piracy?'. Of those who expressed an opinion (32% in this instance did not), 78% replied yes, and 22% no. In March 1938, out of all those questioned, 7% were in sympathy with Franco and 57% with the Republic, the remainder expressed no opinion. *Gallup International Public Opinion Polls: Great Britain 1937-1975* vol.1. 1937-64, George H. Gallup, (ed.), (Random House, New York, 1976) In another poll published in the *News Chronicle* on 25 January 1939, 72% supported the Republic and 9% supported Franco, the remaining views were unidentified.

despondency of the dole queue, or Jewish militants fighting anti-Semitism.[15] They came from a variety of backgrounds, although many were from the working class, and, along with those from other countries, they shared a belief in the vital importance of resisting fascism. The Brigades played a significant role in the battle to save Madrid and then fought in many other campaigns until they were withdrawn from action in October 1938.[16] However, as the Brigades were no more than a small part of the Republican Army, their contribution lay in the powerful effect they had on morale as symbols of international solidarity, rather than only in terms of their military impact.

Historians of the Spanish war have carried out a great deal of research into the diplomatic and economic relationship between Spain and Britain and on political opinion in Britain, particularly that of the Labour Party and trades unions.[17] However, historians of the interwar period often make no mention of the response amongst British people to the war in Spain, notable above all for the widespread 'Aid Spain' campaigns in support of people in the Republic. Although certain aspects of the campaigns have featured in some studies, the only book to focus specifically on this subject is *The Signal Was Spain: The Aid Spain Movement in Britain 1936-39* by Jim Fyrth.[18] In addition to information about the organisation of national and local groups, the book gives details of the work carried out by numerous individuals. His research soon revealed the extensive involvement of women in the campaigns. He noted that many of the

---

15 Richard Baxell carried out research on the social and political composition of the British volunteers who were amongst the total of 40-60,000 from all over the world who joined the International Brigades during the course of the war. See Richard Baxell, *British Volunteers in the Spanish Civil War: The British Battalion in the International Brigades, 1936-39* (Warren & Pell Publishing, Pontypool, 2007. First published by Routledge/Cañada Blanch Studies on Contemporary Spain, London, 2004). K. W. Watkins states that between an eighth and a quarter were unemployed and that 3% were Jewish, though there are now indications that at least 10% would be a more likely figure. *Britain Divided: The Effect of the Spanish Civil War on British Political Opinion* (Thomas Nelson & Sons, London, 1963), p. 168.

16 The Republican Government decided that the International Brigades should be withdrawn after the last offensive across the River Ebro, in the hopes that this would change the attitudes of the Western powers towards intervention.

17 See for example Enrique Moradiellos, *La Perfidia de Albión: El Gobierno británico y la guerra civil española* (siglo veintiuno editores, sa., Madrid, 1996); Watkins, *Britain Divided*; T. Buchanan, *The Spanish Civil War and the British Labour Movement* (Cambridge University Press, 1991); 'Divided Loyalties: The Impact of the Spanish Civil War on Britain's Civil Service Trade Unions, 1936-39', *Historical Research*, 1992, 65 (156), pp. 90-107.

18 Jim Fyrth, *The Signal Was Spain: The Aid Spain Movement in Britain, 1936-39* (Lawrence & Wishart, London, 1986). Hywel Francis included a chapter on Spanish Aid in Wales in *Miners Against Fascism: Wales and the Spanish Civil War* (Lawrence & Wishart, London, 1984). Articles include Michael Alpert, 'Humanitarianism and Politics in the British Response to the Spanish Civil War', *European History Quarterly* vol.14, no.4, October 1984, pp. 423-439.

leading figures were women, and that together with those who went to Spain in the medical and relief services, and others who staffed local committees, ran children's homes and organised food collections, they had remained 'hidden even from feminist history.'[19] To begin to rectify this situation, the same author was then joint editor with Sally Alexander of *Women's Voices from the Spanish Civil War*, a collection of extracts from memoirs, letters and interview transcripts.[20] However, there is a need for a more sustained analysis which seeks to understand women's participation in a phenomenon which has been largely overlooked, perhaps forgotten due to the impact on popular memory of the Second World War which followed so closely afterwards, or marginalised because of the difficulties in assessing a movement which was united more in spirit than as a politically cohesive force.

In some respects, this study has a broad canvas, the women who feature here came from a variety of backgrounds and represent many shades of the political spectrum, not just from left to right, but also varying in degree from ardent party activists to those who had a different agenda, such as the Quakers. Extensive research has already been carried out on the role of women within party political groups during the thirties, but there is now an awareness of the need to broaden the definition of political participation to include the areas in which women are typically more active.[21] This study therefore relates to other research on these areas of high female participation, for example, within local and community groups, self-help projects, protests, reform movements and revolutions.[22] Not only has it been shown that the definition of political participation should be more inclusive, it has also been argued that it should be fundamentally rethought. The traditional division between what is a 'political' as opposed to a 'moral' response has resulted in often unconvincing interpretations regarding the extent of women's engagement with politics.[23] Why, to give one example, has war been considered a 'political' activity, but a rejection of war defined as a question of 'moral principle.'[24] These definitions were, in themselves, reflections of a specific

---

19 Fyrth, *The Signal Was Spain*, p. 23.
20 Jim Fyrth and Sally Alexander (eds), *Women's Voices from the Spanish Civil War* (Lawrence & Wishart, London, 1991).
21 See for example, Sue Bruley, *Leninism, Stalinism and the Women's Movement in Britain 1920-1939* (Garland, London & New York, 1986; Pamela Graves, *Labour Women: Women in British Working-Class Politics 1918-1939* (Cambridge University Press, 1994).
22 Vicky Randall, *Women and Politics* (Macmillan, London, 1982) pp. 40-47.
23 Janet Siltanen and Michelle Stanworth (eds), *Women and the Public Sphere* (Hutchinson, London, 1984).

political perspective. Within the terms of a broader definition, many of the women who feature in this research could be regarded as having interests which were deeply political, and the distinctive qualities of these concerns form a recurring theme through the following chapters. Chapter 2 seeks to understand more about the motivational forces that led to women's involvement. Chapter 3 is concerned with those who worked in the many campaigns in Britain, and Chapter 4 with those in Spain, primarily in medical units and relief organisations. Chapter 5 explores women's communication of their opinions and feelings about the war to others. The focus of Chapter 6 is the impact of the war, on both the lives and the memories of this group of women. Chapter 7 assesses what has been learned from this study and looks forward to future areas for research.

The decision to focus upon women, rather than to adopt a more strongly 'gendered' approach, was made only after careful consideration. The use of gender as a mechanism for historical analysis in some ways remains problematical, although research which has engaged with these issues has done much to increase understanding of the roles of men and women in war. [25] But acceptance of the importance of gender studies in a historical context does not obviate the need to explore the role of women in areas which have been overlooked or ignored. This study seeks to bring women into the historical picture of the British response to the war in Spain, whilst presenting an opportunity to explore at least some of the ways in which gender relates to this subject. Perhaps a point will be reached when women are integrated into a redefined historical analysis, but this aim is unlikely to be achieved quickly. Until then, as others have pointed out, the aim to 'give voice' to women's past experience should not be abandoned, because 'to do so would be to accept an existing framework of scientific knowledge whose epistemologies systematically marginalise or exclude women.'[26]

A deeper and broader understanding of the past can be achieved

---

24 Susan Bourque and Jean Grossholtz, 'Politics an unnatural practice: political science looks at female participation,' in Siltanen and Stanworth, *Women and the Public Sphere*, p. 118.
25 Problems are discussed by Joan W. Scott, 'Gender: A Useful Category of Historical Analysis', *Gender and the Politics of History* (Columbia University Press, 1988) pp. 33-41. Studies of gendered issues and war include Margaret Randolph Higonnet and Jane Jenson (eds), *Behind the Lines: Gender and the Two World Wars* (Yale University Press, New Haven & London 1987); Joanna Bourke, *Dismembering the Male: Men's Bodies, Britain, and the Great War* (London & Chicago, 1996); Penny Summerfield, *Reconstructing Women's Wartime Lives* (Manchester University Press, 1998).
26 Selma Leydesdorff, Luisa Passerini and Paul Thompson, *International Yearbook of Oral History and Life Stories: Gender and Memory* vol. IV (Oxford University Press, 1996) pp. 6-7.

through the creative use of varied sources and by a combination of methodologies, each of which can offer a different perspective. To the techniques used for analysis in the field of history can be added those of sociology, literary criticism, visual arts, media studies and psychology. All material relating to women's involvement in the Spanish Civil War was therefore of value in this study, not only traditional archival sources such as the minutes of committee meetings, but also literature and poetry, pictures and photographs, and various forms of written and oral narratives. Sources always have intrinsic limitations and aspects of their validity may be challenged, but debates have been particularly intense in the field of oral history. This study draws significantly on a substantial number of interviews, and makes extensive use of other forms of personal testimony, such as autobiographies and memoirs.[27] In view of the centrality of this type of evidence in this study, an outline has been given in Appendix II of some of the issues raised regarding their use, together with a summary of the framework in which the interviews carried out during this research were conducted.

Through its focus on personal testimony, this study resonates with those that include the 'emotional' within the historical analysis. Others have noted that feminism and oral history converged in the development of both methodology and interpretation, and that 'Both came quickly to recognise personal feeling as an important focus of investigation...'[28] In the pursuit of objectivity, human emotions have often been ignored in the writing of history, but here they have a place as an essential aspect of these women's lives.

One of the main aims of this study is to convey a sense of the personalities of these women as individuals. Profiles have been included to familiarise the reader with some of those who appear frequently in these pages.[29] Rather than merely summarising their words, quotations have been used as much as possible in the belief that character will be communicated to some extent through narrative style. There is now a wider awareness amongst historians that such narratives are

---

27 Eighteen interviews were recorded as part of the research for this study, fifty-nine other interviews recorded previously by others were also used as sources. See 'Sources and Bibliography' for details.

28 Leydesdorff *et al.*, *Gender and Memory*, p. 5. One study worthy of note on the emotions is *An Intimate History of Killing: Face-to-face Killing in Twentieth-Century Warfare* (Granta, London, 2000, first edition 1999), in which Joanna Bourke confronts the range of feelings, from exhilaration to agonising guilt, that men and women experience when engaged in 'sanctioned blood-letting' during wartime.

29 See Appendix I.

directed towards an 'audience', and that there is a significant interaction between audience and narrator. In view of this, there is now a tendency for oral history studies to include information about those who have carried out the interviews.[30] The historian may decide that, as complete objectivity is an unattainable goal, it is preferable to acknowledge their role more fully. The proposal that inter-subjectivity should replace the myth of objectivity in history is now more widely accepted. No history reaches us un-mediated, and historians, rather than simple realists, are indeed myth-makers themselves.[31]

In writing of these women, and of the events in which I too participated such as the return of the Brigaders to Spain that began this chapter, I have found myself inevitably contributing to the process of shaping the memory of the past. As a historian, I am sharing in the process of myth-making, not by the invention of anything untrue, but by selecting some details and discarding others in order to produce a narrative of past experiences. What historians have referred to as the 'mythologising' or 'legendising' of past events has become a subject for study.[32] There are few such legends that can provide a framework within which to analyse the women who feature in this research, but through sharing their memories with each other and with the public at large, these women made a significant contribution to the 'collective memory' of the war.[33]

'When people come together to remember', write Jay Winter and Emmanuel Sivan, 'they enter a domain beyond that of individual memory.'[34] The act of 'gathering bits and pieces of the past and joining them together in public,' can begin a process of what they have termed, 'collective remembrance.'[35] In the many acts commemorating war, in the unveiling of memorials, the meetings, lectures and literature,

---

30 Summerfield, *Reconstructing Women's Wartime Lives*, pp. 21-22.
31 See the discussion of Hayden White's theories from *Metahistory* (Baltimore, 1973) in Leydesdorff et al., *Gender and Memory*, p. 12.
32 For example, Alistair Thomson used oral testimony 'to question and explore a legend that provided a safe refuge for many of the interviewees,' rather than as a public affirmation of their lives. *Anzac Memories: Living with the Legend* (Oxford University Press, 1994) p. 237.
33 The word 'legend' has been selected for use in the remainder of this study, as being perhaps slightly less ambiguous in meaning than 'myth', the definition of which continues to oscillate uneasily between foolish delusion and higher truth. The narrative legacy of 'myth' has been described as 'aligned with low oral, as opposed to high lettered tradition', an association which has also coloured perceptions of its value. Marina Warner, 'Myth', *The Independent*, 30 August 1996.
34 Jay Winter and Emmanuel Siven (eds), *War and Remembrance in the Twentieth Century* (Cambridge University Press, 1999) p. 6.
35 Ibid., p. 6.

we are exploring 'the intersection of private memories, family memories and collective memories.'[36] By considering not just the role of British women during the Spanish Civil War, but also the ways in which they remembered the war, this book has become linked to the field of remembrance studies. All the chapters that follow not only seek to understand the engagement of these women with a war in another land, but may also come to form a small part of how they are remembered in the future.

---

36 Jay Winter and Emmanuel Siven (eds), *War and Remembrance in the Twentieth Century* (Cambridge University Press, 1999) p. 9.

CHAPTER TWO

The Clarion Call:
Women and the Melioristic Motive

PATIENCE DARTON:
I was purely political. I was so terribly browned off with the state of England and nothing being done about it - and there were the Spaniards doing something about it... I realised that - I don't know how I had the sense, but I did.[1]

2.1 Patience Darton as a young nurse.

1   Patience Darton, AJ, 8 March 1996.

PENNY PHELPS:

It didn't dawn - I wasn't consciously aware - I didn't go to Spain for any political reasons - there was a need somewhere. I mean, it's like you see a gap and you think, 'Oh, dear, that's dangerous,' or 'they need help, and so I thought I could perhaps help in some small way.[2]

2.2 Penny Phelps as a young nurse.

These two nurses who worked near the front lines in Spain viewed their motives for doing so in opposing terms, one saying that she was 'purely political', and the other that 'political reasons' had not motivated her at all. This gives rise to the question, why did women in Britain become involved with the war in Spain, a country most of them had never visited and which was culturally and politically unfamiliar territory? They were not the citizens of a country at war, subject to the dictates of their government. For most of them, the question was one of personal choice. But merely to state that these women were motivated by what they considered to be a 'just cause' would be a gross generalisation which would fail to explain why, amongst the

---

2   Penny Phelps, AJ, 22 February 1996.

mass of the populace, these particular women responded as they did. Answering this seemingly simple question becomes a challenging task, due in part to the inherent complexities of the nature of women's involvement with the Spanish war. Not only was there a wide diversity in the degree and manner of their participation but, in addition, these women held a great variety of beliefs and were representative of a wide section of the social spectrum.

How then to begin the analysis? On initial examination of the roles of these women, a straightforward division between political and humanitarian motives would appear possible; a few female politicians, writers in the left-wing press, and party activists could be placed in the former category, 'Quakers' and others who cared for refugees and the wounded could be classed as humanitarians. However, the reality, apart from minimal numbers at both extremes of the scale, is that most women were motivated by concern on both levels, the personal and the ideological were inextricably linked in varying measures, sometimes altering through time and experience. An alternative strategy would be to separate the women into categories of representative types, for example, nurses, writers, grass-roots campaigners etc., and then proceed to explore the driving forces motivating each group. But, a generalised approach based on typologies could reveal more about conceptions of role definitions than the nature of the motivational forces in play. Beyond these methodological considerations, further issues arise which relate to the question of how to identify a force as elusive as 'motivation' with any degree of confidence.

An exploration of the individual narrative past can provide one starting point. Issues associated with the use of these sources have been well documented in other studies, some of which are discussed in Appendix II, but for the purposes of this chapter, one point in particular requires clarification.[3] A distinction should be made between the first-hand description of motives given by an individual in the course of a personal narrative, and those which are imputed by the historian through an examination of the motivating factors in an individual life history. However, in both instances, the re-constructive aspects of the nature of memory should be considered. It has been argued that narratives reflect the conscious or unconscious desire to

3 See Appendix II. Paul Thompson discussed many of these issues in *The Voice of the Past* (Oxford University Press, 1988, first edition, 1978); Penny Summerfield has given a helpful recent summary in the introduction to *Reconstructing Women's Wartime Lives* (Manchester University Press, 1998).

'compose' a life history with an internal logic.[4] Oral historians have noted that whilst certain individuals may be adept at distinguishing their own motives 'then', from what they would now consider to be more valid explanations, others are less aware of the re-constructive processes of remembering the past.[5] Even when the historian is basing an analysis of motivating factors on 'unwitting testimony', rather than the answers to direct questions, the research will still be affected by the selection or omission of memories that each individual has used to achieve 'composure'. This leads to an examination of motivational sub-text which forces historians close to boundaries shared with psychologists, despite the variance in the intent behind their work. Such a path can lead to new and fertile historical ground, or to becoming mired in the swamps of pseudo-psychology. Despite these perils, an increased awareness of the potential of this type of approach can enable historians to enrich their analysis.[6] Viewed from this perspective, narratives become a way of helping us to understand individuals and their subsequent views of past motives, rather than just the events of the past.[7]

Although it could never be claimed that motivation is no more than a response to irresistible forces, identifying key motivating factors does help us to trace the paths these particular women chose in their lives and to identify certain common patterns. The first part of this chapter seeks to understand the relationship between these women as individuals and the significant influences they experienced in their early years. The second section examines the subsequent interaction between such early determinants and the responses of the maturing women to wider issues and events. Through recollections of childhood and youth, this chapter aims to tease apart the main strands

---

4   The use of the word 'composed' relates to the research of the Popular Memory Group at the Centre of for Contemporary Cultural Studies in Birmingham. It was argued that we 'compose' our memories to rationalise our past and present lives. 'Composure' in this sense has an ambiguous meaning referring both to our construction of memories using public language and cultural meanings, and to the need for a feeling of composure which can only result from the alignment of our past and present selves.

5   This theme has been the subject of much historical discussion. See for example Alessandro Portelli, 'The Peculiarities of Oral History', *History Workshop* no. 12, 1981; Trevor Lummis, *Listening to History* (Hutchinson Education, 1987); Alistair Thomson, *Anzac Memories: Living with the Legend* (Oxford University Press, 1994); Patrick Hagopian, 'Oral Narratives: Secondary Revision and the Memory of the Vietnam War', *History Workshop* no. 32, 1991.

6   See for example, Ronald Fraser, *In Search of a Past* (Verso, London, 1984). For a discussion of this subject, see for example Raphael Samuel and Paul Thompson (eds), *The Myths We Live By* (Routledge, London & New York, 1990) pp. 6-7.

7   This theme recurs in the second part of Chapter 6, in which women's retrospectives view of the war are considered.

from the inter-twining threads of predisposition, influence, and significant events in the formation of attitudes leading to involvement with the Spanish Civil War.[8]

NATURE AND NURTURE

The first theme to emerge with striking regularity from this collection of memories is one of concern for others, manifestations of an early awareness of suffering and injustice in society which remained important elements in the subsequent lives of many women in this study.[9] Penny Phelps experienced such feelings as a small child, amidst others who reacted very differently.

> I remember the Zeppelin coming down over Cuffley, it got caught in the search lights above the railway, high. And I can remember the bang, bang, I presume of the anti-aircraft, and seeing this Zepp being caught and disintegrating and coming down, and everybody was shouting and clapping - but I, young as I was, had no [similar] feeling. I just felt terrible, terrible, that this should have happened and the people being burnt.[10]

After almost eighty years, early memories of these women often include reference to the wounded soldiers from the First World War and the vividly remembered impact of their arrival on the childhood scene, a mutilated revelation of the realities of the adult world. Frida Stewart, who drove an ambulance to Spain during the war, wrote of the memorable occasion when she was about six years old and the Red Cross brought some of the wounded to a garden party in her grandfather's grounds at Longworth.

---

8   Scientific debates on the relative significance of social as opposed to biological factors in dictating individual development are not included here. For the purposes of this study, it is presumed that both are influential to a certain extent.
9   For this chapter, profiles were constructed of 45 women who were involved with the war in different ways. They were selected from the main group of more than a hundred because of the availability of information on their early lives. Unfortunately, many interviews from the 1970s and 80s only cover the period of the civil war. Sometimes the records remaining of a woman's involvement are in the form of articles and reports of events concerning the war, which contain little or no personal material.
10 Penny Phelps, AJ, 22 February 1996. A similar incident involving a Zeppelin was recalled by Priscilla Thornycroft, who although too young to understand what was happening, retained the impression of her mother's intense reaction to the suffering of the people being burned. Priscilla Thornycroft, AJ, 28 April 2000.

...they wore bright blue hospital clothes, some had an arm missing, or a bandaged head, and were pushed about in wheel-chairs, others limped on crutches having lost a foot or leg at the Front. We children were part of a pageant, produced for their entertainment and each of us represented one of the Allies. I was Japan, and brandished a red and white flag with the circle and rays of the Rising Sun. It might have been fun to parade about in a scarlet kimono, but the sight of the mutilated spectators in blue spoiled all my youthful pleasure in the afternoon.[11]

Others, like Kathleen Gibbons and Marjorie Jacobs, were deeply affected by similar memories.

Coming home from school when we were at Edlington - the wounded soldiers up on the tram, up at the top there - I remember to this day with their wounded hands and wounded legs and one soldier, if his legs were all right, he'd take - I was only a little child, about 7 or 8 or so - taking me onto his knee and I can remember the smell of the wounds in the whole place... I used to cry for them when I got home.[12]

I can remember the First World War - the people coming home, the men coming home with their arms cut off and lost their legs, in little gangs, walking in the gutter and playing mouth organs and begging. That's the only way they could get any money to help to keep the families. I remember that very, very plainly. These things stick, you know.[13]

This last comment, 'These things stick', highlights the significance of these memories within this group of women. The majority of children at the time must have seen the wounded soldiers, but for these women, the impression is still vivid, and has been selected from a vast collection of memories to be recounted as an unforgettable experience in their lives.

Other examples of memories reflecting social awareness illustrate

11 Frida Stewart, unpublished memoirs, p. 7. It is interesting to note that there are two versions of this last sentence, the alternative being 'the sight of the mutilated spectators in blue spoiled any possible enjoyment that afternoon.' Having known Frida Stewart, it seems probable that this second version is the amendment, as she always had faith in the good nature of others, and would have presumed that others shared her sadness to the same degree.
12 Kathleen Gibbons, AJ, 6 August 1998.
13 Marjorie Jacobs, AJ, 2 August 1996.

an early recognition of the injustices of the class system. Cora Blyth was later to marry an impoverished Republican refugee without the approval of her parents. As a child, she had also formed firm friendships with those outside the appropriate social circles.

> [My mother] was very class conscious and I had a very, very good friend - the only friend I had because I didn't go to school till I was ten and I had nobody to play with - and when I was seven, I met the little girl from two doors away who was the daughter of - I think he was a house painter - and my mother wasn't at all pleased with that... and would not sort of have her into the house, which made me acutely embarrassed, because I realised. And I was always worrying about why the maids couldn't sit out in the garden, you know, why they couldn't have more days off - which didn't go down with my mother very well. So, I must have been sort of socially conscious from an early age.[14]

Another woman with a similar curiosity about the rigid divisions in society was Leah Manning, a teacher and Labour MP who became a dedicated leading light on several committees concerned with Spain and was largely responsible for bringing four thousand Basque refugee children to Britain.

> Every morning, before we were up, the step-woman came, a great coarse apron tied round her waist and a man's flat cap on her head. I sometimes watched her out of my bedroom window, with her clanking pails, as she whitened the steps and polished the brass letter-box, knocker and bell. Then Emma [...a distant and indigent relative who lived with us...] would emerge from the area steps with a steaming cup of cocoa, some door-steps of bread and dripping and sixpence. I thought it terribly mean of Emma not to ask the step-woman to eat her breakfast in the kitchen.
> 'Why don't you ask the step-woman into the kitchen to drink her cocoa?' I asked pertly.
> 'Ask no questions and you'll be told no lies,' Emma returned.[15]

Jessica Mitford, one of the younger daughters of Lord Redesdale,

---

14 Cora Blyth, AJ, 5 August 1996.
15 Leah Manning, *A Life for Education: An Autobiography* (Victor Gollancz, London, 1970) pp. 18-19

hit the headlines when she 'ran off' to Spain with Esmond Romilly who had been fighting with the International Brigades. She writes of her childhood and the 'early dawning of self-consciousness, the discovery of other people's reality' and 'disturbing vivid glimpses of the real meaning of poverty, hunger, cold, cruelty.'[16] The ragged children she could see on her train journey into London and the newspaper stories of those who lived in one room, dying of cold, caused her to fret and fume at her inability to think of a solution. She joined an organisation called the 'Sunbeams' that arranged for correspondence between a rich child and a poor one. Rather than just send the usual occasional gift of old clothes and toys, Jessica determined that her 'Sunbeam', Rose, now aged fourteen, must be rescued from her life in the slums of London, and brought to the family estate. She was offered the post of 'tweeny' or between-maid, but in practice, the plan failed to live up to the expectations of either of the girls. Jessica was somewhat dismayed to find that although their correspondence had been 'eloquent', after greeting each other at the station they became completely tongue tied and sat in silence for the whole drive home. Rose cried herself to sleep and refused to eat. Two days later, she returned to London leaving Jessica to worry and puzzle over whether this was her fault in some way, or due to the arduous work of a 'tweeny'. She herself recognised the link between this early memory and her later ideas.

> As the months and years dragged slowly by, like the watched pot that never boils, the sad and embarrassing memory of Rose gradually receded, to be replaced much later by new and more revolutionary notions of how to solve the world's ills.[17]

Class differences in the education system were noted at school by Patience Darton, whose family were living in greatly reduced circumstances with all the accompanying 'embarrassment' of unpaid bills. Nevertheless, her parents managed to afford the fees for what was considered a cheap private school until she was fourteen. She recalled her distress and anger at school when the few scholarship girls were picked out for humiliation as a result of their impecunious backgrounds.

---

16 Jessica Mitford, *Hons and Rebels: An Autobiography* (Victor Gollancz, London, 1961) p. 40
17 Ibid. p. 42. Other examples of attempts to help poor children include that of Francesca Wilson, who later worked with the Quakers in Spain. As a child she saved her sweets to give to poor children, but her unwrapped sticky black liquorice drops were not appreciated as much as she had expected. *Francesca Wilson: A Life of Service and Adventure* edited by June Horder (Horder, London, 1993) p. 6

Every year at the beginning of the year, they used to say, 'Now girls, your fathers have all bought your school books, your own school books, but you see these girls - your fathers are paying for their books, and they have our second-hand books and they have to keep them very clean and look after them.' And I was horrified at this public business - anyway I thought they were clever girls to get there, which we weren't, we were there because our parents did pay, and I thought it was very un-Christian.[18]

Micky Lewis became a lifelong campaigner for the Left due to this type of empathy with others and her underlying sense of responsibility.

I know it sounds a bit corny - but I used to have this argument with a girl. She used to say - I always remember this argument, like at school - she used to say, well, like if somebody hurt somebody else, it wasn't your business. But I always said it was, it was your business. If somebody else got hurt it was your business to care.[19]

2.3 Micky Lewis.

18 Patience Edney (née Darton), IWM 8398. The perspective of a scholarship girl on the seg-regation of those to be given free books can be found in an interview with Bessie Wild by Sue Bruley, 8 September 1977, during the research for her thesis, later published as *Leninism, Stalinism and the Women's Movement in Britain 1920-1939* (Garland, New York & London, 1986).
19 Micky Lewis, AJ, 7 July 1996.

A similar sense of responsibility compelled Frida Stewart to work for many 'causes' throughout her life, and for the peace movement in particular. From her viewpoint as a small child, the First World War seemed to have been going on for ever, and by 1918 she felt she must try to do something to help bring peace. This unselfish desire was combined with contrasting self-interest typical of a child.

> At last though, hopes [of peace] rose and as my eighth birthday approached I began to add a special plea to God to arrange for the war to end that day. Two days before - November 9th - the Kaiser had abdicated and the German Republic was set up; the air was full of talk of surrender and peace, though we were warned not to be too hopeful. I redoubled my pressure on God and, when the news came through on the 11th at midday that the Armistice had been signed that morning, I felt immensely responsible and as important as if it had been all my own work![20]

Many of these narratives indicate the presence of a predisposition not only towards identification with the sufferings of others but also of this characteristic determination to do something about it. This current of meliorism, the belief that the world can be improved by human effort, underpins their attitudes to society and politics. For example, of Nan Green, one of the British women most closely involved with the war in Spain, her son wrote,

> She was a highly moral person, the transference of her inherited faith in God becoming one in the possibility of mankind improving its lot by its own efforts; not so much a belief that heaven on earth was possible, but one that posited there was no point in waiting for it to arrive unaided.[21]

What factors, other than a possible straightforward inherited disposition, may have contributed to this determination to employ positive action to bring about change? One force which should be considered is that of family dynamics. Many women in this study refer to their role in the family as that of 'the rebellious child', firstly

---

20 Frida Stewart, unpublished memoirs, pp. 7-8.
21 Martin Green, introduction to his mother's memoirs, 'A Chronicle of Small Beer,' p. 5. Nan Green worked in Spain for much of the war as an administrator in the medical units. See Chapter 4.

challenging parental values and then, later, often the wider status quo. The reason for this tendency may, in part, be due to hereditary characteristics, but another possible contributory factor, still the subject of some controversy, is that of birth order. Extensive research by Frank Sulloway for his book, *Born to Rebel*, has led him to the conclusion that siblings cultivate distinct niches within the family in order to maximise parental investment.

> That siblings jockey for family niches, including that of 'the family radical' is evident from the interdependent relationship between birth rank, sibship size, and radicalism. Firstborns tend to respect the status quo, but the second of two children is distinctly radical. As sibship size increases, lastborns continue to be the most radical family members.[22]

He and others working in this field believe that middle-born children in particular tend to rebel out of compassion for others rather than hatred or fanaticism, making them what he terms, the most 'romantic' revolutionaries.[23] His research on various groups of 'rebels' has been supported in some studies and contested in others, but it should be noted here that there does seem to be a degree of resonance between his findings and the birth order of the women in this study.[24] It is interesting to reflect that the majority of this group could undoubtedly be considered open to ideas which challenged conservative traditions in some way and that there are very few firstborn children amongst them.[25]

Many of the women studied here were well aware of their rebellious characteristics and commented upon them during interviews or in their writings. Lillian Urmston, a nurse in Spain, is one such example. She was proud of her mother's 'gypsy' ancestry and would

---

22 Frank J. Sulloway, *Born to Rebel: Birth Order, Family Dynamics, and Creative Lives* (Abacus, London, 1998. First published in Great Britain by Little, Brown and Co., 1996) p. 98.

23 Ibid., p. 287, quoting from a study by Rejai and Phillips in 1983.

24 Sulloway's arguments are largely supported by Louis H. Stewart, *Changemakers: A Jungian Perspective on Sibling Position and the Family Atmosphere* (Routledge, London & New York, 1992) pp. 57-58, and contested by Judith Rich Harris in her book *The Nurture Assumption* (Bloomsbury, London, 1998).

25 In the course of this research, it has only been possible to collect information on birth order and sibling numbers for 35 women who were involved with active support for the Spanish Republic, excluding those such as Quakers, who were willing to help both sides. There were only 2 first-born children amongst this group, but family size and other factors contributing to the statistical complexities of this subject make it impossible to include a detailed discussion here which could add anything of significance to the thousands of cases used in Sulloway's analysis.

wander off with gypsies as a little girl, being brought home again safely just as people were thinking of sending out the search parties. She
identified even more strongly with her paternal ancestral inheritance.

> [My father]was always anxious to instil into me that I was a descen-
> dent of Jack Cade, the rebel. My mother hated this idea that Jack
> Cade was always instilled into my mind and the more my mother
> disliked it, the more I wallowed in the story... The more I've read
> about him since, the more proud I am that in a small way perhaps I
> tried to carry on his tradition.[26]

Other children adopted a similar rebellious identity when carving
their own niche in the family. Nan Green was born between two pairs of
siblings, and adolescence for her was a period of upheaval during
which time her mother died and the family descended into the lower
middle class. The two elder children could remember their mother in
good health and both had a 'snobbish, High Anglican and exclusive
schooling which coloured the rest of their lives,' whilst the two younger
ones were unable to remember much of their mother at all and settled
comfortably into State schools. Unable to identify with either pair, her
experience was of a mother who was an 'anxious, near helpless invalid'
and small private schools with unqualified teachers. These factors she
believed contributed to her development as the 'Black Sheep' of the
family, and by the time she had begun work in a long succession of
clerical jobs she was 'already a rebel, though not a very open one.'[27]

Penny Phelps was another rebellious child. Born fifth in a family of
ten, she experienced the humiliations that can accompany extreme
poverty. In her early years, she had to stand on the street selling the
mint grown by her father for a 'penny a bunch', dreading the approach
of her school friends who jeered at her misfortune. Resentful of
her onerous duties of looking after the younger children which led
her to miss school or fall asleep in class, she grew to hate a lifestyle
centred around the degradation of queuing for the pawn shop and the
incessant drunken fights outside public houses. Sometimes anger at
her situation exploded into rebellion.

---

26 Lillian Buckoke (née Urmston), Tameside 203. Nancy Cunard, a writer on the Spanish war,
   was also proud to be the descendent of the Irish rebel, Robert Emmett, who had been
   hanged for leading an insurrection. Charles Duff, 'Nancy Cunard: The Enigma of a
   Personality' in Hugh Ford (ed.), *Nancy Cunard: Brave Poet, Indomitable Rebel 1896-1965*
   (Chiltern Book Co., Philadelphia, New York, London, 1968) p. 189.
27 Nan Green, 'A Chronicle of Small Beer'.

And I always remember being very angry at one time and I thought, 'Well, they'll be sorry if I was to die,' because my mother put me upstairs for something I wouldn't do...so I thought I'd take some paraffin oil...but of course, I drank this paraffin oil but nothing - I was very, very, sick. [Laughter]. So then I thought I would get out onto the corrugated roof and get down, and then I heard my mother talking to a neighbour underneath and I was stuck halfway so I couldn't get back and finally my mother wanted to know what [laughter] the noise was upstairs on the roof. And finally they got the ladder and brought me down - I got a good whacking of course.[28]

Meanwhile, Frida Stewart was growing up in an environment far removed from this unrelenting pressure of poverty. In a happy and secure Cambridge home, she was the one singled out from the five children to be called the 'holy terror' by her nurses, a child who committed such heinous sins as pushing over the grandfather clock to draw attention away from her new baby sister.[29] She became the exception to the family norm of very high academic achievement, preferring music and the joys of escaping schoolwork to go bird-watching in the nearby fields and copses. She recalled entering her teens cheerfully 'unaffected by the family's discouraging comments on my shocking school reports and fortified by a clear vision of a glorious career as a super-musico-ornithologist.'[30]

Leah Manning also gave her own assessment of the influences in her childhood. She considered herself extremely fortunate to remain in England and be brought up by her grandparents, rather than emigrate to Canada with her parents.

I loved the idea of being the petted youngest member of a family of grown-ups, rather than the eldest daughter of a rumbustious brood whose intake was one per annum.[31]

From the age of six years onwards, she enjoyed a sheltered upbringing with her adored grandfather and kindly grandmamma, the uncles who were grown up young men still living at home, and a step-uncle, nearer her own age. In her autobiography she comments on her

---

28 Penny Phelps, AJ, 22 February 1996.
29 Frida Stewart, unpublished memoirs, p. 2.
30 Ibid. p. 25.
31 Leah Manning, *A Life for Education*, p. 12.

small rebellions, 'occasional fits of quite inexplicable naughtiness', which seem to consist mainly of wandering off, following organ grinders, bands, circuses, and the impressive funeral processions with black horses and mourners. She saw this as a tendency which continued into adult life, when she 'never could resist a procession or a demo - May Day, Votes for Women, Hands off Russia, Anti-fascist mobs, Ban the Bomb,' even riots which she recalled, 'landed me in a French jail from which I had to be rescued by the British Consul.'[32]

The childhood of Charlotte Haldane was perhaps more temp-estuous than most. The daughter of a German father and American mother, she was born in London in 1894.[33] Due in part to her intense affection for her English nanny, she identified herself as English from an early age by choice as well as birth. Her childhood she describes as being passed in 'a state of more or less permanent emotional rebellion,' against the draconian discipline of her German governess. Her mother's disciplinary efforts only succeeded in developing this intransigence further, and her father was described in her memoirs as a despot who 'overruled and frustrated my every ambition and aspiration.[34] To what extent this background contributed to her later rejection of social conventions to follow her own radically militant path is a matter for conjecture. However, she was certainly amongst the most outspoken on the subject of her life as an ardent feminist and suffragette, an atheist, and Comintern agent.[35] Few middle-class women in those days were prepared to leave their husbands, risking social ostracism and the loss of a child, as she did after meeting J. B. S. Haldane, saying, 'However, rightly or wrongly, when once I have resolved on a course of action, I cannot be deflected from it by threats nor by fear of the consequences.'[36]

The childhood of Ellen Wilkinson, who later became famous as the MP for Jarrow, illustrates several of the issues relating to family dynamics, a subsequent path into politics and significant involvement with the war in Spain. As a child, she was described by contemporaries

---

32 Ibid. p. 24.
33 An ardent Communist Party member during the thirties, she spent some time working in Paris helping International Brigaders on their way to fight in Spain and was also the Secretary of Dependants Aid, the group helping to support families of International Brigaders and those who returned home wounded, see Chapter 3.
34 Charlotte Haldane, *Truth Will Out* (George Weidenfeld & Nicholson Ltd., London, 1949) p. 304.
35 Sulloway would probably see Charlotte Haldane as a firstborn driven to radicalism through extreme parental conflict. *Born to Rebel*, p. 293.
36 Haldane, *Truth Will Out*, p. 24.

as the 'Fiery Particle', and the 'Elfin Fury' because of her red hair, her diminutive stature, and her hot temper. Her rebellious tendencies were in evidence even at elementary school and developed alongside a growing moral indignation at the social evils she encountered.[37] Apart from following the fairly common pattern of early defiance frequently demonstrated by women in this study, Ellen Wilkinson is also representative of many others in that she shared a close relationship with her father. She admired him as a 'tremendous figure' for the determination with which he had overcome the deprivations of his childhood and lack of education through sheer 'ruthless driving power'.[38] As his favourite daughter, she would accompany him to lectures on the contemporary debates surrounding evolution, exploring the subject further by reading together.

This type of father/daughter relationship seems to have had a strong influence on certain women in this study, occasionally acting as an introduction to a political approach to life from an established party activist to a new recruit, but more frequently, as in the case of Ellen Wilkinson, providing early intellectual stimulus leading to the desire to explore new ideologies. Ellen had joined the Independent Labour Party by the time she was sixteen, and however much she admired her father, she did not share his apolitical views which were based on the tenet, 'I have pulled myself out of the gutter, why can't they?'[39] Similarly, Isabel Brown, the prominent Communist activist and well-known speaker for the 'Aid Spain' campaigns, remembered her father as her 'first formative influence' who gave her a 'wider outlook than most girls of that age and that time had', but whose influence she felt was rather on the formation of her character than on her political views.[40] Previous studies have questioned the supposition that daughters generally adopt the political views of their fathers, pointing out that much of the early research simply failed to distinguish between 'paternal' influence and the much stronger effects of combined 'parental' influence.[41] Thora Silverthorne, however, is

---

37 Betty D. Vernon, *Ellen Wilkinson* (Croom Helm, London, 1982) pp. 4-5.
38 Betty Vernon writes that Ellen Wilkinson's father was working as a half-timer in a cotton mill at the age of eight and head of the household by the age of twelve. The only formal education he had was at Sunday School where he learned to read and write. *Ellen Wilkinson*, p. 4-5.
39 Ellen Wilkinson in the Countess of Oxford and Asquith (ed.), *Myself When Young By Famous Women of To-day* (Frederick Muller, London, 1938) p. 399.
40 Interview with Isabel Brown by Sue Bruley, 3 September 1976.
41 For a short review of research questioning the views expressed by those such as Lazarfeld in the sixties, see Vicky Randall, *Women and Politics* (Macmillan Press, London, 1982) pp. 48-49.

representative of those who clearly followed in their father's foot-steps. A theatre nurse in Spain who later went on to form the first trade union for nurses, she came from a mining family in South Wales. Her father was a very active member of the Communist Party and meetings were often held in their house. She was 'always joining something or other, ...never the Girl Guides or anything like that, but always getting leaflets round, doing anything I could in the Labour Party and the Communist Party - always involved.' She was very much aware of her father's influence, describing him as 'a big man in my life,' a 'marvellous', 'wonderful', 'fine man.'[42] There are other similar examples where a close bond was formed between father and daughter based on interest in politics. Mary Docherty, a lifelong grass-roots activist on the Left who worked in the 'Aid Spain' campaigns, often went to 'propaganda meetings' with her father in Scotland. During her dinner hour at school she collected and read his *Daily Herald* so that she could discuss working-class issues with him. Her memoirs are not only dedicated to him but are entitled *A Miner's Lass*, indirectly confirming his importance in her view of her own identity.[43]

Fathers are frequently remembered for their positive influence, either politically, intellectually, or as examples of generosity, sometimes despite their own poverty. Perhaps not surprisingly in view of the widespread poor social conditions in Britain at the time, mothers are more often referred to in the context of the hard lives they led, rather than as role models. However, the impact of illness, death, unemployment and poverty on mothers often resulted in a first-hand awareness for daughters about the effects of social depriva-tion and suffering, and thus set them on a path which led to their involvement with the war in Spain. Catherine Collins remembers her mother singing the 'Red Flag' whilst doing the washing for her family of ten, saying 'I've got to take my venom out on something.'[44]

Maternal illness featured prominently in many recollections of childhood, sometimes ending in untimely death which would have been avoidable under better conditions. Elsie Booth, the youngest child in a family frequently reliant on the humiliating Public Assistance, had no doubts about the cause of her mother's early death. Trying to make ends meet after her husband died, she spent a year scrubbing floors, leading her daughter to firmly believe that

---

42 Thora Silverthorne, AJ, January 1996.
43 Mary Docherty, *A Miner's Lass* (Lancashire Community Press, Preston, 1992).
44 Catherine Collins, IWM 11297.

'What killed her really was the bloody worry of living.'[45] The pawn shop had dominated the daily routine of Elsie Booth's childhood, as her mother made repeated visits to exchange working clothes for Sunday clothes and back again, and the children argued over whose garments should be taken. Although her mother had voted for the Conservative Party, Elsie Booth reacted to these childhood experiences by choosing socialism and marriage to a trade unionist who went to Spain in the International Brigade.

There are a few cases in which mothers could be considered as adventurous role models, perhaps influencing the readiness of their daughters to go to a foreign country at war. Priscilla Scott-Ellis worked as a nurse in the areas held by Franco. Bored with the London social season, and saddened by the death of a Spanish aristocratic friend in Franco's airforce, she decided to go to Spain, perhaps inspired by the example set by her mother who had run a hospital in Egypt during the First World War. Also working in this Egyptian hospital was the mother of Gabriel Herbert, seemingly the only other British woman to have left a record of working for Franco's medical services in Spain.[46] When Patience Darton announced she was going as a nurse to Spain to help the Republic, her mother attributed this to the family 'pioneering spirit.' As a small child, Patience Darton had listened enraptured to her mother's stories of the three years she spent in the wilds of Canada as a young woman, visiting her brothers who were 'opening up the colonies and doing noble deeds.'[47] Mothers were also referred to as the focus of philanthropic traditions in families with comfortable financial circumstances. This is evident in the case of Frida Stewart, whose mother was 'always doing good works', bringing them up 'with all the right attitudes towards refugees and poverty and making a better world...'[48] Priscilla Thornycroft's mother came from a Fabian background, with a circle of friends that included Eleanor Marx, George Bernard Shaw and Bertrand Russell. Growing up with a mother who held strong views about injustice had a great effect on the children.

---

45 Elsie Booth, Tameside 756.
46 Priscilla Scott-Ellis (ed. Raymond Carr), *The Chances of Death: A Diary of the Spanish Civil War* (Michael Russell Ltd, Norwich, 1995), and Mrs Alexander Dru (née Gabriel Herbert), letter and short memoir sent to Michael Alpert, 4 April 1982, about her work of organising supplies. See also Chapter 4.
47 Patience Darton, AJ, 8 March 1996.
48 Frida Stewart, AJ, 30 March 1994.

Our mother was extremely kind hearted, and I guess that had a big influence on all of us. We couldn't see anything suffering without wanting to help. I should think that probably was a big influence on the whole family because we all became what you might call 'do-gooders' - ghastly people for other people, but we thought it was normal.[49]

In general, apart from their role in teaching reading, mothers are much less frequently mentioned in the context of intellectual development than fathers. However, this particular type of parental influence forms just one strand of a thread which runs consistently through the early lives of the women in the sample, namely, a strong desire for education. This was the route to political involvement for a substantial number of women in this study. On numerous occasions, they speak of their love of reading when young, of their later determination to educate themselves at evening classes or in political groups, and of the importance of the advent of the Left Book Club in their lives.[50] Reading was described as almost the 'only joy', books were 'devoured'.[51] Despite a lack of empirical evidence on their mental capabilities, interviews and personal accounts reveal their questioning approach to life, ability to re-evaluate and analyse, and their continuing interest in current affairs, all factors indicative of intelligence. Although much of the research undertaken by Hess and Torney was carried at a time when IQ tests were erroneously viewed as being culturally neutral, this does not entirely invalidate their findings on the interaction between intelligence and politicisation. Their research in this area supports the notion that the women in this sample may have responded to early political influences partly as a result of their high intelligence.[52]

---

49 Priscilla Thornycroft, AJ, 28 April 2000. Priscilla Thornycroft became a member of the Artists International Association, see Chapter 5.

50 These groups were organised along 'Popular Front' lines for discussions on the issues raised by the series of left-wing books published by Victor Gollancz. The appeal for unity which the Club represented resulted in a membership of 60,000 and even a Popular Front by-election victory in Bridgewater in 1938. Ben Pimlott, *Labour and the Left in the 1930s* (Cambridge University Press, 1977) pp. 157-8. See also Chapter 3.

51 See respectively, Nan Green, 'A Chronicle of Small Beer', p. 17;Valentine Ackland, *For Sylvia: An Honest Account* (Methuen, London, 1986, first published by Chatto & Windus, 1985) p. 114 also Horder (ed.), *Francesca Wilson*, p. 14.

52 Robert D. Hess and Judith V. Torney, *The Development of Political Attitudes in Children* (Aldine Publishing Co., Chicago 1967) p. 223 states that 'The intelligence of the child is one of the most important mediating influences in the acquisition of political behaviour. In general, the effect of high IQ is to accelerate the process of political socialisation for children of all social status levels.'

Some of the women from poor working-class backgrounds were able to take advantage of the scholarship system. Isabel Brown only needed her first term's fees at High School because she soon won a scholarship, 'being imbued with a voracious thirst for knowledge.'[53] But at this time, education for girls outside the school system was not unusual. The daughters of the wealthy were still sometimes educated by governesses, or by other members of the family. The author, Sylvia Townsend Warner, who wrote and campaigned ardently for the Republican cause, had little formal education after her exclusion from school when very young for disrupting the class.[54] As an only child, she was in the unusual position of being in constant competition for her father's attention with the boys who were his pupils at Harrow School. A brilliant teacher, he not only influenced her by his rejection of traditional thinking, but also because he encouraged her to read widely, allowing her the run of the library, and to think for herself.[55] Others missed considerable periods at school as a result of serious illness, a fairly common occurrence at this time. Ellen Wilkinson is one such example. From six to eight years of age, as a result of a series of childhood diseases, she remained at home where she was taught to read. On returning to school, she refused to do the subjects she hated, but nevertheless was able to claim proudly that after the age of eleven 'I paid for my own education by scholarship until I left university.[56] Her desire to stretch her mind and her self confidence can be seen later on at school, when, having barely heard the word, 'socialism', she agreed to stand as the socialist candidate in a school election. To prepare herself, she borrowed books written by Robert Blatchford and 'went into the election an ardent, in fact a flaming, socialist.'[57]

Childhood illness was also experienced by Frida Stewart. She spent many months in bed with a cardiac condition during adolescence, 'a fine opportunity for reading and listening to music.'[58] This time was spent in the house of her grandfather, 'a grand old liberal with a tremendous social conscience'. She recalls that in addition to working her way through the supply of records and literature, '...although it bored me dreadfully, I read "The Times" every day so as to be able to talk to

---

53 May Hill, *Red Roses for Isabel* (May Hill, London, 1982) p. 2.
54 It was said that she mimicked the teachers and distracted the other pupils, see Wendy Mulford, *This Narrow Place: Sylvia Townsend Warner and Valentine Ackland. Life, Letters and Politics, 1930-51* (Pandora, London, 1988) p. 6.
55 Ibid.
56 Quoted in Vernon, *Ellen Wilkinson*, p. 6.
57 Ellen Wilkinson in Oxford, *Myself When Young*, p. 406.
58 Frida Stewart, unpublished memoirs p. 26.

him about something serious and grown-up when he visited my bed-
side, and together we shook our heads over the sad state of Britain's
affairs.'[59] Nevertheless, she continued to consider herself 'a dullard',
despite the academic recognition of her later published books.[60]

Could such extended periods of auto-didactic education have offered
an opportunity to develop individuality and a greater tendency to independence of mind? This could be so in the case of Katharine, Duchess of
Atholl, a Conservative MP, who, given her strictly conventional upbringing, could have been expected to conform to traditional patterns of life
established for upper-class women. She was a lonely child, despite her
older step sisters and younger siblings. Often ill and confined to the
house, she read a great deal, becoming a rather bookish and intellectually precocious child.[61] She gave up her aspirations to become a
musician on her marriage, but, having a serially unfaithful husband
and no children she turned again to intellectual pursuits and to political
activity. Although a staunch Conservative, the independence of her
opinions became increasingly apparent as she matured, evident in her
outspoken campaigns against female circumcision in the colonies, her
position on Indian affairs, and in her fervent support for the Spanish
Republic, which eventually resulted in the loss of her Parliamentary seat.

Given the predominance of religious belief within British society
during the early decades of the 20th century, the influence of religion
in its various forms cannot be discounted. Many of women in this
study questioned their religious traditions, and often rejected religion
altogether.[62] Unfortunately, those who were involved with the war in
Spain expressly as a result of their religious convictions have left little record of their early lives. Amongst the Quakers who worked with
Spanish refugees, Edith Pye is one such example. She did not join the
Friends until she was thirty-two but no information has been found
which offers insight into her decision.[63] Norma Jacob, who helped to

---

59 Ibid., p. 27.
60 Books by Frida Knight (née Stewart) include *The Strange Case of Thomas Walker: Ten
    Years in the Life of a Manchester Radical* (Lawrence & Wishart, London, 1957); *University
    Rebel: The Life of William Frend 1757-1841* (Gollancz, London, 1971); *The French Resistance
    1940-1944* (Lawrence & Wishart, London, 1975).
61 Sheila Hetherington, *Katharine Atholl 1874-1960* (Aberdeen University Press, 1989) p. 6.
62 The limitations of this study as a representative sample of women who were involved with
    the war in Spain are discussed in Appendix II. Those who were motivated by religious
    beliefs may just be less likely to have produced accessible narratives, rather than being
    less numerous.
63 Entry on Edith Pye by Sybil Oldfield, *Dictionary of National Biography: Missing Persons*
    edited by C. S. Nicholls (Oxford University Press, 1993). In practice, British Quakers
    worked almost entirely in the Spanish Republic, but gave aid to those who needed it
    without discrimination on political grounds. See Chapter 4.

organise refugee relief for the Friends in Barcelona, joined on her marriage to an American Friend, but before that, her only contact with them had been her tutor at Oxford.[64]

In contrast to these two women, Noreen Branson felt 'frightfully relieved to be an atheist.' Forced to go to church every Sunday as a child, she had been 'bored stiff'.

> And this went on and on - and then, when I was sixteen, somebody said, 'People only believe in this because they want to.' And this was like a wonderful release, you know. I suddenly thought, 'Of course, that's true, I can throw it all aside, you know. [Laughter] Yes, it seemed like a sort of confinement.[65]

For Isabel Brown, amongst others, a questioning mind and a thirst for knowledge brought religious disaffection. During her adolescence, she had become 'caught up in the ritual and music of the local parish church.'[66] She recalled how on Good Friday she would suffer when thinking about the crucifixion, 'the nails and the horrors of it.'[67] However, this early unquestioning faith was undermined by prolific reading, firstly on comparative religions and then of books which challenged the basis of her religious beliefs.[68] But the education on offer through the more socially aware sections of the Church could initially satisfy an appetite for learning. Patience Darton was greatly attracted to a heady combination of religion and concepts of social justice. As a young girl, she went to a Young People's Fellowship run by Canon Skelton at St. Albans Cathedral, a man she considered 'a very great leading socialist Christian', although 'the word "socialism" was never mentioned.'[69] She attended lectures on 'The Church and Social Order',

64 After marrying Alfred Jacob, a birthright Friend from Pennsylvania, Norma Jacob went with him to Barcelona. Oral History Interview #31 American Friends Service Committee 1989. Unfortunately, the interview gives few details of her childhood. Francesca Wilson, although a Friend by birth, was taken into the Plymouth Brethren aged four when her mother became a convert. However, she remained on the Monthly Meeting listings of the Friends, despite having no particular religious conviction as an adult and having no commitment to a neutral position over the war in Spain. Nevertheless, the relief work she did in Spain and elsewhere was either directly for the Quakers or under their auspices. She resigned from the Friends in the early 1950s.
65 Noreen Branson, AJ, 26 January 1996. Noreen Branson was active in the Aid Spain campaigns and was the wife of an International Brigader, see Chapter 3.
66 Hill, *Red Roses for Isabel*, p. 3.
67 Interview with Isabel Brown by Sue Bruely, 3 September, 1976.
68 Ibid., and Hill, *Red Roses for Isabel*, pp. 3-5.
69 Patience Edney (née Darton), IWM 8398, and Patience Darton, AJ, 18 March 1994, respectively.

covering themes such as Internationalism, Trades Unions, Imperialism, Poverty and Housing. Although full of admiration for the social principles of this teaching, she nevertheless was unable to suppress the disturbing questions that arose in her mind.

> I felt this was the right thing, this was proper, this was the way life was - or should be - to know about those things and to do it. And it fitted very nicely with my own mind because I was very religious, but I had terrible doubts, terrible doubts, appalling doubts, which I didn't like to say much about because I thought they were so bad, about poverty - not poverty, poverty didn't matter so much I don't think, as pain, and wickedness, and sin, and rules being made for you that weren't made by you. I mean, it's rather mean to be put into the world and told you mustn't do this and you must do that, but you didn't make those rules, and then you were blamed if you did wrong. I thought that was very hard. The worst was about pain, pain for people who hadn't deserved it or earned it, and children being in pain, and animals being in pain. And it wasn't only man that was terrible with animals, but forest fires started by lightning and things like that, which burnt the little birds and terrified things. And anyway, animals have a rather nasty life killing one another - I thought that didn't fit in with a loving God. And it worried me terribly because I thought it was wicked to have those thoughts.[70]

The interaction between religious and political belief is a theme which occurs in the lives of many women in this study. Patience Darton recalled that when she was training to be a nurse and attending St. George's Church in Holborn, 'well known to be left wing,' people sort of zoomed in, to and fro, from the Communist Party to it, and out again, mostly women, young girls.'[71] Micky Lewis described how the Jewish members of the Young Communist League would discuss religious and political affiliation. She recalled with amusement that they would ask each other 'What comes first, are you a Communist or Jewish?' and they would reply 'We're Communists first', adding, 'A good job the rabbi wasn't listening.'[72] Catholic women in this study

---

70 Ibid.
71 Patience Edney, (née Darton) IWM 8398. She also goes on to make the interesting retrospective observation that although she didn't remember many men doing this, 'they made rather a lot of the men, now I come to think of it, the few who were there.' See also the quote from Nan Green's son above which refers to his mother's 'transference' of faith.
72 Micky Lewis, AJ, 9 July 1996.

were similarly faced with the necessity of prioritising religious or political belief. According to Catherine Collins, this was a problem which some Catholics were loath to confront. In her early teens she remembers that despite the fact that the priests used to condemn Communist militancy, the Catholic Communists still went to church but sat at the back.[73]

Methodism was a strong influence in Ellen Wilkinson's background, as her father was a Methodist preacher and family social life revolved around the Wesleyan Chapel. However, in her teens, she remembers, 'I was utterly bored with religion and sermons, ...sick of the discussions as to what this or that text meant.'[74] She was soon to find a substitute in the excitement of spreading the socialist message of the ILP on the street corners and beyond.

> The details of that first [ILP] branch meeting remained etched on my mind while a first love affair at the same time remains dim... Mere boys seemed very uninteresting creatures to the solemn High Priestess of Politics that I had persuaded myself I was.[75]

But it was hearing Katharine Bruce Glasier speaking on the subject of 'Socialism as a Religion' at a meeting the following week that Ellen Wilkinson later recalled as the dawning of her ambitions.

To the undersized girl listening in the gallery, this woman, not much bigger than herself, seemed the embodiment of all her dreams, all her secret hopes. To stand on the platform of the Free Trade Hall, to be able to sway a great crowd as she swayed it, to be able to make life better, to remove slums and underfeeding and misery just because one came and spoke to them about it, ...that seemed the highest destiny any woman could ever hope for.[76]

She returned home from the meeting 'so bright of eye and full of enthusiasm' that her mother became suspicious.

> Nothing could ever convince Mother that while I had plenty of boyfriends - as every co-educated girl has - I was honestly more interested in politics than love affairs. But father understood. To

---

73 Catherine Collins, IWM 11297. The Catholic Church in Britain was outspoken in support of Franco making the position very difficult for Catholics who felt their loyalties lay with the Republic, see Chapter 3.
74 Ellen Wilkinson in Oxford (ed.), *Myself When Young*, p. 412.
75 Quoted in Vernon, *Ellen Wilkinson*, p. 20.
76 Ellen Wilkinson in Oxford (ed.), *Myself When Young*, p. 414.

him I poured out the whole speech, my determination to work for socialism. 'I had rather you become a missionary,' he said. 'What future can there be for a girl in politics?'[77]

Her later success in the world of politics did not cause her to discard completely her religious beliefs, unlike other women in the sample who held strong religious convictions in childhood and then appear to have transferred this deep level of commitment to a political ideology. Could there be shared predisposing factors in the personalities of these women which led them to respond positively to the notion of either religious or political commitment? Did the fact that both systems shared many of the same characteristics relate to their appeal? Just like left-wing political groups, 'Religion achieves its often positive effects through social cohesion and social support...at the cost of isolation from other bodies and risk of prejudice against those of other faiths.'[78] For Micky Lewis as a member of the Young Communist League, bonded by the solidarity of shared conviction in the face of opposition, a belief in the ideals of Communism were the equivalent of religious moral values.

> We didn't get, we gave. It was always giving dues and subscriptions and collecting money. And it was so idealistic - well, I think it should be - we gave gladly. We gave gladly to the Party, that was our so-called - as charities are today, we believed in giving to a Party that would raise people, not keep giving like the begging bowl it is today.[79]

Mary Docherty's memories of her attendance at Sunday Schools illustrate another aspect of the links between politics and religion, this being the way in which political groups at times elected to mimic familiar religious formulas. Such traditions are noted amongst the Owenites in the 1830s and 1840s, who held Sunday meetings in their Halls of Science where a 'sermon' would be given on some social topic, and 'hymns' sung. Some of these establishments even provided their own form of service for weddings, funerals and child-namings, 'a pilfering of the sacramental rites' which 'did not increase the Socialists' popularity with the clergy, particularly when these

---

77 Ibid. p. 415.
78 B. Beit Hallahmi and Michael Argyle, *The Psychology of Religious Behaviour, Belief and Experience* (Routledge, London & New York, 1997) p. 229.
79 Micky Lewis, AJ, 9 July 1996.

ceremonies were then invested with "blasphemous" content.'[80] Mary Docherty attended a Proletarian Sunday School where the children discussed politics at home and abroad, and learnt to recite precepts which followed a quasi-religious format.

> Thou shalt inscribe on thy banner,
> 'Workers of all lands unite'
> You have nothing to lose but your chains,
> You have a World to Win.
>
> Thou shalt not be a patriot
> For a patriot is an International Blackleg
> Your duty to yourself and your class
> Demands that you be a citizen of the World.
>
> Thou shalt not take part in any bourgeois war
> For all modern wars are the result of the clash of
> economic interest
> Your duty as an internationalist is to wage class war
> Against all such wars.
>
> Thou shalt teach Revolution, for Revolution
> Means the abolition of the present political state
> And the end of Capitalism and the raising in their place,
> An Industrial Republic.[81]

The social parameters for the women in this study varied from a childhood submersion in deep political waters such as this, to a sheltered upbringing in the peaceful backwaters of philanthropic drawing-room society. But, nevertheless, factors such as gender and intelligence had combined with family dynamics and other early environmental influences to produce individuals who would be predisposed to respond actively to the causes they were to encounter. Nature and nurture had united to ensure that for these women, the foundations were firmly laid on which concern about the issues raised by the Spanish Civil War would be constructed.

---

80 Barbara Taylor, *Eve and the New Jerusalem: Socialism and Feminism in the Nineteenth Century* (Virago, London, 1983) p. 225 * note.
81 Quoted in Docherty, *A Miner's Lass*, p. 28. She had first attended a Church Sunday School then, before going to the Proletarian Sunday School, went to one run by the ILP where she was taught to 'Love Learning which is the Food of the Mind'.

ISSUES AND IDEOLOGY

This collection of narratives can now be used to follow the responses of these women to the forces operating within British society and at international level, and to identify certain common experiences which were the direct precursors to involvement with the Spanish Civil War. Some strands remain clearly discernible, for example, early awareness of the sufferings of others may have been transformed into humanitarian work, and a childhood recognition of social injustice had frequently developed into a belief in socialism and anti-fascism. However, the key motivator for almost all these women was empathy, and without doubt, the prime objective was practical action.

The difference between men and women in the way they express their relationship with politics has been researched in a variety of other studies.[82] It has been noted that in their recollections, men typically cite the political overview and rarely mention instances of individual distress, primarily seeing the need to organise labour and to establish a hierarchical movement.[83] This pattern also occurs in the interviews carried out for this study. Not only do men have the firm expectation that a broad political analysis is what the interviewer requires, they are also unlikely to mention the emotional context of their life history unless specifically asked to do so.[84] Women regard political activity primarily as a means of dealing with the problem of suffering and introduce a personal perspective with much greater frequency.[85] The division for women between a 'personal' motive, and a 'political' one is often very unstable.

The personal and the political were closely related for Jessica (Decca) Mitford. Her early awareness of social conditions outside the bastions of privilege had become the basis for developing political ideas, part of a dynamic package wrapped up with a desire for

---

82 For an international perspective on this subject see Joni Lovenduski and Pippa Norris (eds) *Gender and Party Politics* (Sage, London, 1993).
83 See for example Pamela M. Graves' study of fifty working-class women and an equal number of men who were active in interwar labour politics, *Labour Women: Women in British Working Class Politics 1918-39* (Cambridge University Press, 1994) Chapter 2, 'Women and men in interwar working-class politics', pp. 72-73 in particular. Gender differences are less apparent in interviews which focus rather more expressly on policy through specific questions, as for example, those carried out by Sue Bruley for *Leninism, Stalinism and the Women's Movement in Britain.*
84 During the preliminary stages of this study, several interviews with men took place that reflect this different approach, for example, those with Bill Alexander, Lord Listowel, and Nathaniel Lewis.
85 This difference was also noted by Graves, *Labour Women*, pp. 46-47.

adventure, and the excitement of falling in love. Her initial commitment to anti-fascism was not just the result of sibling rivalry, as she
pointed out when writing of a conversation with her sister, Unity
(Boud), a recent recruit to the British Union of Fascists.

> 'Don't you long to join too Decca? It's such fun,' she begged, waving
> her brand-new black shirt at me.
>   'Shouldn't think of it. I hate the beastly Fascists. If you're going to
> be one, I'm going to be a Communist so there.'
>   In fact, this declaration was something more than a mere auto-
> matic taking of opposite sides to Boud; the little I knew about the
> Fascists repelled me - their racism, super-militarism, brutality. I took
> out a subscription to the *Daily Worker*, bought volumes of Communist
> literature and literature that I supposed to be Communist...[86]

Jessica Mitford is described as 'having read herself into socialism
at the age of fifteen,' but although many of these women become politically conscious through books, others entered into the political
world through personal contact with others already involved.[87] As
has already been mentioned, fathers were sometimes instrumental in
this role, but other relationships outside the family could also exert a
key influence, particularly those with admired males, often future
husbands. Many studies have concluded that from childhood there
are differences relating to politicisation between males and females. In
the sixties, for example, it was suggested that women relate to the
political system more through trust and reliance on political figures
than their male peers, placing more faith in the representatives of
what they believe to be an inherently good system.[88] Feminist historians have since drawn attention to the many flawed assumptions in
some of this earlier research.[89] But however justified their criticisms,
there is no doubt that for some of the women in this study, ardent
young men with new and exiting political beliefs had an earth-shaking

---

86 Mitford, *Hons and Rebels*, p. 49. Unity had recently become acquainted with Oswald
    Mosley at the house of her sister Diana, who became his wife.
87 Neal Ascherson, *Independent on Sunday* 28 July 1996, p. 20.
88 Hess and Torney, *The Development of Political Attitudes in Children*, p. 222.
89 The questions raised concerning the research of those such as Hess and Torney, and Fred
    Greenstein are discussed in Susan Bourque and Jean Grossholtz, 'Politics an unnatural
    practice: political science looks at female participation'; Goldie Shabad and Kristi
    Andersen, 'Candidate evaluations by men and women', both in Janet Siltanen and
    Michelle Stanworth (eds), *Women and the Public Sphere: A Critique of Sociology and
    Politics* (Hutchinson & Co., London, 1984) See also Randall, *Women and Politics*, pp. 60-61.

impact in more ways than one. The narratives of women like Noreen Branson, Kathleen Gibbons and Cora Blyth illustrate this point.

> I participated in a sort of thing called the 'Lend a Hand Club' which used to put pantomimes on for school children, free of charge all over East London. I used to act and sing in these pantomimes as a sort of evening pastime. Then one of the members put on a special charity show at the 'Scala Theatre' I think it was, and it was there that I first met Clive, because he had a walk-on part as a soldier. And after the final performance there was an evening party which we went to and we got talking, and it was there that I got to know him. And we went to Lyons' Corner House which in those days was open all night, after the party was over, and sat there till six o'clock in the morning. And he was a socialist of course, and I was frightfully interested in this because I'd never met a socialist before, and about four weeks later we got married. [Laughter][90]

> [Danny] was a hero, in my opinion, of the Irish struggle, and he was lovely and cuddlesome and he was alone and he was poor and there was nobody looking after him... He undertook my education about more than one thing - not just about sex or anything like that, but political education as well - value, price and profit and all sorts... He first of all made me aware there are two classes in society, and I'm not in the most favoured one, and if you ever want to improve your circumstances, we've got to fight to do it - nobody's going to do it for you.[91]

> My parents were just Conservatives by habit and I had no particular political views, as I say, concerning the Civil War, I remember the pamphlets from Franco saying that the 'Reds' were anti-Christ and asking for money, and I sort of took this in. But, I was learning French and Spanish and I went to Normandy to stay with a Protestant pasteur... And his son, Francis, was the first great love of my life - I fell completely in love with him. I was very plain, 16 or 17, and here was a beautiful young man of about 23 with great big eyes - as his mother said, 'Il a les yeux doux.' Well, he'd been to Barcelona and he had had the bombs around him and so on, and when I made

---

90 Noreen Branson, AJ, 26 January 1996.
91 Kathleen Gibbons, AJ, 6 August 1998.

an idiotic remark about Franco he tore a strip off me and told me about the Republic and the legitimacy of it, and how hard pressed they were - and of course, that converted me completely.[92]

Although these three women all met young men whose enthusiasm for politics led them to became involved with Spain, they did not actually go there during the war. However, Kate Mangan was determined to follow the man she loved, Jan Kurzke, when he went to fight Franco. In 1933, Jan Kurzke had fled Germany because of his commitment to Marxism and anti-fascism.[93] The following year he met Kate Mangan, a former student at the Slade School of Art.[94] As a result of their relationship her life was to take a dramatic turn. Kate Mangan's unpublished memoirs tell of her search to find him in Spain when he joined the International Brigades.[95] Despite the fact that she had received no news of his whereabouts after leaving Paris, and had failed to convince Spanish Medical Aid to allow her to take out supplies, she left London and risked crossing the border into Spain without a visa.

From the time Jan left, I intended to get to Spain though I never told anyone the real reason. If getting to Spain had entailed an interview with the Prime Minister or the Pope I should have had no hesitation in trying it. Lack of money and a complete lack of 'Left' political affiliations did not hamper me.[96]

On her arrival, she found occasional work as an interpreter in Barcelona, then became a secretary to Hugh Slater, a friend from her days at the Slade, before eventually moving to Valencia to work in the press office.[97] Whilst searching for Jan Kurzke, Kate Mangan became caught up in the romance and excitement of the early months of the

92 Cora Blyth, AJ, 5 August 1996.
93 Jan Kurzke & Kate Mangan, 'The Good Comrade', unpublished ms, Jan Kurzke Papers, Archives of the International Institute for Social History, Amsterdam. See also Paul Preston, *We Saw Spain Die: Foreign Correspondents in the Spanish Civil War*, (Constable, London, 2008)
94 Kate Mangan (née Foster) was born in Sedgley, Staffordshire in 1904. She married the Irish-American left-wing writer Sherry Mangan in 1931. They divorced in 1935.
95 Kate Mangan and Jan Kurzke, 'The Good Comrade', unpublished memoir edited by Charolotte Kurzke , Jan Kurzke Papers, Archives of the International Institute for Social History, Amsterdam.
96 Mangan, 'The Good Comrade', p. 53.
97 Through Hugh Slater, Kate also met Patience Darton when she was nursing Tom Wintringham in Valencia. See Chapter 4 of this book and also Paul Preston, *We Saw Spain Die. Foreign Correspondents in the Spanish Civil War*, (Constable, London, 2008).

war, becoming more committed to the Republican cause. 'When I reached Spain' she wrote, 'my political ignorance was such that I had barely heard of Marx and Lenin.'[98] In her memoirs, she compares the enthusiasm she discovered at political meetings in Spain with the 'profound discouragement' she usually felt when listening to political speakers in Britain and other countries.[99]

> In Spain, I suddenly felt that I was in the presence of real freedom and truly self-governing people. They cared about what was said because they knew it would be acted upon. Their discussions might be amateurish and their efforts bungling but they were at least out of the field of abstract demagogy and in the field of practice, everybody taking their part in trying to improve society and win the war at the same time. There was a terribly bewildering welter of opinions and talk but it was all so alive and there I grew keen on politics for the first time, and was firmly convinced that if ever these people should be conquered and suppressed it would be a scandalous waste and shame, for they had just begun to live.[100]

Eileen Blair was also determined to find work in Spain that would enable her to be closer to her husband, Eric, better known as George Orwell, who was fighting with the POUM militia. Her letters continually demonstrate concern for her husband's health and welfare but give no indication of any personal deep political affiliation, and at times quite the contrary. Whilst still in England, shortly after Orwell had first arrived on the Aragon front, she wrote to her friend to say she was leaving for Spain on the following morning, making arrangements by telephone with contacts in Paris.

> I leave in a hurry, not because anything is the matter but because when I said that I was going on the 23rd, which has long been my intention, I suddenly became a kind of secretary perhaps to the ILP in Barcelona. They hardly seem to be amused at all. If Franco had engaged me as a manicurist I would have agreed to that too in exchange for a salvo conducto [safe conduct pass] so everyone is satisfied.[101]

---

98 Mangan, 'The Good Comrade', p. 419
99 For the views of other women on party political meetings in Britain see Chapter 3.
100 Mangan, 'The Good Comrade', p. 65.
101 Peter Davison (ed.) *The Lost Orwell* (Timewell Press, London, 2006), p. 68. Davison, *The Lost Orwell* p. 68.

The repercussions of her decision to accept a post in the ILP offices in Barcelona were to be bring her into a dangerous world of left-wing party political struggles.[102]

There are other examples of women whose involvement in politics was perhaps deepened through personal relationships. The marriage of George Green to Nan Farrow was one such instance. Through her work in an insurance office Nan Farrow had already learned about the conditions in which miners and others were working. She knew the inadequacies of the compensation they were given when injured, and the paltry amount allocated to their widows. She began to read Fabian pamphlets and to vote for the Labour Party.[103] An enthusiasm for rambling led to her meeting George Green, a cellist with plenty of idealism but few prospects of financial security. However, her father's outrage at the idea of 'tying herself to a wandering musician' did not prevent the marriage.[104] Commitment to anti-fascism led both George and Nan Green to Spain during the civil war, a difficult decision to make with

2.4 Nan Green.

102 See Chapter 4.
103 Nan Green, Tameside 180 and 'A Chronicle of Small Beer', p. 20.
104 Green, 'A Chronicle of Small Beer', p. 23. For more on the relationship between George and Nan Green see a chapter on Nan Green by Paul Preston, *Palomas de Guerra: Cinco mujeres marcadas por la guerra civil* (Plaza y Janés, Barcelona, 2001) published in English as *Doves of War: Four Women of Spain* in 2002 by HarperCollins.

2.5 Nan Green with her children
before leaving for Spain.

2.6 Margot Heinemann.

two young children to consider.[105] Another partnership with a strong political dimension was that of Margot Heinemann and the poet and Communist activist, John Cornford. They met in Cambridge as students in October 1934, and the brief years until his death in Spain at the end of 1936 had a significant impact on her life and work.[106]

Apart from individual relationships of a personal/political nature, women in this sample often responded enthusiastically to a mixture of the social and the political. The numerous and widespread local left-wing groups, particularly those directed specifically towards a youthful membership such as the Young Communist League and the Labour League of Youth, offered not only educational opportunities, but also abundant organised social activities. Commitment to one of the thousands of these local groups often led directly to involvement with the many campaigns connected with the Spanish Civil War. A heady combination of classes in political theory and a packed social agenda of camps, rambles, and rallies changed the lives of members and opened their eyes and minds to a new world. 'I only really started living when I joined the Communist Party,' said Elsie Booth, 'before that, life was nothing really.'[107] Marie Jacobs, unable to afford to continue her education at school, joined the Hackney Young Communist League. There, they had political classes given by Communist Party leaders, and a packed programme of trips to Sadler's Wells Opera, the Old Vic, and the cinema. She describes it as 'the best social club we ever went to.'[108] Micky Lewis had first joined the Labour League of Youth, but found it was 'too whimsy' so left to join the Young Communist League, which was perceived as much more dynamic. There, she recalled with enthusiasm,

> ...we learned all about the set up of Capitalism and how it led to Fascism and how it led to wars... We used to go on cheap holidays together where we used to have classes - schools, you know, week schools on politics and whatever - used to love them - wish they had them now.[109]

---

105 Nan Green decided that she could go to Spain to carry out administration work with the medical units because Wogan Philipps generously offered to pay for the children to go to a boarding school of her choice. In view of the poverty in which they were living, she chose to send them to Summerhill, knowing that A. S. Neill and his staff were in sympathy with the Republican cause.
106 See Chapter 6.
107 Elsie Booth, Tameside 756.
108 Marie Jacobs, IWM 13819.
109 Micky Lewis, AJ, 9 July 1996. Others felt equally enthusiastic, for example Marjorie Jacobs, AJ, 2 August 1996.

Membership of such groups was only one way in which awareness grew of the appallingly low standard of living prevalent in certain parts of Britain in the thirties. Frida Stewart left Cambridge to work at the Manchester University Settlement in Ancoats, producing plays and music with groups of unemployed men. There she became aware of their struggle against poverty, admiring their good humour and pride despite living conditions which came as a revelation to her.

> At first it was difficult to get used to the monotony of the streets, the fog, the soot, the whole murk-ridden atmosphere; it could hardly have been more different from Cambridge - that grimness, those smoky black gaunt industrial buildings looming out of the mist and rain above row upon row of small grimy dwellings... Later on I got used to the lack of light and colour, and almost enjoyed the effects of factory chimneys soaring against stormy skies, the belching of smoke into windy patterns, the harsh black and grey symphony of the great industrial town. I well realised though, that for me there was always an escape from the darkness to the green radiance of Cambridge.[110]

2.7 Frida Stewart.

---

110 Frida Stewart, unpublished memoirs, p. 62.

Coming in to close contact with 'life on the dole', the 'damp and dry rot', the 'hungry children' and 'the eternal battle against dirt and soot' made her revolt against her 'make-believe palliative job' of creating a world which evaporated as soon as the curtain fell, leaving only a reality of grim hopelessness.

Some of the nurses who went to Spain had encountered much suffering as a result of poverty when they were working 'on the district'. As a midwife in East London during 1936, Patience Darton found mothers weak from malnutrition and repeated pregnancies.

Their houses were quite fantastic, 90% of them were appalling - old barracks, well, tenements, crawling with bugs, alive with bugs, dripping with bugs, and everyone lousy. There was no lighting at night in the main part, in the stairs. There'd be gas in the rooms, worked off a penny in the slot, which you had to take your pennies most of the time, and a gas cooker on the stair... Of course there wasn't any heating in the rooms and there wasn't any water - there probably wasn't any water in the house - you had to go out for the water - the tap, down, outside. A loo outside for tipping away things, but sometimes we had to carry away the afterbirth - no way of getting rid of it if there wasn't a neighbour who would see to it for you, you had to bring it back to the hospital. And the poverty was so extreme with unemployment of that sort, that we've no idea now - they had a table and chair each, a table and two chairs for a husband and a wife, if there were other children you might have another chair or two. Half the time the children were crammed on to the one mattress, and you had to park them around, get the neighbours up to park the children out so that you didn't deliver the mother on top of the children in the bed. Usually there weren't sheets. There was quite often a blanket or sometimes coats and things on top. We used to take a sheet to deliver on, a draw sheet thing. And we used to take newspapers to put round us, to put our things on, to stand the chair on that you were going to sit on while you had to wait for it, because you could see the bugs on them then - on the newspaper, and you could hear them falling, tss, tss, you know, little cricky noise on the newspaper. The stairs were danger-ous because the things were all gone, the railings were all gone for firewood, and the uprights had gone, you only had the - just left to walk on. You used to put your penny in the gas for the thing on the landing and ask somebody to keep an eye on it for you. But if they couldn't, I mean quite often somebody else would come out with their kettle and put it on because they just needed that much.[111]

Her portrayal of this aspect of life for certain women in Britain, mainly those in the families of the unemployed, graphically illustrates the conditions which had led to an increase in maternal mortality in the previous decade.[112] The doubling of the number of dwellings considered to be 'unfit' during the thirties and the serious overcrowding highlighted by an LCC survey in 1936, would have contributed to the fact that in the 1930s it was four times as dangerous to bear a child as to work in a coal mine.[113] Statistics show an overall improvement in conditions for working-class women and children in the thirties, but these figures reflect a rising standard of living for those in work, many of whom were employed in the new industries in the south of England. The figures mask the underlying deprivation of the unemployed who were enduring the indignities of the 'Means Test', particularly in the regions of Britain where the heavy industries had collapsed.[114] As a schoolgirl, Lillian Urmston would cross the road to avoid the people queuing outside the Labour Exchange in Stalybridge, some of whom she knew.

They were standing there looking hungry, depressed and ashamed, and I used to feel ashamed that I'd even glanced at them because I felt it was adding to their misery. And then I heard stories of the way they were treated, when the money was pushed across the counter it was often pushed so that coins fell onto the floor, when the man had to touch his cap and pick them up they were told 'Hurry up, hurry up, there's a long queue behind you, you know, get out of the way.'[115]

This in retrospect she saw as 'political inklings beginning in me, but I didn't recognise them as such in those days.'[116]

111 Patience Edney (née Darton), IWM 8398. See also Lillian Buckoke (née Urmston), Tameside 203, for similar experiences in the Manchester area.
112 Margaret Mitchell, 'The Effects of Unemployment on the Social Condition of Women and Children in the 1930s', *History Workshop Journal* 1985, no.19, Spring, pp. 105-127, quoting Margery Spring Rice, *Working Class Wives* (London, 1981, 2nd edition) p. 19, fn. 1.
113 Ibid., pp. 111-112, quoting Russell, *The Long Campaign* p. 260; C. Pallet, 'Housing' in A. H. Halsey, *Trends in British Society* p.303, Table 10.9; *Overcrowding Survey*, LCC, 1936.
114 For more on the Means Test, see for example, Noreen Branson and Margot Heinemann, *Britain in the Nineteen Thirties* (Weidenfield & Nicholson, London 1971) Chapter 3.
115 Lillian Buckoke (née Urmston), Tameside 203.
116 Ibid.

2.8 Ellen Wilkinson with Jarrow marchers, 1936.

Other women were brought directly into contact with the problem
of poverty through the phenomenon of the Hunger Marches. Many
such marches took place during the thirties, and Ellen Wilkinson
has become famous for joining one group on the 'Jarrow Crusade'
in October 1936. Thora Silverthorne, as a nurse already active in
politics, was naturally one of those who helped to treat the blistered
feet of hunger marchers.[117] Penny Phelps' instinctive desire to help
the marchers on humanitarian grounds was to trigger her departure
for Spain. When nursing in Hertfordshire, at a friend's suggestion,
she went to help treat the feet of the marchers during their overnight
rest in Hertford.

> And honestly, when I realised how some of them - their feet - so
> what did I do? I took it off my own bat to get the ambulance, one of
> them was in such a dire state, I just rang for the ambulance and then
> got him sent to the hospital. In the morning I got called [sic] over
> the coals by the matron.[118]

Penny Phelps' immediate resignation from the hospital followed
this meeting with matron. To what extent this can be attributed to a
reluctance to remain after such a ticking-off, or to matron wishing to

---

117 Thora Silverthorne, AJ, 3 January 1996.
118 Penny Phelps, AJ, 22 February 1996.

remove an undesirable influence, appears a little unclear. In the interview she recalled that, 'I left and went straight to the Spanish Medical Aid, and they took me straight away, and before I could say anything, I was off to Spain.'[119]

Perhaps not many women were affected in such a dramatic way by contact with the marchers, but for those living in more sheltered environments in the days before pervasive media coverage, a Hunger March could be an eye-opening experience. Margot Heinemann recalled the impact the marchers made on her as a student in Cambridge.

> It was always, I think, both things in my mind, the question of poverty as well as the question of war, and I certainly remember there was a demonstration to go out to greet the contingent of hunger marchers from the north-east coast who were passing through Cambridge. And we marched out to meet them at Girton and marched back with them... They slept in the Corn Exchange as far as I remember, and medical students were organised to dress their blisters and deal with their feet. And there was a meeting in the town in the evening which was addressed by the leader of the contingent, Wilf Jobling... And I remember that as a landmark because it was the first time it had ever occurred to me that the working class could have a leading role, or a central role in politics... He was a very fine speaker and he was an unemployed miner, and afterwards was killed in Spain.[120]

Injustice and exploitation at work also acted as a stimulus for women's political involvement on a wider scale. For Ethel MacDonald, a small injustice resulted in a meeting with Glasgow anarchist, Guy Aldred, and a lifetime commitment to revolutionary politics. In an article entitled 'Chance Changed These Readers' Lives', she explained how this had happened.

> Early in 1933 the Labour Exchange sent me after a job as a waitress at Dumfries, but when I arrived I found the whole thing was a fake, and I had to hitch hike back to Glasgow. I went to see a well-known Socialist [Guy Aldred] to ask him to fight my case. He invited me to act as his secretary and assist in the office he was opening. As a result of that I was invited to Barcelona to act as a radio

119 Ibid.
120 Margot Heinemann, IWM 9239.

announcer. As a working woman with no ambition beyond my class, it seems to me that Chance certainly changed my life.[121]

It seems unlikely that Chance was the only factor at work in this dramatic transformation from un-ambitious working woman to someone who became the 'Scots "Scarlet Pimpernel", a legend in Spain.'[122] Little is known of her early life other than that she was one of a family of nine, that she left home aged sixteen and was said to have 'never returned except for a casual visit.'[123] However, perhaps something of her nature as a child can be deduced from her father's description of her as a 'stormy petrel.'[124] Other left-wing activists in this study remembered the difficulties encountered when attempting to encourage other women to become politically involved at work. Elsie Booth worked in a cotton mill where women regularly lost fingers trying to fill their quotas, a misfortune she too suffered.

The mill girls used to think I was mad when I took an interest in politics because they'd never heard of it you see. They used to go to a dance or stand at the corner talking to boys, that was their life. And when they knew that I'd joined the Communist Party, well, they all expected me to pull a bomb out from under my coat.[125]

Attempts to get them to come to political meetings would be met with the retort, 'Oh, shut up Bolshie, we're not interested.'[126]

These efforts to improve working conditions and build a better society were sometimes further stimulated by visits to the Soviet Union where concerted efforts were being made to improve life for the masses.[127] In 1935, Frida Stewart went to the Theatre Festival in Moscow

---

121 'Chance Changed These Readers' Lives', *The Leader* London, February 1938. Quoted in Rhona M. Hodgart, *Ethel MacDonald: Glasgow Woman Anarchist* (Kate Sharpley Library, London, undated) pp. 3-4.
122 Obituary of Ethel MacDonald, *Glasgow Evening Citizen*. Also quoted in Hodgart, *Ethel MacDonald*, p. 20.
123 Guy Aldred, 'Ethel MacDonald Tribute', *The Word*, January 1961, p. 18.
124 *Glasgow Evening Citizen*, Friday 2 December 1960. Also quoted in Aldred, 'Tribute', *The Word*, p. 19.
125 Elsie Booth, Tameside 756.
126 Ibid. The Communist Party had about 14% female membership at this time. The views of some of these grass-roots members, recorded by Sue Bruley, give an interesting insight into their political attitudes towards issues other than the war in Spain, for example, on the family, birth control, prostitution and homosexuality,
127 Isabel Brown, Felicia Browne, Charlotte Haldane, Yvonne Kapp, Rose Kerrigan, Leah Manning, Molly Murphy, Priscilla Thornycroft and Bessie Wild were amongst those who also visited the Soviet Union before the outbreak of the Spanish Civil War.

on a trip organised by the British Drama League. Full of idealism and hope, she described how she reacted to their efforts to build a new egalitarian society.

>...the experience of seeing Russia with one's own eyes was electrifying, and I felt I'd had a glimpse of a new world - an unforgettable periscopic peep into the bright future of the Soviet children and young people, with its promise of plenty for all of them (if only peace prevailed) and of health and culture and equal chances.[128]

Mary Docherty was part of a group chosen to go to the Soviet Union through the YCL in 1929 for a Children's International meeting. Already suffering from TB, contracted as a result of being 'run down in health' after years of childhood poverty, her happy memories of visits to the theatre in Moscow and New Year fireworks contrast starkly with her recollections of playing with a brick for a doll as a child in Scotland. When the others returned home, she remained behind in a sanatorium near Yalta, where her TB was cured.

>The time I spent in the Soviet Union was something I will never forget. I felt a different person, no worry about where the next meal was coming from, free to go where I pleased, everyone doing everything they could to make me happy. This made me feel I belonged there. When I was in Moscow, I would look around and say to myself, 'All this belongs to the workers. No capitalist class.' While I was there it also belonged to me as a worker.[129]

Florence Farmborough's experience in Russia took place two decades earlier and could not have been more different. She first went there as a governess in 1910. In the preface to her published diaries she explains why she felt compelled to set out on a path which would lead to the dangers of nursing on the Russian front during the First World War, and then to working for Franco during the Spanish Civil War, reading daily propaganda bulletins in English on Spanish National Radio.[130]

---

128 Frida Stewart, unpublished memoirs, p. 74.
129 Docherty, *A Miner's Lass*, p. 78.
130 These broadcasts were also published in book form and are strongly pro-Franco and 'anti-Red'. Florence Farmborough, *Life and People in National Spain* (Sheed & Ward, London, 1938).

2.9 Florence Farmborough.

I always knew that I should have to travel. The longing was strong within me from my earliest years. As the fourth of a family of six children, there were few obstacles in my way when, still in my teens, I expressed the wish to go abroad. My feet were restless with the urge to wander and my eyes strained after the veiled ways ahead, eager to behold all that the wide, wonderful world held in store for me.[131]

The record of her years as a Red Cross nurse with the Russian army is both detailed and fascinating. Remarkably, she also took photographs throughout much of the turmoil. An interview recorded

131 Florence Farmborough, *Nurse at the Russian Front: A Diary 1914-18, with 48 Photographs by the Author* (Constable, London, 1974).

in 1975, by which time she was eighty-eight, brings her personality into sharper focus in certain ways than either her books or her photographs. In the imperious tones of a bygone age, rolling the 'R' in Russia and sounding the 'H' in words such as 'why', she relates her experiences with a slow precise delivery, revealing her talents as an orator as she describes the blighted battlefields.

> I don't think in any war would you see a battlefield as you saw in the First World War. The battlefields were great wide open places lined and marked here and there by zig-zagging trenches, some of them very deep, the Russians' very shallow - and innumerable, long, long, wide spaces covered with wire entanglements... In going over, we have walked over them, we have seen on the entanglements bits of human beings. We have found them lying - you will see my photographs - lying on the ground, they were dying, decomposing. They had no time to bury them.[132]

Her experiences of the First World War were to have a great impact on her future attitudes, but for the majority of women in this study, born later than Florence Farmborough, the late 1920s and early 1930s were the key years during which their horizons were broadening. This was a period during which, for them, the hopes for social reform were coupled with a growing awareness of wider events. The international issue causing most concern, and which would become linked inseparably to the Spanish Civil War, was the rise of fascism. The process of becoming aware of this as a danger occurred in a variety of ways, and anti-fascist attitudes reflected several areas of concern. One of these was the concept of racial purity. In Britain, the anti-Semitic rhetoric and violence of Oswald Mosley and the British Union of Fascists were met by mass opposition, and, not surprisingly, the demonstrations against his marches were attended by many of the politically active women in this study.

Margot Heinemann was particularly conscious of this aspect of fascism and was among the Cambridge students who reacted to this 'menace' by attending such demonstrations. At Mosley's Hyde Park meeting of 1934, she recalled the slogan 'Drown Mosley in a sea of working-class activity'. In retrospect, she thought the slogan sounded

---

132 Interview with Florence Farmborough, Peter Liddle, 1975. Liddle Collection of First World War Archive Materials, Brotherton Library, University of Leeds.

'rather curious', but nevertheless believed it gave an accurate impression of the occasion, during which two thousand Fascists, Unity Mitford included, were surrounded by over a hundred thousand anti-fascists being kept back by police.[133] Mass protests of this type have passed into popular memory as a shared experience and a triumph for the Left which 'put the nail into any further progress of fascism' in Britain and 'exposed it to the nation.'[134] Women frequently state proudly, 'I was there' when asked if they joined in these protests.

But although BUF activities were taken very seriously by many of the women in this study, perhaps the events taking place abroad were of even more concern. Simple holiday trips sometimes brought home the nature of the changes taking place in Europe. Margaret Powell went hiking with a friend in Germany in the thirties and was left with an indelible impression of the marching youth and anti-Semitic attitudes that was to develop into an abhorrence of fascism and all it stood for.[135] These sentiments were behind her decision to nurse in Spain and then to work with refugees in Yugoslavia and Germany. Others had similar experiences whilst on holiday, and watched with disbelief as the situation worsened. Through her musical interests, Frida Stewart encountered the ideals of the 'Wandervogel' when attending a fortnight's music festival in Germany to promote Anglo-German friendship in 1931.

> The musical side of this visit was very interesting and worthwhile. I felt much more doubtful about the ideological background... I could not accept the theories they propounded, which seemed suspiciously like those of the young National-Socialists I had met in 1928, nor the expressions 'flaminess' and 'feeling with the blood', nor the semi-religious symbolism of dancing by fire-light and such like ritual.[136]

---

133 Margot Heinemann, IWM 9239.
134 Kathleen Gibbons, AJ, 6 August 1998. For more on Olympia, see *Fascists at Olympia: Statements From:- The Injured, Doctors Who Attended the Injured and From Eyewitnesses* which includes statements from women such as Vera Brittain, Storm Jameson, Naomi Mitchison, Pearl Binder and Phoebe Fenwick Gaye amongst the male eye-witnesses. For more on Cable Street see Noreen Branson and Margot Heinemann, *Britain in the Nineteen Thirties*, pp. 292-294 which tells of how the windows and roofs were alive with women hurling down bottles at the police who were trying to force a way through for Mosley and his Blackshirts, 'making the road thick with the glass of old sauce and vinegar bottles, their smell sharp in the air.'
135 Sam Lesser speaking about his wife, Margaret, AJ, 10 April 1996.
136 Frida Stewart, unpublished memoirs, p. 42.

When she suggested that the goodwill tours be extended to include non-Teutonic countries, a shocked silence ensued. Over the following two years, she heard of conditions in Germany from the Jewish exiles taking refuge with her family in Cambridge, and in letters from her sister in Frankfurt, which she read with 'horror and incredulity.' By 1933, she says, 'The thought of what was happening in the Germany which I had loved and which now seemed to have gone mad, kept me awake at nights.'[137] Elizabeth Crump was at University in Germany in 1936, and was 'thoroughly anti-Nazi' without realising the full implications of what was happening.

> You just saw the trappings of the thing, you know, all these people dressed in black and all these students that I knew went on midnight walks with torches and this sort of thing - and there wasn't a Jew left in the town.[138]

2.10 Elizabeth Crump.

A further issue within fascist ideology causing concern was that of the role of women and the ideal of a return to 'Kinder, Kirche, Küche,' children, church and home. Apart from a tiny minority of 'feminists' who thought that the BUF offered a way forward for women through

---

137 Ibid., p. 47.
138 Elizabeth Crump (m. Thornycroft), AJ, 23 October 1996.

the corporate structure, those who were active in the fight for women's rights were inevitably anti-fascist to some extent.[139] At parliamentary level, both Eleanor Rathbone, the Independent MP and famous 'New Feminist', and Ellen Wilkinson, a former suffragist, became involved as anti-fascists with the war in Spain. At the grass-roots, Molly Murphy was perhaps unique as a former Suffragette who became a nurse in Spain. Born in 1890, as a sixteen year-old she joined the Women's Social and Political Union led by the Pankhursts, together with her mother who had been 'the mainstay' of the family for years. Molly Murphy's feminist views can be linked to childhood misfortunes after her father resigned from his job as manager in protest over the rejection of a pay claim for the men in his department. He announced that he 'would become a worker at the bench and fight with them for better conditions.' 'That sounds very fine and noble,' wrote Molly Murphy in her memoirs, 'but coming from a man with a family of six to provide for, it was just plain silly.' Unemployment followed, and they were forced to move to the slums of Salford, from which her mother resolved to escape as soon as possible. In this she succeeded, becoming the breadwinner, moving the family to a better environment and forcing her husband, 'like it or not, to play second fiddle', until he left permanently.[140] Molly Murphy became the organiser for the Sheffield Branch of the WSPU, but by that time was becoming more interested in socialism. This she dates from a brief glimpse of the life led by some of the WSPU leaders, shortly after she was released from arrest for chalking advertisements for a meeting.

> I arrived at the big house just as the footman was handing tea to a group of the lady's friends. She had invited them to meet Mrs Pethwick Lawrence and the latter had just made an appeal for funds. 'Well,' I said to myself, 'there should be some funds amidst this opulence,' but behold the lady of the house sitting in a most lavishly furnished room with a massive silver tea service before her, expounding on 'sacrifice'. 'Yes, she said, 'all of us have many demands made upon us and yet we must get more people to support us. It is no use people saying they cannot afford any more. There are always ways and means, if it is only cutting out the fish course at

139 See for example the fascinating series of articles on the theme of 'Work for Women' and their role in the Corporate State by Olive Hawks in *The Blackshirt* in 1937, 11, 19, 25 September, 9, 16, 23, 30, October, 6, 10, and 20 November.
140 Molly Murphy, memoirs, 'Nurse Molly' p. 5, National Museum of Labour History.

breakfast and giving that.' 'Cutting out the fish course' was almost too much for me who had never seen a fish course at our breakfast table. I nearly exploded with suppressed laughter. I thought a lot about it... The more I thought about it the more I wondered what such as myself and my mother and Annie Kennie, the mill-worker, could have in common with such as these ladies of the big house.[141]

For Molly Murphy the fight for the enfranchisement of women became 'a very positive phase of the human struggle for socialism and not something apart from it.'[142] She would have been well aware of the risk of losing the hard fought gains for equality if fascist policies to restrict women to the home were to predominate.

2.11 Celia Baker.

Noreen Branson was very active in the Co-operative Women's Guild, helping in the efforts to make birth control available to more women. Members of the Guild, she recalled, were particularly aware of Nazi policies concerning women. Celia Baker learned of these policies in a more unusual way. As a member of a group of actors known as Rebel Players, she performed in a play called 'Mädchen In Uniform',

141 Ibid., pp. 13-14.
142 Ibid., p. 23.

which was based in a girls' school in Germany. It was, she recalled, 'a great eye opener about Germans and their attitude to women.'[143] The women of the Six Point Group, as part of their campaign for women's equality, published a pamphlet entitled *Women behind Nazi Bars*. This had been written by their Honorary Secretary, Monica Whately, who later became deeply involved with the Spanish Civil War. Their Annual Report comments on the pamphlet's success.

[The pamphlet] revealed so forcibly the degradation of women under Fascist dictatorships and contained a moving call to women to band themselves together as a protection against this world-wide menace. Hundreds of thousands of copies were printed and circulated by the Women Shoppers' League, and the document was sold in the streets of the West End, where for many years no feminist publications had been offered for sale.[144]

This was not the only group to disseminate information on this theme. The Six Point Group sent a representative to another organisation, Women Against War and Fascism. Elsie Booth also belonged to this group. She went as one of seventy British delegates to the first international congress, held in Paris in 1934, attended by a total of 1,200 women. Here she would have come into contact with the head of the Spanish delegation, Dolores Ibárruri, 'La Pasionaria,' who was soon to become internationally famous for her call to defend the Republic. The aims of the participants at the congress were later summarised in a bulletin for circulation to prospective British members.

The objects of the world movement are to rouse women to a realisation of the ever-increasing menace of fascism and war, to enlist their support in combating these evils, and to uphold and further their rights and liberties. In this country, the movement is attempting to draw women together in the struggle against all forms of war preparations, such as increased armaments and military propaganda and teaching; to support similar efforts in other countries; to bring home to women the special dangers that fascism holds for them, and the consequent importance of their guarding and extending their existing political and economic rights; and to work

---

143 Celia Baker, AJ, 20 May 1997.
144 Annual Report of the Six Point Group, November 1935 - November 1936, Fawcett Library, London Guildhall University.

for better conditions for women in industry, and for the improvement of social services for women and children.[145]

This statement appears to encapsulate the predominant hopes and
fears of the majority of women in this study during the early thirties.
But those who had been particularly responsive to the idea of pacifism were faced with a crisis of conscience.[146] As their belief in the
possibility of peace through collective security in the League of
Nations began to fade, many modified their views to allow for the
necessity of fighting in a 'just war' in response to the rise of the fascist
dictators. Noreen Branson and Leah Manning had both been pacifists
as a result of personal loss through war. Noreen Branson's father was
killed in the First World War, and Leah Manning had been devastated
by the death of her greatly admired young step-uncle at Mafeking.
Both women had changed their views on pacifism by 1935. Noreen
Branson had shifted from her former anti-war position after participating in the demonstrations against Mosley's Blackshirts in London.

> I thought it was right to fight for a good cause, but that was a differ-
> ent story to an imperialist war that wasn't a good cause, you know,
> imperialist powers fighting one another. But fighting for freedom
> was, by that time, something I'd become completely convinced
> about the need to do.[147]

The results of the Peace Ballot in 1935 showed Leah Manning that
the British people supported collective action against an aggressor
nation. This, combined with what she had seen on her visit to Spain in
1934 following the severe repression of the Asturian miners uprising,
forced her to throw off her long-cherished pacifist ideals.[148]

Others followed a similar path from hopes for maintaining peace to
the realisation that war was inevitable. Betty Harrison, one of the
many women who helped to raise funds for refugee children from
Spain, had thought she was a pacifist until 1936, then recognised that
pacifism 'was not really tenable as far as I was concerned. If I'd been

---

145 The Women's World Committee Against War and Fascism, Bulletin no. 4, March/April
     1936, Marx Memorial Library, Box D5 (XII).
146 For an interesting discussion on the relationship between femininity, pacifism and
     aggressive combat see Joanna Bourke, *An Intimate History of Killing: Face-to-face Killing
     in Twentieth-Century Warfare* (Granta, London, 2000, first edition 1999) pp. 309-14.
147 Noreen Branson, AJ, 26 January 1996.
148 Manning, *A Life for Education*, p. 142. Leah Manning also wrote an account of the repression
     in Catalonia and Asturias entitled *What I Saw in Spain* (Victor Gollancz, London, 1935).

in Spain, I would have been fighting so I was no longer a pacifist.'[149] As an art student, Priscilla Thornycroft joined the Artists International Association, seeing their activities not only for 'free art, democracy and against fascism,' but as part of the campaign for peace, because, 'You see, we really believed that we possibly could stop another war.'[150] The writers, Sylvia Townsend Warner and Valentine Ackland were both active on Peace Councils before campaigning on behalf of the Spanish Republic. Eleanor Rathbone was on the General Council of the League of Nations Union. At first an ardent supporter of progressive international disarmament, she gradually moved to a position favouring tough foreign policy and became a thorn in the side of the British Government, 'whose foreign policy she came to regard as not merely lacking in elementary perception of cause and effect, but in the end as cowardly and dishonourable.'[151]

2.12 Eleanor Rathbone addressing a suffrage meeting, July 1925.

Her book *War Can Be Averted: The Achievability of Collective Security* contains a strong indictment of the British policy of Non-intervention in Spain.[152]

149 Betty Harrison, interviewed by Sue Bruley, 31 August 1976.
150 Priscilla Thornycroft, AJ, 28 April 2000.
151 Mary D. Stocks, *Eleanor Rathbone: A Biography* (Victor Gollancz, London, 1949) p. 222.
152 Eleanor Rathbone, *War Can Be Averted: The Achievability of Collective Security* (Victor Gollancz, London, 1938. See also Chapter 5.

In certain cases, personal experiences from other fields of warfare exerted a direct influence over attitudes to the Spanish conflict. Florence Farmborough surely found it impossible to view the situation in Spain in anything other than a light coloured balefully by her experiences at the Russian front. With the escalation of the Revolution in Russia, the situation had grown worse for her medical unit, and they were ordered to make their way back from the front 'as best they could'. Surrounded by deserting soldiers, she faced very real dangers in all the confusion of 1917.

> That night not one of us slept; we were very cold and we were afraid. All around us were drunken, unruly men, drunken with freedom as well as with alcohol. Bands of them were passing through Botushany after dark; shouting, singing, swearing their way past our hiding place - yes, hiding place. It had come to that; we had to hide, because we were afraid of our own soldiers. As they passed we would hold our breath, and speak in whispers... And more than once, during that black, dreadful night, we heard a peasant-woman's shrill, desperate cry for help.[153]

Her admiration was given to 'the religious, right minded, public spirited, faithful men' who were attempting to maintain order and preserve traditional values amidst the thousands of deserters.[154] Her sympathies naturally lay with her friends in Moscow, whose comfortable lives had been severely disrupted by the *Bolsheviki*. After her arduous journey home, she went to Spain and lectured in English at the University of Luis Vives in Valencia. For her, the outbreak of the civil war in Spain was the 'second Red Revolution' she had witnessed, 'the direct and inevitable result of Russian plotting and propaganda, on the part of the International Communist,' a transfer of fears that would have been difficult to avoid.[155]

Few women in this study had actually been to Spain in the years before the war. Those who had were usually already firmly established on their political path, therefore their views were confirmed, rather than formed, by the experience.[156] Winifred Bates perhaps knew Spain better than most British women as she had spent quite long

---

153 Farmborough, *Nurse at the Russian Front*, p. 363.
154 Interview with Florence Farmborough, Peter Liddle, 1975.
155 Farmborough, *Life and People in National Spain*, pp. 2-3.
156 NB: See footnote opposite.

periods there on several occasions. Fascinated by Spanish culture and traditions, she and her husband spent a year in the villages of Catalonia in 1931, learning to speak the language and talking to the local people they met. She believed, 'I knew what was going on and what was important was, I knew what the people felt.' She was particularly interested in their attitudes towards the Catholic Church, noting that most men in the mountain regions stressed that it was the women who supported the Church. However, she was told by the younger girls that they only went to church, 'because our mothers made us or told us to,' and that they didn't want to go to the 'Daughters of Mary', the only youth organisation in the village for girls. She believed that this was why they 'adapted so quickly to the modern youth organisations and the political ones and so on, that were set up during the war.'[157]

Another woman who also had close contact with Spain before 1936 was Helen Grant, who first went to Spain as an Oxford undergraduate to learn the language. There she formed friendships with many who supported the Republic in the early thirties, including the leading Spanish intellectuals she met through her studies at the famous 'Residencia de Estudiantes' in Madrid. Her recollections of those days include first meeting Federico Garcia Lorca in the gardens of the composer, Manuel de Falla, 'where a French singer sang some of Falla's songs and he reduced her to tears by trying to get her to capture the Andalucian rhythm.'[158] Before going to Spain, she remarks that she 'wasn't really conscious of what was the difference between Communist and Labour,' but she became a firm supporter of the

---

156 For example, Charlotte Haldane made two brief trips to Spain during 1933, firstly accompanying her husband to a scientific and literary conference in Madrid, then shortly afterwards, as a tourist with friends. Ellen Wilkinson had been a member of a delegation from the British Committee for the Relief of Victims of German Fascism which went to Spain in 1934 following the Asturian miners uprising and the subsequent severe repression. Leah Manning had also visited in 1934 (see note 138 above). Felicia Browne was touring Spain to study El Greco murals and to attend the People's Games in Barcelona. She enrolled in a militia group as soon as the fighting began. In contrast, Kate Mangan, who said she had little interest in politics before the civil war, had spent the winter of 1935-36 in Spain with Jan Kurzke.

157 Interview with Winifred Bates, under her second married name 'Sandford', Tameside 192. She and her husband were on holiday in the Pyrenees with a friend they had introduced to the Communist Party, Rosaleen Smythe, when the war broke out. All three were soon working for the Republic in Spain. Winifred Bates used her knowledge of Spanish to work for the Medical Aid Committee, visiting British personnel, sorting out their problems and writing articles about their work. Rosaleen Smythe had administrative skills and was able to work in the medical units keeping the vital records of the dead and wounded. Rosaleen Smythe, AJ, 10 April 1999.

158 Talk given at the Cambridge Union, 'Spain and Me', c. April 1980, papers of Helen Grant, Girton Archive, Cambridge, p. 8.

Republican cause, and 'a passionate socialist.'[159] Helen Grant is unusual in that she became interested in politics through first-hand involvement in Spanish events before the war, such as the student revolt in Granada in 1929. In this she differs from the majority of women whose political attitudes had been formed outside Spain and were applied to the Spanish situation after the outbreak of the civil war. The little knowledge that the ordinary grass-roots activist in Britain had of Spain before the war was to increase dramatically when the campaigns to aid the Republic began to take priority over other activities.[160]

For the few women with first-hand experience of Spain, bonds had been already forged through friendships and familiarity that would be strong motivating factors for involvement with the war in some way. But what of the thousands of other women who were to make this foreign war their concern? Do the narratives in this study suggest that their motivation was the unavoidable consequence of accumulated forces, given their life trajectory up to that point in time? At this juncture, one should perhaps reflect on the possibilities of being seduced by the teleological notion that their paths to involvement with the war in Spain show evidence of inevitability, or even of design. Both the individual whose memories are being explored, and the historian as explorer, may find that their perceptions of a clear highway along which motivations march to their inescapable conclusion are, to some degree, the result of their position as constructors of the past. How tempting it is, some would argue, to find the building blocks for a retrospective stairway to a 'composed' purpose in a life history, when the mixture of past experiences in some cases may only be pebbledash. However, what can be clearly seen is that in this conjuncture, when Spain became a gravitational field attracting a mass of people, women were drawn within its orbit, not only because it was the 'cause' of the day, but because for each of them, the conflict was a reflection of their varied concerns. The extension of these concerns to Spanish issues was therefore a somewhat predictable, rather than a predestined, response.

At the beginning of this chapter, two nurses gave their own evaluation

---

159 Helen Grant, IWM 13808. Her obituary refers to her as a 'passionate socialist', *The Times*, 13 June 1992. For her views on the Republic and the causes of the war, see her pamphlet, *Rebellion in Spain* (Birmingham Council for Peace and Liberty, undated).

160 Apart from the interviews carried out expressly for research on the Spanish Civil War, the priority given to campaigning for Spain during this period is mentioned in some of the interviews for the Labour Oral History Project in the National Sound Archive, and in those carried out in the course of individual research, for example, in the interviews by Sue Bruley in the 1970s.

of their level of political involvement with the civil war, reaching very different conclusions. Now it can be asked, were their motives so diametrically opposed? The traditional definition of politics as an 'activity' which regulates the allocation of resources has been challenged by those who view politics as the working out or 'articulation' of power relationships within society. As such, rather than being defined as an essentially deliberate activity taking place in the public sphere, politics permeates all areas, and does not necessarily demand participation on a conscious level.[161] These disparate notions of the political are reflected in the views held by the women in this study. Patience Darton perceived her motives as 'political', even though she had no affiliation to a particular party at the time, and very little knowledge of politics in general. Her commitment to Communism began in Spain and perhaps retrospectively informed her opinion. Penny Phelps emphasised that her involvement with Spain was not 'political' in any way, but before the war she had friends who were Jewish and, through them, she felt the presence of fascism as a 'threat', saying, 'I felt it because it was a persecution of people who were striving for existence.'[162] Whilst home on leave from her nursing duties in Spain, she spoke at fund-raising meetings for medical supplies and made her views clear.

> I don't know what this government is doing. They don't seem to want the Spanish people to win. We must help them to change the awful conditions of life out there.[163]

The desire to build a better society could be considered fundamentally political, even when expressed in primarily humanitarian terms.

When women party activists are giving their own assessments of their motives for campaigning against Franco, they also at times have difficulty in defining the 'political', for example, claiming to be 'caught up' in the opposition to 'the racism and the fascism rather than the politics.'[164] The narrative of Celia Baker illustrates that the degree of political commitment, as well as the definition, may be largely a matter of perception. Joining the left-wing 'Unity Theatre' group allowed her

---

161 Randall, *Women and Politics*, pp. 7-11.
162 Penny Phelps, AJ, 23 February 1996.
163 *An Abbreviated Verbatim Report*, "English Penny: The Experiences of Penelope Phelps, an English nurse in Spain", as told by herself in a speech at Welwyn Garden City, May 6th 1937, printed report, Penny Phelps, personal papers.
164 Naomi Wolff, quoted in Daniel Weinbren, *Generating Socialism: Recollections of Life in the Labour Party* (Sutton Publishing, Stroud, Gloucestershire, 1997) p. 111.

to combine a love of acting on the stage with her political interests, although she never became a member of any particular political party. Politics, she recalled, had been a part of her background, but she believed she had 'never burned passionately about politics,' adding, 'I never understood Communists who could be so involved.' Nevertheless, her political commitment would appear to be both deep and active. As a girl, she went with her mother to help prevent Oswald Mosley and the British Union of Fascists marching through the East End of London, because, 'Fascists were anathema.' She performed in numerous plays to raise money for Spain on the grounds that the people were victims of 'a terrible injustice' being denied their choice of government. When the civil war ended, she 'mourned the death of Spain' and would not go there whilst the 'fascist dictator' was in power. When asked by her daughter what she had done as a member of the League of Nations to try to prevent the Second World War, she replied,

> 'I marched.'
> She said, 'Did you do any good?'
> I said, 'No, but I had to march.' [Laughter][165]

It would seem therefore, that for Celia Baker, the concept of 'passionate' political commitment perhaps included the necessary element of membership of a political party and adherence to a party line, certainly not considered essential pre-requisites for activists in this age of single-issue politics.

Undoubtedly, there were some women who became Communist Party members because of the active approach the party was taking on Spanish issues. Frida Stewart, not a member of any political group before Spain, decided to 'go the whole hog and join the Communist Party,' partly because she knew about the International Brigade and 'they were the kind of people that I admired.'[166] Others were discontent with the lack of action in the Labour Party on Spanish issues and so left to join the Communist Party instead.[167] But party membership was just one of the ways through which the women in this study demonstrated their concern about the war in Spain. As

---

165 Celia Baker, AJ, 5 May 1997.
166 Frida Stewart, AJ, 11 December 1995.
167 See for example, Beryl Barker, IWM 13805. For more on the attitude of the Labour Party see Chapter 3.

political activists with a strong interest in international events, as followers in the footsteps of women volunteer nurses since Florence Nightingale, as the mainstays of charitable traditions, and as mothers who could share the fears of other mothers for their children, all these women could see in Spain a new focus for their energies. 'Spain' was the clarion call that offered an opportunity to which they could respond, whatever the mixture of the personal, the ideological, the humanitarian and the political on which their motivation was founded. They believed they could help in a practical way, from the smallest contribution to the greatest commitment. The melioristic motive was to them, the essential inspiration.

> People don't seem to understand how it felt, but it was perfectly clear that if you *really* saw what was happening, you felt you had to *do* something about it.[168]

---

168 Noreen Branson, IWM 9212.

CHAPTER THREE

Committee Culture:
Women and Mobilisation

ISABEL BROWN, well known as a Communist speaker, and Katharine, Duchess of Atholl, a Conservative MP, were in the cafeteria at the House of Commons. The Duchess had suggested having tea together to discuss a rather sensitive issue. As members of the National Joint Committee for Spanish Relief, they had resolved never to use the platform of the NJC to further their own political ideas. Appearing as speakers together at meetings had proved very successful, the Duchess attracted those with money, and Isabel Brown was renowned for the amounts she could collect from a crowd. However, the Duchess frequently finished her talk by saying that the democratically elected government in Spain, 'isn't even a Red government.' Isabel Brown had been criticised by her 'own people' for appearing on a platform with someone who made remarks with such derogatory implications. She had decided to avoid further joint public appearances. When the Duchess discovered the reason Isabel Brown no longer wished to continue the successful pairing, she decided to try to put things right in the congenial and intimate atmosphere engendered by the presence of a teapot.

Mrs Brown, I want to apologise, I understand what you must feel. And I of all people should be the last person to use that phrase, 'It wasn't even a Red government' in that tone of voice because what are the newspapers calling me? The Red Duchess.[1]

Her apology was accepted. The Duchess never used the phrase again and Isabel Brown recalled that they resumed their amicable

---

1   Isabel Brown, IWM 844.

practice of sharing a platform for Spain, despite their vastly different views on other issues.

3.1 Isabel Brown.

Isabel Brown's anecdote introduces the theme for this chapter, that of women's activism for Spain in Britain, primarily in response to the needs of those in the Republic.[2] The working relationship established between Isabel Brown and the Duchess of Atholl was characteristic of one of the fundamental factors in the success of many of the committees for Spanish aid, a spirit of co-operation across both political and class divisions.[3] Many of the campaigns connected with the Spanish war involved a significant proportion of women, both as prominent committee members and at grass-roots level. In the pamphlets produced by many of the newly formed groups both nationally and locally, the names of hundreds of women are listed, representing all social classes. Those who were establishing committees knew very

2 Women who were working in Spain for extended periods during the war feature in Chapter 4. Chapter 5 examines the ways in which women communicated their concerns about the war in Spain to others.
3 Other studies have also noted the possibility that predominantly female campaigns could be more effective than masculine movements because of their ability to transcend class. See Rohan McWilliam on the campaign to repeal the Contagious Diseases Acts, *Popular Politics in Nineteenth Century England* (Routledge, London & New York, 1998) pp. 74-5.

well that 'if you could get a Lady somebody into your committee, it helped a great deal.'[4] Lady Hopkins, Lady Noel Buxton and Lady Thomson are listed as supporters of the Eastern Counties Foodship for Spain, for example, along with intellectuals and local dignitaries such as the Mistress of Girton College, the Principal of Newnham, and Mrs Rackham JP. At the other end of the social scale were the thousands of un-named working-class women who bought stamps for a few pennies each week in the Milk Clubs organised for children in Spain, and the factory girls who gave money from their hard earned wages in regular pay-day collections towards some aspect of Spanish relief.[5]

Organisation took place at every level to mobilise activity. British women were working to help those in Spain through international groups, such as the Women's World Committee Against War and Fascism and the Artists International Association, through national groups like the Women's Co-operative Guild and their branches, and in towns and villages through local committees.[6] However, the organisational structure and functioning of the groups concerned with the war in Spain are not the primary subject of this chapter.[7] Here, they are relevant rather as the framework within which women's individual perceptions of the conflict can be explored. Through women's own words more can be added to our knowledge of those who were playing high-profile roles, but who nevertheless receive rare mention for their efforts in this context, and much can be learned about those whose voices are seldom heard at all.

This chapter is based predominantly on material relating to those who were involved with support for people in Republican Spain.

---

4 Frida Stewart, AJ, 11 December 1995. Frida Stewart was responsible for the formation of the 'Aid Spain' groups in Hull and York and helped establish others.
5 The British Youth Foodship Committee sold stamps for a halfpenny each to buy milk for a children's home near Madrid. The Co-operative Union sold milk tokens for threepence and sixpence and by December 1938, had collected £23,000. Jim Fyrth, *The Signal Was Spain: The Aid Spain Movement in Britain 1936-39* (Lawrence & Wishart, London, 1986) p. 247 & p. 257; Collections in factories were common. Mary Freeman remembered collections amongst the girls in the hat factory where she worked. IWM 842.
6 Some of the work done by women in the international groups is discussed in Chapter 6. For details of work for Spain carried out by the Women's Co-operative Guild see the Annual Reports at the LSE, MF 68. The Fifty-Sixth Report, p. 8, states that individual members contributed £363 10s 10d which was sent to Spain through the International Co-operative Alliance, 898 branches also sent money, food and clothing to Spain, 127 branches contributed through local aid committees, milk tokens were sold in 426 branches, knitted garments contributed by 124 branches and 144 Basque children were either wholly or partially maintained by Guild members.
7 Appendix II lists some of the groups that were encountered during the course of this research. Although the list is not the result of a systematic search and makes no attempt to be comprehensive, it serves to illustrate the variety of groups that were concerned with Spain.

There were several notable examples of British women working in what they viewed as 'Nationalist' Spain, but women did not play leading roles in the few committees that were established here in support of the Nationalist cause.[8] The general absence of women holding prominent positions in some of the best known right-wing groups is apparent in an article published in *Labour Research*, 'Franco's Followers in Britain.'[9] In the article, a diagram links the members of The Friends of National Spain to the Cliveden Set and so to the Cabinet, through the Londonderrys to the Anglo-German Fellowship, and also to the British Union of Fascists, and Franco. Only one woman, Lady Londonderry, is mentioned in the lists of inter-connected Lords, Viscounts, Dukes, and other prominent men.[10]

Despite the wealth of many of his British supporters and the publication of *Spain*, a glossy propaganda journal, relatively little money was raised for Franco in Britain in comparison with the amounts collected to benefit the Republic.[11] To assess the degree of support given by women to the few efforts at fund-raising for the Nationalists is difficult. Most of the British campaigns supplying relief to the Nationalists were dominated by the Catholic Church.[12] The Catholic Press, outspoken in support of Franco as the leader of a crusade against an anti-Christian Republic, launched appeals for funds and some of their female readers would doubtless have responded.[13] Groups such as the 'Bishops' Committee for the Relief of Spanish Distress' made collections in church congregations, and contributions from women included wealthy benefactors like Lady Houston, who donated the considerable sum of £700.[14] The funds were used to provide medical equipment and ambulances for a field hospital and mobile unit behind Franco's lines.[15] The supplies were

---

8 For more information on these women, see Chap. 4 for Priscilla Scott-Ellis and Gabriel Herbert in Spain with medical units, and Chapter 5 for Florence Farmborough's broadcasts from Spain.
9 'Franco's Followers in Britain', *Labour Research* May 1938, pp. 107-8.
10 Lady Londonderry is listed for her role on the Basque Children's Repatriation Committee.
11 *Spain*, published monthly by Spanish Press Services, London.
12 For more on the role of the Catholic Church in Britain see Michael Alpert, 'Humanitarianism and Politics in the British Response to the Spanish Civil War, 1936-9', *European History Quarterly* vol.14, part 4, 1984, pp. 423-440, particularly pp. 428-430; Tom Buchanan, *Britain and the Spanish Civil War* (Cambridge University Press, 1997) pp. 118-120.
13 *The Catholic Times* and *The Universe* both ran appeals. See Alpert 'Humanitarianism and Politics in the British Response to the Spanish Civil War', p. 429.
14 *Catholic Herald* 4 December, 1936, p. 1. In total, the Bishops' Committee raised £14,500 during the course of the war, see Buchanan, *Britain and the Spanish Civil War*, p. 119.
15 See for example 'Ambulance for Spain is Blessed: Archbishop Hinsley blessing the ambulance which is being sent to the Nationalist Army by the Bishops' Committee for the Relief of Spanish Distress', *The Universe* 18 December, 1936; 'Ambulance Sent to Spain by Bishops' Fund' *The Universe* 30 November, 1936.

usually ordered and dispatched by a British woman, Gabriel Herbert, but no British medical teams were recruited as Franco did not welcome foreign humanitarian aid workers.[16] Apart from 'eye-witness' accounts of escapes from the war zone, British women wrote relatively few articles and letters in support of Franco in the press.[17] As hostesses to gatherings of those who made policy decisions, women on the right may have been exerting their influence on Franco's behalf in the drawing rooms of Britain, but this type of evidence has proved elusive.

In contrast, there is abundant written and oral evidence relating to the substantial numbers of British women who joined different groups in order to direct their efforts towards the people in the Republic. Indeed, the very diversity of these groups has made it difficult to produce a definitive history of their work. Jim Fyrth attempted this task in *The Signal Was Spain: The Aid Spain Movement in Britain*, a title that reflected the main purpose of his book, this being to present a history 'from below', that would give an impression of the feeling of the times and the extent of the activity that took place.[18]

The documentary and oral evidence shows that tens of thousands of people were engaged in organising marches, demonstrations, concerts, socials, bazaars, dances, rambles, film shows, plays, street theatre, appeals from union platforms and pulpits, and door-to-door collections in support of Aid for Spain. More than a thousand committees working for some part of the campaign have been recorded. Every city had several, almost every town and many villages had their own. Millions of people attended the events and gave money, food and clothes.[19]

These events were frequently covered by the press particularly at local level, and the larger meetings were reported in national newspapers. The prevailing view of the campaigns expressed in the extreme right-wing press was that 'Charity Begins at Home.' Aid should not therefore be given to help those in Spain whilst in Britain the unemployed and their children were starving.[20] Examples from

---

16 See Gabriel Herbert, Chapter 4.
17 See for example 'Eye Witness Story of Spain: Liverpool Teacher's Vivid Account', *Catholic Herald* 7 August, 1936, p. 15; 'Franco's Island' by Lucy Heath Pearson, *Action* no. 91, 13 November, 1937, p. 6. Other articles in support of Franco include 'Franco - A Close-Up', written by his English teacher, Dora Lennard de Alonso, *The Morning Post* 20 July 1937, p.10.
18 Jim Fyrth, 'The Aid Spain Movement in Britain, 1936-39' *History Workshop Journal* Issue 35, 1993, p. 155.
19 Fyrth, *The Signal Was Spain*, p. 21.
20 See for example, 'Spain or Britain First', *The Blackshirt* 23 January, 1937; 'Charity Begins at Home', *The Blackshirt* 6 February, 1937, p. 6; 'Will Bristol Support Spain? Poverty at its Doors, and yet - ', *Action* no. 63, 1 May, 1937, p. 6; 'Basques Before Britons in Birmingham' *The Blackshirt* 9 October, 1937, p. 8.

The Blackshirt, the newspaper of the British Union of Fascists, illustrate the nature of the propaganda in use at the time. A cartoon opposing the provision of medical supplies shows an anti-Semitic personification of Communist 'Internationalism' saying to a down-trodden woman and child, the victims of 'British Problems', 'You must wait - I am saving Spain.' The female figure of 'Spain' is however, being strangled in his murderous grasp, the dagger of 'Medical Supplies' in his other hand ready to strike her unconscious form.

On another occasion, the BUF expressed their views on a rally for Spanish relief in an article entitled 'The Great "Help-the-Spanish-Church-Burners" Campaign in Trafalgar Square.'[21]

3.2 A cartoon from *The Blackshirt*, 23 January 1937,
'You must wait – I'm saving Spain'.

Sandals and carmine toenails blended with the exotic odours of the far from mystic East. While haircuts were conspicuous by their absence. At least two workers were present, both strangers to London, who had strayed in the Square mistaking it for Petticoat Lane. The 'intellectuals' were there in force. Contrary to reports the men could be distinguished from the women. Their voices were higher pitched.[22]

In addition to news on the progress of the war, *The Times* carried let-ters of appeal for Spanish aid, and occasional summaries of committee

---

21 The rally, organised in London by the Communist Party, collected £695 for Spanish relief. *Daily Worker* 8 September, 1936, p. 1.
22 'Church Burners on Parade', *The Blackshirt* 12 September, 1936, p. 8.

meetings. On 24 December 1936, the formation of a National Joint Committee for Spanish Relief was reported as having taken place at Friends House on the previous day. A meeting to discuss the need for such a committee had already been held in November, attended by many of the British women who were to have a high profile roles in connection with the Spanish war. Representatives from thirty-eight aid organisations met in the House of Commons, with the purpose of co-ordinating the work for Spanish relief.[23] Isabel Brown attended on behalf of the Spanish Medical Aid Committee, the group she had helped to establish less than a fortnight after the start of the war. Edith Pye represented Save the Children, and both the Salvation Army and the Society of Friends sent women delegates. Amongst the prominent members of the NJC were the Duchess of Atholl who was elected Chairman, and the Independent MP Eleanor Rathbone who became a Vice-chairman.[24]

Local 'Aid Spain' Committees rapidly proliferated. Glasgow for instance, had at least twelve, and in London there were committees in most boroughs and in each of the outer suburbs. Approximately 180 different organisations eventually came under the 'umbrella' of the NJC, many with their own local branches.[25] Attempts to calculate the amounts raised for Spanish relief overall are therefore fraught with difficulties, not only as a result of the number and variety of groups involved, but also because much of the aid sent to Spain was in the form of goods, such as the tins of food collected by the British Youth Foodship Committee, or the garments produced in response to the Duchess of Atholl's knitting competition.[26] A figure of £2,000,000 is

---

23 The aims of the NJC were reported in *The Times* on 24 December, 1936, p. 5, as follows: 'The aim of the committee is to attain as full co-operation as possible among the organisations concerned, particularly by establishing a means of sharing information as to needs and as to what is being done by the various bodies to meet them, and by co-operation in appealing for funds. The co-operating bodies will retain full freedom in the organisation of their own work in Spain. Any central fund that might be established would be regarded primarily as supporting the co-operating organisations.' The number of aid organisations present is given by Fyrth, *The Signal Was Spain*, p. 201.
24 The other Vice-chairman was the Earl of Listowel.
25 Fyrth, 'The Aid Spain Movement in Britain', p. 155. Spanish Medical Aid, for example, established around 200 local committees, raising funds to send trained medical staff, ambulances and equipment to the Republic. Also affiliated to the NJC was the Basque Children's Committee, established in the Spring of 1937 when almost 4000 refugee children were brought to Britain by Leah Manning. As the children were cared for without any government support in small colonies throughout the country, part of the fund raising work was carried out by committees at local level.
26 The competition was a national variation of many local campaigns organised around knitting for Spain. See for example the photograph in the *Daily Worker*, 12 December, 1936 of women in the window of the People's Bookshop in Lavender Hill, Battersea, under the banner 'We are Knitting for Spain'. Also reproduced in Mike Squires, *The Aid To Spain Movement in Battersea, 1936-1939* (Elmfield Publications, London, 1994) p. 12.

sometimes given, in recent terms possibly as much as £100,000,000.[27]

The NJC was careful to emphasise that they intended the aid to be sent 'wherever the need is greatest'. In practice, this meant that the committees formed what could be called the 'backbone' of support in Britain for the Republicans. It is important, however, to point out that no organisation could aptly be described as the 'head', perhaps least of all the National Government in Britain. The policy of 'Non-inter vention' was maintained, despite considerable pressure from a large section of the public, and even though it was clear that the policy was working strongly in favour of Franco's forces. Eleanor Rathbone compared the attitude of British Ministers towards Spain to that of 'a housewife, anxious to be rid of a litter of unwanted kittens, who, as she hands them over to the executioner, remarks perfunctorily, "Poor little things".'[28]

No single political party should be seen as the 'brains' behind the campaigns. The disparate approaches of those who were motivated to become involved prevented the domination of one particular political group over all. In the House of Commons, MPs who were concerned about the war formed a cross-party Parliamentary Committee for Spain.[29] Women in this group had worked together across party lines on other issues, so found co-operation over Spanish issues a natural extension of the way they had collaborated during previous campaigns.[30] The subject of non-intervention was one of the key issues for debate in relation to Spain. The Labour MP, Ellen Wilkinson spoke in the House with great fervour about the way in which the policy worked in favour of Franco, warning MPs of the dangers of inaction in the matter of the Spanish war, and accurately judging that 'things are not going to settle themselves until there has been a great deal more human misery.'[31]

---

27 Even conservative estimates put the amount in excess of £1,000,000. See Alpert, 'Humanitarianism and Politics in the British Response to the Spanish Civil War', pp. 436-437.

28 Eleanor F. Rathbone, *War Can Be Averted: The Achievability of Collective Security* (Victor Gollancz, London, 1938) p. 66.

29 There were five women amongst the thirteen members of the Committee, the Duchess of Atholl (Conservative), Eleanor Rathbone (Independent), Ellen Wilkinson and Edith Summerskill (Labour) and Megan Lloyd George (Liberal).

30 One of the functions of this Committee was to make sure that information on the situation in Spain was available for MPs to use in the House. This work was often carried out by Margaret Stewart, secretary to the Liberal MP who had founded the group, Wilfred Roberts. According to Jim Fyrth, 'When, for instance, Herbert Morrison spoke in the House on Spain, he did so almost verbatim from notes supplied by Margaret Stewart.' *Signal Was Spain*, p. 217. See also Frida Stewart, unpublished memoirs, p. 111

31 Ellen Wilkinson, *Hansard* 6 May, 1937, 1357- 1364.

Official party policy relating to members' involvement with the committees varied. Communist Party membership was relatively small in Britain, but as the approved policy at this time was to promote united action against fascism, it was not surprising that the enthusiasm of their members sustained many of the campaigns to 'Aid Spain'. For the first year of the war, the official Labour Party line was to support the policy of Non-intervention. However, the rank and file within the Labour movement were often determined to take action, despite the lack of urgency shown by their leaders. At a meeting held in 1976 on the theme of British support for Spain, a speaker, probably Angela Tuckett, recalled in precise tones how she and her friends applied pressure from the grass roots.

When the news [of the outbreak of war] came through in Bristol there were a few of us rehearsing in Bristol Unity Players. We instantly stopped the rehearsal and each one of us went off to contact his own organisation and report back the same evening as to what could be done and was being done. Somebody was sent off, of course, to the Trades Council Secretary and brought back the rather sad news, 'nobody's interested in Spain, it's holiday time and it certainly can't be put on the agenda until a branch raises it, and I don't think they will...' So we discussed what we should do and we felt the most important thing was to get them shifting and so, noticing that one of them, of course, was a councillor, we said, 'Right, we'll go out immediately this Sunday with a little leaflet,' which yours truly scratched together, 'and collecting sheets,' which we most illegally invented then and there, 'and we'll collect in this man's ward.' So the following Tuesday it was my pleasure to go and see him and say, 'Now could you, Mr So and So - Brother So and So - do anything about it?' He said there was no interest, so we said, 'Well, we have collected all this money in your own ward.' Hah! They moved - the Trades Council and the Bristol Borough Labour Party quite soon after became very helpful.[32]

Nevertheless, the Labour Party leaders preferred to restrict any expression of international solidarity to their own centralised channels

---

32 Angela Tuckett is not named on the recording made at the meeting held to commemorate the 40th anniversary of the war, but her identity has been verified by others. Tameside 232. The audience seems to have been composed of many people who had themselves been activists in some way, as there was knowing laughter when she declared that she would not name names of those who had been insufficiently active.

and were certainly not keen for their members to become involved in the loosely controlled 'grass-roots up' type of structure adopted by many of the 'Aid Spain' committees.[33] Organisations linked to the Labour Party, such as the trade unions and the Women's Co-operative Guild, were instructed to follow official Party policy and keep away from any such 'Popular Front' style campaigns which would entail Labour Party members working alongside members of the Communist Party. However, these instructions were frequently ignored and party members worked for both party-political and broader-based 'humani-tarian' committees.[34] By attempting to impose these restrictions on the rank and file members of the Party, the Labour leaders suffered a loss of credibility in the eyes of their activists.[35] As Tom Buchanan has pointed out, the leadership had constructed 'if not a folly, a house of crystal - beautiful in its ideologically pure structures but lacking in humanity and vitality, meaning little to ordinary members.'[36]

One of the difficulties which dampened the Labour leaders' enthu-siasm for greater support of the Republic was the possible alienation of their substantial Catholic membership. For British Catholic men and women on the Left, the issues surrounding the civil war raised complex and difficult problems of loyalty. Working-class Catholics had to solve the dilemma of choosing between the call from the Left to uphold the Spanish Republic and workers' solidarity, and the cry of the Catholic Church to support Franco and their religion. Never-theless, Catholics who supported Franco generally remained within the party structure, even if only because there was no alternative organisation that could answer their particular needs.[37] Catholic

---

33 The complex relationship between various groups within the Labour movement and the 'Aid Spain' campaigns are examined in some detail by Tom Buchanan. See for example, 'Divided Loyalties: the Impact of the Spanish Civil War on Britain's Civil Service Trade Unions, 1936-39' *Historical Research GB* 1992 65 (156) 90-107 and 'The Role of the British Labour Movement in the Origins and Work of the Basque Children's Committee, 1937-9' *European History Quarterly* vol. 18 (1988) 155-174. The subject is also discussed by Fyrth, *The Signal Was Spain*, pp. 213-216. For a regional perspective see Squires, *The Aid Spain Movement in Battersea*.

34 The significance of patterns of multiple membership has been discussed by David Berry, who argues that overlapping multiple membership of associations that are heterogeneous in social composition, and cross-cutting to allow the spread of social contacts and commun-ications channels, contribute both to social integration and democracy. *The Sociology of Grass Roots Politics: A Study of Party Membership* (Macmillan, London, 1970) pp. 112 & 128.

35 See for example, C. Fleay and M. L. Sanders, 'The Labour Spain Committee: Labour Party Policy and the Spanish Civil War' *The Historical Journal* 28, 1, (1985) pp. 187-197.

36 Tom Buchanan 'Britain's Popular Front? Aid Spain and the British Labour Movement', *History Workshop Journal* 31, 1991, p. 69.

37 Certain unions were deeply divided on the issue, and the potential existed for a serious breach between the Church and Party. For a discussion on these issues see Tom Buchanan, *The Spanish Civil War and the British Labour Movement* (Cambridge University Press, 1991) Chapter 5.

women in the Labour movement were, however, amongst those who took action over this issue. Women telephonists resigned from their union, protesting on religious grounds against a grant made to the Spanish Workers' Fund.[38] At a meeting of the TUC in 1936 Bertha Quinn of the tailor's union voiced her concern that 'Red outrages have been perpetrated in Spain', and the following year protested against the resolution of her own union to send fraternal greetings to Spanish trade unionists.[39]

Other Catholic women strongly defended the Republic. Monica Whately, an LCC councillor who had been to Spain as a member of a Church delegation of both Catholics and Protestants, addressed Catholics through the pages of the *Daily Worker*.[40] She stated that she had no alternative as the Catholic press would not publish her article 'Let Catholics Know the Truth', which highlighted the large numbers of priests fighting with the Fascists and their use of churches as ammunition stores.[41] Along with many Catholics, she believed that the Republic was anti-clerical rather than anti-Christian as a result of many years of oppression by the Church in Spain.[42] Others, like Noreen Law, were also rejecting the official Catholic view of the war.

I went to a convent and I was in the sixth form and there were a couple of people, I think they were priests, came to tell us about the Spanish Civil War. But it was very biased, and Franco was supposed to be absolutely marvellous, you know, God's gift, and the government of the country was wicked, and so forth. And they were talking about the way Franco took as mercenaries the Algerians and the Moroccans, and they said, 'Any questions?' So I said, 'Yes, I understand that the Moroccans are Muslims - or Mohammedans, as we called them then - how is it that they were prepared to fight for a Catholic cause?' And the headmistress looked at me - I wasn't very popular. I can't remember what reply I got now, but it was something

---

38 Ibid p. 178, fn. 48.
39 TUC CR 1936, p. 432, quoted in Buchanan, *The Spanish Civil War and the British Labour Movement*, p. 189. The *Catholic Times* noted her stand, and contrasted her attitude with that of the 'weak-kneed' Catholic officials within the Labour movement. *Catholic Times* 20 August, 1937, quoted in Buchanan, *The Spanish Civil War and the British Labour Movement*, p. 189.
40 For details see *New Statesman and Nation* 17 April, 1937. Cited in Buchanan *The Spanish Civil War and the British Labour Movement*, p. 188, fn. 85.
41 Monica Whately 'Let Catholics Know the Truth' *Daily Worker* 27 August, 1936, p. 4.
42 For the arguments of Spanish Catholics in support of the Republic see Frances Lannon, *Privilege, Persecution and Prophecy: The Catholic Church in Spain 1875-1975* (Clarendon Press, Oxford, 1987) pp. 211-214.

very anodyne, and obviously not particularly honest, and that really started me thinking.[43]

In strongly Catholic areas, feelings could run high. Marie Stevenson, a Catholic living in Fife, later recalled that she had her 'first and only experience of violence,' when she was collecting door to door for Spanish Relief. She called at the house of a woman who had been a former class-mate at school and was promptly pulled into the house, and thrown on the table with the words, 'How dare you come here after being brought up as we were brought up, and you turning your coat to be a Communist.' Only the face of a colleague at the window put an end to the assault.[44] However, this was an isolated incident, and the majority of Catholics she called upon contributed something to the collections, although she remembered them as being 'a bit dry about it.'

Faced with the complexities of this vast collection of assorted organisations, many historians have drawn the distinction between those which claimed 'humanitarian' motives and those with a manifestly 'political' agenda. Indeed, on the level of a formal study of the organisational structure of the campaigns, this approach can be justified and appears adequate. However, the picture becomes less clear when the perspective shifts from policies to people. This alternative people-orientated view produces results which can complicate, or at times, conflict, with the traditional structural approach. The description given by Hywel Francis of Spanish Aid in Wales reflects the type of difficulty that can arise.

> There was little apparent involvement from political parties or religious bodies in Carmarthen so that the support was clearly humanitarian throughout, although most of the activists would have described themselves as socialists.[45]

As multiple membership of both political and humanitarian groups was a common factor in the 'Aid Spain' campaigns, it seems inappropriate to attempt to maintain the notion of a political/humanitarian division at the level of grass-roots activity. Tom Buchanan writes of

---

43 Noreen Law in Daniel Weinbren, *Generating Socialism: Recollections of Life in the Labour Party* (Sutton Publishing, Stroud, 1997) pp. 99-100.
44 Marie Stevenson, IWM 13802.
45 Hywel Francis, *Miners Against Fascism: Wales and the Spanish Civil War* (Lawrence & Wishart, London, 1984) p. 127.

the 'beguiling simplicity' with which the Spanish Medical Aid Committee 'channelled the humanitarian impulse in a political direction.'[46] By viewing the political and the humanitarian as separate spheres, it is easy to hint at a calculated manipulation of naïve good intentions. However, as discussed in the previous chapter, for many British women involved with Spain no such clear division existed. Broad political and humanitarian concerns were, for them, inseparable, just two sides of the same coin. This suggests that it would be overly simplistic to regard the members of such committees, who often worked concurrently in both 'political' and 'humanitarian' groups, as little more than devious political opportunists.[47]

Another area of conflict relates to the question of whether this mixture of political and humanitarian activity be classed as a 'movement.' Tom Buchanan believes that 'the "Aid Spain" movement did not exist, at least not in any concrete form and certainly not in a way that is helpful to historians analysing this period.'[48] The lack of an overall 'national identity' to the campaigns led him to ask, 'What, indeed, *united* these diverse phenomena beyond a broad internationalist sympathy with the people and workers of Spain and a hatred of fascism?'[49] Jim Fyrth, after many interviews with those who were active in the thirties, places these issues at the very heart of people's concerns, therefore essentially, 'the main political question of the time.'[50] In his analysis, the response to these concerns took on an identity as the 'Aid Spain movement'. Many women in this study would share his view, Margot Heinemann amongst them.

And every demonstration, every Communist Party demonstration, every May Day demonstration, every united action, every meeting, this question of Spain would come up - the solidarity with Spain would come up.... These great anti-fascist turn outs that prevented Mosley marching through the East End, the slogan raised from the people was 'They shall not pass'. We saw what we were doing there as the same as was being done in Madrid, so that everything, whatever it was about, turned into a solidarity action with Spain. I think

---

46 Buchanan, *Britain and the Spanish Civil War*, p. 93 and p. 101.
47 A similar debate has taken place in Australia in relation to the Australian Spanish Relief Committees. See Judith Keene, *The Last Mile to Huesca: An Australian Nurse in the Spanish Civil War* (New South Wales University Press, 1988) p. 67.
48 Buchanan, 'Britain's Popular Front?', p. 70.
49 Ibid., p. 71.
50 Fyrth, 'The Aid Spain Movement in Britain', p. 162.

it is Arnold Wesker's play, 'Chicken Soup with Barley', which begins in Cable Street. The curtain goes up and the people are rallying to stop Mosley marching through the East End, and the stage direction says the 'Himno de Riego', the Spanish anthem, is being played on an old gramophone. And that's exactly how it was - Spain was seen as part of everything we did here and everything we did here was seen as part of solidarity with Spain.[51]

She was not alone in feeling that she had been part of a movement and that, as Elizabeth Crump put it, 'the whole thing linked up.'[52] For the purposes of this study therefore, the concept of a 'movement' is of value because it is an important element in the understanding of women's perceptions of their work for Spain.

Arguments which discount the notion of a movement because it 'did not exist as a national political entity and had no institutional basis,' have much in common with the approaches, now considered somewhat questionable, that have traditionally marginalised women's political involvement.[53] Both the women's movement and the 'Aid Spain' movement fall outside the tightly structured expectations of a traditional historical approach and have therefore perhaps suffered from the imposition of unsuitable paradigms. Nineteenth century feminism has been labelled as 'irregular and unscientific', but in her study of Victorian feminism Philippa Levine has countered the dismissal of the movement in these terms.[54] She argues that although at first glance we see a 'women's movement splintered into a series of single issue campaigns to fight educational, or sexual or employment battles,' in reality 'they were not entirely separate campaigns; they drew on the same core of women whose political analysis saw each individual campaign as one facet of a broader aim and purpose.'[55] A similar pattern can be seen in the case of the 'Aid Spain' campaigns where on many of the committees, just as in the women's movement, party politics and their divisive nature were largely discarded in favour of a loosely affiliated organisational structure in which 'women of conservative mould are allied with

---

51 Margot Heinemann, IWM 9239.
52 Elizabeth Crump (m. Thornycroft), AJ, 23 October 1996.
53 Quotation from Buchanan, 'Britain's Popular Front?', p. 62.
54 K. E. McCrone, 'The Assertion of Women's Rights in Mid-Victorian England' *Canadian Historical Association Historical Papers* 1972 pp. 49-50. Quoted in Philippa Levine, *Victorian Feminism 1850-1900* (Hutchinson, London, 1987) p. 18.
55 Levine, *Victorian Feminism*, p. 14.

those of radical temperament.'[56] Viewed in the wider context of the traditions found in this type of broad-based movement, the concept of an 'Aid Spain' movement becomes a phenomenon of historical value, particularly interesting to those who study women's distinctive engagement with the public sphere.

To mobilise most successfully, women appear to require both a wide choice of activity and an ongoing fluidity within the organisational structure. As Martha Vicinus has pointed out in relation to the early feminist movement, 'A woman could work locally or nationally, in a broad-based or single issue organisation, as a full time activist or as a silent partner.'[57] The same could be said of many of the 'Aid Spain' campaigns. The committees were dealing with matters particularly relevant to the concerns of many women and were also readily accessible to those who were not normally activists. It is possible that women were more eager to participate in these campaigns partly because of the lack of a hierarchical, male-orientated, structure. Noreen Branson remembers the door to door collecting for Spain from women as highly rewarding.

> When you went round - Spain was an exception in this way - because if you went round knocking on doors, arguing for this or that, they would usually pretend that they didn't know - particularly if you were canvassing for candidates, Labour or not, they would always say, 'I must consult my husband', - that was very much a habit. Spain was an exception in this way; they always rushed back to get a tin of milk or something, immediately.[58]

Women felt there was something they could do, however small, to contribute. Celia Baker remembered that her mother and a friend,

> ...in the back of beyond in Hackney, stood there and people came and gave tins, whatever, soup or whatever. There were all these little organisations that wanted to do something, you know, everyone wanted to do something.[59]

---

56 Ethel Snowden, *The Feminist Movement* (1911) p. 21. Quoted in Levine, *Victorian Feminism*, p. 159. The 'umbrella' provided by the National Union of Women's Suffrage Societies fulfilled a similar function to that of the National Joint Committee for Spanish Relief.
57 Martha Vicinus, *Independent Women: Work and Community for Single Women 1850-1920* (University of Chicago Press, Chicago & London, 1985) p. 249.
58 Noreen Branson, AJ, 26 January 1996.
59 Celia Baker, AJ, 20 May 1997.

What has remained in Celia Baker's perception of the campaigns is the way in which they could involve everyone on different levels, the attitude that everybody could 'do their bit' in a way which was to carry on into the years of the Second World War.

The inclusive nature of these campaigns can be contrasted with the more exclusive characteristics of traditional party political organisations. Some of the women who feature in this chapter commented on the difficulties they and others experienced when attempting to participate in these groups. Elsie Booth was one of the women who tried to attend Communist Party meetings despite having to overcome the tremendous obstacles faced as a working-class woman with children.

> You had to come home from work and see to your kids, and then you had to go and bring one out of the nursery and - no washing machines - you had to go to the public wash house with an old trolley and bring it back. I had to leave my son in the house minding the baby so if you still had to go to a meeting - well, that was it - that was your problem... I knew what my own mother went through, you know, and I'm not going to die when I'm bloody forty-eight - so you sort of had to put an extra spurt on and try and assert yourself, which was very hard to do. This is the reason why it was always a struggle to get women in the Party, really, in the thirties, because - I don't care what anybody says - the men domineered the women, especially in the working-class areas. The ordinary working woman didn't really have much of a chance unless you really did assert yourself - you couldn't walk out and leave the kids, somebody had to mind them, didn't they?[60]

Younger women were less restricted. Micky Lewis, an active campaigner in the Young Communist League, experienced a great sense of group solidarity, only mentioning gender in response to direct questioning.

> Because we fought - we were together - the way we were in the YCL, probably because of that, we didn't find this business of lack of equality so much.[61]

---

60 Elsie Booth, Tameside, 756. For the pattern of women's membership in the Communist Party see Sue Bruley, *Leninism, Stalinism and the Women's Movement in Britain 1920-1939* (Garland, London & New York, 1986) Chapter 8.
61 Micky Lewis, AJ, 9 July 1996.

Marjorie Jacobs thought gender equality prevailed in her local Communist Party branch but then, as an afterthought, confirmed that there were limitations to that equality .

> We were accepted pretty well as equals. We used to go to meetings, men and women, you know, we were only young at the time, altogether. I can't remember us being trained as speakers from the platform, it was always the men who were talking and the men in the trade unions as well.[62]

Some women found it difficult to attend meetings because of the cultural traditions surrounding appropriate behaviour for women. Bessie Wild for example, commented on the fact that trade union meetings were often held in public houses and she was 'a bit shy about going into pubs in those days.'[63] Rosaleen Smythe came to London as a young woman in the early thirties. Her interest in politics faltered temporarily when confronted by the reality of the traditional political meeting.

> I went to a few Labour Party meetings and I found those extremely boring - there were all these - what looked like old men, you know, probably thirty or something, with these stiff collars, sitting around, you know, moustaches.... I don't recall any women in the meetings. I didn't stay very long.[64]

Her impressions of the Labour Party meetings are replete with images that re-create the atmosphere of exclusion which has been an aspect of organised politics for so long, even within radical and reformist groups. Both Chartism and Owenism had high levels of female participation at first, declining as formalisation and centralisation increased.[65] After the First World War and the completion of the first stage of female enfranchisement, women had flocked to join the Labour Party, keen to be included in the class struggle for social

---

62 Marjorie Jacobs, AJ, 8 August 1996.
63 Bessie Wild, interview by Sue Bruley, 8 September 1977.
64 Rosaleen Smythe, AJ, 10 April 1999. Rosaleen Smythe joined the Communist Party through her friendship with Winifred and Ralph Bates, participating in demonstrations against Oswald Mosley and eventually going to Spain to help with the administration work in Spanish Medical Aid units. See also Chapter 4.
65 See for example, Barbara Taylor, *Eve and the New Jerusalem: Socialism and Feminism in the Nineteenth Century* (Virago, London, 1983) pp. 220-221; Dorothy Thompson, *The Chartists* (Temple Smith, London, 1984) pp. 122-127.

justice. Some women even hoped that they could bring a new approach to the movement, transforming it into 'something greater and more uplifting for the whole of humanity.'[66] But despite the influx of a hundred thousand women into the Labour Party by 1922, only a few managed to rise to the level of policy making. Pamela Graves has commented on their relatively low profile. 'The thousands of women members, it seems, disappeared without trace into national organisations run by men.' She wonders if 'the silence implies that Labour women were either so similar to their male comrades in their political ideas and activities that they merged unnoticed into their ranks or so different that they were unable to find an accepted place in the mainstream movement.'[67] When women attempted to campaign together on an issue such as birth control, resolutions passed at the Women's Conferences were prevented from proceeding further. The National Executive Council did not consider it to be a party political issue suitable for discussion at national conference level. By the thirties, women in the Labour movement were less likely to be challenging male notions of what were acceptable topics for policy making. The war in Spain created many problems for the Labour leadership, but at least it did not create problems of division on gendered lines.

In addition to the complexities relating to organisational structure, there were also distinct regional and local differences in the 'Aid Spain' campaigns throughout Britain.[68] A few examples will give the flavour of this diversity from the perspective of women's activities and their memories of the work. The economic problems of certain areas in Britain have become part of popular memory through the images of the hunger marches and the dole queues. Nevertheless, despite the trials of their daily lives, people in deprived areas gave as much as they could to Spain. Women in some parts of Wales were amongst those in greatest difficulties, but in Rhondda for example,

---

66 Mrs Fawcett (National Federation of Women Workers), speech at the Labour Party Annual Conference 1918 *Labour Party Report* (1918) p. 104. Quoted in Pamela M. Graves, *Labour Women: Women in British Working-Class Politics 1918-1939* (Cambridge University Press, 1994) p. 1.

67 Graves, *Labour Women*, p. 2.

68 See for example Michael Herbert, 'Anti-Fascism in Manchester 1932-1940', MA Thesis, Department of Economic History, Manchester Metropolitan University, 1996; Squires, *The Aid to Spain Movement in Battersea* (1994); Nigel Todd, *In Excited Times: The People Against the Blackshirts* (Bewick Press, Tyne & Wear, 1995). Francis, *Miners Against Fascism* has a few passing references to women, for example, he notes on p. 121 that on two flag days for Spain in Ammanford, a significant feature was that a total of 43 women had been involved. Oral testimony from various parts of Britain has been collected by Daniel Weinbren and published in *Generating Socialism*, Chapter VI.

there was a strong awareness of the international situation and of the war being fought in Spain. As Lilian Price, the wife of a Brigader, recalled, 'There was always something going on, collections up the Valley, although God knows, they didn't have much to give because they were half starved.'[69] In October 1936, the *Daily Worker* recorded that the women had managed to donate £2 to Aid for Spain.

> In spite of widespread unemployment and dire poverty in the Rhondda Valley, the women have determined to give all the help they can to the Spanish democrats. 'We in this district', writes a member of the Tonypandy Working Women's Guild, 'know what Fascism stands for. At this moment we have 36 workers waiting their trial at the Assizes for putting up a fight against Mosley and his Blackshirts.'[70]

Extracts from the oral testimonies of several Sheffield grass-roots activists indicate the nature of work for Spain taking place in many large towns and cities in Britain. Beryl Barker, brought up in the Labour Party and the Co-op Movement, joined the Communist Party at the time of the Spanish war.

> In Sheffield at that time we had a Left Book Club group which met every Friday evening in a Vegetarian café, called the 'Sunshine Café', and we had regular speakers, each month we discussed the book of the month. And at the time that the Spanish Relief campaign was underway we were urged to form a support group. We used to meet in the evenings and on Sunday mornings and do door to door collections for non-perishable foods - tinned foods, packet foods and so on - and also money. My mother was interested in the Spanish war and she agreed that our house should be a depot if we made a collection on our estate - it was a Council estate at Southey. A man came up from London, I think his name was Alf Bowyer, and he had a van. We used to go into the area, and he had a loudspeaker on the van. He always played a record of Paul Robeson, singing 'Sometimes I feel like a motherless child.' We also had a campaign for knitting 4 inch squares to make up into blankets and people would give us odd balls of wool and so on for this. And then another thing I remember is

69 Interview with Lilian May Price, South Wales Coalfield Collection, University of Wales, Swansea.
70 *Daily Worker* 13 October, 1936, p. 3.

that Isabel Brown came, because she was the champion money collector for Spanish Relief and she did a City Hall meeting I believe, and she
also went round the clubs, working-men's clubs, speaking and collecting. I can remember going along myself to one or two working-men's
club to do the actual going round with the tin after she'd spoken.[71]

Wyn Hawkins and Marion Hague were both in the Sheffield YCL,
and remembered Spain as 'really the main part of our activity for two
years.'[72] Many of the youth groups in Sheffield worked together
through the broad-based Youth Peace Council. During the war in Spain,
through this group, YCL members co-operated in fund-raising with
those in the Labour League of Youth, the Co-op Youth and other organisations such as the Woodcraft Folk.[73] Someone was out collecting
every night, but special efforts were made to distribute leaflets on
Wednesdays round the housing estates and to make collections on
Fridays - pay day. There were meetings when people returned from
Spain, field days for Spain at the Clarion Cycle Club, and concerts
by the Sharrow Glee Singers. Wyn Hawkins, a former Methodist,
collected from two chapels, but was unsuccessful at the Church of
England. The wife of a Brigader, Win Albeye, was also in Sheffield, and
remembered helping with the collections at some of the big meetings.
Rather than recalling information about the dates or the specific
nature of the events, after fifty years, it is often the details of the
unfamiliar that remain with surprising clarity.

I remember the Duchess of Atholl in a funny hat and Robert
Boothby, and as I was a collector I was near the front, and [laughter]
he'd got suede shoes on and - it's funny how little things stick in
your mind - [laughter] I'd never seen a man in suede shoes before.[74]

There were many different local committees for 'Aid Spain' in London.
Press coverage of the bazaar and cabaret organised by the North Battersea Women's Co-op Guild captures the character of many similar events
in which women were frequently engaged, for this, as in other causes.[75]

71 Beryl Barker, IWM 13805.
72 Wyn Hawkins and Marion Hague (née Barber) IWM 13832.
73 See also The Woodcraft Folk Archive at the London School of Economics, for example, a
   receipt to the Woodcraft Folk from the Sheffield Youth Peace Council, Subcommittee
   Spanish Youth Foodship, YMA/WF 204 Solidarity Archives 1937-39.
74 Win Albaya (Albeye), video interview with Maria Delgado, 1986.
75 'Battersea Ambulance for Spain: Bazaar and Cabaret at the Town Hall', *South Western Star*
   26 February, 1937, p. 5. Reproduced in Squires, *The Aid Spain Movement in Battersea*, p. 21.

Their aim in this instance was to collect enough money to send an ambulance to Spain. The text speaks of the 'bold chalkings' used to advertise the occasion, and of the stalls, 'glistening with silver foil,' which were 'well laden with goods of the useful sort, plus things to eat.' The photograph shows 'the lady stallholders', members of the Spanish Aid Committee, who for the most part were in Spanish costume, 'borrowed plumes' which 'became them admirably.' The Chairwoman of the Committee, Mrs Bowler, was quoted in the text, speaking of the determination of the women to make the event a success and ensure that that the Battersea ambulance would soon be in Madrid. Her formidable presence in the centre of the photograph gives the clear impression that this objective would, without doubt, be achieved.

3.3 The photograph from the *South Western Star*, 26 February 1937, used in 'Battersea Ambulance for Spain: Bazaar and Cabaret at the Town Hall', with the caption 'Mrs Saklatvala opening the bazaar. The ladies seated are members of the Spanish Aid Committee. Mrs Bowler, the chairwoman, is the central front figure.'

This type of traditional fund raising, based on local social events that are regarded almost exclusively as the province of women, has been the subject of study in relation to other areas of women's mobilisation. Sue Bruley in her research on the role of women in the unemployed movement between the wars, noted the attitudes within the National Unemployed Workers' Movement to this form of activity. A circular asked branches to organise social events to keep up the morale of the unemployed, emphasising that this work 'must not be relegated simply to the women's committee.' The implication was, however, that in reality, these events were taking place largely as a result of women's efforts.[76]

Elements arising from traditions of female philanthropy can be discerned in the involvement of some middle and upper class women with the campaigns for Spain. The philanthropic foundations for the Duchess of Atholl's parliamentary career have been noted by Stuart Ball, who points out that she was devoted to public works rather than to a political career in the conventional sense. Her emphasis upon philanthropic public duty was, he believes, 'the product of Victorian ideals of the role appropriate to women of her social station.'[77] In Cambridge, these influences were significant amongst a group of women that included Frances Cornford, whose son, John, had been killed fighting with the Brigades in Spain during the first year of the war, and Jessie Stewart, who had been one of the early students at Newnham College. After her marriage to a Fellow of Trinity College who later became Dean of Chapel, Jessie Stewart's strong social conscience kept her constantly occupied. Her daughter, Frida, remembered that her mother was 'always working for some good cause,' attributing this to her upbringing in a 'very do-gooding family.'[78] Apart from frequently welcoming refugees into her home during and after the First World War, Jessie Stewart's work included prominent roles in the Cambridge Society for the Care of Girls, and the running of a Girls' Club. This background of philanthropic work, and the fact that two of her daughters were preoccupied with Spanish issues, resulted in her own involvement with causes connected with the war.[79] The breadth of her concerns, from local to international level, reflects the change that had taken place for many women of her class in the nature of their interests. In the early years of the nineteenth century, women had shown little interest in foreigners and were predominantly involved with those charities that dealt with children and childbirth, with servants and women who could be

76 Sue Bruley, 'A Woman's Right to Work? The Role of Women in the Unemployed Movement Between the Wars' in Sybil Oldfield, *This Working Day World: Women's Lives and Culture(s) in Britain 1914-1945* (Taylor & Francis, London, 1994).

77 Stuart Ball, 'The Politics of Appeasement: the Fall of the Duchess of Atholl and the Kinross and West Perth By-election, December 1938', *Scottish Historical Review* vol. LXIX, no. 187, April 1990, p. 52

78 Frida Stewart, AJ, 11 December 1995; Frida Knight (neé Stewart), IWM 13801.

79 Two of her daughters have been mentioned above, Margaret Stewart was secretary to Wilfred Roberts, often referred to as 'MP for Spain' and Frida Stewart drove an ambulance to Spain and was involved extensively in refugee work.

classed as the 'deserving poor'. However, to carry out their philanthropic duties to the full, hundreds of thousands of women found
that they had to interest themselves to varying degrees in the work-
ings of government and administration at local and national level.[80]
They had become increasingly aware of wider political issues
through extensive involvement in the anti-slavery campaigns, and of
their own need to put off the 'slave *spirit*' in the women's suffrage
movement.[81] As Chapter 2 has shown, the First World War and the
rise of fascism further increased awareness of events happening
abroad. At the time of the war in Spain, interests of women like
Jessie Stewart, although largely enacted at local level, were international in scope. The photograph showing her amongst others with a
truck bearing the slogan 'Cambridge to Barcelona: Help to Send
More', is an appropriate illustration of this attitude.

3.4 'Cambridge to Barcelona' collection for Spanish Relief,
Jessie Stewart on the far right.

---

80 Research has shown that more women were involved in philanthropic work than in any
other type of work at that time, including domestic service. F. K. Prochaska, *Women and
Philanthropy in 19th Century England* (Clarendon Press, Oxford, 1980) pp. 224-5. For
women's early involvement in local government see Patricia Hollis, *Ladies Elect: Women
in English Local Government 1865-1914* (Oxford University Press 1987).

81 See for example, Clare Midgley, *Women Against Slavery: The British Campaigns, 1780-1870*
(Routledge, London and New York, 1992); Emmeline Pethick-Lawrence spoke of the 'slave
spirit' in *My Part in a Changing World* (Victor Gollancz, London, 1938) pp. 150-151, quoted
in Martha Vicinus, *Independent Women: Work and Community for Single Women 1850-1920*
(University of Chicago Press, Chicago & London, 1985) p. 256.

Margot Heinemann had been studying in Cambridge just before the war and was part of the very active anti-fascist circle within the University, meeting John Cornford and joining the Communist Party. Her thoughts on the relationship between the students and the working classes reflect the typical discourse of left-wing politics of the thirties.

> We are all, as it were, the natural allies of the working class, it wasn't a question of crossing over from your middle class background to find yourself a niche in the working-class movement, but of trying to unite all these kinds of people on the basis of a conscious desire to combat fascism and war and to see the potential of their own disciplines fulfilled in practice. That was the kind of basis of a kind of People's Front approach and it was really under the impetus of that, that Cambridge students became so very broadly left-wing and organised such tremendous solidarity with Spain.[82]

Students in the women's Colleges noted their contributions to the campaigns in the *Girton Review* and the *Newnham College Roll*. The Girton Group of the University Socialist Club made collections in College and 'knitted innumerable garments both for the government forces and for the civil population.'[83] The Spanish Society was also influenced by 'the unhappy situation in Spain; which has diverted the interests of its members from literary to more practical matters.'[84] Newnham College hosted a Basque children's concert and a Resident Fellow, Inez Isabel MacDonald, was amongst the Cambridge women who were very active in the ongoing work of supporting a local colony of refugee children from the Basque region in Northern Spain.[85]

The events surrounding the arrival of the Basque children, brought

---

82 Margot Heinemann, IWM 9239.
83 *Girton Review*, Michaelmas Term 1937, p. 33.
84 Ibid., p. 29.
85 Flyer for 'Basque Children's Concert at Newnham', papers of Frida Stewart. Inez Isabel MacDonald also worked with refugees in Spain, writing of her experiences in 'Summer in Murcia in 1937', *Newnham College Roll* January 1938, pp. 39-45. See Chapter 4.
86 *See opposite page*] Yvonne Cloud (Kapp) produced a contemporary account, *The Basque Children in England* (Victor Gollancz, London, 1937). Dorothy Legarreta wrote a chapter on 'The Basque Refugee Children in Britain' as part of her international study, *The Guernica Generation: The Basque Refugee Children of the Spanish Civil War* (University of Nevada Press, 1984). Jim Fyrth puts the arrival and care of the children within the context of the 'Aid Spain' campaigns in Britain in *The Signal was Spain*, and Buchanan looks at 'The Role of the British Labour Movement in the Origins and Work of the Basque Children's Committee', pp. 155-174. A regional view is given by Don Watson and John Corcoran in *The North East of England and the Spanish Civil War 1936-39* (McGuffin Press, London, 1996), and Adrian Bell explores the impressions of the children themselves in *Only for Three Months: The Basque Children in Exile* (Mousehold Press, Norwich, 1996).

here in May 1937 to escape the heavy bombardment, and their subsequent care, have been studied from various different perspectives.[86] In
this instance, the theme is explored through the words of some of the
British women who worked to bring the children to this country and
contributed to their care after arrival. After the bombing of Guernica, the
Basques, isolated from the remainder of the Republic, faced imminent
defeat. Bilbao and the surrounding towns and villages were repeatedly
attacked from the air. The Basque Government appealed to other countries
for help in the evacuation by sea of refugees. France, Belgium, Mexico and
the Soviet Union accepted many thousands, sometimes in family groups.
The Duchess of Atholl and Ellen Wilkinson were amongst the signatories
of a letter to *The Times* on 1 May 1937, written as part of the campaign by
the NJC to bring children to Britain.[87] Leah Manning was in the Basque
Country preparing the children for evacuation and sending telegrams to
British MPs and religious leaders imploring for support.[88] The British
Government was less than enthusiastic about granting permission for
refugees to come to this country, but, despite opposition from the Foreign
Office, eventually reluctantly agreed to allow the entry of 4,000 children
with their teachers and priests.[89] This was on the strict understanding
that no government funding would be required and that in the interests
of political fairness, children should be chosen from political backgrounds corresponding proportionally with the numbers of representatives of the parties in the Basque Parliament.[90] A new group, the Basque
Children's Committee, was formed to arrange for the care of the children.
Many familiar names re-appeared as members of the new Committee,
and usually over half those present at committee meetings were women.[91]
Doctors Audrey Russell and Richard Ellis were flown over to examine the
children selected from 10,000 applicants. On the 21 May, 3,889 children,
219 women teachers and helpers, and 15 priests sailed from Bilbao.[92]
Leah Manning described the voyage on the *Habana* in her autobiography.

---

87 See also Michael Alpert, 'Humanitarianism and Politics in the British Response to the
    Spanish Civil War', p. 433.
88 Leah Manning, *A Life for Education: An Autobiography* (Victor Gollancz, London, 1970) p. 130
89 For more details on those who opposed the idea see Buchanan, *Britain and the Spanish
    Civil War*, p. 110.
90 For an example of how the requirements of political selection failed to work in practice,
    see Bell, *Only for Three Months*, p. 34.
91 Those attending meetings included, for example, the Duchess of Atholl, Eleanor Rathbone,
    Dame Janet Campbell, Dr. Audrey Russell, Lady Layton, Edith Pye, Leah Manning, Mary
    Sutherland, Ellen Wilkinson, the Hon. Mrs Gilbert Rollo, Miss Frida Stewart, Miss Arne,
    Miss Todd, and Mrs. Wilfred Roberts. Minutes of the Basque Children's Committee. Papers of
    Frida Stewart.
92 263 children who were signed up did not actually sail. Legarreta, *The Guernica Generation*, p. 106.

At last the night of departure arrived. The quay was a thick, black mass of parents, defying bombs as the children, some happy and excited, some in tears, were taken aboard in orderly companies. Head to tail the señoritas laid out our precious cargo - on the bulk-heads, in the swimming pool, in the state rooms and along the alley ways, for all the world like the little *sardinas* about which they were always singing; and out there, in grey waters, two ships of the British Navy stood by to guard our going. I don't know if sea-sickness can be brought on by hysteria; if so, that was what my children suffered from. For two dreadful days and nights, Richard, Audrey and I slipped and slithered from one pool of diarrhoea and vomit to another, giving drinks of water and assuring them it wasn't the fascists who had stirred up the troubled waters against them.[93]

The children disembarked in Southampton on 23 May 1937. A tented camp had been prepared for them in fields at Stoneham, organised with massive voluntary help from local workers, students and youth groups.[94] Isabel Brown had been amongst the welcome party at the docks, and later that evening experienced what she later recalled as 'one of the most excruciating moments of my life.'

I'd been living in Northumberland during the 1914-18 war and knew nothing about bombing. But those Basque children had known it, and the first evening, just as it was coming dusk, some aeroplanes came over. We were not at war - but to them aeroplanes in the sky were - and we had near panic in the camp... Thank God there were a number of Spaniards, teachers and priests and so on there that could help calm the situation. But I use that instance to show what they had come from because we hadn't experienced what we were to experience later on. I used it in my appeals.[95]

However, despite Leah Manning's blithe assertion that the camp was 'organised marvellously by the English Committee', there were

93 Leah Manning, *A Life for Education: An Autobiography* (Victor Gollancz, London, 1970) p. 131.
94 Even the Duchess of Atholl dug trenches according to Bell, *Only for Three Months*, p. 48. See also Jim Fyrth, *The Signal was Spain*, pp. 223-4.
95 Isabel Brown, IWM 844. The extent of the children's fear of planes is discussed by Laura Watts in 'An Analysis of the Primary Source Material Related to the Basque Children's Camp, North Stoneham, Summer 1937'. Some of the oral sources she examines contest the view that the children were so afraid, others agree. LSU History Department, 1989.

problems. The first few days were chaotic, the volunteers were plentiful but inexperienced. There were inevitable language difficulties, some
of the children spoke only the Basque language and few of the British
helpers understood Spanish. Many of the children were aware of the
complex political divisions creating conflict in Spain and fights broke
out between children from the different political groups in the camp.
Some of the older boys kept heading off into the town although they
were supposed to be under quarantine.[96] Food queues could also cause
problems as Kathleen Holmes, a volunteer worker at the camp, recalled.

> I went along the next morning early, and when I arrived there was
> the tent with the food with bread and milk, and the children were
> queued up and there was a bread cutting machine, and no one
> seemed to be cutting the bread and the children were crying
> because they were hungry. So I took hold and started trying to cut
> the bread. Well, it was an old machine that was very blunt, and the
> bread was very new. I wasn't getting on very well and then a priest
> came along and he said something to me, and I thought he wanted
> to take over and cut the bread for the children, and so I stood back,
> and expected him to start slicing the bread, instead of which he
> stood there. And there was a Spanish girl there who spoke some
> English and she said to me, 'He's asking you for a slice of bread.'
> And I got very angry because I thought I'm trying to cut bread for
> the children who are really crying and hungry and I thought he
> should wait. [Laughter] I indignantly went on cutting the bread to
> the best of my ability, and the girl herself, the Spanish girl, gave him
> a piece of bread and he went away, and I felt furious that he wasn't
> attempting to help the children... I didn't know much about Spanish
> Catholic priests.[97]

She, amongst others, also remembered how the children's behaviour
had been influenced by living in a country at war.

---

96 For life in the camp see Bell, *Only for Three Months*, pp. 51-61.
97 Kathleen Holmes, IWM13817. She was angered further when she heard that when a torren-
tial storm flooded the camp, local men had been instructed by the priests to stop digging
trenches round the children's tents and attend to their tents first. The testimony of an
un-named woman helper from the Women's Co-operative Guild refers to similar feelings
towards a group of British nuns who, when faced with the newly arrived children
requiring anti-septic baths, seemed more concerned about 'saving their souls than they
were about saving their sores.' *Of Whole Heart Cometh Hope* Centenary Memories of the
Co-operative Women's Guild, 1983, p. 40.

I found one tent that hadn't got a señorita allotted to it so I sort of took the children under my wing and they began to rely on me to come night and morning to see how they were. They learned how to get their food and so on but they needed an adult to take an interest in them. And one thing I noticed, which was rather remarkable, the children of course were getting plenty of food but they started saving their bread - they got more bread than they needed, and they hid it under a blanket in the centre of the tent. And I had a little dog that used to come up with me and they were very fond of him and they were always trying to get my dog to eat some of this bread because it got staler and staler and he didn't want it. I thought it was a very curious thing for children to do, and then I read a story by Jack London and he described how a sailor who'd been near starvation, they found out that he lined the sides of his bunk with bread, you see. So I thought of that, that's the sort of thing people do when they get food after they've been starved.[98]

During the remainder of the year, colonies were established for the children throughout Britain run mainly by local committees and a variety of organisations, including the Salvation Army and the Catholic Church.[99] Not all experiences of the colonies were pleasant ones, some were austere and in a few, standards of care inadequate. The Committee also had to deal with problems relating to some of the older boys who were 'difficult to handle.'[100] The majority of the children were more fortunate and found themselves in happier circumstances. This was certainly true in the case of the twenty-nine children who were sent to Cambridge. They had been together before they left Bilbao, living in a hostel run by Spanish Socialists for children whose fathers had been killed in the war. María Luisa, who was six years old when she arrived, had very happy memories of the colony.

We were very fortunate in the people who were involved in looking after us. You know, I think a great deal of thanks has to go to them -

---

98   Kathleen Holmes, IWM 13817.
99   Around 90 colonies were established in 1937, dropping to about 40 by mid-1938. Legarreta, *The Guernica Generation*, p. 116 and a full list of British colonies in Appendix VII. The same list is reprinted in Gregorio Arrien, *Niños Vascos Evacuados a Gran Bretaña 1937-40* (Asociación de Niños Evacuados el 37, 37. an Atzerriraturiko Haurren Elkartea, 1991) p. 202.
100 See minutes of the Basque Children's Committee, for example, 20 July, 1937, papers of Frida Stewart. Copies also in the papers of Wilfred Roberts, Modern Records Centre, University of Warwick.

Mrs Cornford, Mrs Stewart. They must have worked awfully hard to make sure we had what we had. And they gave their time unstinting-ly and tried to involve us in things.[101]

Jessie Stewart edited a record of life in the hostel, published as a booklet containing photographs, essays by the children and contributions written by helpers.[102] A report by Mrs E. E. Cooke describes the reception at the station organised to greet the children and illustrates the concern of the volunteers for their charges.

The children arrived by train shortly before 5 o'clock on 17th June - a day when Cambridge weather at its worst was countered by Cambridge hospitality at its best. They were met by a crowd numbering several hundred and by a small fleet of cars, which, after a brief welcome, took them off to the YMCA Hall, where there was awaiting them a large tea - including an iced cake bearing what was hoped to be a cheerful inscription in the Basque language - to which several local firms had contributed. Members of the Town Council were present and a speech of welcome was made by Councillor Peek, Mr. E. W. Hawkins, of Trinity Hall, acting as interpreter. The children were naturally tired after a railway journey which had brought them from Southampton to Cambridge via Bletchley, and rather subdued in their unaccustomed surroundings; but the warmth of their welcome combined with the warmth of their cocoa to induce happier faces before their first introduction to Cambridge was over.[103]

The children initially lived at the Vicarage in Pampisford, a rather dilapidated large house a few miles from Cambridge that had been specially repaired for them by local volunteer craftsmen and students. They later moved into a large house in the town, lent to them by one

101 Quoted by Bell, *Only for Three Months*, p. 66.
102 *'Recuerdos'; The Basque Hostel at Cambridge* edited by Jessie Stewart (Cambridge Daily News, undated, c.1939).
103 Mrs E. E. Cooke, 'Arrival in Cambridge' in *'Recuerdos'* edited by Jessie Stewart, pp. 4-5. According to Tony McLean, who taught the children in Cambridge when he came back from Spain, the efforts of the committee to welcome them with a cake iced in the Basque colours and singing the Basque National anthem may not have been appreciated properly by the children in this group. Although they came from Bilbao, they were not Basque nationalists and didn't speak the language. They later asked if they could replace the photograph in their colony of the leader of the Basque Nationalist Party with one of the President of the Republic, Azaña, but they did not object to learning the Basque songs and dances. Tony McLean, IWM 838.

of the Colleges. Photographs in the booklet show the children playing in the garden, preparing their own magazine, practising carpentry and painting, and at a party held for them in the Labour Hall. Their education was undertaken with great care in all respects, with sports and drama included. Music lessons were provided by Rosita Bal, a former pupil of Manuel de Falla.[104]

They Embraced Our Cameraman.

Appearing for the first time on any stage in dresses and dances of their own devising, a party of eight Basque children delighted a large audience at the Kettering Central Hall on Wednesday evening. Here are six of the girls in one of their characteristically Spanish dances. The children speak little English, but with Southern vivacity they clustered round our photographer (whom they called the "Photo Man") after this picture had been taken and warmly embraced him.

3.5 'They Embraced Our Cameraman': Basque children dancing in Kettering.

The children's ability to perform their national songs and dances resulted in a proliferation of concert tours, in which the children, usually dressed in Basque national costume, raised considerable amounts of money towards their own upkeep.

---

104 The children's activities were also preserved on film by P. A. L. Brunney. This film, 'Children of Spain', shows the daily lives of the children and special occasions, such as tea at the Stewart's home, Girton Gate, and on holiday at the mill owned by the Cornfords. It was shown on many occasions at fund-raising meetings. Private collection of Mr. Brunney, Cambridge.

The Basque Children's Committee in London appointed Frida
Stewart as Concert Secretary who organised tours with a group of
talented children selected from various colonies. The Cambridge artist,
Gwen Raverat, donated a wood-block of refugees fleeing Spain which
was used to advertise such occasions. Frida Stewart used any contacts
she had for the purposes of arranging tours. Her brother Ludovick's
former teacher at Eton, W. Hope-Jones replied to her request for a
venue, giving a vignette of life within the academic establishment and
casting interesting light on the forces at work within British society. In
his letter, Mr Hope-Jones stated his willingness to help provide an
opening for a Basque children's concert at Eton, but before approach-
ing the headmaster, he attempted to assess the value of the cards they
held in favour of the proposal. His own worth he estimated at minus 3,
having been convicted of thinking for himself and being 'tainted by
Bolshevism.' P. C. M. G. Evans, who taught Spanish and had done a
great deal to help refugees, was also only worth minus 1, as a result
of his interest in causes not fashionable within Etonian circles.
C. A. Gladstone, head of Modern Languages, was in favour of the concert and would be worth plus 20. However, it was Frida Stewart's own
value that he believed would prove the deciding factor.

Forgive my disgraceful forgetfulness; such memory as I ever had
died of old age thirty years ago. I have been rummaging through all
the Stewarts I have known, and I can't place Ludovick; but I may
well have known him without ever gathering his Christian name.
Evans and Gladstone both suspect you of being the daughter of the
Rev. H. F. Stewart, DD, a Fellow of Eton. If this is true, our fortunes
are made; Fellows count 1000 each, and even in such a diluted form
of sanctity as a daughter, surely they are worth 100. Do try to decide
that you are a Fellow's daughter: if you can manage it the walls of
Jericho will fall flat at the first blast of the trumpet. But if not, what
other allies can you whack up from your end? They could join forces
with mine in a mass attack on the fortress.[105]

Despite the apparent failure of this particular enterprise, Frida
Stewart was inspired by many successful fund-raising concert tours
all over England to try more lucrative possibilities.

---

[105] Letter from W. Hope-Jones, Eton College, Windsor, 21 November, 1938, to Frida Stewart.
Papers of Frida Stewart.

Swiss winter-sports centres seemed ideal places for money-raising, and the hotels would obviously provide large audiences of wealthy people (whether they would be sympathetic to the Republican cause was problematical, but they could not fail to be moved by the children). There is nothing like reaching for the highest possible star, and I got in touch with the manager of Suvrettahaus, the great St. Moritz hotel, who happened to be in London in November. To my delight he was friendly and quite sympathetic, and agreed to have seven children and two or three helpers to stay for two nights and for them to give two cabaret shows at the hotel. With a written agreement to this effect I was able to approach all the other resorts with pre-ordained success. We got fixed up at Pontresina, Davos, Gmund, not to mention Zurich and Wintertur; and Swiss Air flew us out, free of charge, from London to Zurich in the middle of December. The whole expedition seems like a dream now: the children were wildly excited by everything, the flight, the snow mountains, the skiing on the nursery slopes, the Bergbahn, and most of all, of course, by the luxury of the hotels in which we performed, ate and slept. To be waited on by dignified gentlemen in tail coats was the height of bliss for the little Basques; they rose to the occasion and sang and danced admirably, raising over £300 for the cause.[106]

As a result of the popularity of the concerts, a music book, *Songs of the Basque Children* was produced, edited by Frida Stewart, with an introduction by the Duchess of Atholl.[107]

Contact with the children had a great effect on the lives of some British women. Cora Blyth was studying Spanish at Oxford and began visiting the Basque colony at nearby Aston, partly to improve her Spanish. After a lonely childhood, the warmth of the atmosphere amongst the children in the colony was to prove irresistible.

We used to go, quite a little party of us, every Saturday. There was the convenor of the Museum of Oxford, his name was Geoffrey Turner - he had been terribly injured by infantile paralysis, he was extremely lame, he had a harness, he had crutches. He used to struggle out on the bus every Saturday with a gramophone hanging from one hand

---

106 Frida Stewart, memoirs, p. 190.
107 *Songs of the Basque Children* collected and edited by Frida Stewart, illustrated by James Boswell, published for the Basque Children's Committee by People's Songs Distributors, proceeds to the Basque Children's Committee.

and a big case of records from the other, and go and play Spanish music to the children, which of course was absolutely lovely. And the place rang with song and dancing. You went into this very bare house where there were no carpets or anything and children would come clattering down the stairs and rush into your arms and welcome you - it was so lovely, they were so lively these children.[108]

Her narrative is greatly enhanced by listening to the recording of the interview rather than just reading the transcript. As Cora Blyth recalls going to see the children, the emphasis on certain words becomes very noticeable, she stresses all the words which mark the contrast between her lonely childhood and the lively colony, that *rang* with *song*, and the *clattering* of feet in the *rush* to greet visitors. The colony became a key influence in her life, for it was there that she met the Republican refugee she was to marry, Luis Portillo.[109]

Reports on the conditions in some of the other colonies reflect the diversity in the care they provided. Frida Stewart was appointed by the NJC as a sort of 'Travelling Officer', to visit the hostels and help to sort out any problems, roaming hundreds of miles in her 'valiant Baby Austin'.[110] She was also to report back to the Committee on the work being done for Spain in various towns, and organise local meetings with speakers on the Spanish question to raise the profile of Spanish relief. This wide ranging remit reflects the flexibility typically required of those who worked in the campaigns for Spain. The extent of Frida Stewart's authority is difficult to determine, but her recommendations were often frankly expressed.

If there are any spare cooks available, could one be sent to replace the sinister looking person here? I have nothing against him except his reputation, and the mess in the kitchen, and his personal appearance, but feel very strongly that he ought to go away![111]

Other hostels offered children an environment in complete contrast to the general disorder and indiscipline of the one above.

Visited the home on Friday evening, children just going to bed, dressed in perfect blue and pink pyjamas, getting into blue and pink

108 Cora Blyth, AJ, 5 August 1996. See also Chapter 6.
109 See Chapter 6.
110 Frida Stewart, memoirs, p. 174.
111 Report from Frida Stewart to NJC, 29 October 1937, papers of Frida Stewart.

blanketed beds, by blue and pink miniature wardrobes! The children look very well and bright. Taken in a party to the cinema every Saturday and out in cars very often with lots of other treats.[112]

In an interview almost sixty years later, she still found the distinctive characteristics of each home fascinating, saying, 'It made me understand how important environment is at a certain age for children - how these children fitted in to their different committees that looked after them.'[113] In some, the children were 'brought into more political circles' as 'the people who came to visit them were the political people locally and they would attend the Labour Party functions and so on.'[114] A Liberal tradition prevailed at the colony in Cumberland where around eighty children were 'under the wing of Lady Cecilia Roberts', the 'imposing and splendid mother' of Wilfred Roberts MP.[115] There were the rather 'Quakerish' ones, and 'arty crafty ones who lived in a forest kind of atmosphere,' in a cottage lent to them by the owner of a stately home. The Catholic homes 'kept themselves very much to themselves,' and she found them rather depressing. In her memoirs however, she points out that despite the lack of jollity, a secondary consideration to their aim of saving souls, 'it would have been churlish of our Committee to complain of the austerity of the young Basque lives, for in fact their bodies as well as their souls had been saved by the humanitarian action of the Catholics, and they were treated with genuine kindness.'[116]

Apart from the concerts in which the children themselves performed, there were many other fund raising activities, some quite prestigious occasions. Yvonne Kapp was amongst those who organised a meeting at the Albert Hall. In her reflections about the meeting many years later, she points out the type of inaccuracies that can arise in the process of 'legendising' events.

---

112 Report from Frida Stewart to NJC, 29 October, 1937, papers of Frida Stewart.
113 Frida Stewart, AJ, 11 December 1995.
114 Difficulties were sometimes encountered by Labour women with their party officials and trades councils when trying to run local colonies for the children through broad-based committees. See for example the case of Mrs Chapman in Dundee discussed by Buchanan in 'The Role of the British Labour Movement in the Origins and Work of the Basque Children's Committee', pp. 168-9.
115 Frida Stewart records that she stayed the night in the Roberts' home nearby, a 'great Liberal house, where even the soap in the bathroom was stamped "The country needs Liberalism".' In view of all the work that the family had done for the anti-fascist cause, she 'felt inclined to agree with the soap.' Frida Stewart, memoirs, p. 176.
116 Ibid., p. 173. Bell gives a figure of 1,200 children as the total looked after by the Catholic Church in Britain. *Only for Three Months*, p. 60.

[The meeting at the Albert Hall] was a great success and we raised a lot of money. It's quite interesting that very recently, somebody wrote a little piece saying what a wonderful effect it had that Picasso had been at a meeting in aid of Spain - but he never was - that his mere presence on the platform, though he didn't speak, had been an inspiration. Well, it's a lovely story but it's untrue because we went to see Picasso in Paris and asked him to come and he said, 'I can't, I can't, I can't.' And he was doing sketches for 'Guernica' - doing sketches all the time for the big thing that he was going to do and he hated flying and we'd arranged an escort to fly with him so there'd be no difficulty for him. So, he couldn't - he would not leave his studio. So what he did was to give us one of the sketches for 'Guernica' of that day, and it's dated and signed and it's the 8th of May and it's the second sketch of the day and we used it as the cover of the programme for the Albert Hall meeting, and the original we had framed and it was auctioned.[117]

Paul Robeson, however, did appear in person and sang to resounding applause, the audience then responding enthusiastically to the appeal for more sponsors for the Basque children. [118]

The question of repatriation created many difficulties.[119] Calls from those wanting the children to be returned as soon as Bilbao had fallen to Franco were loud and strong on the grounds that the danger from bombing was over. Headlines in the anti-Republican press referred to the Basques as 'The Duchess of Atholl's Boomerang' and quipped 'Put all these Basques in one exit.'[120] At the meetings of the Basque Children's Committee, long debates centred on concerns regarding the authenticity of the requests for the return of the

---

117 Yvonne Kapp (née Cloud), interview with Mike Squires 1 March, 1994. Shortly after the Albert Hall meeting, she visited the Basque children at the Stoneham camp and then wrote her book, *The Basque Children in England*.
118 Paul Robeson sang at many such fund-raising concerts and also toured Spain where he sang to the International Brigades. Charlotte Haldane acted as his guide and interpreter. See Charlotte Haldane, *Truth Will Out* (Weidenfeld & Nicholson, London, 1949) pp. 124-131. The amount of ten shillings a week that had been calculated as necessary for the support of each child was much higher than that deemed sufficient for the children of the unemployed, a fact which provoked much criticism from those opposed to them being brought to this country. See for example, 'Report on Conference of the National Joint Committee for Spanish Relief: Conditions for Return', Millicent Fawcett Hall, London, Saturday, 2 October, 1937, papers of Frida Stewart.
119 See for example, Minutes of the Basque Children's Committee, 1 October, 1937; Legarreta, 'Repatriation from England', *The Guernica Generation* (1984) pp. 211-225; Fyrth *The Signal was Spain*, pp. 231-233.
120 *Action* 31 July, 1937, p.3; Quoted in several interviews and in Fyrth, *The Signal was Spain*, p. 231

children, and the pressures that were possibly being put on those parents who did write. One such instance occurred in the colony in Theydon Bois and Leah Manning's report is recorded in the minutes of the Committee.

> One of the boys had received a letter from his parents. The letter said that everything was now normal and food plentiful in Bilbao and that the boy must remember that he had not gone to England to escape bombs but to carry on his education. When that was finished he must come back and join the Black Arrow Regiment [Spanish Fascist Youth Group]. Mrs Manning reported that the child, on receiving this letter, became highly excited as he said that he knew his father would never wish him to join the Black Arrows. He pointed to a small tear at the corner of the letter which he said his father had put as a pre-arranged signal to the child that nothing in a letter with a torn corner was to be believed. She therefore submitted that pressure was being brought on the parents in Bilbao to write these letters to the children to be used for propaganda purposes by the Nationalists.[121]

Under the ever increasing pressure, partly financial in nature, to return the children, the Committee attempted to check the requests and arrange for some to be escorted back to the Basque Country.[122] The parting could be painful for the children and for those who had cared for them. Nell Badsey, who had been responsible for running a colony of Basque boys in Tynemouth, accompanied a group of children to the border for repatriation. An article in the local paper reported her concerns about the children who had been 'fearful and uncertain' at the prospect of returning as they did not wish to go.[123] A letter in *The Times* calling for the immediate repatriation of all the children was countered by the Duchess of Atholl, in which she explained the need for caution.

> It would be a dishonourable breach of trust if they were to be returned to Bilbao, where, in the absence of their parents, they would

---

121 Leah Manning, minutes of the Basque Children's Committee, 28 July, 1937. Leah Manning was closely associated with the colony in Theydon Bois and it was named after her.
122 The Basque Children's Repatriation Committee wanted all the children to be repatriated, to be placed if necessary in orphanages run by the Spanish Fascist Party. FO W18373/37/41, 20 October, 1937: Duke of Wellington to Eden. Quoted in Alpert 'Humanitarianism and Politics in the British Response to the Spanish Civil War', p. 434.
123 Nell Badsey, *Shields Evening News* 21 April, 1938, p. 7. Quoted in Watson and Corcoran, *The North East of England and the Spanish Civil War*, p. 82.

almost certainly be put into reformatories or other institutions, there to be in the insurgent authorities' own phrase, 're-educated', i.e. brought up to believe that the cause for which their parents are fighting and suffering is not merely misguided but wicked.[124]

Eventually just over 400 remained. Some of these were orphans, the parents of others had been imprisoned by Franco, there were some who had been told by their parents not to return and others whose families could not be traced.[125] Those who returned to Spain often experienced great hardships, and sad letters were written asking to come back to Britain again.[126] Of those who remained, some were adopted or fostered, and three hostels remained open to care for the others until they were old enough to earn a living. The commitment made by some British women to help children whose lives had been threatened by war, was therefore to last many years.[127]

One aspect of women's involvement with Spain has received even less attention over the years than others; the mothers, girlfriends and wives, family and friends of those who went to fight or work in Spain.[128] Women's memories of their experiences in this context are often vivid, sometimes distressing. Charlotte Haldane could have prevented her son from going to Spain in the International Brigade as he was still underage. However, she chose not to do so. The scene she describes would elicit sympathy from many parents, although perhaps her son might have wished for a less explicit rendition of his appearance.

At the end of November, one evening when I was having an attack of influenza, Ronnie came into my bedroom. He announced quietly and firmly that he had joined the International Brigade, and was shortly leaving for Spain. I looked at my son. He was tall and lanky, overgrown for his age. His enormous velvet-dark eyes blazed from his thin angular face, which was pale as cheese, and on which the acne spots stood out vividly. He had the pathetic nobility

---

124 Duchess of Atholl, *The Times* 7 February, 1938 in reply to a letter from Sir Arnold Wilson, February 1st 1938. Quoted by Bell, *Only for Three Months*, pp. 103-4.
125 The question of repatriation of the Cambridge children was reported in 'Young Exiles From Spain: Cambridge and the Basque Children - Need For More Subscribers', *Cambridge Daily News* 19 March, 1938, MML Box B1, File C, 12a.
126 See for example, letters to Miss Picken, MML Box B-2: B/7, B/10.
127 See Chapter 6.
128 The focus here is on the experiences of women only. However, Natalie Suart of De Montfort University wrote a doctoral thesis on the families of those who went to Spain, including fathers, sons etc.

and panache of the adolescent completely vowed to a cause (any cause), the espousal of which would free him from the oppression of his personal problems. Just so, at his age, with the same pitiable gallantry, I had vowed myself to the cause of Woman's Suffrage. I could either burst into tears, in maternal fashion, or restrain myself and be gruffly paternal. I chose the later alternative, which was at least less embarrassing to us both. 'You silly little fool,' I barked at him. 'What use would you be? Why, you can't even shoot.' 'Oh yes I can,' he answered, without raising his voice, but squaring his shoulders. 'I did PT at school.' I was helpless, trapped. You cannot have your cake and eat it. You cannot have your propaganda, either, and deny to your first, most loyal convert, the right to accept and act upon it. He was only doing what, had I been of his age and sex, I would myself have done. But he was sixteen years old and I was his mother. Was I perhaps sending this child of mine to glory, death, wounds, mutilation, disfigurement? It was a heinous responsibility I had piled up for myself.[129]

3.6 Charlotte Haldane at a fund raising sale for Spanish Aid.

Her son was wounded in the arm, and returned home 'thin as a lamp-post, but perfectly well,' in the Autumn of 1937.[130] Charlotte Haldane was not alone in feeling that it would be hypocritical to have

129 Haldane, *Truth Will Out*, pp. 93-4.
130 Ibid., p. 123.

spoken of the need for action and then, faced with the possibility of the loss of loved ones, to have put obstacles in their path. This theme recurs in various forms in the sources used for this study. The contrast between a stylised written presentation of this subject and oral testimony is apparent in the words of Kathleen Gibbons. Her short written piece on 'The International Brigade' relates in heroic style the parts played by her husband and his two brothers, and makes brief mention of her own attitudes.

> As partners, Danny and I were both prepared to face the price we might have to pay for partaking in this struggle. We took the decision with our eyes open; no delusion as to its risks, dangers and desolation. It had to be faced - and won, if we could help it. Within a few days of Christmas he was gone from home.[131]

This formal style conveys her commitment, but perhaps less of her character, than her oral response to a question about her feelings when Danny went to Spain.

> Well, how could I feel? I didn't object but, broken hearted of course. What could you do? A duty, you know, it's no good spouting opinions if you're not prepared to sacrifice something for them when the rub comes you see, and that's the way it had to be. Luckily I was able to earn, I mean already I was earning enough to keep the bloomin' house going - 'cause Danny earned bugger all [laughter], one way and another... He never felt that the reins were on him because I wouldn't be able to manage if he went and pursued the interests which he felt obliged to follow, you see - put it that way.'[132]

Facilitating the actions of the other partner in a relationship was therefore often an active, rather than just a passive, contribution. This impact of a breadwinner's political commitments on the family finances was also mentioned by Rose Kerrigan.

> Of course, I've never stopped my husband - let me put it this way - because I have the same views as him, I've never stopped him from doing anything. He became, as you call it, a professional revolutionary and we lived on very little money, when he was a skilled engineer

---

131 Kathleen Gibbons, 'The International Brigade', papers of Kathleen Gibbons.
132 Kathleen Gibbons, AJ, 6 August 1998.

and could have earned good money. But you never asked why in all these things so that I've always just turned out and done my bit to keep the finances going and keep our heads above water as it were, financially... I have done my part like that as the back-room boy, the back-room woman.[133]

3.7 Rose Kerrigan with her daughters, June 1938.

Rose Kerrigan was amongst the women who had young children to consider as well as themselves when their husbands went to Spain. In some cases, such as that of Elsie Booth, it was difficult to refuse the pressures to agree.

---

133 Rose Kerrigan, Tameside 197 and IWM 796. Sue Bruley discusses this point in her study of women in the Communist Party, pointing out the irony in that 'just as capitalism required a subordinate sex to service its male workers, the revolutionary party needed a subordinate sex to service its male revolutionaries so that they could fight capitalism.' *Leninism, Stalinism and the Women's Movement in Britain*, p. 124.

I don't regret it because I know he wanted to go, and I knew he should go. But you know what it's like, he kept asking me, 'I want to go to Spain', and you've got a baby eighteen months old, and although I was a member of the Communist Party myself - I read the *Daily Worker*, I knew all about it, and I went to the meetings - but you don't want your own to go, do you? And I knew he should go, but he wouldn't go until I said 'Yes', you see, but of course, he was always maundering me. [Laughter] So eventually, I gave in at the end. [134]

3.8 Elsie Booth sitting behind Sid Booth (centre foreground) and friends.

Elsie Booth was taken down to the Communist Party office to verify her agreement, her husband being firmly told to leave the room. 'He's not pushing you, is he?', the party official asked. 'Oh, no, no,' she replied, 'I want him to go.'[135] The normal practice at this time was to keep the planned journey secret to avoid the possibility of being detained by the British authorities who had threatened prosecution under the Foreign Enlistment Act of 1870.[136] The week between the meeting and her husband's departure was one Elsie Booth never

---

134 Elsie Booth and Mary Freeman, Tameside 215 and IWM 842.
135 Elsie Booth, Tameside 233.
136 Although no prosecutions were actually brought under the act, volunteers were forced to be more discreet. They usually began their journey by taking a weekend excursion to Paris by rail, a trip which did not require a passport. Bill Alexander, *British Volunteers For Liberty: Spain 1936-39* (Lawrence & Wishart, London 1982, paperback edition with corrections 1986) pp. 41-49.

wanted to go through again, 'because I didn't know what I was doing in wishing him gone or wishing he wasn't going.'[137]

> The night he was going, I went to the station, he didn't want me to go, but I went... I couldn't feel myself walking.... As that train went out it - it was a terrible feeling. [Crying] And you couldn't tell anybody, you see, you lived in a little street and you couldn't tell the neighbours, and of course, after a few weeks, all the neighbours thought he'd deserted you, you know - they didn't understand. Then you had your family saying 'What has he left you for? Has he deserted you? So you had all this to deal with. Very hard it was.[138]

Unlike women in Britain during the Second World War, surrounded by others whose husbands had also gone to war and an abundance of war-work opportunities, Elsie Booth was unable to find work.[139] The mills where she had been employed were on short time, other jobs were scarce and she had her children to look after. She relied on support from party comrades who gave them meals, and on the money from the Dependants Aid Committee. This group had been formed in June 1937 at the instigation of the Communist Party but with broad support for appeals from some religious leaders, MPs and groups such as trade unions.[140] The donations were principally used for direct aid to the families of Brigaders, but also helped in other ways, providing convalescent holidays, artificial limbs and parcels for prisoners. The Honorary Secretary first appointed was Charlotte Haldane, who wrote that she threw herself into the job with alacrity, speaking at meetings and writing an appeal to be published every day in the *Daily Worker*. In an article she wrote for *Woman To-Day* she emphasised how the task of helping to support the wives and children of Brigaders would be particularly suited to women.

> In asking the readers of *Woman To-Day* to help this work, I feel that it is a task that will particularly appeal to women. It calls for enthusiasm and patience, which are feminine qualities though not

---

137 Ibid.
138 Elsie Booth and Mary Freeman, Tameside 215 and IWM 842.
139 For more on women and work in the Second World War see Penny Summerfield, *Reconstructing Women's Wartime Lives* (Manchester University Press, 1998).
140 For details of supporters see Fyrth, *The Signal was Spain*, pp. 215-6. For Dependants Aid receipts and payments accounts see also MML Box 39/B/2. By the end of 1938 the total income stood at £63,543.

prerogatives. Particularly at present do we want regular weekly guarantors, who will agree to give us anything from a shilling upwards. Every housewife knows what a difference it makes to have a regular budget on which to rely; and that is what we are aiming at.[141]

Even though donations were fairly substantial, when the money was divided between so many dependants there was often barely sufficient for basic needs. Elsie Booth usually received 30 shillings a week from Dependants Aid, this was reduced to 25 shillings when there were not enough funds coming in. 'Sometimes you couldn't pay the rent,' she said, and 'one time I had to pawn my wedding ring because the baby was ill.' [142]

Narratives from women who did not want their husbands to go to Spain are rare. However, as they would be less likely to be interviewed or to leave written testimony than the wives of those who supported their husbands' decision to go, no conclusions can be drawn as to whether this was a common occurrence or not. A male perspective on this subject can be found in the memoirs of Harry Stratton, *To Anti-Fascism by Taxi*, in which he records the 'very bad three weeks' he spent before coming to a resolution.

Winnie and the kids posed a big enough problem, but to complicate things still further, Winnie was pregnant. I looked at the wider aspects of things though as well, and in principle it seemed that if Fascism could be stopped in Spain, and thereby possibly a second World War be averted, that this would be in everybody's interest including that of my family. I spoke to Charlie (Williams) about it, and he told me that if I decided to go, Winnie would be given a weekly allowance from a fund organised by Charlotte Haldane. So I decided to go, but knowing that Winnie would be opposed to my going, and not wanting a confrontation on the issue, I used the pretext that I was taking on a new job in Southampton. Winnie accepted this. She had never, from 1930, gone along with my new ideas, and if I told her that I was going to fight in Spain she would not have accepted my reasons.[143]

---

141 Charlotte Haldane, 'They Are Fighting For Us', *Woman To-Day* September 1937, p. 10. In addition to her work for Dependants Aid, Charlotte Haldane also spent some time in Paris during 1937, working as a 'receptionist' for the groups of British volunteers on their way to Spain. For her account of this work see *Truth Will Out*, pp. 101-123.
142 Elsie Booth and Mary Freeman, Tameside 215 and IWM 842.
143 Harry Stratton, *To Anti-Fascism By Taxi* (Alun Books, Port Talbot, West Glamorgan, 1984) p. 28

In Spain the letters he receives from his mother contain little notes from his children, but he writes, 'Winnie had taken things rather badly and had not replied to my letters, had not in fact written at all.'[144] He begins to worry about the impending 'event' and to wonder if he can get leave when the baby is due, if he is still alive. When he eventually arrives home, he learns that she had slipped and fallen and there had been a miscarriage. Although Winnie did not greet him on his return, he writes, 'slowly and painfully things mended between us and we began to discuss the future.'[145]

Communication with those in Spain was a further problem for those left behind. Not only did some, like Elsie Booth, find difficulties in affording the postage, but, inevitably, there were delays in receiving up to date news from the front. Encouragement to write was given to those at home by the wife of a Brigader from Manchester.

We cannot send back to our menfolk stories of equal heroism, but they appreciate more just hearing what is happening at home, the ordinary humdrum gossip of everyday life, which so often seems dull to us but to them must be refreshing indeed.... It is just this normal kind of life that we are leading which Fascism would destroy and which our husbands and brothers are defending so nobly.[146]

Celia Baker wrote to two Brigaders in Spain who had been working with her in Unity Theatre. The group had put on many productions to raise money for Spain, the most well-remembered being the mass declamation of *On Guard for Spain*.[147] The letters she received were clearly intended to be read by all the members of 'Unity' beginning, 'Dear Comrades,' and maintaining an unremitting optimism suitable for public consumption. Bruce Boswell writes of high morale, 'despite some pretty hefty knockings about.' Ben Glaser, although writing of the plight of refugees and the civilian deaths from bombing, finishes by saying, 'We are going into action united and strong, confident of victory.'[148] Both men died at the Ebro in 1938.

144 Harry Stratton, *To Anti-Fascism By Taxi* (Alun Books, Port Talbot, West Glamorgan, 1984) p. 41.
145 Ibid., p. 51.
146 *Woman To-Day* November 1937, p. 13.
147 For more on the work of Unity Theatre relating to the war in Spain see Colin Chambers, *The Story of Unity Theatre* (Lawrence & Wishart, London, 1989) pp. 82-88.
148 Bruce Boswell, Barcelona, undated; Ben Glaser (Glazer), 24 May, 1938. Papers of Celia Baker, since donated to the Marx Memorial Library. See also the more personal letter from Ben Glaser to Celia Sevitt, 18 August 1938, in which he admits to feeling 'more than a little lonely' due to the death of comrades. MML Box D7 B/1.

The optimism of women left at home could be soon shattered by bad news from the front or the anxiety of uncertainty. Win Albeye's husband was the son of a Spanish family who had settled in Sheffield. He had volunteered to fight in Spain after hearing La Pasionaria speaking on the radio. No news was heard of him for several months after he left. Win Albeye meanwhile attended meetings for Spanish Aid.

It was a packed meeting - I don't know who the speaker was, but somebody came down the side of the hall and beckoned me to come out and I went out and outside this person gave me a piece of paper with a phone number on, and said would you go and ring this number, it's something connected with you. I went outside and it was a dark winter's night, and I found a phone box - it's still there by the way - and I went inside and my hands were absolutely trembling and I managed to make out this phone number and I rang, and somebody the other end said, 'There's been a very great battle in Spain, at Jarama and there's been a lot of casualties but that's all we know.' Well, I'll never forget that moment - I just sort of felt like a jelly. But, we heard no more after that, and then about the last week in February I got a letter. It was just simply a short letter and it said that he'd been in the battle, but he didn't mention the name, he said he'd been on active service, and he just said that he was now stationed at Albacete, and he gave me an address and he said it would be all right for me to write. Well, of course, I was absolutely over the moon then.[149]

In July 1937, he came back, but, she remembered, 'He never told me any details, you more or less had to wait patiently until you got a little bit of information then you had to build on that.'[150] A reluctance to talk about experiences was not uncommon. When Rose Kerrigan's husband came back from Spain he seemed very different.

There was a terrible change in him - he was very, very much - he was quite morose - I don't know whether I should really say this - he seemed very within himself. He was really going grey, and this was because of the people he'd seen who had died in Spain, with having to take their effects home and with having to go and see some of their people.[151]

149 Win Albeye (Albaya), video interview by Maria Delgado, 1986.
150 Ibid.
151 Rose Kerrigan, Tameside 197 and IWM 796.

Peter Kerrigan returned to Spain as a *Daily Worker* correspondent. Others were wounded and needed care at home before going back again. This was the case for Kathleen Gibbons when Danny came home to convalesce. When he went back to Spain, life became even more difficult for her.

I went to Marie Stopes and thought I'd got a proper fitting for once in my life, because he was coming home after being wounded - dum-dum bullet in his back - it had been three months till he came home. And, lovely treat - I'd be able to make love to him. He was only home about five weeks in all I think it was, when he went back, and a fortnight later I'm realising something's changed - I was pregnant - oh dear... It was probably because I hadn't done the thing properly or something and it didn't work. [Laughter] So the die was cast - then, perhaps, I wouldn't have my David now, so, [blows a kiss to photograph of son, David] you can't have all the treats in this world without suffering something to get them can you? But it was a very great shock at the time.[152]

A few weeks after his return to Spain, Danny was a prisoner in Burgos, not to see his new son till he was three months old. Noreen Branson's husband, Clive, was also taken prisoner. He was amongst those imprisoned in San Pedro, and then was moved to an Italian prison camp where his artistic skills proved useful.

I suddenly began getting a few letters from Clive. And then of course, I received all these drawings through the post - these drawings of people. And I took them up to show to Isabel Brown, who was wildly excited because some of the people had been missing and they hadn't known that they were prisoners. So it was sort of absolutely - it was most marvellous. And she got hold of everybody and told them they must come and look at them, and they were all thrilled of course, the relatives, you see, to know what was happening to their, to their sons and husbands and whatever it was.[153]

For some women, the news they were given was of the death of someone they loved.[154] Leila Berg's *Flickerbook*, described as a

---

152 Kathleen Gibbons, AJ, 6 August 1998.
153 Noreen Branson, AJ, 26 January 1996.
154 A figure of 526 is usually given as the number of British Brigaders who died in Spain.

'reliving rather than a remembering', gives snapshots of her emotions when she hears news that first one lover, then the next, has been killed in Spain.[155] She had refused their offers of marriage, not wanting to marry anyone, 'Even though I know you're supposed to marry everyone when there's a war on; that's what girls are for.'[156] The extracts which follow give glimpses of her thoughts after a letter from Alf had arrived from the front.

> Someone has nicked his harmonica. Yes, yes, I rush to get him a new one. I am so happy to get him something that he has asked for. I scrape together everything I can, and get him such a proud, gleaming one.
>
> Have I been silly? Is this what he wants? Perhaps I should have bought him a very simple ordinary mouth-organ? After all - *Stardust* - it doesn't need something so gleaming - so ostentatious...
>
> A ragged wallet has come.
>
> So stiff. The blood has dried now.
>
> Inside a tattered birth certificate.
>
> All he possessed.
>
> I am down as his next of kin. And in receipt of all his possessions.
>
> Did he get the mouth-organ in time? They die so fast in Spain.
>
> I shouldn't have spent the whole morning choosing the best. Perhaps it would have caught an earlier post and got there sooner, and he could have played it longer...
>
> I sit on the top of the bus, at the front, and want to smash my fist through the glass. To feel the blood, real blood, trickling down.
>
> The real raw pain.
>
> I hold fast and don't do it.[157]

In 1935, on a visit to Cambridge with a friend, she had met John Cornford and the others in his student circle. In December 1936 she read the news of his death in the *Daily Worker*.[158] Amongst the poems he wrote in Spain, 'Heart of the Heartless World', written for Margot Heinemann, has made the depth of their relationship well known. The blunt question put to Margot Heinemann many years later in a recorded interview strikes the listener as insensitive.

---

155 Leila Berg, *Flickerbook* (Granta Books, London, 1998, first edition 1997) back cover.
156 Ibid., p. 192.
157 Ibid., pp. 228-9.
158 Ibid., p. 193. She writes of the photograph of him in the newspaper and wonders if anyone will know that he is 'doing the Cambridge Clutching Hand?' This was apparently a popular mannerism amongst the Communist student group which she describes on p. 161.

So when you got the news of his death you must have been shattered, were you?[159]

Her reply in clipped tones, 'I was, rather,' seems a masterpiece of restraint. She quickly continued with a factual description of the process by which she was informed.

> He told me not to believe any reports unless they came from party head-quarters - this one did, so I took a bit of leave from school. I hadn't been well actually, I'd had a couple of weeks off at the end of the previous term - I suppose it was really all a bit too much - and I went down to London to see whether this was really true and whether they knew any more about it. They didn't know much but they had checked carefully - they didn't release information until they'd checked as carefully as they could - and I saw Harry Pollitt. He saw all the families of the people who'd been killed, himself, as far as he could. Again, one of the legends is that Pollitt was one of these inhuman characters that sent young men up to the front to die. In fact he was always quite as distressed as the families themselves - he was the most humane, kindliest of men. And he said was there anything he could do for me, having confirmed that the news was true. And I said well, no, nothing really. I mean, he obviously meant are there financial problems or are you expecting a baby or anything like that. And I said no, there was nothing, but I wasn't very happy just teaching school in Birmingham, I would like to do something more useful, more directly helpful to the cause I believed in - take my mind off this tragedy. And he said he couldn't do anything about it immediately but he'd bear it in mind and he'd try and think of something.[160]

Through his contacts, she was employed by the Labour Research Department, 'just what I needed really because it was very intensive, very interesting work.'

Frances Cornford, John's mother, suffered a serious depression from 1934-1940. Her son, Hugh, later wrote that 'She told me later that the worst feature of her long illness was that she felt numb inside, and could not grieve for John.'[161] Margot Heinemann received a sympathetic message from John's father.

---

159 Margot Heinemann, IWM 9239.
160 Ibid.
161 Extract from the unedited version of a memoir of Frances Cornford by her son, Hugh, written as an introduction to a book of her selected poems.

He wrote a very beautiful letter to my parents actually, saying that he hoped this - I wouldn't allow this to maim my life. It was an appalling loss for them of course, this brilliant boy.[162]

Confronted by either temporary, or in some instances, permanent loss, many women, Margot Heinemann included, turned to the constructive action and friendship to be found in the campaigns for Spain.[163]

So one sought refuge in activity and of course, in the round of solidarity for Spain, meetings - Arms for Spain, selling papers for Spain, all this kind of thing, as well as research into British investments in Spain, all this kind of thing, in which the whole left-wing movement was engaged at that time. [164]

Bereaved wives at times seemed to wish to become substitutes for their dead husbands, committing themselves to his beliefs and metaphorically picking up the rifle he had let fall.

I regret very much to hear of my husband's death in Spain, but I am proud to know he died for a cause he held so dear. I will do all in my power to continue his good work, and I have decided to join the Communist Party, of which my husband was an honoured member.[165]

Another letter illustrates an attitude often encouraged in war-time propaganda, and perhaps not unusual amongst women committed to long term revolutionary or militant struggles, that of offering sons as the next generation of warriors.

I have just received news about my husband's death. It was a great shock. I had hoped for the best, we were devoted to each other. He never lived to see his first son born. He is very like his Dad. I shall bring him up a true fighter and to hate Fascism.[166]

---

162 Margot Heinemann, IWM 9239.
163 Other women who referred to being active in the Aid Spain campaigns whilst their husbands were away included for example, Noreen Branson, Rose Kerrigan and Win Albaya.
164 Margot Heinemann, IWM 9239.
165 Letter from the widow of Charles Goodfellow (2nd in command of British Battalion) 'Proud of their Husbands' *Daily Worker* 3 September, 1937, p. 4.
166 Mrs Mackie from Sunderland writing to Dependants Aid Committee on the death of her husband Bob at Brunete. Quoted in William Rust, *Britons in Spain: The History of the British Battalion of the XVth International Brigade* (Lawrence & Wishart, London, 1939) p. 137.

PICKETING FOR SPAIN

WITH biting winds and the weather at zero, over fifty women from the Labour Party, Co-operative Guilds and other organisations, picketed the Foreign Office for a week. On Tuesday, January 31, a letter was handed into the Foreign Secretary by the Women's Committee for Peace and Democracy, stating: " That the continuance of the policy of depriving the Spanish Government of its right to buy arms with which to defend the people, is not only becoming clearly inequitable to all and leads a savage slaughter in Spain, but also increases the dangers of a European War. We therefore ask that the policy of the British Government in this respect be changed and facilities to acquire armaments to be given to the Spanish Government. We also ask that everything be done to send large supplies of food to Spain. The reports of the starvation of children is heartrending, and there can be no doubt that the majority of the British people would enthusiastically support steps taken to alleviate this situation. We demand the full protection of British shipping engaged in carrying food to Spanish Government ports."

. This letter was signed by a number of prominent women including Lady Violet Bonham Carter, Dame May Whitty, Dr. Edith Summerskill, M.P., Miss Rebecca West, Mrs. Philip Guedalla, Miss E. Rathbone, Mrs. Evelyn Sharp Nevinson, Mrs. Wintringham, Mrs. Leah Manning, Mrs. Naomi Mitchison. An answer was received from the Foreign Secretary in which he states: " I would refer you to that passage in Mr. Chamberlain's Speech in which he says, ' I repeat that in my view a reversal of the policy of non-intervention must inevitably lead to the extension of the conflict in Europe.'

(*Continued on page* 8)

3.9 *Woman To-Day*, February 1939, 'Picketing for Spain'.

Elsie Booth, as a Brigader's wife, could be speaking for many of their families when she said, 'So that's why I always say, them that was left behind suffered just as much.'[167]

As the war drew to a close, women in Britain continued to campaign for Spain with what can only be described in rather hackneyed terms as 'grim determination'. By February 1939, the sad story of the war for the supporters of the Republic in Britain can be seen in the weary face of the woman holding her placard that appeared in *Woman To-Day*.

Nevertheless, the article, 'Picketing for Spain,' also illustrated the tenacity of women in their campaigns, and their willingness to work together.

> With biting winds and the weather at zero, over fifty women from the Labour Party, Co-operative Guilds and other organisations, picketed the Foreign Office for a week. On Tuesday, January 31st, a letter was handed into the Foreign Secretary by the Women's Committee for Peace and Democracy...[168]

The Aid Spain campaigns present a rare opportunity to study the mobilisation of substantial numbers of women in Britain during a period when this country was not at war. Although women were usually working alongside men on the broad-based committees, their numbers, and sometimes their previous experience of this type of work, made it possible for them to avoid the usual pattern of subordination, and to fulfil their potential to a greater degree. Instead of having to battle for recognition, they could work effectively in many ways within a loose structure that suited them and that made optimum use of their varied capabilities. Those who would never have become involved with formalised politics could express a different kind of political concern, in which an activity as simple as knitting could become a practical demonstration of support for a particular cause. As far as women were concerned therefore, with their

---

167 Elsie Booth and Mary Freeman, Tameside 215 and IWM 842.
168 'Picketing for Spain', *Woman To-Day* February 1939, p. 6. The article stated that the letter, asking that the Spanish Government should be allowed to buy arms and for more food to be sent to Spain, had been signed by a number of prominent women including Lady Violet Bonham Carter, Dame May Whitty, Dr. Edith Summerskill MP, Miss Rebecca West, Mrs Philip Guedalla, Miss E. Rathbone, Mrs Evelyn Sharp Nevison, Mrs Wintringham, Mrs Leah Manning and Mrs Naomi Mitchison. *Woman To-Day* was, at this time, under the editorship of Charlotte Haldane and had become the voice of the Women's Committee for Peace and Democracy, formerly known as the Women's' World Committee Against War and Fascism. See Chapter 5.

commitments to work, home and family, the variety of things they could do to help gave them the flexibility they needed to become involved.

Today, committees are often viewed with a degree of contempt, more likely to impede action than to facilitate it. For women in the thirties, committees were a successful mechanism for organising a direct, and if necessary, a rapid response to an urgent need. Local meetings relating to the war in Spain could be held in places and at times that allowed women to attend, and there was practical work to be done in which all could share with no dichotomy arising between the interests of the male and female members. This type of work, in which women have played a significant part, is frequently overlooked and undervalued. Nevertheless, despite the lack of any financial reward or even of wider public recognition, committee culture remained a firmly ingrained aspect of life for women in this study who saw it as a means to help others. Faced with a crisis in the modern world, whether international or local, Frida Stewart would say with indefatigable resolve, 'We must form a committee,' and proceed to mobilise those around her into action.[169]

---

169 For more on the life of Frida Stewart after the war, see her profile in Appendix I.

CHAPTER FOUR

'A Woman's Work in Wartime': Women in Spain

'WRITE AN ESSAY on "A woman's work in wartime",' a teacher instructed her pupils as the 'war to end all wars' raged in Europe.[1] After the Spanish Civil War this task would have become considerably more demanding. Not only were women's traditional war-time activities expanded and developed in Spain, but the disquieting phenomenon of women in typical masculine roles was brought dramatically to public attention. The images of Spanish women taking up arms in defence of the Republic appeared in newspapers across Europe in the early days of the war, and posters emphasising their importance to the war effort in heavy industry abounded in the cities that remained in Republican hands. The majority of British women who went to Spain were involved with the care of the casualties of war, but the Spanish posters depicting saintly nurses in pristine white uniforms bore little resemblance to the cruel realities of nursing near the front lines. Here, British women were working alongside volunteers from other countries and contributing to the surgical and medical advances that saved the lives and limbs of thousands.[2] Many thousands more would have surely died without the help of those who worked in refugee centres, where displaced women and children could receive the basic necessities of life.

However, the purpose of this chapter is not the compilation of a guide indicating which British women did what, where and when in Spain.[3] The principal aim here is to reach a greater understanding of

---

1 Winifred Bates, a pupil during the First World War, describes this episode in her undated memoir, 'A Woman's Work in Wartime', MML Box 29/D/7.
2 See for example an article by R. S. Saxton MRCS Eng., 'The Madrid Transfusion Institute', *The Lancet* 4 September, 1937, p. 606, and 'Medicine in Republican Spain' by the same author, *The Lancet* 2, 751, 1938.
3 Some of this type of information can be found in the profiles of individual women in Appendix I. See also Jim Fyrth, *The Signal was Spain: The Aid Spain Movement in Britain 1936-39* (Lawrence & Wishart, London, 1986).

the experience of the Spanish Civil War for the British women who remained in Spain for some time during the conflict. Many of the themes have been suggested by the words of the women themselves, selected for their significance in the life of a particular individual, or because a common theme has arisen in several different narratives. Inevitably therefore, this chapter primarily reflects the perspectives of the women whose memories have entered the public sphere for a variety of reasons. Sadly, there are many others who appear as no more than names in the records, perhaps only remembered in private family legends.[4] The experience of some British women who were in Spain during the war included the work of conveying the urgency of the situation to the public at home. The ways in which they expressed their views are discussed in Chapter 5.

With seemingly only one brief exception, British woman did not fight at the front in Spain.[5] The role of female combatants is therefore largely unexplored here, although mention should be made of its relevance through absence. Studies on gender and war have highlighted the attitudes which generally dictated women's choices.[6] There are British women in this study who would perhaps have taken up arms had the possibility been open to them. But these women, who were potentially 'The Ferocious Few', had to look for other, more acceptable ways to join battle.[7] However, in general, women's recollections of their interaction with war differ markedly from those of men, not only because the experience was in itself typically different, but also because their distinctively gendered perspectives are reflected in the narrative form.[8] Warfare, although involving entire

4   The methodological implications of such a process of self-selection in relation to this study are discussed in Appendix II.
5   Felicia Browne, killed in action, 22 August 1936, see this chapter below.
6   For an excellent study of this subject see Joanna Bourke, *An Intimate History of Killing: Face-to-face Combat in Twentieth-Century Warfare* (Granta, London, 2000, first published 1999), particularly Chapter 10, 'Women go to War'. See also Kris Rothstein, ' "This Is Where War Is": British Masculinity and the Spanish Civil War' MA Dissertation, Department of Sociology, University of Essex, 1996
7   Jean Bethke Elshtain contrasts the role of women she refers to as 'The Ferocious Few' with those she calls 'The Noncombatant Many' in *Women and War* (Harvester Press, Brighton, 1987)
8   A striking example of this can be seen in the unpublished memoirs of Kate Mangan (née Foster) and Jan Kurzke, 'The Good Comrade', (Jan Kurzke Papers, Archives of the International Institute for Social History, Amsterdam.) They were both in Spain during the first year of the war. Jan was fighting in the Brigades until he was wounded, Kate was working in the rearguard and attempting to find him. Originally their intention was to publish their memoirs together in one book, but the differences in style and content made this impossible. The focus of her narrative is on Jan, whereas he never mentions her at all. My thanks to Charlotte Kurzke for allowing me to read her parents' memoirs.

populations, takes place in an arena largely controlled by men. They establish the parameters and the rules of the game and afterwards are renowned for their tendency to tell war stories and write war memoirs. The masculine perspective of war is also emphasised by historians, who commonly give priority to the military and political aspects of the conflict.[9] Histories of the war in Spain frequently focus on the internecine strife taking place on the Left. In such scenarios women may only appear as a fleeting presence, perhaps as an idiosyncratic element on the battlefield, or in their rare capacity as prominent political figures. Women in general may receive mention as victims of war, but the words of an individual woman are likely to feature only if they can be construed as evidence of political persecution or dissent. Such approaches cast but the merest glimmer of light on women's interaction with the war, and in some senses, obscure the nature of the relationship.

As discussed in previous chapters, when women have been strongly committed politically, they have commonly seen participation in a hierarchical political structure as a means to reduce suffering, rather than as a way to construct a power base. Although often identifying deeply with the 'political' implications of the war in the broadest sense, few British women played an active role in the factional conflicts of the Left in Spain, many were manifestly uninterested in these party political struggles and others rejected involvement in such matters entirely.[10] This chapter therefore is not a study of the machinations of political parties but of the experience of the war as perceived and expressed by women, forming a synthesis dependent upon the perspective of a female historian. As such, it offers an approach to the war differing from that of the accepted norm.

Estimates have been made of the numbers of British women who worked in Spain during the war, but as complete records are not

---

8 cont] When reviewing the narratives of Spanish men and women relating to the war, Shirley Mangini pointed out this difference between the vantage point of men and women. She agrees with Estelle Jelinek, who noted that that females emphasise not so much their political and historical connections, but rather their personal relationships with others. *Memories of Resistance: Women's Voices from the Spanish Civil War* (Yale University Press, New Haven & London, 1995) p. 58. See also the discussion on women's descriptions of battles further on in this chapter.

9   The tendency to conflate 'war' with 'combat' has also had a significant impact in the field of literature, leading to the frequent exclusion of women's texts on war. Margaret Higonnet, 'Another Record: A Different War', *Women's Studies Quarterly*, 1995, vol. 23, part 3/4, pp. 85-96

10 The party political affiliations of a handful of the British women who were working in the medical units in Spain are listed in International Brigade files. MML Box D7 A/2

available, figures remain uncertain.[11] Numbers fluctuated as some returned home and new volunteers arrived. Women doctors, still something of a rarity in Britain, were few in Spain, but there were numerous British women working as nurses and administrators in the medical units and hospitals, and in the refugee centres, such as those run by the Society of Friends.[12]

Less than a month after the war started, organised groups of volunteer medical staff began leaving for Spain.[13] None of the women studied here have spoken of pressure being brought to bear to persuade them to volunteer, other than the insistent demands of their own sense of what was right. Molly Murphy wrote that the appeal for nurses 'rang a bell in my heart,' feeling that it would be 'nauseating' to continue the private nursing she was doing 'when splendid young men were dying on the international battlefield of Spain because there were so few nurses and doctors to help them to keep alive.'[14] At first she was told that her services would not be required, but in January 1937 she received a telegram asking if she was still available. The elation that followed her previous depression was expressed in almost religious terms, 'When I received the telegram calling me, it seemed like a ray of light amidst the greyness of the day.'[15] Margaret Powell was also not accepted initially. She had gone for an interview with the Spanish Medical Aid Committee as soon as the war broke out, but was told by Leah Manning that she should finish her midwifery

---

11 References to over seventy women from Britain who were working for some time in the medical and refugee services have been noted during the course of this research and many more went to Spain for short periods. Jim Fyrth estimates that there were more than 170 English speaking women volunteers involved in this type of work. Those from Australia, New Zealand, South Africa, Canada, and America are not included in this study. Jim Fyrth and Sally Alexander (eds), *Women's Voices from the Spanish Civil War* (Lawrence & Wishart, London, 1991) p. 29, fn. 1

12 Dr Audrey Russell worked with refugees, mainly in Catalonia. In *Trueta: Surgeon in War and Peace: Memoirs of Josep Trueta* (Gollancz, London, 1980) there are references to an ENT surgeon, Miss D. Josephine Collier arriving in Barcelona with Audrey Russell early in 1938, bringing a car full of medical supplies. Portia Holman worked in the medical units in Spain shortly before she qualified as a doctor. Angela Guest, although not a qualified nurse, worked in the medical services in Spain until the end of the war and later became a doctor serving with the WHO.

13 One of the first groups to leave for Spain was an ambulance unit organised by the Spanish Medical Aid Committee which left on 23 August 1936. Jim Fyrth refers to eight women amongst the doctors, medical students, nurses, and drivers, these being a German doctor who had come to England in 1934 called Ruth Prothero, two nurses from Australia, Aileen Palmer and Margot Miller, four nurses from Britain, Thora Silverthorne, Doris Bird, Jean Woodifield, and Elaine Bell, and one British administrator, Rosita Davson. *The Signal was Spain*, pp. 48-50

14 Molly Murphy, unedited version of autobiography 'Nurse Molly', p. 126. Museum of Labour History. She first volunteered her services in October 1936.

15 Ibid., p. 127.

training. On the day that her training formally ended, she left for Spain.[16]
Some women had to re-apply before they proved successful. Lillian
Urmston saw an appeal for medical volunteers in the *News Chronicle*.
Having qualified as a nurse, she had joined the Territorial Army
Nursing Service. She was not involved with party politics, but her
sympathies always lay with 'the underdogs', in this case, the
Republicans, who were 'short of everything and needed nurses far
more than any others.' Feeling 'bitterly disappointed' when she
received no reply after bombarding Spanish Medical Aid with requests
to go as a nurse to Spain, she eventually sent them a telegram,
demanding to know why they hadn't replied. Early in 1937, she was
granted an interview by the secretary, George Jeger. After many
questions concerning her background, he asked her to explain why
she had written 'politically disinterested' on her application form. She
recalled his amusement at her reply,

Well, I've never heard of any organisation employing nurses that
wanted nurses who were politically minded. Religion and politics
are like sex in hospitals, never discussed.[17]

He was persuaded that she was suitable volunteer material by her
determination to gain experience of nursing under wartime conditions
in readiness for the 'total' war she saw looming ahead. On handing in
her notice however, she, amongst others, discovered that the reaction
to her reason for leaving was far from favourable.

I was requested to be ready to go at anytime and they would send
phials through the post of anti-typhoid - anti-typhus serum and so
on for me to take. So I gave in my notice immediately and I had
about three weeks leave due and the sisters who ran the nursing
home refused to give me the leave. They refused to pay me my
uniform allowance which was overdue and they threatened me with
all sort of dire things, including a solicitor's letter if I left them. They
also confiscated from my bedroom the phials of serum which I
had to have.[18]

---

16 24 March 1937. Short memoir by Margaret Powell, 13 July 1980, papers of her daughter,
    Ruth Muller.
17 Lillian Buckoke (née Urmston), Tameside 203.
18 Ibid.

Fortunately, a doctor working at the nursing home was a Quaker who was prepared to give her the necessary injections. However, she was not allowed to take even a few hours off duty although she was 'suffering agony from all the shots.' Mary Slater also remembered working on night duty in pain after her injections because she felt 'I dare not tell them at work I had got them.'[19] The hospital where she worked had already insisted that she must pay £5 for not giving a month's notice. As she did not have such an amount, the sum was eventually paid by Spanish Medical Aid.

Patience Darton was training in midwifery at the British Hospital for Mothers and Babies during the summer of 1936. She greatly admired the strength of character of the matron who had founded the hospital, 'an absolute darling, a real fighter'.[20] Matron however, strongly disapproved of her plan to go to Spain, calling it 'an emotional extravagance.'

> I was very upset with this because I was very fond of her and it seemed to me quite straight forward... She thought it was an emotional thing on my part - which was probably true, it was - but it was quite a sensible emotion I thought. I was very downcast by that but it didn't stop me in the least.[21]

Armed with her determination to 'change things', not only the generally low standards of midwifery care that were the matron's concern, but the fundamental causes of the poverty she witnessed around her, Patience Darton set off to volunteer. Having no idea how to get to Spain, she went firstly to the offices of the *Daily Herald*. The staff responded enthusiastically and, knowing that the *News Chronicle* had been running an appeal for nurses, took her there in a taxi. From there she was taken to the Spanish Medical Aid offices and, after a brief interview, was accepted. Patience Darton gives detailed information on the subsequent outfitting of the volunteer nurses, in particular the lack of the Committee's foresight in providing appropriate clothing for service near the front line. She complains justifiably about the unsuitability of 'three silly little blue frocks with white collars and turned back cuffs', of the difficulties cross-over overalls that kept uncrossing and opening up, and the impracticality of the all-in-one men's overalls

---

19 Mary Slater, Tameside 181. Mary Slater was from Lancashire, a former worker in a cotton mill who had attended Hillcroft College for women, then trained as an SRN in London.
20 Patience Edney (née Darton), IWM 8398
21 Ibid.

when you were at the front amongst 'very low bushes, terribly low bushes, and if you wanted to get out to the loo for a pee, you had to take all your top off.' Other criticisms relate to the fact that underwear, stockings, shoes, and sanitary towels were not supplied, and as initially they were unpaid volunteers, often with no resources of their own, these deficiencies could prove troublesome. The only solution for Patience Darton was to borrow from other nurses.[22] The Committee was also unaware of certain aspects of protocol in the Republic regarding dress. Fifty years after the war, she still had several of the white square head-dresses, unused, because when she was in Spain, 'anyone who wore head-gear of any sort was considered a fascist.'[23]

For Patience Darton, as for most women in this group, the decision to go to Spain had taken place on an intensely personal level. Her parents knew nothing of her decision until she had been accepted as a volunteer.

And I went back and told mother, who gulped a bit. I must say, I was very hard hearted, it never occurred to me that she'd mind about it.... She certainly didn't like the idea very much but she swallowed and accepted the fact that I was going to do it anyway.... I didn't consider what my father thought about it, never occurred to me to ask him or discuss it.[24]

Perhaps some potential volunteers were dissuaded by outside influences, but the parents of these young women were probably already aware of the futility of arguing with such determined offspring. Frida Stewart recalled her mother's attitude to her plans to drive an ambulance to Spain.

I think she [mother] knew me well enough to know that I wouldn't be quite mad and do totally idiotic things, she trusted me to look after myself. And she knew from her own background - if you want-ed something and you felt you could do it, you had to do it. She'd gone - was one of the very early Newnham students in the face of a lot of resistance from her family.[25]

---

22 This situation changed after she joined the IB after which she received 10 pesetas a day. See below.
23 Patience Edney (née Darton), IWM 8398
24 Ibid.
25 Frida Stewart, AJ, 11 December 1995.

Parental anxieties paled into insignificance in comparison with the overriding urgency of the conflagration beginning in Spain. For nurses like Thora Silverthorne, aware of the political issues at stake, there was a duty to be fulfilled.

And the family were a bit apprehensive of course - going all the way to Spain - but I took it all as a matter of course, this was part of a Spanish war against the Fascists.[26]

Margaret Powell decided not to try to explain such anti-Fascist feelings to her family, merely saying that she was motivated by a sense of adventure. She believed that they would have been proud of her if she had wanted to go to China or Africa as a missionary, but that they would not have understood her 'real reason' for wanting to go to Spain.[27] According to an article in the *Daily Express*, Dorothy Rutter had not told her mother about going to Spain, she had kept it to herself so that her mother would not worry.[28]

In marked contrast to the self-determination apparent in the narratives of most of these women, the involvement of Diana Smythies with the war occurred at her father's insistence. Major Hugh Pollard was a right-wing fire arms collector who 'couldn't resist adventures'.[29] His eighteen year old daughter, Diana Smythies, became an important member of a small group that played a key role in the early days of the war. She acted as 'camouflage' in a plan to fly Franco from his semi-banishment in the Canary Isles to North Africa.[30] She knew nothing of Spanish politics, but just did as her father asked, taking her best summer apparel, hats, gloves and seersucker dresses, in order to act the part of a tourist and make it appear more convincing that the group were on holiday. A friend, Dorothy Watson, blonde and pretty, was considered to be 'another ready made one', to play this role. In an interview many years later, Diana Smythies recalled that although she didn't have any particular wish for this adventure, it was difficult to refuse, 'rather like, you know, being cowardly, so one had to say yes.'

---

26 Thora Silverthorne, AJ, 3 January 1996.
27 Powell, 'Memoir', 1980.
28 'British Nurses in Spain Send News, "O.K. - Love" ', *Daily Express*, 12 March 1937, p. 5.
29 All quotations in this paragraph are taken from an interview with Diana Smythies, IWM 7371.
30 Luis Bolin, correspondent of the monarchist paper *ABC*, chartered the plane from Croydon. Douglas Jerrold, a right-wing publisher, had been responsible for contacting Hugh Pollard, who then agreed to include his daughter, Diana and another girl, possibly an employee, in the group.

She remembered her mother's somewhat despairing reaction to the plan, 'I saw the face - you know - here we go again, oh dear, they may none of them come back - she didn't think it was at all suitable - nor was it.' The outward flight with Captain Bebb in the Dragon Rapide involved landings in France, Portugal and Morocco and was fraught with difficulties, including a drunken radio operator and nearly running out of fuel. Diana Smythies carried secret papers for Franco hidden in a copy of Vogue, feeling 'very unreal.' But, without doubt, the plane would not have succeeded in reaching Las Palmas if not for the presence of the two girls. As the situation in Spain worsened, aerodromes were closed. They had landed at an airfield in Spanish Morocco, where after a 'lovely lunch' the commandant told them that they would not be allowed to continue.

> Father said, 'There are no facilities for women, are there, you see? I can't leave these beautiful ladies in such a situation.' And then, people had very good manners, even if they might be going to kill you, they would apologise, they didn't just shoot you like they do on ITV! And so he [father] said if we were to have our holiday disrupted in this way, 'perhaps you could allow us to go as far as Gran Canaria, because there's a sympathetic government there and they can impound the aeroplane and it would be a lot better than having us stuck here on this heap of sand to your great disadvantage.'[31]

Following this call to uphold the values of chivalry, they were allowed to proceed. The mission was completed successfully, Franco was able to arrange for the Army of Africa to be transported across to mainland Spain in German planes, and the course of the war changed in his favour. The girls returned to England, and were later offered a decoration of 'Golden or Red Arrows' by Franco for their efforts on his behalf. However, Diana Smythies wanted no further involvement with the war, 'I thought, never again, no more adventures of this kind.'[32]

For many other women however, the departure for Spain and the first journey were memorable experiences in which the excitement of new adventures were unmarred by the realities of war. Thora Silverthorne remembered with deep emotion the day in August 1936 when she left for Spain with the first medical unit from Victoria

---

31 Diana Smythies, IWM 7371.
32 Ibid.

Station. Young and enthusiastic, dressed smartly in her nurses uniform, she recalled thinking 'My God, we're going to take part,' whilst the crowd of thousands cheered and applauded as they departed.[33] Patience Darton, as a member of the congregation of St. George's in Holborn, was given 'a good send off' when she left for Spain.

> ...they had a great 'bidding' prayer from the Church. First of all it was mentioned in the service and then I was seen off down the steps, with all the congregation and Father Roberts, and there was Haile Selassie, but he didn't know quite what was going on [laughter] - anyway, he was dragged out to do it.[34]

Many of the women went first to Paris, then endured a crowded and slow train journey across France. A recurring theme in the narratives is their delight at the warmth of the welcome they received from local people when they eventually arrived in Spain. Molly Murphy wrote of her train journey to Albacete, during which the nurses were singled out for a special welcome at every stop, and were repeatedly presented with oranges, grapes and dates.[35] Patience Darton arrived in Valencia, delighted by the orange trees, the flowers, and the sunshine.

> And the trams were like - I'd never seen anything like it in England - the crowding, people jammed all the way round, holding on to the little rails round the outside, round the windows and jammed tight on to the back, all hanging on round the edges of things, not quite on top, but all but. And they put me on to this and said where I had to get off, and I couldn't hold on to anything, I held on to people. I got my feet on and I was held on and they took my bags. And when we got to the hospital, ever so many people got off the tram to help me across, they were terribly excited about this English nurse come to help Spain... And I thought this was very sweet and very welcoming.[36]

Not all journeys were without unpleasant incidents. Some had their first experience of bombing soon after crossing the border. Dorothy Davies, a nurse who was on her way by plane to work in a children's hospital run by the Society of Friends, did not at first realise

---

33 Thora Silverthorne, AJ, 3 January 1996.
34 Patience Edney (née Darton), IWM 8398.
35 Molly Murphy, 'Nurse Molly', p. 128.
36 Patience Edney (née Darton), IWM 8398.

that the clouds of dust and stones she saw rising into the air from the city of Barcelona were caused by an air raid.[37] Bombs just missed the train which took Molly Murphy to Barcelona.[38] On the way to the Aragon front, Lillian Urmston's train was constantly stopping because of fire from enemy aircraft. Her journey had already been fraught with difficulty when she and her companion, the Australian nurse, Dorothy Low, were detained in Port Bou. Although they had passports and visas, they were unaccompanied and nobody arrived to meet them as planned. They were detained by the authorities and spent the day locked in a hotel room furnished only with iron bed frames.[39] Eventually they were taken out to eat, under guard, and noticing two men who looked English in appearance, were fortunate to find that one was the lorry driver who had been sent to collect them. The remainder of their journey however, was marked with the cheers, clenched fist salutes, food and drink, typical of the exuberant welcome given by ordinary Spanish people.[40]

Medical personnel were to find themselves working in many difficult situations, not only as a result of being in a country at war. Those British nurses who came into contact with the medical care on offer in some Spanish hospitals at the start of the war register a marked degree of dismay. There was no nursing tradition in Spain similar to that of Britain. Nuns carried out some nursing duties, but the general care of a patient was usually the responsibility of the family. Standards of hygiene and asepsis were often low. Priscilla Scott-Ellis only had brief training before becoming a nurse for Franco's forces, but was amazed at the lack of sterile precautions she witnessed when posted to a surgical unit. After remarking that the head wound they were dressing 'bled like a pig and one could see his brains pulsating', she does not mince her words as she writes in her diary,

I was absolutely horrified at the dirtiness of the doctor. His ideas of antisepsis were very shaky and it gives me the creeps to see the casual way they pick up sterilised compresses with their fingers etc. I am not surprised that so many of the wounds get infected.[41]

37 Dorothy Davies, 'Six Months in Southern Spain', undated, Box D2:AC/1, Marx Memorial Library.
38 Molly Murphy, 'Nurse Molly', p. 128.
39 Those who detained them are not specifically identified.
40 Lillian Buckoke (née Urmston), Tameside 203.
41 Priscilla Scott-Ellis, *The Chances of Death: A Diary of the Spanish Civil War* edited by Raymond Carr (Michael Russell Publishing Ltd, Wilby, Norwich, 1995) 3 February 1938, p. 33.

On her arrival in the Republican zone, Patience Darton nursed Tom Wintringham who was failing to recover from his wounds in a Valencian hospital.[42] Kate Mangan, who had come to Spain searching for the German International Brigader, Jan Kurzke, was in Valencia when Patience Darton arrived. In her memoirs, she described Patience's appearance in detail.

When the nurse arrived for Tom she causes a sensation. She was a lovely, earnest creature called Patience. She was tall, thin, angular and virginal. She had a mass of ash-blond hair done up in a bun, but usually covered by a white kerchief. Her face was pointed and eager, with a full mouth, rather large nose and very striking, very blue eyes... She looked like the kind of beautiful hospital nurse one dreams of...[43]

As a suspected typhoid case, Tom Wintringham had been given no food and had not been washed, in case of 'chills'. Knowing this approach had been superseded, Patience Darton introduced a new regime of care, despite feeling rather intimidated by the form she had to sign taking sole responsibility for the outcome of her changes. She re-opened his badly infected wound to allow drainage and he rapidly improved. However, in contrast to these grim accounts, British nurses often speak highly of Spanish surgeons they encountered in the medical units, praising their surgical skills and emphasising the lifelong bonds of friendship that were formed. Under bombardment and continually facing the challenge of maintaining standards through improvisation, Thora Silverthorne worked as a theatre nurse with the Catalan surgeon, Dr Moises Broggi, forming a friendship that lasted until her death in 1999.[44]

Initially, most of the British medical personnel were sent by Spanish Medical Aid to Grañen, a hospital on the Aragon front. In January 1937, this policy changed and the majority were attached to the International Brigades.[45] As the war continued and new fronts opened up, they were to be found working in many diverse locations and with volunteers of many nationalities. Much of the work was done

---

42 Tom Wintringham had been wounded at the battle of the Jarama whilst Commander of the British Battalion.
43 Mangan, 'The Good Comrade', p. 344.
44 Thora Silverthorne, AJ, 3 January 1996.
45 The International Brigades and the attached medical staff were incorporated into the Republican Army later in 1937.

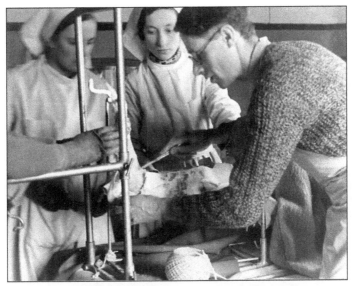

4.1 Thora Silverthorne with Dr Alex Tudor-Hart
in a field operating theatre.

in mobile hospital units, frequently moving in order to be near the
fighting wherever it was occurring. Sometimes a specially converted
ambulance, an 'auto-chir', was used for operations and the wounded
were nursed in tents. Buildings were converted to hospitals where
possible, but as the war progressed, nurses found themselves working
in trains, disused railway tunnels and towards the end, in a cave near
the river Ebro. On arrival at such a unit, the incoming casualties were
assessed, and given emergency treatment if necessary. Those needing
immediate surgery were sent into the operating theatre but the less
seriously injured were usually taken to the base hospital. This system
of 'triage' was but one of the many innovations which increased the
survival rate of battle casualties during the war in Spain. Apart from
the benefit of receiving care much more quickly due to the presence
of units nearer the front lines than before, other advances included
new methods for blood transfusion, improved abdominal surgery and
fracture repair, and techniques to treat wounds which avoided the
onset of gas-gangrene.[46]

46 For more detailed information on this subject from a nursing perspective see articles by
Lillian Urmston, 'English Nurse in Spain', *Nursing Mirror* 13 May 1939, pp. 231, 234; 20 May
1939, pp. 273-4; 27 May 1939, 293; 3 June 1939, pp. 335-6; 10 June 1939, pp. 368-9; 17 June
1939, pp. 403-4; 24 June 1939, pp. 435-6. An overview is given by Fyrth, 'Medical
Advances', Chapter 10, *The Signal was Spain.*

4.2 Hospital train and wounded men.

4.3 The cave hospital near La Bisbal de Falset, 1938.

In the areas controlled by Franco, there seems little evidence to suggest that similar advances were taking place.[47] To date, only the diaries of Priscilla Scott-Ellis give the perspective of a British nurse in the 'Nationalist' medical units. However, another British woman, Gabriel Herbert was acting as an intermediary between the medical services for Franco's forces and the Bishops' Committee for the Relief of Spanish Distress, a group founded by British Catholics who wanted to help Franco. Funds were raised for two ambulances and to supply an 'Equipo Anglo-Español' for medical services at the front. After her first visit behind the insurgent lines she told the *Daily Sketch* 'When I arrived with our ambulance, there was only one other surgical unit for the whole of the insurgent forces - and that had been captured from the 'Reds.'[48] The 'equipo' was based firstly near Vitoria and from there, members of the team were sent out to man first aid posts at the front. Later, they moved to Huesca. Gabriel Herbert was an exception to a strict rule that members of the team must all be Spanish. Her role, she wrote, was to act as 'a sort of enlace, or middle man who could travel more freely than the Spanish could, between frontiers; report to the Committee, and act as their representative.'[49] As her Spanish improved she could record requests for supplies, collect the orders in London and convey them back to Spain.

> There were one or two embarrassing moments for me, a confusion between the meaning of words, 'agujas' meaning needles, and 'angulas'. It was pointed out, very kindly to me that what I was asking the bewildered Committee to send us, urgently, was 10,000 baby eels of different sizes.[50]

As she travelled to and fro, several individual members of the London Committee came with her to meet the staff on the 'equipo' and see the work being done. The relationship between the Committee and the 'equipo' is described as 'very easy' with a 'natural trust between

---

47 Dr Nicholas Coni has carried out research on the medical advances made in Spain during the civil war and has found numerous articles by doctors working in the Republic in the British medical journals on this subject, but few references from those who were working for Franco in any of the Spanish, British, German or Italian journals. *Medicine and Warfare: Spain 1936-1939*, (Routledge/Cañada Blanch Studies on Contemporary Spain, London, 2007).
48 'These Heroes are New Crusaders: Peer's Sister Tells of Spanish Bravery,' *Daily Sketch*, 26 November 1936. Gabriel Herbert was the sister of Lord Howard of Penrith.
49 Letter from Mrs Alexander Dru, (née Gabriel Herbert), 4 April 1982 to Michael Alpert, papers of Prof. M. Alpert, University of Westminster, London.
50 Ibid.

them' and a 'wonderful lack of 'red tape and bureaucratic interference.'[51]
    As the war continued, in all the confusion of retreating and advancing lines and shifting fronts, medical personnel arriving in Republican Spain were frequently faced with a bewildering succession of locations. Molly Murphy arrived in Albacete, the International Brigade Headquarters, in January 1937. She soon heard that she was to leave for a hospital near the Madrid front. Her first taste of life as a nurse in Spain was in the inky blackness of a cold and rainy winter's night.

> When we arrived in the early hours of the morning in the deepest darkness it all seemed so weird and grim. Fighting had been hard and fierce in recent days. The hospital was crowded to capacity. Every bed was occupied and wounded men lay on mattresses covering every foot of space. All was dark and the nurse was moving about the place with the aid of a shaded torch. The black-out had to be very complete.[52]

4.4 From left to right, sitting: Molly Murphy
and Nurse Wilson, and standing: Nurse Bell,
Dr Reggie Saxton and Rosaleen Smythe, Spain 1937.

---

51 Ibid.
52 Molly Murphy, 'Nurse Molly' p. 129.

She describes a pattern of work which was similar to that experienced by many of the women in the medical units, frequent moves and working conditions unlike anything she had ever known before.

Everything here was in short supply and especially nurses. Regulation hours of work meant all hours. Never did we get a house for conversion where there was a laid-on supply of water. Always the water had to be carried, rarely less than a quarter of a mile. There were no windows. All had been shattered by blast from bombs. One had to get used to the breezes blowing through the place, to rats scurrying across our beds, to bats flying around in the night, to living with wounded men groaning with pain, to working until one was completely exhausted, to fall asleep on a blood soaked mattress and to wake up with a start finding wounded men on either side.[53]

Working by the light of candles and giving blood transfusions in a glimmer of illumination from cigarette lighters were common occurrences, according to an article written by another nurse, Margaret Powell.[54] Adjusting to such conditions was difficult and was exacerbated by their struggles to adapt to a different diet. Lillian Urmston remembered that all the new arrivals from Britain had severe constipation for about a month until their swollen stomachs learned to cope with a diet consisting largely of beans.[55] These complaints were echoed by Molly Murphy, who wrote home of 'a touch of stomach ache', and added, 'I can assure you sanitary arrangements are such that chronic constipation is a gift from the Gods.'[56] To add to these problems, Patience Darton comments on the prevalence of dysentery, and that nothing much could be done about it, 'we just all had it', and that she suffered from it 'off and on nearly all the time.'[57]

Molly Murphy also wrote home about the scarcity of opportunities to have baths, or even wash. For her birthday the theatre staff gave her the present of enough hot water to wash her feet, and 'promised for my next birthday to give me some more for the rest of my body!!!'[58]

---

53 Ibid., p. 130.
54 Margaret Powell, 'Nurses There Work in Wards Lit By Cigarette Lighters', *Daily Worker*, 7 January 1938.
55 Lillian Buckoke (née Urmston), Tameside 203.
56 Molly Murphy, letter to Bill and Gordon, April 1937, Museum of Labour History.
57 Patience Edney (née Darton), IWM 8398.
58 Molly Murphy, letter to Darling old boys, 10 March 1937, Museum of Labour History.

When 'lousy' she was not alone in preferring to keep the information to herself. One of the younger nurses, who thought her rash was the result of a food allergy, was forced to face the truth when Molly Murphy caught one of the culprits. 'You won't tell anyone, will you, Murphy?' she begged.[59] Sometimes 'green' young nurses found themselves working under these conditions, bearing responsibilities beyond their wildest dreams. As a trained fever nurse, Penny Phelps was put in charge of controlling an epidemic of scarlet fever amongst the Garibaldi Battalion. When she arrived, the ward was full of sick men, one of whom she realised had typhoid.

> I went in and it - stench - and there was pots of urine, you know, all overflowing with urine, bits of bread and crusts all over, no pillows, people in clothes and on clothes, and it was terrible, and the windows were closed. And I thought, 'God, what am I in for?' And then I looked as I walked by and I thought, 'God, that man's ill.' And I went up, and I thought, 'God, he's almost moribund.' And I talk about lice, you could imagine them that they'd be running off with people.[60]

4.5 Penny Phelps (centre) with the staff at Quintanar, 1937.

59 Molly Murphy, letter to Bill and Gordon, April 1937, Museum of Labour History.
60 Penny Phelps, AJ, 22 February 1996.

In addition to attending to those who were ill, she organised staff for a programme of thorough disinfection, fumigation, and inoculation for the entire battalion of 600 men. When the International Brigades became part of the Spanish army, she states proudly in her memoirs, 'Now I was Lieutenant Penny Phelps of the Spanish Republican Army, medical officer to the Garibaldi Battalion of the 15th International Brigade.' However, she adds modestly that 'Luckily, about two months later, the Republican Government de-militarised all women and I gladly returned to being a nurse.'[61]

Even though the medical staff were forced to face the horrific injuries and the death of their patients repeatedly, each person remembers certain occasions with particular clarity. The reasons for such vivid recall vary, usually there is some factor over and above the grim reality of the 'run of the mill' death and destruction. In the cases involving children, such a response was acute. During the final retreat through Barcelona, Ann Murray was with a group evacuating casualties to France.

> We found a whole lot of children, of, dozens of them, with their hands off, completely off. The Italians had dropped anti-personnel bombs marked 'Chocolatti' [sic]. The children were picking up these things - they hadn't had chocolate for years - and they just blew their hands off. This Spanish surgeon that I worked with, he was in tears. We all were. This sort of thing was so horrible, it left a big impression on me.[62]

In December 1995, shortly before her death, this was the one memory she selected to painstakingly record in an uncertain hand on her application form for honorary Spanish nationality as a member of the International Brigades.[63] Others were similarly affected by incidents involving children. Priscilla Scott-Ellis, normally blasé about the many injuries she had seen, was upset by the case of a twelve year old girl who had been playing with a hand grenade and had received severe injuries when it exploded. She wrote, 'I think I minded seeing her being treated and operated on more than anything else I have seen so

---

61 P. Fyvel, (née Phelps, m. Feiwel), *English Penny* (Arthur H. Stockwell Ltd., Ilfracombe, Devon, 1992) p. 38.
62 See Annie Murray in Ian MacDougall (ed.), *Voices from the Spanish Civil War: Personal Recollections of Scottish Volunteers in Republican Spain 1936-39* (Polygon, Edinburgh, 1986) p.73.
63 Photocopy supplied by Bill Alexander, Secretary of the International Brigade Association.

far. I can't bear to see children hurt.'[64] Penny Phelps was enjoying a short break in the café of a small town square when the petrol station opposite received a direct hit.

And I can always remember the children playing round on the other side with the mules, and you know, there was the carts and the petrol station with lorries filling, I mean, to be re-fuelled, and this terrible, terrible explosion - you didn't know quite what happened. I mean, I went off my chair, and all I could think of - and then I remembered, the children, the children, and all I got was a child, picking it up. And I can remember the trembling - I can even now - holding its leg and it was wiggling.[65]

Was the child unconscious or already dead? The narrative varies on retelling, but the significance of the event lies in the contrast between the initial normality of the scene and the speed of its obliteration. A similar theme emerges from the painful memories of Patience Darton.

One of the times we were machine gunned, we'd got quite a lot of refugees in the truck with us. Obviously, we picked them up, and one woman with a little baby - small child, must have been about two - and the baby was killed, machine gunned, and she wouldn't believe it - it was all so quick. We got out and we ran and they machine gunned us and the baby was killed, and she got back in the truck with this dead baby - it took about three quarters of an hour the machine gunning - and she wouldn't believe it, she couldn't believe it, that one moment she was holding her live child and the next moment there was a dead baby in her arms. And she didn't know what to do - how can you bury someone when you're away from your village with nothing and didn't know where her husband was. [Sigh] Machine gunning refugees is terrible, terrible.[66]

Patience Darton also remembered with grief the cases where her instinct to help those who were suffering was thwarted. Two Finns with fatal chest wounds, 'never forget them, such beautiful creatures, great blonde things', are remembered because nobody could speak Finnish to help them send their last messages home. She recalls with

---

64 Scott-Ellis, *The Chances of Death*, 4 June 1938, p. 101.
65 Penny Phelps, AJ, 22 February 1996.
66 Patience Edney (née Darton), IWM 8398.

sadness that as the Finns were not Jewish, the common practice of using Yiddish as a common language was of no avail.[67] Whilst working in a disused railway tunnel, she was caring for several Spaniards who had been picked up from an abandoned hospital during the retreat. They were already dying from gas gangrene, no longer a problem in her section due to improved techniques in dealing with wounds. These men were imprinted on her memory, 'an absolute nightmare - and they wouldn't die. We filled them up with morphia, there was no treatment.'[68] The fact that they took four days to die despite such massive amounts of morphia is recalled again in another interview ten years later. Her degree of distress does not seem to diminish.[69] On the other side of the lines, Priscilla Scott-Ellis faced a similar situation.

> The little Moor with the bad stomach wound was dying in agony so Pepe told me to give him a double dose of morphia which is another thing I hate doing as it is just cold blooded murder... It is silly to mind that, as it merely means he will die quickly and painlessly instead of slowly and in agony.

4.6 Priscilla Scott-Ellis as a nurse in Spain.

---

67 Patience Darton, AJ, 18 March 1994 and IWM 8398.
68 Patience Edney (née Darton), IWM 8398.
69 Patience Darton, AJ, 18 March 1994.

Exhausted by a day and a night on duty, she left the Moor to die in
the care of the Lieutenant whose greatly valued batman he had been,
and 'went miserably to bed with a guilty conscience.'[70]

Guilt also arose in some narratives as a result of feelings of failure
or the inability to do enough. An influx of wounded involved the need
to make life and death decisions that haunted the dreams of Margaret
Powell for many years.

> I didn't know who to let die first. I started to look after an older
> man but he made me see that I must see to a younger man across
> the room. I proceeded to do this and as I held up the container
> of blood for a transfusion, I saw the older man die. The young
> one screamed - they were brothers. The older was the regiment's
> commissar. I wanted to run away.[71]

The use of blood transfusions saved many lives in Spain. When it
was not possible to use stored supplies from donors in the cities,
the nurses, wrote Margaret Powell, 'behaved like vampires', waylaying
lorry drivers going back and forth to the front, taking a pint of blood in
return for a swig of rum. In several narratives, women recall with
amusement how they gave so much of their own blood that they
almost fainted.[72] Giving blood, particularly by direct transfusion, was
not only a practical way of helping but must have also taken on
symbolic importance for women who could not fight themselves, but
who felt their blood was empowering those who could. As Nan Green
said, 'Blood goes from your arm and colour comes to his lips - it was
an experience I wouldn't have wanted to miss.'[73] In such dramatic
situations, Winifred Bates felt a sense of guilt because she had a rare
blood group that was best avoided for general use.[74] During the Ebro
offensive she visited the hospital set up in a cave near the village
of La Bisbal de Falset.

70 Scott-Ellis, *The Chances of Death*, 19 May 1938, p. 94.
71 Powell, 'Memoir',1980. Her husband, Sam Lesser, spoke of her recurrent nightmares about
    this event in an interview about his wife, AJ, 10 April 1996.
72 For example, Margaret Powell, Nan Green, Patience Darton. For more details on blood
    transfusion in Spain, see the series of articles by Lillian Urmston, 'English Nurse in Spain',
    Nursing Mirror, especially 19 June 1939, no. 5, and the film, *Blood Donation in Spain*,
    Educational and Television Films Ltd., 247a Upper Street, London N1 1RU.
73 Nan Green, IWM 13799.
74 Winifred Bates had varied tasks in Spain, see below for more on her work visiting British
    nurses and helping to sort out their problems, and Chapter 5 for more on the articles she
    wrote about their work.

It is so hard to make a man, and so easy to blast him to death. I shall
never forget the Ebro. If one went for a walk away from the cave
there was the smell of death. In the beds beside the soldiers were
women and children brought in from the villages round about after
bombing raids. I do not know if the girls who worked with me were
ever aware that under my placid countenance I had a secret sin, the
sin of jealousy. Many a time they had been called upon to give their
blood to a soldier in a transfusion. I, being a rare and not very useful group, had never been called. It hurt a little, to know that I was
not useful. Up in the cave an Englishman was dying. I watched the
doctor give him the universal group from the ampoule, and he said,
'If this does not do we'll take you.' I have since seen pictures of elab-
orate blood transfusions in hospitals with all the performers
dressed up in white. In the cave, work was more direct. I sat down
on the floor, stuck my legs under the bed and put my arm on the
table. It was a simple matter. There was nothing in it, but it eased
my vanity and helped my self respect.[75]

4.7 Leah Manning and Nan Green in Spain, 1938.

75 Bates, 'A Woman's Work in Wartime', p. 22.

This un-named patient could perhaps be the same man who is remembered both by Nan Green and by Leah Manning in their memoirs. Nan Green recalls how during a visit to the cave, Leah Manning, the former Labour MP who had organised the evacuation of the Basque children to Britain, sat up all night holding the hand of a dying man she had known before the war.[76] From Leah Manning's memoirs, we learn that this Brigader was in fact Welsh, and that he had joined the Brigades after hearing her speak at a meeting about the war in Spain.[77] Unidentified in all their accounts, the dying man is an 'unknown soldier' who becomes a powerful heroic symbol representing many other Brigaders who met a similar fate.

Other patients are remembered for similar symbolically heroic reasons. Both International Brigade members and Spanish soldiers are referred to for their tendency of 'deserting to the front', determined to leave the hospitals and return to the fighting as soon as possible, taking great exception to 'being out of it' and 'raring to go back'.[78] Frida Stewart wrote home from Murcia, 'There are a terrible number of "mutilados" here from the IB. Splendid people and marvellously brave and of course anti-Fascist to the bone. They are all champing to get back to the Front.'[79] However, there were a few who were trying desperately to leave the front, and as anaesthetic was in short supply, the common policy was to restrict its use in the case of self-inflicted injuries of the hand or foot. But they were not treated entirely without sympathy according to Patience Darton, who stated that the usual practice was to make them totally drunk instead.[80]

The treatment of the enemy wounded is another theme which emerges from the narratives, in order to make the point that they did receive medical care, despite protests. Ann Murray recalled one such occasion.

We got a wounded Fascist in. He was a Fascist officer, a high sort of ranking Spanish officer. And of course, we had to treat everybody, you know. But the young Spaniards, the casualties were shouting at us 'Leave him to die, leave him to die.' But of course we were just

---

76 Nan Green, 'A Chronicle of Small Beer', unpublished memoirs, p. 70.
77 Leah Manning, *A Life For Education: An Autobiography* (Victor Gollancz, London, 1970) pp. 135-39
78 Patience Edney (née Darton), IWM 8398.
79 Letter to Mummy, Hotel Victoria, Murcia, Spain, 16 May 1937, papers of Frida Stewart, copy also in MML, Box B4, C3g.
80 Patience Darton, AJ, 18 March 1994.

there to treat all the people. We weren't sorry though, when that man died because he looked a nasty little man.[81]

Franco's use of Moorish troops added the dimension of race to the problems of treating enemy wounded. As historic enemies, racial tensions already existed between Spaniards and Moors, and the reputation of the Moors for extreme cruelty intensified feelings against them.[82] Patience Darton spoke frankly about the deep racial conflict that had to be overcome when a Moor needed medical attention.

There was one Moor I remember, a Moorish prisoner we'd taken, a Franco Moor, very badly wounded in the neck. God, how he hated us, he used to give terrible looks to us, he didn't trust us at all, he expected we'd kill him the same as they killed people. But he was admitted amongst the others, and he ought to have had a blood transfusion, and the [Spanish] chaps got together and said they weren't going to give the blood of the women of Spain to the Moor.[83]

She was full of admiration for the nature of Spanish Republicans when these prejudices were overcome. She recalled, 'When I looked round, he was getting one - this lot of sheepish faces as he got his blood transfusion.'[84] The infamy of the Moors also affected the nurses. Lillian Urmston spoke of their fears during forced retreats on hearing the approach of unidentified vehicles.

I must confess, we were scared of the Moors, they had treated the people in some parts of Spain with such atrocity, rapes galore, that I'm afraid we all worried about that, and that was when people started to talk about things like venereal disease, that it would be worse to have that...We had that awful feeling that we ought to damn well hide or get under a patient's bed, but as - if the Moors were there, they often went into wards and killed the patients - we knew damn well if the worst came to the worst to hide anywhere

---

81 Annie Knight (née Murray), IWM 11318.
82 The Moorish occupation of Spain began in 711. The Reconquest started shortly afterwards but the Moors were not completely expelled until after the fall of Granada in 1492. Moorish troops had been used in the violent suppression of the Asturian miners in 1934. Infamous for their treatment of prisoners and in newly occupied regions, during the civil war they became a focus of terror for civilians in much of Republican Spain.
83 Patience Edney (née Darton), IWM 8398.
84 Ibid.

near a patient would be a disaster. We used to look at each other afterwards and someone would say to me, 'Lillian, what happened to your knees?' and I said 'Why?' and after the crisis was over, when it turned out to be our trucks and ambulances, my knees would knock for hours on end, and other girls would go deathly white and vomit.[85]

Margaret Powell was forced to face her fear of the Moors when she had two as patients. They had 'lost their legs and were rotten with maggots' by the time they were found in 'No Man's Land' after the battle of Huesca. When they died she was sad, they had been so 'gentle and uncomplaining' and had 'kissed our hands in such a heart-breaking way' to show their gratitude.

Wounded Moorish soldiers were nursed by Priscilla Scott-Ellis in the regions controlled by Franco, but, although they were not 'the enemy', treating them raised other problems for her.

I am beginning to loathe the Moors. They are so tiresome, always quarrelling and yelling at one. It makes me mad to have a lot of filthy, smelly Moors ordering me about. I don't mind what I do for them if they ask me and appear pleased, but the trouble is that they are almost all very low class and just shout and snatch things and swear, or worse, become cheeky and make lewd remarks in Arabic and laugh at one. Every time I had just finished a bandage they wanted a different-sized one and pulled the whole thing off again. The trouble is that they are doing their period of fasting and eat nothing till dinner, so are all very irritable. However, I love the work; even if I am getting to dislike the people intensely, I still like their wounds, which is after all the main point.[86]

Her dislike of the Moorish patients seems to have been based much more on class difference than on racial distinctions. The treatment of enemy 'Red' wounded is also mentioned by Priscilla Scott-Ellis in her diaries.[87] However, it appears that she was only involved in the care of Spanish prisoners, as another entry in her diary refers to eighty-five prisoners from the International Brigades, 'mostly American and some English', who were being held nearby and who

---

85 Lillian Buckoke (née Urmston), Tameside 203.
86 Scott-Ellis, *The Chances of Death*, Sunday, 14 November 1937, p. 11.
87 Ibid. See examples 10 May 1938, p. 90 and 12 May 1938, p. 92.

'will all be shot as the foreigners always are.'[88]

The actual business of fighting and the strategies of war played little part in the experience of the majority of these women. Felicia Browne was a notable exception to this general rule because she was already in Spain when the war broke out and had enlisted in a militia unit whilst it was still possible for a woman to do so. She was killed during an attempt to blow up a munitions train. According to the report made shortly afterwards, although under heavy fire, she was trying to help a wounded member of the group - a manner of death appropriately symbolic for a woman in battle.[89] The narratives of the British women who were in Spain tend to say little of either the detail of individual campaigns, or of the overall battle strategy. In part, this may be due to the fact that the information was not commonly available at the time, as Molly Murphy pointed out in her autobiography.

> It was not possible for us to follow the fortunes of the war as a whole. Indeed, sometimes we had not the slightest notion of where we were in relation to the general line of the war, and we were so engrossed in the work that was thrust upon us by the war in our immediate area that we learned our location on the map later on.[90]

Although this may also be the experience of many male combatants, there is a tendency for men to attempt to fill the gaps in their personal experience with retrospectively gained details. Keen to clarify the overall picture of war, they include this information in their narrative, but women rarely do so.[91] Penny Phelps' descriptions of military strategy showed her lack of interest in the fine details.

> ...and then afterwards, this wretched what's-a-name, they gained ground and they were very jubilant, and then there was the counter-attack which they lost a bit but didn't lose completely, but they

---

88 Scott-Ellis, *The Chances of Death*, 12 March 1938, p. 52. Although this was a common occurrence, especially in the case of wounded Brigaders, some were at times imprisoned until an exchange of prisoners could be arranged. For details of British International Brigaders as prisoners see Bill Alexander, *British Volunteers for Liberty: Spain 1936-39* (Lawrence & Wishart, London, 1986, first published 1982) pp. 183-195, and Carl Geiser, *Prisoners of the Good Fight* (Lawrence Hill, Connecticut, 1986).
89 Report by Georges Brinkman, Barcelona, 30.8.36. MML, Box 21/B/1a.
90 Molly Murphy, 'Nurse Molly', p. 132.
91 Many examples of such male narratives of the Spanish Civil War are to be found in the Sound Archives of the Imperial War Museum.

were pushed back and then there was another bit, and it was back-
wards and forwards, and then suddenly they lost and they were being
pushed back and that's when we were being pushed back then to
retreat - it was terrible to hear, you know.[92]

Patience Darton was a rarity in mentioning that she felt her
interest drawn to the intricacies of warfare.

> You know, it is fascinating being in an army - the whole military
> thing is fascinating... You can't help it. You are interested in battles
> and what happened, and the mistakes and the mess up, and what
> weren't mistakes and what you did do and little chiseling things and
> a whole lot of things - you are sucked into it. Not from wanting to
> glory in it but because it is fascinating.[93]

The most keenly expressed interest in the fighting activity is to be
found in the diaries of Priscilla Scott-Ellis, particularly when she was
nursing Franco's forces during the Teruel campaign. Nevertheless,
despite being given an explanation of 'what was what' by some
German soldiers, she does not choose to include this in her diary.

> We left the car and climbed up the hill to where lots of German
> guns were placed. The Germans were amicable and lent us glasses
> and explained what was what. The noise was incredible, a continual
> roar like thunder with intermittent different-toned bangs. The sky
> was full of aeroplanes shooting up and down the Red trenches and
> the whole landscape all around was covered with pillars of smoke.
> Bit by bit we wandered from one hill to another amongst all the anti-
> aircraft and look-out posts until we were quite close to the action.

'Too enthralled to leave,' her description of the battle continues with
far more references to the sounds of machines, bombs, and cannon,
than to strategy. No mention is made of the victims of the air raid even
though she was close enough to say, rather confusingly, that 'One
could see Teruel about ten kilometres away, hidden in a cloud of smoke.'
She also refers to her Spanish aviator friends with some detachment.

---

92 Penny Phelps, AJ, 22 February 1996.
93 Patience Darton, AJ, 8 March 1996. See also the memoirs of Kate Mangan, who wrote after
     seeing news reels in Valencia, that she had discovered that methods of waging warfare
     were interesting 'when one had one's heart in the cause.' 'The Good Comrade', p. 78.

It was so strange to sit in the sun watching it all going on and recognising the aeroplanes and thinking 'There goes Ataulfo, then Prince Ali, over there Alvaro, etc.' It seemed like a strange dream.[94]

She returned the next day to a position even nearer the front, surprised that no one seemed to mind their presence. She was amused to hear the orders for attack being given to Ataulfo's unit by telephone, and would 'have loved to have phoned him from there.'[95] These entries in her diary are set amongst pages of graphic descriptions of the horrific injuries of the soldiers she was nursing. She seems able to separate the battles she witnessed from their effects in human terms, despite her detailed knowledge of the sufferings caused by warfare.

The experience of Priscilla Scott-Ellis in the 'Nationalist' zone differs markedly from other British women in Spain because occasionally she was able to escape from the arduous work in the medical units to visit her friends in the Spanish aristocracy. This abrupt move from one world to another was mainly possible thanks to her prize possession, a car provided by her father. One day she would be surrounded by 'some thirty or more groaning corpses,' the next she would have returned to what she viewed as 'normal life'.

I was very ashamed of turning up to dinner at the Grand Hotel [Zaragoza] in my filthy uniform, with burst shoes and torn stockings, my face unpainted and my hair on end. We joined Arnold Lunn for dinner. He is out here writing articles about 'Red Horrors' and collecting more material for speeches. It seemed strange to be sitting in a large hotel talking to Arnold and eating good food with the right amount of knives and forks. I saw Ataulfo over the other side of the room with some other aviators and a lot of empty bottles. He came over to talk to us, and was quite bottled and in splendid form. Then he tootled off with his friends to beat up the town.[96]

She could then relax at the 'perfectly huge and beautiful house' of her Spanish friends, having hot baths, playing cards and socialising with German and Spanish members of the Condor Legion.[97]

---

94 Scott-Ellis, *The Chances of Death*, 17 February 1938, p. 40.
95 Ibid., 18 February 1938, p. 41.
96 Ibid., 9 April 1938, p. 69.
97 Her Spanish friends were 'Prince Ali', the Infante Alfonso d'Orleans Bourbon who was a first cousin of the King of Spain, his wife, the Infanta Beatrice, who is referred to as 'Princess Bee', and their sons. The Orleans family were living in a requisitioned 'Moorish' villa at Epila, near Zaragoza at this time.

There were only limited possibilities for a temporary relief from
pressure for the nurses in the Republican zone. For Molly Murphy,
older than most of the others, interludes between battles were to be
used for 'having a wash and brush up,' and 'letting our people at home
know we were still in the land of the living and reading our letters.'[98]
But free time could also be spent in curious ways. Patience Darton
spent May Day 1938 in the hospital at Valls, amongst a group of about
thirty medical personnel and the locals from the surrounding villages.

We had extra food and things sent for it, to celebrate, we decorated
the place up. And we had a spitting competition. Spaniards are very
good at spitting, and some of the Americans - 'Tex' we used to call
him, Tex was a marvellous spitter, he could aim. I don't know how
they got so much spit ready to spit with, because I dry up if I try to
spit and I can't sort of get it going. But Tex could [laughter] - always
seemed to have plenty to go and he could aim right across, so could
the Spaniards - wasn't a thing I cared for - it was quite a well known
thing. And we had a target up on the side of an ambulance to be spat
at, and we put the people further and further away - and they got really intent on, you know, doing better than the Tex. And it was as serious as can be - we had absolute hysteria watching this because they
stood there, sort of churning round with their mouths getting a good
gob going then - 'buong' - you see, [laughter] either booed or cheered
by the surrounding crowd. It was a very good competition. Tex won.[99]

In the convalescent hospital at Valdeganga, Nan Green tried to
brighten up the Saturday nights dances which were organised for the
patients and local villagers.

Half or more of our patients were sufficiently mobile to dance, but
there was great difficulty about partners for them. Village girls in
those days could not be touched before marriage by any man other
than their fathers or brothers, and to have danced with a stranger
was likely to ruin their chance of a husband. I prepared, and recited
each Saturday night, an earnest plea to regard these wounded men
as their brothers, but only a few of the bolder ones responded; the

98 Molly Murphy, 'Nurse Molly', p. 132. Also amongst the older nurses with nursing experience
    from the First World War was Winifred Wilson. *North Mail*, 2 April 1937, in Don Watson and
    John Corcoran, *The North East of England and the Spanish Civil War, 1936-1939*, (McGuffin
    Press, London, 1996) p. 42.
99 Patience Edney (née Darton), IWM 8398.

rest danced with other girls, while our poor patients danced with
one another.[100]

What of love? Why is so little said of such a powerful force in the
many narratives of the British women who were in Spain. That numerous romantic attachments developed during this time, despite, or
perhaps partly due to, the proximity of war, cannot be doubted. It may
be that the reluctance to speak of such matters is simply because
private lives were regarded as more 'private' by women who were
young in the thirties, or that the women considered the subject to be
of little interest to the interviewer. Perhaps self-defence mechanisms
prevent discussion of topics which expose one's own vulnerabilities
to a prurient world. The historian as interviewer generally avoids the
subject, not wishing to play the role of a tabloid journalist in pursuit
of a 'kiss and tell' exposé. Nevertheless, there are occasional brief
references to liaisons which were merely transitory. Nan Green,
viewed as 'very, very correct' by her contemporaries, admits in her
memoirs to 'falling victim to an ephemeral affair with a patient, a man
much younger than myself.'[101] This relationship, which 'had exploded
- and gone out like a rocket', became a 'stain' on her conscience.
Determined to write an honest account of her life, she nevertheless
seems at a loss to explain this episode. Rather than examining any
personal needs, she attributes it to the 'over-charged atmosphere'
due to living at a high altitude, believing 'we were all infected with a
touch of mountain-sickness and lived in a permanent state of mild
excitement.'[102] Madge Addy formed a relationship which reflected a
deeper commitment. In 1938, as a leading nurse at the hospital at
Uclés, she was in frequent contact with the head of the Manchester
Medical Aid Committee, discussing the progress of the 'Manchester
Ward' in the hospital and arranging supplies of equipment. In one
letter she deviates from this topic to discuss a subject which is
causing her concern.

> Can you bear me to talk about myself? There are so few people I can
> really have a heart to heart talk with. I have written to my husband
> to ask him if he will divorce me. I know he won't let me divorce him,

---

100 Green, 'A Chronicle of Small Beer' p. 63.
101 Ibid., p. 67. The opinion on Nan Green was given by Frida Stewart, AJ, 11 December 1995.
102 This is a reference to the hospital at Valdeganga. See Green, 'A Chronicle of Small Beer'
    p. 60.

so I have told him if he will do so, I will give him grounds. I think you will believe me when I tell you that the idea is abhorrent to me, but apparently there is no other way and when our affairs are quite settled, I am going to marry Mr Holst. I am very much attached to him, and although he holds a very important position here, he is unaffected and simple in his tastes and is liked by everyone... In the meantime, Spain and the hospital come first, I have pledged myself to both for a year, then I am hoping to be able to turn my thoughts seriously to some kind of happy future...

Yours in the fight, Madge.[103]

The conspicuous understatement of emotion in this extract is surpassed in the narrative of the theatre nurse, Thora Silverthorne, who merely states when referring to the experience of falling in love in Spain that 'I linked up with Kenneth Sinclair-Loutit and later married him.'[104] The significance of the 'unsaid', may be associated with distressing emotions surrounding memories. In the interviews she gave over the years, Patience Darton always spoke of 'my particular lot of Germans' in the International Brigade, with immense admiration, describing them as 'marvellous, wonderful and young and full of zeal and glory.'[105] Recalling her time with them, she never mentioned individuals, but paused in her dialogue, seeming to slip away from the present. In 1986 she said that Spain held too many 'ghosts' for her to ever want to return. However, by 1996 she had changed her mind and decided to accept an invitation from Spain to attend the commemoration of the sixtieth anniversary of the war. In an interview before leaving, for the first and last time, she spoke of why she had been so reluctant to return.

The memories upset me terribly... A chap I was deeply in love with, a German, was killed on the Ebro. I'm going to make efforts not to go back to all those places where I was with him. His death altered my life, but I've tried to make up for it.[106]

---

103 Letter from Madge Addy to Dr Nat Malimson, 7 September 1938, p. 4, MML Box D1, File A7.
104 Thora Silverthorne, AJ, 3 January 1996. Other marriages include that of Susan Sutor, a nurse from Scotland, who married Dr Aguiló, the Spanish surgeon in charge of the medical unit where she was working. There may be other cases in which reticence could possibly be due to the question of the legality of some 'marriages' which took place in Spain. Worries of this nature may have subsequently led to questions of conscience for the women concerned, and British social conventions of the thirties would have demanded discretion.
105 Patience Darton, AJ, 8 August 1996.
106 Patience Edney (née Darton), 'Carried Away to War' by Tunku Varadarajan, The Times, 2 November 1996, pp. 1-2.

She died in Spain a few days later.

References to sexual matters are rare indeed, whether of a personal or more general nature. Spanish soldiers are recalled with pity for their exceptionally ghastly shouts after being wounded in the groin and waking in hospital to find their 'manhood was taken away.'[107] More explicit episodes feature in the diaries of Priscilla Scott-Ellis who recorded her opinions of men with candour. She describes nursing a 'head wound' who was 'half mad and quite terrifying'.

> My unpleasant experience was very funny. The over-sexed head wound suddenly threw off his bedclothes, let out a wild shout and produced his penis, he then left it to its own devices and proceeded to spray fountains in all directions. I rushed for the pot and chased after the fountain, but it was so damned elusive that I finally had to grab the thing and hang on. I thought he would never stop. How any nurse can look at a man, let alone touch him, I don't know, after all the unattractive things one has to do with them.[108]

In this collection of memories, spontaneous references to any perceived gender-based inequalities are few and far between. When asked directly, interviewees usually say that they were not aware of such matters at the time.[109] However, the decision of the Republican government to re-assert traditional gendered stereotypes and recall women from the front after the first few months of the war did affect a British woman, Sybil Wingate.[110] In his *Spanish Diary*, John McNair records that she came to see him in the Barcelona ILP office, offering to work voluntarily as his secretary.[111] In January 1937 she informed him that she was joining a group of Spanish women who were going to the Aragon front as nurses and stretcher bearers. A few weeks later,

---

107 Lillian Buckoke (née Urmston), Tameside 203.
108 Scott-Ellis, *The Chances of Death*, 23 March 1938, p. 61. Susan Kingsley Kent discusses how nurses in the First World War felt about their patients' sexuality, and how they often referred to the wounded not as human beings but as broken objects or body parts. *Making Peace: The Reconstruction of Gender in Interwar Britain* (Princeton University Press, New Jersey, 1993) pp. 67-73.
109 For example, when Norma Jacob was asked if she had been inspired by the fact that a woman, La Pasionaria, could have such a large leadership role, she replied, 'Never occurred to me.' Norma Jacob, interview with Karin Lee, American Friends Service Committee, 31 March 1989, #31, pp. 13-14.
110 Sybil Wingate, from the family of military and exploring renown, was later a member of the Labour Spain Committee. She was in Spain carrying out post-graduate research when the war began and decided to stay on to assist the Republic.
111 John McNair *Spanish Diary* (Greater Manchester ILP Branch Publication of articles and pamphlets first published in the *Socialist Leader* 1974).

she and other women were being instructed to withdraw from the front but, 'supported by all the contingent which had grown to respect and admire the work she was doing', she chose to remain. John McNair went to look for her and found her in one of the villages near Huesca, dressed as a militia man and looking 'smart and capable'. She was not at all pleased to see him and believed that she was carrying out useful work with the unit. 'I agreed with her completely', wrote McNair, 'but had to insist, and we arranged to go back the next morning to Barcelona.'[112]

Kate Mangan also writes of the withdrawal of women from the front which took place whilst she was in Barcelona shortly after her arrival in Spain. She encountered two people she knew who had joined an anarchist militia, but relations with any anarchists were 'distinctly hampered' by the hostility of her socialist friends. She feared that if she saw too much of them, she would 'get a bad name' and would lose a promising job offer. She records that the anarchist *milicianas* had been asked to leave the front, though had not yet been forced to do so, and those who insisted on staying were 'to be relegated to cooking and clerking jobs.' She gives a fascinating account of her excursion to a vegetarian 'anarchist lunch', and makes good use of her talent for giving vivid portrayals of the characters she meets.

> This was a family that might have come from *Seven Red Sundays*.[113] The mother, fat, kind and motherly, talked of the worry it had been when she often carried bombs concealed in her shopping basket, and there was a blind brother who used to make hand-grenades, the kind in old tins, in the cellar, as he was not good for much else. There was a pretty younger son, who clung to his father's hand but was already a good shot, so his old dad boasted, and there was a thin, straight, beautiful and forbiddingly serious daughter, who was a militiawoman, and a fanatical spectacled son, also in the militia who was a school-teacher.[114]

Later, in Valencia, she met some Polish International Brigaders on leave from the front and asked them what had happened to the militiawomen.

---

112 Ibid., p.17.
113 *Seven Red Sundays* by Ramón J. Sender is a novel set in Madrid in 1935 about a revolutionary uprising of working men.
114 Mangan, 'The Good Comrade', p. 79.

'Ah, it is serious now,' they said, 'we don't want girls in it; it is too hard for them. Those we had in the beginning we have sent behind the lines to work in the administration. Why even the cooking is not fit for women. They cannot life the great cauldrons of soup and our cook is a butcher by profession.'[115]

The relative emancipation of British women in comparison with Spanish women is noted in certain narratives. Nan Green was particularly aware of the reactionary attitudes of some male Spaniards and at times, attempted to introduce notions of equality to Spanish women.

I went to an Anarchist commune where they had seized the land and distributed it and everything, invited as a guest and I sat down at the table with the other chaps I was with and the women served us - they stood up while we ate. And after we finished - I was disappointed about this, you see, and I made up my mind to go and speak to them. Before I got up, I lit a cigarette and then I went over to the women and said, 'Why didn't you sit down?' and they said, 'Oh, in this village we don't sit down until the men have finished.' So then we had a long, long talk about women, but the first thing they wanted to know was did women smoke in England, and which was the correct hand, and which the correct fingers to hold the cigarette, and they had heard this - some kind of fairy tale that in England there were shops where you could buy frocks ready made and was this true, and all sorts of questions they wanted to know. So I gave them a good talk about women's - well, there wasn't women's 'lib' in those days - how women should be equal to men and they were really open-eyed and very delighted about it.[116]

Another such instance of reactionary attitudes was recounted with mock outrage by Patience Darton.

We were in an Anarchist village which didn't care at all for having us anyway, 'the 'Carlos Marx' hospital. And they didn't like foreign nurses either - we were very 'uppish'. And the Anarchists are, on the whole, rather backward about women - they weren't at all sure women should learn to read and write... I'm still annoyed with them

---

115 Ibid., p. 96.
116 Nan Green, Tameside 180. See also Nan Green on the reluctance of a local mayor to include a woman speaker in a fiesta to boost morale. 'A Chronicle of Small Beer' p. 70.

because we used to go and bathe in the river in perfectly
respectable bathing dresses - proper built up tops and things, well
away from the village - very hot summer. And they didn't like this
because they didn't approve of it, so they stopped us doing it - they
said we frightened the mules! And I haven't forgiven them yet![117]

She also had a running battle with a Spanish Political Commissar who
discriminated against women in the important matter of cigarette quotas.

I had a terrible quarrel always with the 'Commissar' who gave out
cigarettes at the hospitals, and to the medical staff, because he was
under the strong impression that women shouldn't smoke because
it deprived the men, and I was under the impression that women
should have as much right to smoke as the men. So we had a
permanent quarrel about this, challenging him on feminine rights.
The chaps supported us even though it did mean one less for them,
one packet less for them, they supported us on principal, it was just
a rather old fashioned Spaniard.[118]

As a 'modern' British nurse, Spanish men found her difficult to
place within their usual clear-cut categories of 'tart' or 'good girl'.
Nevertheless, she was treated with great respect, although they found
it very amusing when at first she confused the Spanish for 'tired',
(cansada), with 'married', (casada) and they would all laugh uproari-
ously when she replied, 'not this morning, thank you' or 'a bit' when
each new arrival asked if she was married.[119] Nurses could also come
to symbolise the women that men had left at home. Margaret Powell
recalled how she was often asked to accompany the men when they
were carrying out burials of those who had died in the hospitals. She
never asked why, but felt it was plain that she was seen by them to
represent an absent wife or mother.[120]

---

117 Patience Darton, AJ, 18 March 1994. In Valdeganga, British nurses had more luck, even
lending costumes to some of the Spanish girls and teaching them to swim. SMAC Bulletin,
October, 1937, p. 4, MML Box 29/B and Box B5, file H. However, despite all the images
showing Spanish *milicianas* in trousers at the beginning of the war, Norma Jacob noted
that the anarchists did not approve when she and other women wore trousers to work
on the Quaker trucks distributing relief. Norma Jacob, interview with Karin Lee,
American Friends Service Committee, 31 March 1989, #31 p. 7, and Norma Jacob, 'The
Spanish Civil War', Appendix A, in Piers Anthony, *Bio of an Ogre* (Ace Books, New York,
1988) p. 232.
118 Patience Edney (née Darton), IWM 8398.
119 Ibid.
120 Powell, memoir, 1980.

Many of the nurses remember the gratitude of Spanish civilians for the nursing care they or their children received. Molly Murphy wrote that she treasured the memory of a peasant family who walked many miles to thank her for nursing their wounded son, bringing her a small gift despite their poverty.[121] But the interaction between British and Spanish women was of special significance and enduring memories of this contact appear in the narratives. Lillian Urmston formed friendships with Spanish girls in her unit and remembered one in particular many years later. Lola had already broken from the traditional Spanish female role by fighting as a *miliciana* at the front until women were recalled to the rearguard. Her parents had been killed in Andalucia but she had escaped with the Republicans as they retreated.

> She was a tiny little thing, Lola, and everybody worshipped her - she was always bright and gay and it was only when she slept at night you realised all the tension that was building up in her. She used to have terrible nightmares, and when we slept out in the open, we were near to the Nationalist lines, we always had to be ready to clap a hand over her mouth when she wakened because she was babbling and screaming with the horror of what had happened in her Andalucian town.[122]

Many of the British nurses were enthusiastic about training the Spanish women who volunteered to work in the hospitals and realised the social implications of what they were doing, as Patience Darton explained.

> And to them it was an enormous thing - we were modern women that they hadn't ever come across, you see. We didn't mind talking to men, we didn't mind throwing our weight around either, which we did a good deal, because you know what nurses are! And without thinking much about it, you see, but a Spanish woman couldn't have done that, and she couldn't have nursed a stranger - she couldn't have touched a strange man, let alone washed him or looked after him. For them it was a tremendous thing they were doing, helping us, and taking part in it - it was an enormous thing, and the men had to accept it, you see, the Spanish men didn't like it particularly.[123]

---

121 Molly Murphy, 'Nurse Molly' pp. 131-2.
122 Lillian Buckoke (née Urmston), Tameside 203.
123 Patience Darton, AJ, 18 March 1994.

There can be no doubt of the importance of this contact with British nurses in the life of some young Spanish women. Aurora Fernandez abandoned her studies to become a volunteer in the medical units.

All the English nurses taught us, the volunteer nurses, how to work, but in such a considerate way, they never showed any 'superiority' towards us. They usually said, 'Could you come and help me?' That was the introduction to do 'together' something... I must stress the non-obtrusive way in which this was done in order not to hurt anybody's feelings. They did not say 'I am going to tell you how to do this,' but rather, 'Come, let us get this ready.[124]

This method was not only 'very soothing', but in the eyes of Aurora Fernandez, 'of high political significance in those days.'[125]
Medical staff were constantly exposed to a variety of stresses, working closely together in conditions which could exacerbate personal and political differences. A theme of some complexity in the narratives relates to the tensions that inevitably arose on different levels. The prolific diary entries of Priscilla Scott-Ellis contain a stream of complaints and gossip about colleagues amongst details of the cases she is nursing in the hospitals under Franco's control.

I am fed up to the back teeth with life, with Spain and mostly with that damn filthy-minded Isabel. I have been frothing against her all day and most of yesterday, and I am damned if I will have her trotting around spying on me and thinking I am misbehaving all the time. And if she does think so, why the hell can't she just come and talk to me about it instead of telling everyone else?[126]

But diaries, despite their immediacy, also have many limitations. Their valuable function as a repository for anger, as in the example above, makes them helpful sources for understanding the youthful emotions of the diarist, but may offer a false perspective regarding the general level of conflict within a particular medical unit.

---

124 Account written by Aurora Edenhofer (née Fernandez), Prague, January 1983. MML, Box 29, File D/9. Other Spanish girls who came into contact with British nurses and wished to emulate them included Josefa from Seville, SMAC Bulletin, October 1937, p. 4. MML Box 29/B and Box B5, file H.
125 Ibid., p. 10.
126 Scott-Ellis, *The Chances of Death* (1995), 12 December 1938, p. 163.

Other documentary and oral sources contain examples of tensions in the units in Republican Spain, usually occurring when a front became less active or during the sporadic lulls between each massive influx of wounded. In her memoirs, Nan Green recalled the times between battles.

There is a lot of waiting about in an army in wartime; when the battle is raging, morale is high and everyone is busy. It is the waiting about, sometimes not knowing what one is waiting for, that brings out the grumbles, boredom, the doubts and discomforts, the homesickness and anxieties that have a bad effect on morale.[127]

It is interesting to note the similarity between these memories and those of Florence Farmborough concerning her experience on the Russian Front in the First World War.

When we worked, we worked as one man, completely in accord, each with the other, everyone helping the other, everyone doing their very best to make life a little bit easier in those tragic, dreadfully difficult times. But, when work had ceased and when for some reason there was a lull in the operations in the front lines, then it was that our nerves began to show that they were getting frayed. We would even quarrel sometimes with each other, we would criticise not only ourselves and our neighbours and our workers, but the government, the administrations, the head command. Everyone came under our scathing criticism. But work was our salvation. No sooner did work begin, then all was well. When we worked it was almost incredible to see what tremendous work was done.[128]

Her words may help to explain why, in the narratives of these women, references to the tensions they experienced are almost always brief and understated. It is highly probable that recollections of administrative problems or derogatory opinions of individual colleagues have dwindled in importance in comparison with the memories of the work carried out together, a valued shared experience which has subsequently come to take precedence over all else. Such selective choices could be seen as part of a process of prioritising past events. One example of this type can be seen through examination

---

127 Green, 'A Chronicle of Small Beer' p. 69.
128 Interview with Florence Farmborough, Liddle Collection, Brotherton Library, University of Leeds. For more on Florence Farmborough in Spain, see Chapter 6.

of archival documentary sources relating to the first few months of the war when the British medical staff were working together in the hospital at Grañen. A memorandum to the Spanish Medical Aid Committee in London consisting of eight points and numerous subsections, contains allegations of general inefficiency which jostle with accusations of political bias against certain individuals. The memorandum ends with the typed surnames of seventeen members of staff, including several nurses who presumably supported the rather acrimoniously expressed complaints presented in the memo.[129] However, two of the nurses whose names were listed gave later interviews making no mention of the incident, consciously or unconsciously omitting the conflict from their narratives. [130]

Even amongst those with a tendency to express their views in a forthright manner, like Patience Darton, there is a reticence to refer to tensions in anything other than general terms. After the hospital at Grañen had been handed over to the Spanish authorities, some of the British nurses were together in a unit at Poleñino. Patience Darton felt strongly that given the scarcity of trained staff overall, having a high concentration of trained nurses in one place was not making the optimum use of their skills. When offered the chance, she seized the opportunity to move on.

What they liked to do was to send nurses up to the little hospital they'd got up in Aragon, where they had six English nurses, of all ridiculous things, six nurses in one tiny little hospital on the dead

129 Spanish Medical Aid papers, Modern Records Centre, University of Warwick, memo dated 30 November 1936, MSS 292/946/41. See also subsequent correspondence, letter from Captain J. R. White to Dr Morgan, 21 December 1936, and reply 5 January 1937, letter from Dr Morgan to Dr Addison, 22 January 1937, 292C 946/2.
130 There are several other examples of later narratives in which conflicts of this type are not mentioned. See for example, Leah Manning, 'Report on Personnel in Spain', September 1938, Spanish Medical Aid papers, MSS 946/539, Modern Records Centre, University of Warwick, which devotes four pages to her efforts to talk to the nurses and resolve tensions surrounding Rosita Davson, the SMAC representative responsible for the distribution of supplies. She does not refer to these problems in her autobiography, only praising Rosita Davson for her skills as a linguist, and her hard work. A Life for Education: An Autobiography (Gollancz, London, 1970) p. 121. After the war, the suspicion held by some of those in the medical units that Rosita Davson had been spying for the British government was fuelled when she became a member of the British Diplomatic Corps. A similar case is that of Molly Murphy who, in a letter home writes critically of the organisational skills of the doctor in charge of her unit. The tensions she felt, whether based on personal or political differences, almost certainly contributed to her prompt departure for Britain. However, they are not mentioned in her memoirs, in which she only states, 'I was at the end of my tether and completely exhausted.' See Molly Murphy, letter to Bill and Gordon, April 1937, Museum of Labour History; Molly Murphy, 'Nurse Molly' p. 139.

front, very quiet front. And they hadn't got any method of putting it in to anything in the Spanish set up, because there wasn't very much of an organised Spanish medical set up, it didn't exist. And one day...a couple of doctors came over from the International Brigade, on the scrounge - they'd heard about the nurses and they came and took two of us. We didn't mind, we were all ready to be abducted... They had a better organisation and they needed nurses, and we obviously, I mean I was still fed up about this, there was another couple sent up from there by then - there were nine of us, in this little - doing nothing. All English, all trained, I found it outrageous. So I was all for it, and off I went. And then it was quite different of course, we were all properly organised, and it was a great boon and a blessing to everybody.[131]

4.8 From left to right, standing: Margaret Powell, Susan Sutor, Ann Murray, Patience Darton; sitting: Agnes Hodgson and Mary Slater, Poleñino, March 1937.

---

131 Patience Edney (née Darton), IWM 8398. The unit based at Poleñino was attached to the Carlos Marx Column, a militia unit controlled by the Catalan Socialists.

Part of the work of Winifred Bates was to help to defuse discord. She saw her role as 'a kind of soft buffer against which they [the nurses] could fling their war-ragged nerves and be soothed.'[132] From April 1937 onwards, she travelled between medical units, visiting the British nurses to try to sort out their problems. She would listen to all their outbursts, believing that it was good for them to 'talk themselves out.' Amongst the many expressions of praise for the unstinting efforts of colleagues, there were also some tirades against others. She describes these as commonly being 'high-faluting tales', which she chose to ignore, 'they were tipped down the scullery sink I keep in the back of my mind for such things, and they went down the drain of time and were lost forever.'[133] Her account tells of the great diversity in political outlook, religious belief and character of more than forty nurses with whom she was in contact. From Scottish Presbyterian to Jewish, from Communist to Conservative, what she admired most was their courage, not only under fire, but when faced with appalling nursing tasks.

4.9 Winifred Bates (left) with Dorothy Rutter (centre) and Lillian Urmston (right) and Spanish patients at Teruel, 1937-38.

132 Bates, 'A Woman's Work in Wartime', p. 11.
133 Ibid., p. 13. Whilst it would be true to say that these tales were, in the main, 'lost forever', Winifred Bates' report on personnel, recently found in the Moscow Archives (545, 6, 88), does bring to light her criticisms of certain women working with the medical units. Her greatest concerns are related to the behaviour of Rose Davson, a British subject of Polish origin who was in charge of the flat used by British medical aid personnel in Barcelona and responsible for the distribution of supplies from the Spanish Medical Aid Committee in London.

There was one [nurse] who worked in a dilapidated old monastery building. One of her patients was a man who was paralysed. At night the rats got into his bed and ate his feet and she would put her hand in his bed and pull them out. Yet that same woman when working at the front made a fuss because there were no toilets.[134]

Disorder and conspiracy frequently loom large in historical studies of the war in Spain. There is a tendency to have unrealistic expectations of 'heroes', and to indulge in retrospective 'cherry-picking' of instances of discord, suffusing all with a lurid hue. This is particularly so in the case of political tensions. Such incidents which emerge from the testimonies collected for this chapter should be viewed within the overall context of the female narrative style, not as part of an imagined lengthy political diatribe. Nan Green, for example, made only brief mention of her own problems as a Communist Party member in interviews and in her memoirs.[135] Whilst in Spain, she had suffered unjust accusations made by another member of the Party, but chose not to 'waste everyone's time just to put myself in the right again' during a critical stage of the war.[136] The defamatory report about her that had been dispatched to Moscow was subsequently corrected.[137]

It has been suggested that in a world of deep political intrigue, Nan Green and others, 'appeared not to want to know what was taking place around them, even when they themselves were in harm's way.'[138] This view is supported by the general absence of references to internal party politics and internecine political clashes in the narratives of the vast majority of the women in this study. Without doubt, many people who were in Republican Spain during the war were affected not only by the civil war between the left and right, but also by the discord amongst the left-wing political parties. The effects were sometimes felt by the staff in the medical units and also, at times, caused problems for British women working in Spain in other capacities. Eileen Blair is a case in point, illustrating how the struggles taking place on the left impacted on

---

134 Ibid., p. 12.
135 Nan Green, Tameside 180, and 'A Chronicle of Small Beer', pp. 60-62.
136 Green, 'A Chronicle of Small Beer' p. 67.
137 It seems most likely that this was the result of Winifred Bates' report sent to Moscow (see note 129 above). She praised Nan Green highly and stated that the charge against her was 'false and actuated by jealousy.'
138 James K. Hopkins, *Into the Heart of the Fire: The British in the Spanish Civil War* (Stanford University Press, California, 1998) p. 286.

innocent victims.[139] In 1937, Eileen Blair went to Barcelona to work in the offices of the Independent Labour Party [ILP], thereby becoming involved in the worst aspects of party political fighting in Catalonia.[140] As discussed in Chapter 2, the motivation for her journey to Spain appears to have been the wish to be close to her husband, George Orwell, rather than any deep political commitment. As Orwell's biographer, D J Taylor, explained 'Eileen is one of the larger silences in Orwell studies.'[141] She flits in and out of Orwell's *Homage to Catalonia*, leaving little of her personality on the pages, except perhaps when he writes on being shot through the throat, 'This ought to please my wife, I thought: she had always wanted me to be wounded which would save me from being killed when the great battle came.'[142]

Extracts from several letters written by Eileen Blair were published in 2001 as part of a collection relating the time Orwell spent in Spain. In a letter to her mother she describes with excitement her visit to the front lines, saying she '*thoroughly* enjoyed' being there. She also writes of her daily life; finding Crosse & Blackwell's pickles and English marmalade in Barcelona, the luxury of having a bath and her worries about money.[143] A later letter, written to her brother, discusses plans for leaving the city to go to Valencia, and the possibility of following her husband should he join the International Brigades to fight on the Madrid front.[144] A further collection of letters she wrote to a close friend came to light more recently.[145] They reveal an ironic and jaunty sense of humour. She writes at great length about her husband, sometimes with undisguised exasperation, but says very little about politics at all, except to explain that she and Orwell decided to call their poodle 'Marx' to remind them that they had never read any of the Russian's writings.[146] In June 1937, after the violent factional fighting of the previous month in Barcelona, both left Spain, afraid

---

139 Eileen O'Shaughnessy married Eric Blair in the summer of 1936 when aged thirty. She had an Oxford English degree and had taught in a girls' boarding school, worked in clerical jobs and had run her own typing agency before returning to study at University College London. She died in 1945 during a hysterectomy operation. See 'Another Piece of the Puzzle' by DJ Taylor, *The Guardian*, 10 December 2005.
140 The ILP was linked to the Spanish Trotskyist group, the Partido Obrero deUnificación Marxista [POUM], suppressed after the events of May 1937 in Barcelona.
141 Taylor, 'Another Piece of the Puzzle'.
142 George Orwell, *Homage to Catalonia*, first published in 1938, also in Peter Davison (ed.) *Orwell in Spain* (Penguin Books, London, 2001), p. 131.
143 Davison, *Orwell in Spain*, Eileen Blair to her mother, 22 March 1937, pp. 9-11
144 Ibid., Eileen Blair to Dr Laurence ('Eric') O'Shaugnessy, 1 May 1937, pp. 15-16
145 Peter Davison (ed.) *The Lost Orwell* (Timewell Press, London, 2006), Ch. II, 'Eileen Blair's Letters to Norah Myles', pp. 62-82.
146 Ibid., p. 72.

they would be arrested by Communists because of their involvement with Trotskyist groups. Fleeing the country in fear for her life certainly demonstrates that Eileen Blair suffered from the consequences of party politics but does nothing to show that she was a committed party activist.

D J Taylor writes of Eileen and her husband, 'The experience of Spain affected the couple in different ways. For Orwell it provided a spectacular validation of his belief in democratic socialism, while definitively undermining his constitution. For Eileen, it had offered among other enticements, a relationship with Georges Kopp, formerly her husband's commander but now languishing in a Republican jail, which is one of the great enigmas of her trip.'[147] By summing up their experiences in such a way, is Taylor misjudging the depth of Eileen Blair's commitment to the ILP, or merely reflecting her lack of interest in party politics and possibly, even the cause of the Republic in general? As is often the case when researching women's lives, little evidence remains to decide the matter. It seems apparent from her letters that as far as the affair with Georges Kopp was concerned, although he was 'a bit gone' on her, he was never a real rival to her husband.[148] When she did manage to spend time with Orwell on the front at Huesca, her devotion to him was noted by other members of the company. 'She worshipped the ground he walked on' was one comment.[149]

Women's 'failure' to analyse political divisions in their narratives has on occasion been judged as a weakness. Such verdicts are merely the imposition of one notion of what is considered to be of momentous importance on the individual perceptions of another, who may have a different perspective entirely.[150] In addition to the possible unconscious rejection of uncomfortable memories or, as some would suggest, the conscious decision to distort the record for posterity, there are other feasible explanations for this. It could serve to illustrate the fact that women were largely excluded from such matters by higher-

---

147 Taylor, 'Another Piece of the Puzzle'.
148 Davison, *The Lost Orwell*, p.71.
149 Ibid., p. 70, fn. 9, Jock Branthwaite quote from Stephen Wadhams, *Orwell Remembered*, (1984), p. 84.
150 For example, Ralph Darlington in his introduction to *Molly Murphy, Suffragette and Socialist: An Autobiography* (University of Salford, 1998) considers the fact that Molly Murphy does not discuss why the Communist Party of Great Britain so readily accepted the class against class strategy in the late 1920s, or go into the reasons why she and her husband left the Communist Party in 1932 as 'failings'. See also Chapter 6.151 Lillian Buckoke (née Urmston), letter to Jim Fyrth, 5 November 1985. MML Box D-1: B/1.

ranking male political figures. Alternatively, it could be that in many cases this is a reflection of a different agenda amongst women, a repudiation of this aspect of politics, rather than of their exclusion by others. As Lillian Urmston stated emphatically, 'Party politics as such were not in my line.'[151] Women are notably absent on a list of alleged 'suspicious individuals' in the Brigades, retrieved from the Moscow archives. The inaccurate entry for Nan Green achieves unique distinction by the need to state in brackets afterwards, 'Note: This is a female.'[152]

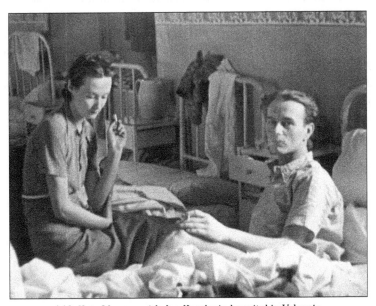

4.10 Kate Mangan with Jan Kurzke in hospital in Valencia.

One British woman working in Spain who developed a keen interest in the complexities of the political divisions on the Left was Kate Mangan. She had arrived in October 1936 and, whilst searching with dogged determination for the man she loved, she turned her hand to various jobs, at first translating and interpreting then working for the press office in Valencia.[153] She wrote several articles for the

---

152 Document 48, 'List of Suspicious Individuals and Deserters from the XV Brigade' (undated), The Russian Centre for the Preservation and Study of Documents of Recent History, in *The Secret World of American Communism*, Harvey Klehr, John Earl Haynes, Fridrikh Igorevich Firsov (Yale UP, Newhaven and London, 1995) p.180.

153 Kate Mangan had a working knowledge of Spanish, having made several previous visits to Spain. Her sister was married to a Spaniard and Kate had lived in Mexico for some time with her first husband, Sherry Mangan.

Manchester Guardian and, through an introduction by V S Pritchett, became a correspondent for the *Christian Science Monitor*. She travelled considerably, meeting and talking to many local people, Spanish officials and visitors, recalling these experiences in her memoirs, written not long after the end of the war. On two occasions, she acted as an interpreter for groups visiting prisons and noted her observations in detail. A party of female journalists were taken to a women's prison outside Valencia, in a former Jesuit monastery. Kate Mangan believed it to be 'an open prison, without locks or bars', but thought that 'the prisoners would know they were safer inside than out.' The inmates were 'very mixed socially' but all had their own cells. 'Some of them appeared to be prostitutes, who had been taken up for spying.' Others were 'very high-born ladies', being held as valuable exchange prisoners, usually for aviators who had been obliged to bale out over enemy territory.

> There was Franco's niece with her baby in a cot covered with netting to keep off flies...There was Millan Astray's sister and a very ugly old lady in black who was some relation of the Duke of Alba but proved rather a bad investment as he did not seem anxious to ransom her.[154]

Eventually, Kate Mangan found Jan Kurzke, the German International Brigader she loved, and so fulfilled her original motive for her journey to Spain. He had been badly wounded but, thanks to her efforts on his behalf, he survived. She managed to arrange for him to be moved to Valencia in order to ensure he was receiving good care. Patience Darton was there when he arrived and helped to look after him. 'The Spanish nurses were too modest to wash him', wrote Kate Mangan, 'but Patience did, and rubbed him with alcohol so he would not get sore from lying in bed.'[155] Eventually when he was well enough to make the journey, Kate organised their journey out of Spain and the pair left together, almost a year after her search had begun.

Due to her husband's work, Mary Bingham de Urquidi was already in Spain when war broke out. Already well accustomed to living abroad with her well-travelled British parents, in 1917 she married

---

154 Mangan, 'The Good Comrade', p. 418. Kate Mangan wrote an article about this visit for the *Christian Science Monitor*, 'Spain's War Prisoners Live in Comfort of Boltless Jail', 7 October 1937.
155 Ibid., p. 398.

Juan Francisco Urquidi, a Mexican diplomat. After postings in Paris, London and Bogotá, he became Minister Counselor at the Mexican Embassy in Madrid. Mary Bingham had qualified as a nurse in New York before her marriage and, on the outbreak of war, whilst her husband and children were by chance on the other side of the lines, she remained in the Republican zone and quickly offered her services to help the wounded. However, her memoirs not only tell of her blood-curdling adventures whilst nursing at the front and in the hospital of the Fifth Regiment in Madrid, but also of her activities as a sort of female Scarlet Pimpernel, helping Nationalist sympathisers escape to safety via the Mexican Embassy.[156]

She is very much the protagonist in her book, *Mercy in Madrid*, and has a keen sense of her own status, exclaiming early on in these lengthy memoirs, 'I couldn't believe that I, Mary Bingham de Urquidi, wife of a diplomat was being sent to the front like an ordinary *miliciana*.'[157] But, as quickly becomes apparent, she soon takes charge of any situation, giving orders to gun-brandishing *milicianos*, senior military personnel and government officials with equal aplomb. Her writing offers a mass of factual information, including dialogue complete with contemporary Spanish swearing, carefully translated into English in the footnotes. Her reaction to the oft-encountered odour of stale sweat is somewhat squeamish, in marked contrast to her pragmatism when faced with violent deaths, horrendous wounds and surgical operations, all described in graphic detail. She never refrains from calling a spade a spade, except perhaps when she writes of finding 'certain articles' belonging to the nuns 'prohibited by the Catholic Church even to married women.'[158]

Through her eyes, the first months of the war are brought vividly to life, and a new perspective of women's work in wartime is added by her descriptions of what was happening within the Embassy, where thirteen hundred people were taking refuge. Mary Bingham's talent for organisation was tested to the full by the cramped conditions and the many difficulties and dangers they were facing. Even with her diplomatic standing, her determination to rescue women prisoners being held in the San Rafael Asylum in Madrid could have had dire personal consequences. Despite a petition of protest signed by

---

156 The hospital of the Fifth Regiment was also known as the 'Hospital Obrero'.
157 Mary Bingham de Urquidi, *Mercy in Madrid: Nursing and Humanitarian Protection during the Spanish Civil War, 1936-7,* Edicions del Sur, Argentina, 2004 (First published as *Misericordia en Madrid* by B. Costa Amic Editores, México, 1975) p. 51.
158 Ibid., p. 109.

General Miaja and La Pasionaria amongst others, also bearing the seals of over a dozen committees in Madrid, she and her husband were recalled by the Mexican government. Before they left in March 1937 the refugees were evacuated from the Embassy. They were taken to Valencia in coaches supplied by the authorities in Madrid to be put on board a French ship. 'I doubt that any other country would have been so humanitarian,' wrote Mary Bingham, 'as among the voyagers there were many political enemies of the Republican Government.'[159] When asked what she would have done if she had been in Nationalist Spain when the war broke out, she replied that she would have tried to work as a nurse, though thought she might have encountered difficulties because she was not a Catholic.

> I have spent almost all my life in Latin countries and have always tried to help the needy. In those countries social service is generally part of the Church which made me very anticlerical. I believe that all religions should serve their spiritual purpose without mixing in politics, such as the Catholics do. My religion is to serve humanity...[160]

The impact of certain British women in Spain was based on both their work and their idiosyncratic characteristics. One such well-known figure involved in medical and relief work was the Commandant of the Scottish Ambulance Unit, Fernanda Jacobsen.[161] The somewhat chequered career of the unit is detailed elsewhere, indicating that Fernanda Jacobsen's efforts to help those on both sides increased the difficulties they faced.[162] Mary Bingham and her husband at the Mexican Embassy were well aware of the way in which the Scottish ambulances transported supporters of Franco by night to Valencia and from there to an English ship.[163] Despite several crises and the departure of many members of the unit, Fernanda Jacobsen remained in Madrid carrying out relief work even after the end of the war. As the unit had faced accusations of helping Fascists escape from the

---

159 Mary Bingham de Urquidi, *Mercy in Madrid: Nursing and Humanitarian Protection during the Spanish Civil War, 1936-7*, pp. 504-5.
160 Ibid., p. 147.
161 The unit was founded by Sir Daniel Stevenson, Chancellor of Glasgow University, and arrived in Spain in September 1936.
162 See Fyrth, *The Signal was Spain* (1986) pp. 181-187, and Buchanan, *Britain and the Spanish Civil War* (1997) pp. 107-109.
163 According to Mary Bingham, the Department of Security and the Police in Madrid were both aware of the activities of the Scottish Ambulance Unit, and the British Consul 'played dumb'. Bingham, *Mercy in Madrid*, pp. 381 & 464.

Republic, it is interesting to note the different perspective in the diary of Priscilla Scott-Ellis, who encountered Fernanda Jacobsen in Madrid after Franco's victory.

> I met Miss Jackson, [sic. Jacobsen] head of the Scottish Ambulance which has been very Red indeed. The Infanta wanted to see her about whether she would go with her on her relief work amongst the population or not. She had two porridge canteens but one had been removed by Auxilio Social. [The Falangist relief organisation] She was furious. An incredible woman, small and square, with a huge bottom. She always dresses in a kilt, thick woollen stockings, brogues, a khaki jacket of military cut with thistles all over it, huge leather gauntlet gloves, a cape also with thistles, and, the crowning glory, a little black Scottish hat edged with tartan and with a large silver badge on it. We all laughed ourselves silly afterwards. She had a dreadful discussion with Prince Ali as to whether she was a Red or not.[164]

4.11 Helen Grant

A more sober picture of the work undertaken by Fernanda Jacobsen in Madrid is given by Helen Grant, a lecturer in Spanish at Birmingham University who knew Spain well. She notes that in addition to dealing with the wounded, Miss Jacobsen also had a list of

---

164 Scott-Ellis, *The Chances of Death* (1995), 3 April 1939, pp. 213-4.

people she supplied regularly with food and that in the early mornings the ambulance distributed hot chocolate to waiting women.[165] Helen Grant's comments were recorded in the diary she kept of her visit in March 1937. She had been asked to act as facilitator and inter-preter for a group sent out by the Society of Friends to assess the relief work being done and to establish what was required to help the growing number of refugees.[166] 'Los Amigos Cuáqueros', as the Friends were called in Spain, carried out extensive relief work during the war, co-operating with other groups, not only at international level but also with both Spanish and Catalan organisations in the Republic.[167] Their involvement had begun in earnest in December 1936, when Edith Pye and others took over five tons of condensed milk, sugar and cocoa to Barcelona.[168] As always, the policy of the Society of Friends was to give aid impartially to all factions in the con-flict. However, as Franco had occupied many of the main areas of food production, the need for help was greater in Republican Spain.[169]

Despite the official policy of impartiality, the political sympathies of individual Friends are sometimes evident. Norma Jacob and her

---

165 Helen F. Grant, 'Spain: 25 March – 18 April 1937', Cambridge University Library, papers of Helen F. Grant.

166 Others travelling out with her included Francesca Wilson, who had extensive experience of refugee work with the Friends, (see Appendix I) and Muriel Davies, the headmistress of a Streatham Secondary School. At this time Helen Grant was a lecturer at Birmingham University. After working for the Foreign Office and the BBC European Service during WW II, she became a lecturer in Spanish at the University of Cambridge and a Fellow of Girton College. Also sent out by the Friends at this time to investigate the progress of refugee work were Cuthbert Whigham, Chairman of the Friend's Service Council, and Janet Perry, a lecturer in Spanish at King's College, London, who was acting as his interpreter.

167 For the first few months of the war, the Friends Service Council joined forces with the Save the Children fund to appeal for food and funds for the growing number of refugees in Spain. Estimates have been made of the numbers of refugees being fed and cared for in Republican Spain. In July 1938 there were about a million refugees in Catalonia alone, which escalated to approximately three million by 1939. Fyrth estimates that by 1939, 150,000 children were being fed by the 'Friends' in Barcelona and 64,000 in the South. *The Signal was Spain*, p. 177.

168 Edith Pye, who joined the 'Friends' in 1908, was a midwife and international relief organ-iser who had been awarded the Legion of Honour for her work in France during WWI. She then worked in Vienna and the Rhur. She also served on the international executive in the Women's International League. During the Spanish Civil War she instigated the forma-tion in Geneva of the international commission for the assistance of child refugees in Spain. Other members of this group were Janet Perry (see fn. 142 above), and Mrs Lothian Small of 'Save the Children'. For Edith Pye see *Dictionary of National Biography: Missing Persons*. For her visit to Barcelona see Fyrth, *The Signal was Spain*, p. 161.

169 Franco rejected offers of assistance from British Quakers, though he did accept a small number of Americans. For more information on the policies and organisation of the 'Friends' in Spain see Farah Mendlesohn, 'Practising Peace: American and British Quaker Relief in the Spanish Civil War. (PhD Thesis, University of York, 1997); Fyrth, *The Signal was Spain*, pp. 158-163, and particularly for their relationship with the Save the Children Fund see Buchanan, *Britain and the Spanish Civil War*, pp. 116-118.

husband had been sent to work in Barcelona by the Friends Service
Council in London because they were the only two Spanish speaking
Quakers in the British Isles.[170] An interview with Norma Jacob reveals
the difference between the views she expressed as a representative of
the Society of Friends and her personal perspective.

> We had to be non-political. In fact, we had to resign from the British
> Labour Party before they took us for the job. We did not belong to any
> political body, we did not express any opinions. I remember having
> a drink in a café somewhere with a friend who was a Communist,
> and he kept saying, 'What are you people doing here? You should be
> with us on the barricades.' And we were trying to explain, 'No, bar-
> ricades are not part of the way we live.' But we couldn't get it
> through to him. 'We know what you're doing, we sympathise, but we
> couldn't do it your way. Not possibly.'[171]

Despite her belief in non-violence and the need to distribute aid
to the children of Republicans and Franco's supporters alike, she
nevertheless viewed the conflict in a mixture of both humanitarian
and political terms. Her hopes, she said had been 'absolutely' for
the Republic.

> Well, anybody who remembers back to the thirties knows there
> were the white hats and the black hats, and Franco's bunch wore
> the black hats.[172]

The fall of Barcelona to Franco she felt was 'the crushing defeat of
something in which one has profoundly believed. Nothing seems to
have been quite the same since.'[173]

As in the other areas of British women's involvement with the
civil war, the story of refugee work in Spain is one of co-operation
across a wide spectrum of beliefs and backgrounds based on shared
concerns. Like Helen Grant, not all the British women who worked
with the Quakers were Friends themselves, but shared their strong
commitment to this type of work. Kanty Cooper, for example, was a
'friend of the Friends', who worked with the Quaker relief team in

---

170 Norma Jacob 'The Spanish Civil War', in Anthony, *Bio of an Ogre*, p. 229.
171 Norma Jacob, interview with Karin Lee, American Friends Service Committee, 31 March
     1-989, #31.
172 Ibid.
173 Norma Jacob 'The Spanish Civil War', in Anthony, *Bio of an Ogre*, p. 235.

Barcelona.[174] The narratives of this group of women are primarily orientated towards the needs of displaced women and children.[175] They visited many children's refugee colonies and schools in the Republic, and the efforts being made to improve children's education are highly praised. Francesca Wilson, who had many years experience of refugee work, commented on 'the admirable combination of order and freedom in the atmosphere', whilst Helen Grant approved of 'the great idea of "educating" children as opposed to "instructing" them.'[176] Edith Pye, after her visits to refugee colonies, hospitals and schools had also been impressed, stating, 'We have come back definitely encouraged by the order and organisation of those parts of Spain we have been privileged to see.' Amongst the immediate practical requirements for food, milk, and clothing, wool for knitting was included, 'so that refugee women may knit for their children and so avoid the demoralisation of idleness.'[177]

The diary of Helen Grant, though only covering a short period, is rich in observations of the political atmosphere in Spain, reflecting her previous interest in the subject.[178] During a visit to the cinema in Barcelona she noted that there were 'Great cheers from the gallery when Stalin's photo appeared on the screen, but only from the gallery.' [Her emphasis] Where she was sitting, surrounded by people who were 'obviously middle class', people kept quiet.[179] She later remarks that she attended a meeting of the CNT-FAI (Anarcho-syndicalists) and the International Anarchists, which she found to be 'rather quiet and boring', as 'most of the speakers gave history lessons'.[180] However, she shows great interest in the practicalities involved in the running of a collectivised drapery firm she toured,

---

174 Kanty Cooper had studied sculpture at the Royal College of Art and had been a pupil of Henry Moore. See *Guardian Woman*, 12 February 1979, 'A friend of the Friends: Kanty Cooper talks to Alex Hamilton,' and Kanty Cooper, *The Uprooted: Agony and Triumph among the Debris of War* (Quartet Books, London, 1979).

175 These narratives include short memoirs, such as Davies, 'Six Months in Southern Spain'; Inez Isabel MacDonald, 'Summer in Murcia in 1937' *Newnham College Roll* January 1938, pp. 39-45; Muriel McDiarmid, *Franco in Barcelona* (United Editorial Ltd., London, 1939).

176 Francesca Wilson *In the Margins of Chaos: Recollections of Relief Work In and Between Three Wars* (John Murray, London, 1944) p. 172. Grant, 'Spain: 25 March – 18 April 1937', p. 23. The educational approach being employed in the Republic was based on the theories of Francisco Giner de los Ríos, founder of the Institución Libre de Enseñanza, see Salvador de Madariaga, *Spain: A Modern History* (Jonathan Cape, London, 1961, 1972) pp. 77-84.

177 Edith Pye, 'Report on Visit to Spain', Friends Service Council, 1937, 033.5 FSC vol. 3/45.

178 For references to her earlier visits to Spain, see Chapter 3.

179 Grant, 'Spain: 25 March – 18 April 1937', p. 4.

180 Ibid., p. 31.

especially in the provision of evening classes for employees and a school for their children.[181] Throughout her diary she takes great pains to note the opinions expressed to her during conversations, whether political or otherwise. She recorded many details of her meeting with the British Consul in Barcelona. His views were noted at length and contrasted with her own, usually opposing, conclusions. Her frank opinion of him was that he seemed 'a coarse man - astute, even intelligent, but with no understanding of conditions.'[182] He was apparently of the opinion that the Spaniards could not be reached by books, and thought it odd that they were showing a sudden enthusiasm for reading. 'My guards downstairs, for example, spend all their day reading but this is just a passing fad.'[183]

After cramming as much as possible into her stay in Barcelona, Helen Grant went on to spend a week in Valencia and then travelled by car to Madrid. On this journey, she took the opportunity to talk at length to the chauffeur, finding him, 'one of the finest men she met in Spain'. She records many of his opinions on the war and politics, noting his intelligent grasp of economics and his faith in the future. 'If I were a guide,' he said, 'I should not show people the works of art. I should take them to talk to the people because the best thing we have in Spain is the people.'[184] This extensive use of direct quotations found in the writings of Helen Grant also occurs in those of Francesca Wilson, creating an intimate style in which detailed conversations with Spanish people are constantly intermingled with their own experiences and observations.[185] The same driver's views also merit a paragraph in Francesca Wilson's narrative, in which he compares the atmosphere in Valencia and Madrid.

'You'll see the spirit there is in Madrid,' he added, 'and you'll understand that we can't be defeated. In Valencia people have too easy a life - too much to eat, too much time for sitting in cafés. They get depressed. They are gayer in Madrid - there is *mucha alegría en Madrid.*'[186]

---

181 Grant, 'Spain: 25 March – 18 April 1937', pp. 24-26.
182 Ibid., p. 8.
183 Ibid., p. 9.
184 Ibid., p. 43.
185 The frequent use of direct quotations, dialogue and reported speech in the narratives of women has been noted in other studies. See for example Selma Leydesdorff, Lusia Passerini and Paul Thompson (eds), *Gender and Memory* (Oxford University Press, 1996) Introduction p. 3 and the contribution from Richard Ely and Alyssa McCabe.
186 Wilson, *In the Margins of Chaos*, p. 177.

His opinion of the situation in Valencia corresponds to Helen Grant's summary of the atmosphere there as 'unsatisfactory'. An air of normality prevailed but, she believed a good deal of money was being made due to the presence of the Government officials who had all retreated to the safety of Valencia from Madrid.[187]

On the way to Madrid, the group stopped for lunch with a peasant family in a small village, which gave Helen Grant the chance to gather views from women on the Church.

An old woman said that she was not shocked by our smoking because they now knew that it was only the Church which had pretended that sort of thing was wicked. Then someone said, 'Yes, the priests told us it was wicked for women to smoke but it did not stop them from seducing the prettiest girls in the vestry.' The old woman talked to me for a long time. She wanted to know about England. She was surprised when I told her it was smaller than Spain and said, 'I always thought Spain was the smallest, poorest country in the world.' Then she turned to the other people and said, 'That just shows they never taught us anything.'[188]

When they arrived in Madrid, the city was under bombardment, their bedrooms had no glass in the windows, but they soon became accustomed to life so near the front lines.

The main impression on walking about Madrid is that nobody even thinks about danger. Nevertheless, the majority of the houses and shops in the Gran Vía have been hit... The telephone building is marked on every storey by shells although the rapidity with which the effects of bombardment are cleared up gives a superficial appearance of order... Although the guns roar almost continually and sometimes they are quite deafening, no one appears to take any notice.[189]

The spirit of the *Madrileños* is a theme to which Francesca Wilson also returns when describing the women of the city.

---

187 Grant, 'Spain: 25 March – 18 April 1937', p. 42.
188 Ibid., p. 44. Helen Grant repeated this story, and some of the others from her diary when she gave a talk at Cambridge University, probably in April 1980, on the theme of 'Spain and Me', Girton Archive, papers of Helen Grant.
189 Ibid., p. 49.

There were queues everywhere. I saw a vegetable cart with carrots, turnips and cabbages. The women behind it stretched in a long line, but they had put their hands on the shoulders in front of them and were dancing and singing. *Mucha alegría en Madrid.* These Madrid women seemed to me astonishing. Not because they stood up to bombardments and air-raids, for danger is a stimulant to strong natures, as we have seen in our own cities. It was not their courage in the battle against the enemy that surprised me, but in the unceasing and inglorious battle against hunger and cold. We met two women who had been in the militia, done sentry duty and fought in the streets. When their party had decided that women were more useful in the rear than at the front, they had, like disciplined soldiers, done a right about turn and opened a crèche, and were now guarding the babies of factory workers with the same zest and energy that they had once put into fighting.[190]

Francesca Wilson's trip to Madrid took place after she had already begun her work in Murcia. Refugees fleeing from Málaga before the city fell to Franco were arriving in Murcia in their thousands. They had endured shelling from warships and machine gunning from aircraft as they retreated along the coast road to Almería. Many had lost children on the journey and did not know what had become of them. About 4,000 of them were living in an unfinished, unfurnished apartment building, with no doors or windows or even many internal walls.[191] After a journey through the dreamlike beauty of April blossoms in the Spanish countryside, Francesca Wilson found herself in the nightmare world of traumatised refugees. 'They surged round us, telling us their stories, clinging to us like people drowning in a bog.'[192] Realising that many of them were 'wild with hunger,' she immediately requested emergency supplies for the children from Barbara Wood, who was in charge of the Friends' warehouses in Valencia and Madrid. But when the cocoa, sugar, milk and biscuits arrived to feed 700 children and pregnant and nursing women each morning, the problems were not over. Although it was relatively easy to control the children, the women, who were afraid that there would not be enough to go round, were another matter.

---

190 Wilson, *In the Margins of Chaos*, p. 179.
191 For a local Spanish perspective on the refugee work in Murcia see Carmen González Martínez, *Guerra Civil en Murcia: Un análisis sobre el poder y los comportamientos colectivos* (Universidad de Murcia, 1999) pp. 128-148.
192 Wilson, *In the Margins of Chaos*, p. 173.

They broke down the doors, they flung down the sentries, they surged into the room, dipped their tin mugs into the scalding vats, fought with each other, tearing each other's hair and the clothes off each other's backs. They shrieked and gesticulated. It was not a breakfast - it was hell.[193]

Fortunately, stalwart re-enforcements arrived over the next few days in the form of four more British women.[194] One of these was Frida Stewart, who had driven an ambulance to Spain at the request of the National Joint Committee. On arriving in Murcia, she was struck by the figure of Francesca Wilson, 'looking as if she had just come from a garden-party in a Sussex village, tall and slim and so very English in a light cotton frock - in contrast to the universal black of the Spanish women.'[195] All the newcomers were welcomed with open arms by this indomitable organiser, who, wrote Frida Stewart, 'had all kinds of other plans which she unfolded as we sat in the hotel lounge that sweltering afternoon. Five of us - a stage army for the relief of Mafeking! Francesca, however, had no doubts that her plans could be put into operation.'[196] In addition to the distribution of food, these plans included organising classes for the children, sewing groups for the women as most of them only had the clothes they wore on the flight from their homes, and the establishment of a hospital for the sick babies and children who were in the refugee centres. Like Francesca Wilson, Frida Stewart found the impact of one of these centres almost overwhelming.

The first impression of the centre was quite unforgettable - the stench that assailed you as you approached the entrance, the sight of the muck heaps and piles of rusty rubbish and refuse, and of the ragged people sitting and leaning in the doorway, the filthy bony little children crawling about in the semi-darkness of the interior. It was all like something out of Dickens at his most sordid, hardly believable that it could exist in 1937.[197]

The dirt and degradation made her feel 'quite sick with anger.' Her thoughts turned to the political implications.

---

193 Ibid., p. 176.
194 Frida Stewart, Kathleen McColgan, Eunice Chapman and Nurse Shaw are named in a report written by Francesca Wilson to the Friends Committee on 9 June 1937 from the Hospital Inglés para Niños, Murcia, papers of Frida Stewart.
195 Frida Stewart, unpublished memoirs, p. 137, papers of Frida Stewart.
196 Ibid., p. 137.
197 Ibid., p. 139.

Why were these people here? What had they done to deserve the suffering, the uprooting, the crowding like cattle in a strange stable far from their homes? Nothing, except to have wanted to live a quiet life under a government of their own choice.[198]

She wrote letters home to Cambridge every few days. They reflect both her commitment to the work she is doing and frustration at not being able to do more. She distributes the supplies to the children, writing to her Mother, 'Poor darlings they are terribly pathetic and clutch their biscuits and gulp their cocoa with such fervour - it takes two hours to queue them up and feed them and even then it seems very little achieved when there's so much waiting to be done.'[199] She also writes of her social activities, and the 'razzle' of a ball, which took place against a background of suppressed tension, explaining that '...you can't be frightfully gay, even at a "Grande Baile" [sic] if your partners have mostly an arm missing or bandaged heads or limbs, as so many have.'[200]

Meanwhile, due to persistence and force of personality, Francesca Wilson succeeded in establishing the children's hospital in a modern villa requisitioned for the purpose by the civil Governor. There was no shortage of patients and an outbreak of typhoid soon ensured that the hospital was filled with babies and children in all stages of fever, delirium, and sickness. Fortunately, most of the children recovered after several weeks of intensive care, in which all did what they could to help with the nursing. Francesca Wilson's report states that as the only trained Sister, Nurse Shaw was wonderful, and that Frida Stewart was 'a perfect brick.'[201] High praise indeed.

By the time Inez MacDonald arrived to take up her post as temporary Superintendent in the summer of 1937, a daily routine had been established for both in-patients and out-patients, two Spanish doctors visiting daily to see the children. On her return to Cambridge where she was a Resident Fellow at Newnham, she wrote an account of her daily life in Murcia for the *Newnham College Roll*.[202] The tone is

198 Frida Stewart, unpublished memoirs, papers of Frida Stewart. p. 139.
199 Frida Stewart, letter to Mother, 16 May 1937, Hotel Victoria, Murcia, papers of Frida Stewart.
200 Ibid.
201 Francesca Wilson, report to the Friends Committee on June 9th 1937 from the Hospital Inglés para Niños, Murcia, papers of Frida Stewart.
202 Inez Isabel MacDonald, 'Summer in Murcia in 1937', *Newnham College Roll* January 1938, pp. 39-45. Well known for her published works as a Hispanist, she befriended many Spanish refugees in England, inviting them to her regular Wednesday afternoon gatherings of students at Newnham. She died in 1955.

restrained, but there is an underlying admiration for the extraordinary 'courage, vitality and gaiety' of the Spanish people, in spite of
the sadness of the conditions in which they live. The wild nature of
Malagan mothers is mentioned once again, with the comment that 'on
the whole, these lawless people who never had the reasons for any
rules ever explained to them before, responded very well to a reason-
able explanation of their necessity.'[203] Her sympathy for their situation is evident in the last few lines when she writes that apart from the
lives they were able to save, they also 'were able to create a feeling, a
positive feeling, of good will, which I feel convinced is of great value
to a nation that is suffering as are the Spanish today.'[204]

The following year, Dorothy Davies, who had previously been the
Matron of a Quaker hospital in the Lebanon, spent most of her six
months in Spain at the hospital. Refugee children continued to arrive,
suffering from a multitude of illnesses, typhoid, pneumonia, TB, measles,
diphtheria, whooping cough, chicken pox, and from malnutrition.
Despite her familiarity with sickness, she did not become hardened to
the 'appallingly high' death rate especially amongst babies. Like the
nurses in the medical units nearer the front lines, an individual child
is of particular concern. She writes of her 'special care' for Dolores
who was severely under-weight. As she improved, her face filled out
'and she looked less like a wizened little old woman', but having
no strength to resist disease, she died when an attack of measles
followed chicken-pox despite all the care Dorthy Davies had given.[205]

The costs of running the hospital had escalated as the number of
beds increased to fifty, and, although because of its origins, it was
always known as 'The English Hospital for Children', the American
Society of Friends took over the expenses.[206] The indefatigable
Francesca Wilson set up ten sewing workshop for refugee girls in
Alicante and Murcia, 'alpargata' workshops for older men, a colony for
fifty older refugee boys at Crevillente, and a summer camp on a beach
near Benidorm.[207] She had been warned many times against beginning

203 Inez Isabel MacDonald, 'Summer in Murcia in 1937', *Newnham College Roll* January 1938, p. 43.
204 Ibid., p. 45.
205 Davies, 'Six Months in Southern Spain,' p. xiii.
206 Many more refugee colonies for children were being set up by Spanish and Catalan child welfare organisations, helped in some instances by funds from the Quakers and from the National Joint Committee.
207 'Alpargatas' are rope-soled sandals with canvas tops that were worn by many Spaniards at this time. Following the summer camp, a colony was founded for thirty girls in a near-by villa.

projects which would entail substantial funds to keep them running, but despite sleepless nights of worry, her response to these cautious voices was unequivocal. 'They spoke with the voice of prudence. But in relief work prudence is not enough. When needs are great, risks have to be taken.'[208] The value of the projects she started was recognised and they continued to be funded from a variety of sources until the end of the war.[209] Without underestimating the contribution of the many men also working in the field of refugee work, it is clear that this was a sphere in within which British women were able to operate confidently and efficiently.[210] The roots of this confidence stemmed from earlier traditions, in which women were seen as the nurturers, symbolic of compassion to the suffering, and as doughty and intrepid female pioneers in far off lands.

The perspective on British women in Spain during the war can be broadened further through following the adventures of Frida Stewart after she left Murcia, determined to experience life in Madrid. Through her writings we can begin to understand not only the response to suffering, but also the exhilarating atmosphere in Spain. We are able to see life through the eyes of a young, intelligent British woman, alone in a capital city at war, far from the safety of home and family, immersed in a foreign culture. What will she make of it? What will she do? How will she feel?

All I wanted was to set foot in Madrid - absurdly like a pilgrim seeking inspiration at a shrine.[211]

A badly poisoned hand prevented her from working in the hospital and she took the opportunity to get a lift on a lorry taking supplies to Madrid. The daily dressings of her hand at the military hospital stopped on the arrival of a new influx of seriously wounded troops, but soon she could type a little and was ready for work. She found plenty to do at the Press Office where she met the 'great swells' in the world of

---

208 Wilson, *In the Margins of Chaos*, p. 192.
209 See Chapter 6.
210 Examples of prominent men include Sir George Young, John Langdon-Davies, Sir Richard Rees. A graphic portrait of the flamboyant Sir George Young is painted by Frida Stewart who knew him well in Spain where his normal attire included a flowing white cloak, white corduroy breeches and broad-brimmed white hat. He was known at the border as 'el hidalgo inglés'. She wrote home that '...he is said to have arrived in Valencia in his usual white corduroys and snow white shoes, clinging to a wicker chair, strapped to an antiquated motor-bike ambulance. I don't know whether to admire him for his courage or condole with him his craziness. There's no doubt about his being both courageous and cracked!' Letter to Mother, 2 July 1937, papers of Frida Stewart.
211 Frida Stewart, memoirs, p. 150.

journalism, Pitcairn, Delmer, Robert Capa and Gerda Taro. She worked for a Canadian journalist, Ted Allen for several weeks, during which time Gerda Taro was killed by a lorry whilst taking photographs at the front. The effect on those in the Press Office was 'shattering' and 'somehow summed up the hateful chaotic waste of life in wartime.'[212]

Frida Stewart was pleased that tribute was paid to Gerda Taro at the Writers' Congress taking place in Madrid at this time. A host of famous authors and poets were attending the Congress, Pablo Neruda, Heinrich Mann, and amongst the British, Stephen Spender and Sylvia Townsend Warner. Frida Stewart wrote home enthusiastically, '...the whole thing was rather exciting and I was awfully glad to get in.' Her letter continued in a light vein.

> Today everyone was going about in shirtsleeves at the writers congress. It was funny to see old Alexis Tolstoi shedding one garment after another. The ones in uniform - Ralph Bates and Renn who are officers in the International Brigade - could not shed poor things. Malraux and the other Frenchmen looked fairly cool but everyone got very excited and hot with all the ceremony and processions and leaping up at very short intervals to salute extra special comrades, and sing the International.[213]

A further task she embarked upon was at the instigation of a formidable American woman who was in Madrid, Anna Louise Strong, a journalist of international renown.[214] On this occasion she decided that Frida Stewart would be a suitable person to edit a Spanish Grammar and Vocabulary Book to be used by British and American International Brigaders. Phrases such as 'Pass the ammo, quick' and 'My gun lock is rusty,' were duly translated for use at the front.[215] She also managed to join one of the tours taking visitors to the front lines.

> And I went up to the front line in Madrid, where in University City they'd got machine guns up facing the outskirts of Madrid where the Moors were entrenched - there were a whole lot of Franco's

---

212 Frida Stewart, memoirs, p. 160.
213 Frida Stewart, letter to Mother, 5 July 1937, papers of Frida Stewart.
214 Anna Louise Strong later went to China where she died in 1986. See Tracy B. Strong and Helene Keyssar, *Right in Her Soul: The Life of Anna Louise Strong* (Random House, New York, 1983).
215 Frida Stewart, memoirs, p. 167. When I interviewed her in 1994, Frida Stewart believed that this book had never been of much use, but I was able to tell her that I had seen a copy in the possession of one of the British Brigaders, Fred Thomas, who had found it very helpful.

army people only two hundred yards away. And they said, 'Would you like to fire a shot at them?' So I fired a shot for freedom. I felt, 'as long as I don't kill anybody I don't mind' [laughter].[216]

Several British women were amongst those whose voices were heard world-wide broadcasting from Madrid, and this visit to the front became the subject of one of several made by Frida Stewart.[217] She felt 'some slight satisfaction' to be challenging the propaganda for Franco being transmitted by General Queipo de Llano, 'even if one could not emulate his atrocity stories, or present the facts in such a horrifically picturesque way as he presented his fictions.'[218]

A telegram from her sister on behalf of the National Joint Committee requesting her return to help with the work of fund-raising in Britain was most unwelcome.

You can't think what the pull of Madrid is! If only you could come out and see you wouldn't dream of wiring anyone to come home... And get the Joint Committee to send me back as soon as possible for it's the only place to be in the world just now.[219]

Guilt at consuming the precious rations available in Madrid seems to have been a strong factor in her decision to return home, combined with the knowledge that she had seen enough at first hand in Spain to be able to carry out valuable propaganda work for the Republic.

When Winifred Bates had been asked as a girl to write an essay on 'A Woman's Work in War Time,' she sat on the hard school bench, sucking the end of her pen, confident of her spelling and grammar, but, as to what a woman could do in such circumstances, her mind was 'as devoid of notions as an empty oil can.' Eventually she came up with two ideas, 'you could make shirts and knit socks, and you could do men's jobs so that they could go to the front.'[220] After her years in Spain during the war, talking to so many of the British women working there and writing dozens of articles about their experiences, she

---

216 Frida Stewart, AJ, 30 March 1994. Kingsley Kent quotes a nurse from the First World War who was also still wondering what happened to the shell she was invited to fire at the 'Boches'. *Making Peace*, p. 64. Jessica Mitford was asked if she would like to fire a shot at the enemy Italian troops near Bilbao. She hit a nearby tree. *Hons and Rebels: An Autobiography* (Gollancz, London, 1961) p. 106.
217 See Chapter 5.
218 Frida Stewart, memoirs, p. 167.
219 Frida Stewart, letter to sister Margaret, 23 July 1937, papers of Frida Stewart.
220 Bates, 'A Woman's Work in Wartime', p. 1.

probably knew more than most just how diverse that work could be and what it could entail. However, her memoir shows that she had learned, not just of women's work, but of the women as individuals, their strengths and weaknesses under pressure during a time of war, and indeed, her own. Such narratives have also made it possible for us to broaden our understanding of what war means to women.

CHAPTER FIVE

'A Far Cry': Women and the Voice of Empathy

It seems a far cry from the comparative quiet of English town and village to the ravaged countryside of Spain, and many of us scanning the newspapers turn away from the pictures of civil war with only one feeling, that of relief that it is so far. Or we look rather unsympathetically at the photos of women shouldering their muskets alongside of their men, half critical, half wondering at this unusual sight. We turn back to the quiet routine of our lives, washing, cooking, shopping, children, husbands, neighbours, either dismissing this race of Amazons from our minds or registering a somewhat muddled resolve that we'll keep out of such troubles. It is not easy to understand (nor do the papers help us to get much clearer) what the Spanish people are fighting for, or to know whether we, in their place would do the same. It seems incongruous, doesn't it, to imagine ourselves together with Mrs Smith across the way and Mrs Green next door marching smilingly off with rifle on shoulder? Who, we ask, would look after the children and what would happen on washing day? And yet those girls and women whose faces confront us each day in the papers are the mothers and wives of Spanish workmen and peasants, with husbands and children and homes, not unlike our own, who have turned from the weekly task of making low wages meet high prices to defend the Government they elected and to whom they looked for some betterment of their conditions.[1]

This article by Magda Gellan in *Woman To-day*, entitled 'The Women's Front in Spain' typifies one way in which the war in Spain was presented to women in Britain, through reference to the phenomenon of the *miliciana*.

---

1 Magda Gellan, 'The Women's Front in Spain' *Woman To-day* November 1936, p. 5.

Woman To-day, a monthly magazine published by the British Section of the Women's World Committee Against War and Fascism, was aimed at the 'thinking' woman, interested in articles on international affairs and social improvements, but also included a smattering of contrasting features such as 'Frocks for Spring Parties' and 'Thumbsucking Infants - Should They or Shouldn't They?'[2] The article quoted above invokes the reader's empathy, asking of them to imaginatively enter into another person's reality. British women were being asked to consider the almost unthinkable, but perhaps rather exciting, notion of being transformed from a mundane housewife into a *miliciana*, leaving behind domestic duties to defend democracy and the chance of a better life for the family. In contrast, the more down to earth reality of British women's traditional role as fund raisers for such causes was depicted on the front cover of the Christmas issue in 1937.

5.1 *Woman To-Day*, Christmas cover, December 1937.

---

2   *Woman To-day* March 1937 and June 1937 respectively. *Woman To-day* was far from representative of women's magazines in general in the inter-war period. Deirdre Beddoe has pointed out that the vast majority of media coverage portrayed the housewife as 'the only desirable image a woman should adopt.' *Back to Home and Duty: Women Between the Wars 1918-1939* (Pandora, London, 1989) p. 4.

However, rather than showing the arduous foot-slogging work involved, the idealised image romanticised door-to-door collections by portraying a well-dressed, wide-eyed and high-browed young woman appealing for 'Milk for the Mothers of Spain', smiling as she stands, tin in hand, daintily adorned with gently falling snow and framed by holly leaves. The readers of *Woman To-Day* could identify comfortably with this image and share her wish to contribute to the appeal.

Articles and pictures such as these can help us to understand not only how women perceived the war in Spain, but also how they attempted to communicate their concerns within the social context of the time. They form one aspect of the theme of this chapter, an exploration of the interactions between British women who were involved with the war and the processes of mass communication. British women not only became the subjects of war-related media coverage themselves on occasion, but were also making use of their renowned proficiency in communications skills by contributing extensively to public awareness of the war. Particularly active in this work were the British women who were able to go to Spain themselves. The effects of such visits, however brief, were frequently dramatic. Not only did they witness the grim actualities of the war at first hand, but they also found themselves to be deeply affected by their contact with the Spanish people. The women who feature in this chapter responded by voicing their concerns in the public sphere. They wrote extensively for newspapers, journals and pamphlets. They spoke at public meetings in Britain, they broadcast from Spain, they kept Spain high on the agendas of their international groups. Rather than merely disseminating information, in the overwhelming majority of cases their aim was to elicit a practical response.[3] Empathy both sustained their efforts and was instrumental in the success of their appeals to others.

It would be difficult to gain an understanding of the work done by the women who feature in this chapter without firstly placing them within the broader framework of the media coverage of the war. Previous studies have explored the attitudes expressed in the British press and the newsreels and have revealed a great deal about the social values prevalent at the time.[4] However, for the purposes of this

---

3   Although this chapter maintains the focus of the study on the role of women, there is no intention to imply that work of this type was an exclusively female preserve.
4   See for example, K. W. Watkins, *Britain Divided: The Effect of the Spanish Civil War on British Political Opinion* (Thomas Nelson, London, 1963); Anthony Aldgate, *British Newsreels and the Spanish Civil War* (Scolar Press, London, 1979); Caroline Brothers, *War and Photography: A Cultural History* (Routledge, London & New York, 1997).

chapter, rather than considering the context of media coverage in its entirety, it is perhaps more pertinent to focus primarily on the attitudes towards Spanish and British women involved with the war. 'The Women's Front in Spain', quoted above, is but one of the many articles published in Britain which evoked the notion of the 'Amazons' to represent Spanish women bearing arms. The identification with the powerful image of Greek mythological warrior women was quickly made in the British press and was drawn upon as required for propaganda purposes. Indeed, the use of the term in this context was not new. During the First World War, British women had been described as 'Our Amazons', and praised for the spirit with which they had undertaken war work.[5] The reference to 'Amazons' in *Woman To-day* was therefore taking place within a wider discourse relating to women and war, in which the self-mutilation of the Amazons had become symbolic of women's self-sacrifice in Spain. Like the Amazons, Spanish women were suppressing their femininity by taking up arms. Bare-headed and in trousers, they became the icons of a revolutionary break with tradition.[6] However, the fact that they retained the essence of their womanly and homely natures was often clearly indicated by those in the press who favoured the Republic. The article in *Woman To-day* stresses the fact that the 'Amazons' have 'husbands and children and homes, not unlike our own.' The *News Chronicle* was keen to emphasise this point in the front-page portrayal of a *miliciana* in uniform entitled, 'Spain's Sister Susie - One of the Amazon army sews a button on the shirt of a loyalist soldier...'[7]

Elsewhere in the media, the phenomenon of the *miliciana* contributed to the fear of a destabilisation of society. There are many examples in which these women-at-arms were denigrated for propaganda purposes. But acceptance of negative attitudes towards women who challenged their traditional gendered roles was widespread at the time, and no resounding objections to this approach seem to have been raised. *The Times* correspondent in Valencia wrote in apparent dismay of 'women, armed and aggressive' taking their place in the front line with men, the primary fear being, 'All that womanhood

---

5   *Daily Chronicle*, August 1918. Quoted in Beddoe, *Back to Home and Duty*, p. 11.
6   Ethel MacDonald on her arrival in Barcelona in 1936, notes that despite the fact that it was difficult to tell the young men and girls apart at a distance because they all dressed exactly alike, as they drew nearer they saw that all the girls had beautifully 'permed' hair and were strikingly made up. Rhona M. Hodgart, *Ethel MacDonald: Glasgow Woman Anarchist* (Kate Sharpley Library, B. M. Hurricane, London, WC1N 3XX, undated) p. 5.
7   *News Chronicle* 10 August 1936, front page.

traditionally stands for is rapidly disappearing.'[8] A photograph of *milicianas* in the *Catholic Herald* was accompanied by the comment 'The recent controversy about shorts in sport may seem to some a trifle less important in view of the conduct (and dress) of certain women in Spain.'[9] Those who listened to the leaders of the British Union of Fascists would have learned that women combatants were in the category of 'atrocities', even attaining distinction as the worst atrocity of all.[10] In the *Daily Express* a selection of photographs under the heading of 'The Terror in Spain,' included one with the caption, 'Amazonian girl soldier carrying pistol and wearing military cap, takes a drink before going into action with Government troops near Madrid University.'[11] The iconoclastic nature of this image was heightened by a wedding photograph nearby of the indisputably modern 'Miss Doreen Evans, racing motorist', who nevertheless had chosen to marry in traditional style with an abundance of bridesmaids and flowers.

The *Daily Mail* portrayed *milicianas* as 'The Women Who Burn Churches', illustrating the article with a photograph in which marching women confront the reader with grimly expressionless faces.[12] The article has been the subject of analysis by Caroline Brothers, who sees the caption labelling them as 'Red Carmens', as a coupling of the notion of the 'ultimately destructive heroine of Bizet's eponymous opera', with 'the value laden qualifier "red" which associated the scarlet hues of the fallen woman with the term's more obvious political connotations.'[13] The photograph and article are discussed within the context of a patriarchal discourse of power, 'which define and delimit acceptable behaviour for women.'[14] This gendered perspective is markedly different from the view that would have been taken by most British women reading these newspapers at the time. The indications are that women on the Left would have perceived the articles and photographs largely in terms of the class struggle. Even in recent interviews during the course of this research, a gendered approach to

---

8 *The Times*, 4 August 1936. Quoted by Frances Lannon in 'Women and Images of Women in the Spanish Civil War' *Transactions of the Royal Historical Society* 1991, pp. 213-228, p. 218.
9 'Europe at the Cross Roads; Spanish Issue Simplifies Itself, Communism Versus Humanity', *Catholic Herald*, 7 August 1936, p. 1.
10 BUF official speakers' notes, Union of Democratic Control Papers, Hull University Library, DDC, 5/373, September 1936. Quoted in Tom Buchanan, '"A Far Away Country of Which We Know Nothing"? Perceptions of Spain and its Civil War in Britain, 1931-1939', *Twentieth Century British History*, vol.4, no.1, 1993, pp. 1-24, p. 10.
11 *Daily Express*, 30 July 1936, p. 20.
12 Ferdinand Tuohy, 'The Women Who Burn Churches', *Daily Mail*, 27 July 1936, p. 10.
13 Brothers, *War and Photography*, p. 89.
14 Ibid., p. 91.

these matters amongst the interviewees is notable mainly by its absence.[15] Frequently, when attempts were made to discuss perceptions of feminist issues, the response was dismissive.[16] Women-at-arms were firmly situated within left-wing discourse as evidence of the determination of the 'Spanish people' to resist the forces of repression. In the *Daily Worker*, the captions to photographs of women bearing arms commonly reflected this view, being entitled for example, 'On Guard for Freedom', 'Ready for the Rebels', and 'To Defend Democracy.'[17] Despite the power of the image as an instrument of propaganda, few women interviewed for this study spontaneously recalled being affected by these photographs. A notable exception from autobiographical sources is Jessica Mitford. Through the photographs of *milicianas* she was able to focus her desires to go to Spain.

> I cut pictures of women guerrillas out of the papers, determined, steady-looking women, wiry, bright-eyed, gaunt-faced, some middle aged, some almost little girls. How to take my place at their side?[18]

Others, like Doris Wood, remembered the significance of media coverage only for the single crucial factor of being 'pro' or 'anti' one side or the other.[19]

One particular 'Amazon' received coverage in both the press and the newsreels.[20] The Gaumont British Newsreel of 'The Blonde Amazon',

---

15 This attitude is reflected in quotations in other studies, for example Wendy Mulford cites a female CP member who said that as far as women activists in the Party were concerned, they thought of themselves not as women, but as Party members. *This Narrow Place: Sylvia Townsend Warner and Valentine Ackland, Life, Letters and Politics, 1930-51* (Pandora, London, 1988) pp. 90-91. Nellie Logan, also in the CP, wrote, 'We were in it together - no time to think of what sex one was - we were human beings wanting a better deal.' Pamela Graves, *Labour Women: Women in British Working-Class Politics 1918-1939* (Cambridge University Press, 1994) p. 159. See also in general Sue Bruley, *Leninism, Stalinism and the Women's Movement in Britain, 1920-1939* (Garland, New York & London, 1986).
16 See also for example, Norma Jacob, Oral History Interview #31, 31 March1989, p. 14, Archive of the American Friends Service Council, Philadelphia. A few contrasting examples are discussed in Chapter 4.
17 *Daily Worker* 29 July, p.1; 1 August, p.1; 17 August, p.1, respectively.
18 Jessica Mitford, *Hons and Rebels: An Autobiography* (Victor Gollancz, London, 1961) p. 78.
19 Doris Wood, interviewed by Maria Delgado, 1986. Other examples include Noreen Branson, AJ, 26 January 1996; Frida Stewart, AJ, 11 December 1995. Amongst the interviews with men who fought in Spain that have been studied for this thesis, Fred Thomas is the only one to spontaneously recall the effect of a specific image. He remembered being deeply moved by a photograph of Republican prisoners, roped together, being led away for execution. He joined the International Brigade shortly afterwards. Fred Thomas, AJ, 22 March 1994.
20 It has been estimated that in Britain during the thirties, eighteen to twenty million people went to the cinema each week. Programmes were changed twice weekly, and each one contained about fifteen minutes of news. For more detailed statistics see Aldgate, *Cinema and History*, Chapter 3.

released on 13 August 1936, shed an interesting new light on a photo-graph that had previously appeared in several different newspapers.[21] This photograph, supposedly showing a group of armed girls marching off to fight, featured in its centre a woman with curled blonde hair in a frilly checked dress, brandishing a deadly weapon in each hand whilst, surprisingly, still managing to retain a smart handbag over her arm.

5.2 Miss Phyllis Gwatkin Williams, 'The Blonde Amazon' of the Gaumont British Newsreel, as she appeared in *The Daily Mail*, 24 July 1936 with the caption 'Armed Girl Communists... marching off to fight the anti-Reds in Madrid.'

A subsequent newsreel revealed in an interview with the 'Mystery Woman of the Spanish Revolution', that 'The "Blonde Amazon" whose picture went round the world is neither "Red" nor "Rebel" but a British schoolmistress, Miss Phyllis Gwatkin Williams.'[22] Questions of verisimilitude were raised regarding the photograph as Phyllis Gwatkin Williams at no point claimed that she actually had been involved in any of the fighting. Similar issues were also the subject of debate regarding the newsreel and have been discussed by Anthony Aldgate in his book, *British Newsreels and the Spanish Civil War*.[23]

---

21 Photo caption, 'Armed girl communists, one wearing a steel helmet and the other carry-ing bayonet as well as rifle - marching off to fight the anti-Reds in Madrid.' *Daily Mail*, 24 July 1936, p.11; 'Madrid Girls Take Up Arms - Armed women marching through the streets of Madrid', *Daily Express*, 24 July 1936, p.1; *News Chronicle*, 24 July 1936, back page.
22 Gaumont British Newsreel, (13 August 1936) 'The Blonde Amazon': Exclusive GB News Interview with Mystery Woman of the Spanish Revolution.'
23 Aldgate, *British Newsreels and the Spanish Civil War*, pp. 113-117.

The testimony of Miss Williams, consisting almost entirely of hearsay, was filmed in her garden after she had returned. Cutting into this footage were lengthy shots of church burnings, armed men and women in the streets giving the Republican salute, and a captive being led away under guard. These were all stock shots taken on other occasions which were used to add authenticity to her statement. The dangers of this technique were recognised at the time, and pointed out in an article appearing in *World Film News*. A method normally used for giving reality to a fiction film had been subverted in the newsreel, which, the article stated, 'we are in the habit of accepting as objective', and had resulted in straightforward propaganda against the Republican Government.[24] The case of 'The Blonde Amazon' was thus the precursor of the current debate relating to the computerised manipulation of media images. It has not been possible to discover how Phyllis Gwatkin Williams viewed the presentation of her story. Had she intended to project such a strong anti-Republican bias, or was her main concern expressed at the end of the newsreel when she stated vehemently, 'And if people could realise how terrible war is, they'd do everything to prevent it.'?

The phenomenon of the *milicianas* was short-lived and the associated images virtually ceased to appear. The recall of women to the rearguard by the Republican Government was commented upon in *Woman To-Day*, in order to counter statements in the Spanish press that this was because they had run away. The 'actual reason' they stated, was 'something unsuspected by cynical journalists,' and rather than the behaviour of the women, it was the 'curious reactions' of the fighting men that had been the deciding factor.

> These men, seeing their women fellow-soldiers fall dead, or lie writhing, lost their heads. Horror, or furious rage, took possession of them; forgetting caution, forgetting rather that military version of caution which is called discipline, they would rush upon the enemy, calling them Butchers and Fascists, and get needlessly killed themselves. And since there was no time to train away this instinctive chivalry, it was thought best to withdraw the women from the fighting ranks.[25]

---

24 Brian Crosthwaite, 'Newsreels Show Political Bias: Editing of Spanish War Scenes discloses partisan views' *World Film News* vol.1, no.7, October, 1936, p.41. See also A. Calder-Marshall, 'Propaganda in the Films' *Life and Letters Today* vol.15, Part 6, 1936-37, pp. 151-161, p. 161; also Aldgate, *British Newsreels and the Spanish Civil War*, pp. 113-114.
25 'A Girl of the Spanish People: A story from the special correspondent of Woman To-Day', *Woman To-Day* December 1936, p. 6.

The heroine of this article, Ramona, who had been fighting at the front, was now to return to the rearguard, where she would be more likely to be shot in a town captured by her enemies, or killed as a civilian in an air-raid. Her change of role is recognised as having implications for Ramona's newly constructed sense of identity. 'To the Fascists' the article concluded, 'this will make little difference, but it will make considerable difference to Ramona, so proud in her uniform, wearing her forage cap so jauntily with the tassel dangling above her bright eyes.'[26]

Both the press and the newsreels soon had plentiful opportunities to present women in their more traditional roles as victims of war.[27] There were no shortages of images of civilians wounded or bereaved by bombardment, or of the bewildered faces of refugees. Occasionally, individual cases arose in which British women were the victims, perhaps becoming heroines in the process. Wounded nurses sometimes came home to convalesce and were featured in the press, stating their determination to return to the front.[28] Those on the Left in Britain would certainly have known of the death of the British artist and Communist, Felicia Browne, whilst fighting at the front near Barcelona in the first weeks of the war.[29] Her decision to join a militia unit had been reported by the *Daily Express* at the beginning of August. The text had defined her, just as Spanish *milicianas* had often been defined, by the rejection of 'womanly' qualities. She not only 'defied' the order to British subjects to leave Barcelona, but she had 'demanded' to be enlisted saying, 'I am a member of the London Communists and can fight as well as any man.'[30] Her farewell at the garrison gates with the words, 'I am not at all afraid, I am fighting for a different country but the same cause,' was soon to be followed by the news that she had been killed.[31] Reading of her death had a deep impact on Nan Youngman, who from that moment, remembered that she 'began to be aware of living in history, aware of what was

---

26 'A Girl of the Spanish People: A story from the special correspondent of Woman To-Day', *Woman To-Day* December 1936, p. 6. The importance of the uniform, i.e. trousers, is noted in the representation of Ramona as a 'feminist' heroine, perhaps somewhat muted by the reference to her stylish approach to wearing the cap.

27 See for example articles such as 'Women and Children Blown to Pieces' *Daily Worker*, 2 November 1936, reproduced in *Cockburn in Spain: Despatches from the Spanish Civil War* edited by James Pettifer (Lawrence & Wishart, London, 1986) pp. 111-13.

28 See for example, Nurse Margot Miller, 'They're in the News' *Woman To-Day*, December 1936, p. 3.

29 For a selection of press cuttings see MML, Box A 12: Bro/1.

30 Sydney Smith, 'London Girl Off to Fight' *Daily Express*, 4 August 1936, front page.

31 Ibid.

happening in a way I never had done before.'[32] She immediately joined the Artists International Association, 'which seemed to me the most tremendous political action,' and helped to arrange an exhibition of Felicia Browne's work as a tribute to her. The drawings Felicia Browne had done in Spain were published in a pamphlet, and the profits donated to Spanish Medical Aid.[33]

5.3 Banner designed by the Artists International Association for an exhibition of the work of Felicia Browne, following her death in 1936.

The war in Spain also formed the backdrop for an ongoing newspaper story early in 1937, seemingly tailor-made for mass appeal, involving a missing heiress, romance, and family scandal. Jessica Mitford's elopement to war-torn Spain with Esmond Romilly, the nephew of Clementine Churchill, was headline news. Esmond Romilly had been fighting in Spain, returning to England after the battle of Boadilla. He was unwell and appalled by the realities of warfare but

32 'The Spanish Civil War: Felicia Browne', in Lynda Morris and Robert Radford *The Story of the Artists International Association, 1933-53* (Museum of Modern Art, Oxford, 1983) p. 31. Nan Youngman had known Felicia Browne as a student at the Slade.

33 The news sheet of the Artists International Association in November 1936 refers to an exhibition of the work of Felicia Browne at the Frith Street Gallery, opened by Viscount Hastings. By the end of the exhibition, 170 drawings had been sold and the profits of £150 were given to Spanish Medical Aid. MML, Box 4D. See also *Drawings by Felicia Browne: Killed in Action with the Spanish Government Militia* (Lawrence and Wishart, London, 29 August 1936) MML Box A 15, 8.

was determined to return as a journalist. Meeting his second cousin, Jessica Mitford, for the first time, soon resulted in an agreement to go to Spain together secretly. Her long held dreams of 'running-away' from the deadly boredom of her life in upper-class society were eventually coming to fruition and she prepared by buying a 'good running-away outfit' with characteristic determination.

> Having pored over pictures of Spanish guerrilla women fighters in the weekly illustrated papers, I knew exactly what I wanted, and found it, a brown corduroy ski suit with a military-looking jacket and plenty of pockets.[34]

There was wild speculation in the press as to their whereabouts, 'Fiancé and Peer's daughter trapped in Peak Hut?', 'Jessica Mitford feared lost in Pyrenees', but they were at last tracked down in Bilbao where Esmond Romilly was working as a correspondent for the *News Chronicle*.[35] Jessica's family made her a ward of court to prevent their marriage, Esmond being threatened with imprisonment if he attempted to marry her without permission. Matters escalated to such an extent that they were told by the British Consul that there would be no British co-operation with the evacuation of women and children from the Basque country unless they both agreed to leave Spain.[36] Fervently committed to the Republican cause, they left forthwith. Both were concerned that the publicity about them had not been beneficial to the Republic. Jessica Mitford wrote sadly that, 'The endless stories about our adventures had driven the war news off the front pages, as well as making a farce of our own convictions.'[37] They were eventually allowed to marry in France, still both only aged nineteen.

Also covered by the media were the adventures of 'Fifi' Roberts, the daughter of a Welsh ship's captain who ran Franco's blockade of

---

34 Mitford, *Hons and Rebels*, p. 94.
35 Ibid., p. 114.
36 Ibid., p. 111.
37 Ibid., p. 116. Another British woman, Angela Guest, was the subject of stories in the British and South African press when she was 'missing' in Spain. David Zagier, a journalist who had been asked by her parents to find her, discovered that she was working in a hospital near S'Agaro and brought back a written message saying 'I am not killed. I am not missing. Salud to all my friends in South Africa', which was reproduced in the *Daily Express*, 17 January 1939. Unpublished memoir of David Zagier, 'Seven Days Amongst the Loyalists: A Tale of Civil War Time in Catalonia', chapter entitled 'Angel was Certainly Not Dead.' Papers of his son, Prof. Don Zagier.

Bilbao in the *Seven Seas Spray*.[38] Florence Roberts was determined to sail with the ship to carry much needed supplies of food to the Basque port. She had written to a friend at home that although her father wanted her to stay behind, as a member of the ship's crew she would be on board, 'Make no mistake about that.'[39] The triumphal arrival of Captain Roberts, his daughter and the valuable cargo was reported world-wide, they had exposed the blockade as a sham and were the heroes of the day, filmed and photographed for newsreels and the press. Basque ships and planes escorted them into the port, thousands thronged the water's edge to greet them and the Basque Government held a dinner in their honour. Apart from general public interest in the event, the details of Florence Robert's voyage had been of special concern to one particular group in Britain. These were the girls of the Penarth County School for Girls, where Florence Roberts had been a pupil. Through the Ship Adoption Society, the girls had adopted the *Seven Seas Spray* and so followed its progress with enthusiasm, receiving a first hand account from Florence Roberts in a letter sent to the headmistress.[40] The *Seven Seas Spray* was soon followed by other British ships bringing supplies to Bilbao, their captains perhaps not wishing to seem to have less courage than a nineteen year old girl. She was soon immortalised in poetry by Edgell Rickword, a 'brave lass' who dared to run the blockade that the British fleet refused to challenge.[41]

Appearing within this wide framework of images and text focusing on the war were the words of women who had seen for themselves what was happening in Spain. Their contributions tend to differ markedly in content and style from the offerings of diplomatic and war correspondents.[42] In

---

38 The *Seven Seas Spray* arrived in Bilbao on 20 April 1937. For details see P. M. Heaton, *Welsh Blockade Runners in the Spanish Civil War* (Starling Press, Pontypool, Gwent, 1985) pp. 44-47, and Robert Stradling, *Cardiff and the Spanish Civil War* (Butetown History and Arts Centre, 1996) pp. 70-1. See also the interview with Fifi Roberts in Part 3 of the Granada TV documentary, 'The Spanish Civil War', and the accompanying book by David Mitchell, *The Spanish Civil War* (Granada Publishing, St. Albans, Herts, 1982) pp. 89-93.

39 Letter from Florence Roberts quoted in Heaton, *Welsh Blockade Runners in the Spanish Civil War*, p. 47. Heaton notes that Florence Roberts was not the only woman on board, the wife of the Chief Engineer, Mrs B. Docker, also sailed with them.

40 Letter to Miss K. Hughes, quoted in Heaton, *Welsh Blockade Runners in the Spanish Civil War*, p. 47.

41 Edgell Rickword, 'To the Wife of Any Non-intervention Statesman', March 1938. It is interesting to note that Rickword refers to 'Potato Jones and his brave lass', seemingly having made the common mistake of confusing Captain Roberts with 'Potato Jones', another Welsh blockade runner.

42 For more on the work of foreign correspondents, including some whose writings reflected the sympathies they felt for the Republic, see Paul Preston, *We Saw Spain Die*, (Constable, London, 2008), published in Spanish as *Idealistas bajo las balas. Corresponsales extranjeros en la guerra de España*, (Debate, Barcelona, 2007).

the mainstream press, most news items on Spain related to the interactions taking place at international level, or to the progress of the fighting, the accounts of which at times sounded like weather reports, 'The cloudless sky was ideal for war in the air... Storms and snowfalls are hindering communications between Madrid and Asturias.'[43] Women writers, for the most part, did not write in this way and were less likely to attempt to de-personalise the conflict. Other studies have noted how by relying on '"public documentary" techniques and fact insistent narratives that downplay "personal-autobiographical" aspects, journalism draws attention to the external, historic events of the war and creates a sense of authority and textual verisimilitude.'[44] However, the traditional tendency of journalistic narratives to 'bury' the narrating I/eye to create a sense of objectivity, was a strategy largely reversed in much of the eye-witness journalism on Spain.[45] Women's writing on Spain frequently allowed space for the 'personal', and empathy, in many cases, overrode detachment. This should not be not be dismissed as a mere trick for propaganda purposes, aiming to obscure objectivity by an appeal to the emotions. It was, in many cases, a reflection of a different agenda. The approach of British women writers often had much in common with the views expressed by the American, Martha Gellhorn, who was also reporting from Spain. She rarely quoted or even mentioned politicians and, on being told that correspondents had a duty to retain their sense of objectivity, is said to have replied, 'To hell with objectivity.'[46]

This type of approach can be seen in the writings of Elizabeth Wilkinson. Whilst employed as a *Daily Worker* correspondent in the Basque Country, she had been amongst the first to arrive in Guernica after the bombing and to describe the results of a new style of warfare, saturation bombing of defenceless civilians.[47] In her articles she

---

43 'No Resumption of Spanish Rebels Offensive' *Manchester Guardian*, 16 March 1937, p.11.
44 Lolly Ockerstrom, 'The Other Narratives: British and American Women Writers and the Spanish Civil War', PhD Thesis, Department of English, Northeastern University, Boston, Massachusetts, June 1997, pp. 33-4.
45 Ibid., p. 33.
46 Martha Gellhorn replying to Drew Middleton. Quoted as 'A la mierda con la objectividad', in *El País* 'Protagonistas Del Siglo XX' no.12, 1999, La Guerra Civil, p. 292. For a wider perspective on the work of foreign correspondents in general, see Paul Preston, *We Saw Spain Die*, (Constable, London, 2008), published in Spanish as *Idealistas bajo las balas. Corresponsales extranjeros en la guerra de España*, (Debate, Barcelona, 2007).
47 Elizabeth Wilkinson, report from Bilbao, 27 April 1937, *Daily Worker*, quoted in Jim Fyrth and Sally Alexander, *Women's Voices from the Spanish Civil War* (Lawrence & Wishart, London, 1991) p. 271. Re. question of exact time of her arrival in Guernica see p. 271, fn. 8. Fifi Roberts was also taken to see Guernica on the same day. She acted as a special reporter for the *News Chronicle*, taking photographs of the bombed town. See Stradling, *Cardiff and the Spanish Civil War*, p. 71 and Mitchell, *The Spanish Civil War*, p. 91.

writes mainly of what she herself is seeing and experiencing, giving her readers a strong sense of the veracity of her reports, 'As I write this... I can see a tremendous pall of black smoke', 'I could feel the intense heat from the tremendous conflagration.'[48] Her short succinct sentences are at times powerful in their simplicity. But it is in her observation of the small details of the tragedies in the lives of ordinary people that her perspective emerges most strongly. From Bilbao she writes of the peasants bringing their cattle into the capital, noticing even the calves with broken legs in the carts.[49] She writes of how the flocks in the fields and the herds of cattle are also being bombed, reporting how people streaming into Bilbao say that the roads are 'strewn with dead and dying cows.'[50] She tries to awake the voice of conscience in each reader, refusing to allow them a sense of comfortable detachment.

> Already the Nazi planes have dropped thirty big explosive bombs
> on the city. They dropped them when you in England were laughing
> and shouting. As I write the sirens, signalling a raid, are sounding
> again. I cannot tell what will happen.[51]

As the 'special correspondent' for *The Christian Science Monitor*, Kate Mangan wrote in-depth articles about the effects of the war on civilians and life in the rearguard. Occasionally she wrote for *The Manchester Guardian*, substituting for her friend, Kitty Bowler. Most of her reports date from 1937 and were based on first hand observations she made whilst working in Barcelona and Valencia.[52] Her first report however, was written from Madrid in January 1937 and reveals her talents for observation and a sense of humour.

> What are still the most expensive, and were the smartest and most
> exclusive cafés, with modern decorations, are unbearably crowded
> with soldiers on leave dressed in everything from Cossack hats and
> sheepskin coats to all sorts of ragged odds and ends. It is a perfect
> babel of languages. These are of the International Column, the
> heroes of the populace, who would give them everything free if they

---

48 Elizabeth Wilkinson, report from Bilbao, 9 May 1937, *Daily Worker*. Quoted in Fyrth &
     Alexander, *Women's Voices from the Spanish Civil War*, p. 272
49 Ibid., 29 April 1937.
50 Ibid., 12 May 1937
51 Ibid.
52 For more on Kate Mangan see Chapter 4.

had anything to give. The soldiers are like schoolboys. Plates piled
with buns are put before them which disappear in the twinkling
of an eye. They bewail the lack of chocolate and jam. Only certain
cafés even have any food at all. The German soldiers are older-
looking than the others and inspire great confidence. Members of
the International Column tell me, 'We all look so tough we frighten
each other!'[53]

Her reports reflect her determination to understand the practical
implementation of the political agenda in land reforms, education
and cultural activities. For example, a lengthy article for the *The
Manchester Guardian* entitled 'The Spanish Peasant', explains why the
timid land reforms first introduced by the Republican government
failed to make an impact. She includes clauses from a contract between
tenant and landowner in which the terms all favour the landowner.
The peasants had no option but to sign, despite the fact that the
majority could not read. She then describes in detail the programme of
collectivisation and training available for rural workers, enthusiastically reporting on the scheme for a travelling agricultural teaching
service.[54] Education is also the subject of a report for *The Christian
Science Monitor*, 'Education Taken to Spain's Trenches: Cultural Militia
Formed by Voluntary Teachers Who Like Work'.[55] Government policy
relating to the preservation of works of art features in her report
'Spanish Art Treasures Saved Despite Dangers of Civil War', which
describes the visit of dignitaries from the British art world to see what
was being done to safeguard Spain's cultural heritage in the major
cities.[56] As the war progresses, the articles reflect her changing
opinion regarding the Catalans in Barcelona. In June 1937, she sees
Barcelona as a 'frivolous' city, full of spies and 'agents provocateurs',
where the people seem indifferent to the conflict going on elsewhere
in Spain.[57] In August, she writes of how they are welcoming thousands
of refugees and writes, 'The eagerness to establish here a Utopia,
immediately, has something very touching about it.'[58] By November
1937, she writes from Barcelona with sympathy for the inhabitants,

---

53 Kate Mangan, writing as 'A Woman Visitor in Madrid, Special to *The Christian Science
   Monitor*, 20 January, 1937. My thanks to Charlotte Kurzke for copies of her mother's articles.
54 Kate Mangan, writing as 'A Correspondent' for *The Manchester Guardian*, 21 May 1937.
55 'Special to the *Christian Science Monitor*', 15 October 1937.
56 Ibid., 11 September 1937.
57 Ibid, 'Spain in War Time', 23 June 1937.
58 Ibid., 'Barcelona Outwardly Normal After Year of Civil War', 21 August 1937.

now 'at their wits' end to know how to provide for this endless stream of homeless and destitute people.'[59]

Winifred Bates was writing with the aim of forming a bond between her readers and the British nurses working in Spain. As she travelled round visiting the staff in the medical units she collected their stories and took photographs.[60] *Spain at War*, for example, used her photographs in 'British Nurse in Spain', a report she wrote about the Scottish nurse, Ann Murray, who was working on a hospital train near the front.[61] Reports by Winifred Bates were frequently to be found in pamphlets about Spain and in the bulletins of the Spanish Medical Aid Committee. The bulletins, for circulation amongst supporters with the request to hand it on to friends, often contained lengthy quotes from individual nurses.[62] In the bulletin for February 1938, Winifred Bates details the work of 'English Penny', Lilian Kenton, Ann Murray and others. Descriptions of the difficult working conditions and the suffering of civilians were recurrent themes. She was able to underline the self-sacrifice of the nurses by using their own words, as in this quotation from an un-named nurse.

> I used to miss the comfortable things that I have given up, the comfortable home in England, but I am beginning to miss them less now because they mean less to me than the comradeship and kindness I have met here.[63]

It was easy for readers to identify with the image of a 'nurse', the 'girl next door' perhaps, or a daughter, an ordinary girl in extraordinary circumstances who was doing her best. Readers could feel that their donations would be well spent in these capable hands. This was essential for the encouragement of a good response to the appeal for more funds, invariably included at the end of the bulletin. Nurses themselves also wrote reports of their work in the form of letters to

---

59 Ibid., 'Refugees Flock to Catalonia As Loyalists Move Capital', 13 November 1937.
60 See Winifred Bates Collection, Photographic Archive, IWM.
61 Winifred Bates on the work of Ann Murray 'British Nurse in Spain' *Spain at War*, Number 7, October 1938, pp. 244-247 (MML Box 25).
62 MML Boxes B5 and 29. Winifred Bates was not always cited as the source of the reports, and was probably responsible for many that had no named author.
63 Un-named nurse on the Aragon front. Spanish Medical Aid Committee, February Bulletin, 1938, MML Box B-5: H/6 p. 4. The frequent use of direct quotations, dialogue and reported speech by women has been mentioned earlier in this book and has been noted by others. See Selma Leydesdorff, Lusia Passerini and Paul Thompson (eds), *Gender and Memory* (Oxford University Press, 1996) Introduction p. 3 and the contribution from Richard Ely and Alyssa McCabe.

be used for fund-raising purposes. Reference has been made in the previous chapter to the letters of Madge Addy, who was writing from what became known as the 'Manchester Ward' in a Spanish hospital at Uclés to the Chairman of the North Manchester Spanish Medical Aid Committee. She would give news of their work and they would try to supply funds for the equipment and supplies she requested. As the war progressed, shortages became more acute.

> ...the Committee sent out a gross of Izal toilet rolls, but they cannot be used for the purpose they were intended for. The director said to me, 'Madge, we were very glad indeed for the paper.' I said, 'What paper?' and he said, 'Well it was really toilet paper, but we are using it in the office, come and see.' And at every desk, by each typewriter is a roll of Izal toilet paper, and the clerks are typing away on it! That will give you some idea of the shortage of everything.[64]

By February 1939, her pleas became desperate as supplies could not always get through. Hundreds of sick and wounded men were arriving from the front, the few clothes they had were infested with lice, and they had often been fighting in bare feet. 'You probably wonder where the things go to,' wrote Madge Addy, 'but you cannot take the shirt, pants and vests off them when they are discharged and send them away without, if you have them.'[65] The latest group however, had arrived with next to nothing, and would have to be discharged 'practically nude' as there were no more clothes to give them. Her patients were dying from lack of food and there was only one syringe in the hospital which she 'guarded with her life.' Her requests were simple, '...please ask Manchester to do its utmost to send money so that you can buy stuff necessary. Don't send anything for me, devote every penny to the hospital.'[66]

Amongst the women who wrote about Spain were some of the so-called 'intellectuals' of the day, although none achieved the fame of Stephen Spender or of W. H. Auden for their work relating to the Spanish war. As Barbara Brothers has found, 'In the narrative of Spanish Civil War writing, women became emblem, bibliographic entry,

64 Letter from Madge Addy, Uclés, Spain, to Doctor Nat Malimson, 17 January, 1939. MML Box D1: A/11,
65 Letter from Madge Addy, Uclés, February 20 1939, Spanish Medical Aid papers, Modern Records Centre, University of Warwick, MSS 946/539.
66 Ibid.

or footnote, equivalent to their role in the social script as attendant - wife or sweetheart.'[67] The writers Sylvia Townsend Warner and her partner, Valentine Ackland, were both leading members of their Communist Party branch in Dorset. They were involved in the founding of their local Left Book Club, and Sylvia was secretary of the Dorset Peace Council. They were ardently committed to the cause of the Spanish Republic, campaigning and fund-raising in a whirl of 'breathless non-stop activity'[68] In September 1936, a plan was put forward by Valentine Ackland in a letter to the *News Chronicle*. She wanted to form a group of self-funded volunteers, if possible with their own cars, 'with a knowledge of First Aid' and a 'willingness to help in every way possible the Loyalists' magnificent cause.' She proposed to take over her own 'small, fast, two seater.'[69] Her well-intentioned but somewhat haphazard scheme did not meet with approval at Communist Party headquarters and never came to fruition.

5.4 Sylvia Townsend Warner (left) and Valentine Ackland (right)
with their hostess, Ascensión, in Barcelona, 1936.

67 Barbara Brothers, 'Sylvia Townsend Warner and the Spanish Civil War', in Mary Lynn Broe and Angela Ingram (eds) *'Writing Against the Grain': Women's Writing in Exile* (University of North Carolina Press, Chapel Hill, 1989) p. 350, Also quoted in Ockerstrom, 'The Other Narratives', p. 16.
68 Mulford, *This Narrow Place*, p. 67.
69 Letter from Valentine Ackland to the Editor, *News Chronicle*, 14 September 1936. MML, Box 29A.

Nevertheless, she and Sylvia Townsend Warner managed to make alternative arrangements to go to Barcelona on their own, without the car, later on that month. Through personal contacts in Barcelona, they circumvented the normal official channels of both the Spanish Medical Aid Committee and the Communist Party in London. The three weeks they spent there attached to an ambulance unit, and their visit to the Writers Congress in Madrid the following year, were formative experiences for both of them, forming the basis of many articles and poems.[70]

In Barcelona they had been inspired by the revolutionary atmosphere of the city and touched by the 'naturally intellectual' capabilities of the Spanish people. Sylvia Townsend Warner was moved to write 'I don't think I have ever met so many congenial people in the whole of my life, liking overlept any little bounds of language.'[71] This view did not extend to some of the British people they met during their stay. In a joint report entitled, 'Party Position in Barcelona' addressed to 'Comrade Pollitt', they stated that they considered it their duty as Party members to return and report on the situation in Barcelona so that the situation might be remedied. They suggested the replacement of certain key personnel they considered to be either 'unfit' or 'failing' to fulfil their functions as responsible Party members. Some of their criticisms were based on what they termed the 'failure to adopt a satisfactory social attitude.' They noted that no stress was laid upon the importance of learning some elements of the Spanish language and, in their view, the situation could be summed up by saying that 'the atmosphere amongst the English in Barcelona' was 'the atmosphere of the English in India.'[72] These views, detrimental to the image of the Party in Spain, were not to feature in any of their published material. Also absent from their work are references to other aspects of Party politics. As Wendy Mulford notes, although Valentine Ackland makes brief mention of the POUM,[73] the revolutionary anti-Stalinist Communist group, as 'the smallest and noisiest of the three parties in Barcelona', nowhere in the writings of either of them on Spain is there any real attempt 'to engage' with issues relating to the Communist

---

70 It seems that their duties in Barcelona consisted mainly of office work rather than actual-
     ly driving ambulances.
71 Letter from Sylvia Townsend Warner to Elizabeth Wade White, 14 November 1936. Quoted
     in Mulford, *This Narrow Place*, p. 89.
72 MML Box C, File 7-1.
73 Partido Obrero de Unificación Marxista.

Party's involvement in the suppression of the POUM.[74] This she attributes to the general belief amongst Communist Party members that the repression had been justified because the 'POUM's utopian non-authoritarian politics spelled certain death to the Republic pitched against the military strength of the Fascist powers.'[75] However, it is also interesting to note that in their omission of such matters from their writing, they are reflecting the common tendency of women to focus their attention on aspects of the war other than the political divisions within the Left.

In the days of their first visit in the Autumn of 1936, such divisions had not erupted into armed fratricidal conflict. Their writings reflect not only their concerns about the broad political issues, but also their preoccupation with the sufferings of the Spanish people at grass-roots level. Valentine Ackland wrote bitterly of the indifference of the British Government and the Press in her poem 'Instructions from England, 1936', combining the themes of passion and sacrifice often associated with the Spanish war.

> Note nothing of why or how, enquire
> no deeper than you need
> into what set these veins on fire,
> note simply that they bleed.
>
> Spain fought before and fights again
> better no question why;
> note churches burned and popes in pain
> but not the men who die.[76]

An article for the *Left Review* written by Sylvia Townsend Warner on her return also has as its theme the struggle of the Spanish people, emphasising the role of the Church in their oppression. She describes how, since the outbreak of war, works of art had been removed from churches in Barcelona and stored in museums. [77] The systematically gutted churches had 'been cleaned out exactly as sick-rooms are

---

74 Valentine Ackland, *Daily Worker* October 1936. Quoted in Mulford, *This Narrow Place*, p. 95. See also review of *Spain To-Day* by Valentine Ackland in *Left Review* January 1937, p. 915.
75 Mulford, *This Narrow Place*, pp. 95-96.
76 Reprinted in *Spanish Front: Writers on the Civil War* edited by Valentine Cunningham (Oxford University Press, 1986) p. 230.
77 Sylvia Townsend Warner, 'Barcelona', *Left Review* October 1936.

cleaned out after a pestilence.'[78] She tells of a particular incident she herself witnessed, relating it to one individual Spanish girl to strengthen the readers' identification with events. It was reported that a religious plaque in the garden of a suburban villa was being used as a private praying centre. Two men were sent by the local Committee to smash it to bits with hammers, carrying out their work like 'decontaminating officers', watched by a small audience.

Among these lookers-on was a servant girl who had been suspected of worshipping before the plaque. She had a religious upbringing, she could neither read nor write. While the hammer-blows fell she watched with painful attention. Her face expressed profound animal fear. But it was not on the men that she fixed her terrified stare. It was the plaque itself which she watched with such bewildered and abject terror.[79]

The message behind these words is clarified by reading a letter in which Sylvia Townsend Warner discusses the relationship between Spanish people and the Church.

I have never seen churches so heavy and hulking and bullying, one can see at a glance that they have always been reactionary fortresses. I did not find a single person of any class who resented their being gutted, though we did find two domestic servants...who felt a certain uneasiness about it, as though God might pop out of those ruined choirs and grab them by the scruff. The not being able to read and write is the crux. A people naturally intellectual, and with a long standard of culture, have thrown off the taskmasters who enforced ignorance on them.[80]

The Writers' Congress took place in Madrid during July 1937, despite the bombardment.[81] Sylvia Townsend Warner and Valentine Ackland were amongst the delegates from Britain, one of the twenty-six countries to participate. Another British delegate, Stephen Spender,

78 Sylvia Townsend Warner, 'Barcelona', *Left Review* October 1936. p. 816.
79 Ibid.
80 Letter from Sylvia Townsend Warner to her friend Elizabeth Wade, November 14 1936, William Maxwell (ed.), *The Letters of Sylvia Townsend Warner* (Chatto & Windus, London, 1982) pp. 41-42. Also quoted in Ockerstrom, 'The Other Narratives', p. 193.
81 In full, the Second Congress of the International Association of Writers for the Defence of Culture.

they viewed as 'an irritating idealist, always hatching a wounded feeling', but this did not detract from the wonderful welcome they had received by ordinary people who greeted them with cries of 'Viva los intelectuales.'[82]

> We learned to hear ourselves spoken of as los intelectuales without dreading words usually so dubious in good intent, without feeling the usual embarrassment and defiant shrinking.[83]

She became captivated by what she termed the 'solid appreciation' of culture that permeated life in the Republic, flourishing despite poverty and illiteracy, believing that writers had at last been 'released from the old fear that by giving one's support as a representative of culture to a cause one had at heart one might be doing that cause more harm than good.[84] Her article on the Congress, 'What the Soldier Said,' explores attitudes to culture in the Republic largely through the story of one Spanish soldier-delegate. 'What the soldier said' she wrote, was 'borne out by a hundred speeches' that they heard from ordinary Spanish people, 'We will fetch peace and culture at the point of a bayonet for the sake of our own happiness and that of our children.' [85] Like many of the women writers on Spain, much of her other work took the lives of ordinary people as a focus, often describing individual responses.[86] In her poetry about Spain, lyrical descriptions of the countryside abound. Seeing the wounded soldiers convalescing on the coast at Benicasim inspired a poem which captured their vulnerability amidst the landscape.

---

82 For this quotation from Sylvia Townsend Warner and more details of the tensions with Spender see Mulford, This Narrow Place, pp. 98-99.
83 Sylvia Townsend Warner, 'What the Soldier Said', Time and Tide, August 1937. Also quoted in Mulford, This Narrow Place, p. 102.
84 Ibid. Also quoted in Maroula Joannou, 'Sylvia Townsend Warner in the 1930s', A Weapon in the Struggle: The Cultural History of the Communist Party in Britain edited by Andy Croft (Pluto Press, London, 1998) p. 96.
85 Ibid. For a more detailed analysis of the article see Ockerstrom, 'The Other Narratives', pp. 44-48.
86 Other examples of writings about ordinary people by women include the tragic story of Benita told by Kanty Cooper in The Uprooted: Agony and Triumph Among the Debris Of War (Quartet Books, London, 1979). Similarly, the American, Martha Gellhorn, well known for her work on Spain is quoted as saying, 'All politicians are bores and liars and fakes. I talk to people.' Obituary by Veronica Horwell, The Guardian, 17 February 1998, p. 18. Other examples by Sylvia Townsend Warner, include 'The Drought Breaks', in which she views life through the eyes of a Spanish woman whose town has been taken by the Nationalists, her husband shot and their children taken away by nuns. Life and Letters Today, Summer 1937. Reprinted in Cunningham, Spanish Front, pp. 244-247. The efforts of Spanish peasants in the Republican Army to gather in crops from No Man's Land whilst under fire is described in 'Soldiers and Sickles in Spain', The Countryman October 1937 pp. 78-79. Peasants and the harsh life they endured were also to form core themes in her novel, After the Death of Don Juan, a political allegory examining the oppression and exploitation of the peasants by the Church and the aristocracy in 18th Century Spain, published in 1938.

Here for a little we pause.
The air is heavy with sun and salt and colour.
On palm and lemon-tree, on cactus and oleander
a dust of dust and salt and pollen lies.
And the bright villas
sit in a row like perched macaws,
and rigid and immediate yonder
the mountains rise.

And it seems to me we have come
into a bright-painted landscape of Acheron.
For along the strand
in bleached cotton pyjamas, on rope-soled tread,
wander the risen-from-the-dead,
the wounded, the maimed, the halt.
Or they lay bare their hazarded flesh to the salt
air, the recaptured sun,
or bathe in the tideless sea, or sit fingering the sand.

But narrow is this place, narrow is this space
of garlanded sun and leisure and colour, of return
to life and release from living. Turn
(Turn not!) sight inland:
there, rigid as death and unforgiving, stand
the mountains - and close at hand.[87]

Both Valentine Ackland and Sylvia Townsend Warner contributed
to one particularly interesting publication designed to stimulate
public interest in the war, *Authors Take Sides on the Spanish War*.[88]
The pamphlet was originally the brain-child of Nancy Cunard after she
had visited Spain in the Autumn of 1936. Nancy Cunard was a perhaps
a 'wild card' as far as propaganda for the Republican cause was
concerned. Rich, unconventional, and individualistic, aptly named
'Brave Poet, Indomitable Rebel'.[89] A friend, Charles Duff, thought that
'she could not be regarded as a "political" person, notwithstanding all

---

87 Sylvia Townsend Warner, 'Benicasim', *Left Review* March 1938. Reprinted in Cunningham,
    Spanish Front, p. 243.
88 *Authors Take Sides on the Spanish War* (Left Review, London, 1937).
89 Hugh Ford (ed.), *Nancy Cunard: Brave Poet, Indomitable Rebel 1896-1965* (Chilton Book
    Co., Philadelphia, New York, London, 1968).

her associations or words', because despite being frequently labelled as 'red', she had little grasp of political ideology, finding systems of any kind repugnant.[90] Another friend, Solita Solano, was aware of an almost elemental force in the personality of Nancy Cunard, and believed that she fought for causes in a 'state of fury in which, in order to defend, she attacked every windmill in a landscape of windmills.' [91] Passionately convinced that the Republicans were on the side of the people in their fight for freedom, on her return from Spain she began to write a stream of articles which were featured in a diversity of publications, including the Associated Negro Press, Sylvia Pankhurst's *New Times*, and Charles Duff's *Spanish Newsletter*.[92] She then came up with the novel idea of letting the public know the views of British writers regarding the war in Spain. She asked them,

> Are you for, or against, the legal Government and the People of Republican Spain? Are you for, or against, Franco and Fascism? For it is impossible any longer to take no side.[93]

Her unashamedly biased question to the writers of Britain for *Authors Take Sides on the Spanish War* brought a stream of replies, overwhelmingly in favour of the Republic. Her division of the 148 replies into 'FOR the Government', 'AGAINST the Government' and 'NEUTRAL?' has been challenged as the object of 'rigging'.[94] How many writers, it has been asked, were intentionally excluded from the poll or chose not to reply at all, and what did such silence signify? Was the 'Neutral?' category engineered to avoid having more than a paltry five replies for the Right? Nevertheless, despite all the conjectures as to the numerical details, the popularity of the pamphlet, and the 127 replies 'For' the Government stand as testimony to the success of Nancy Cunard's effort to inform the public about issues relating to the war in Spain. Women writers were fairly well represented in the pamphlet.[95]

---

90 Charles Duff, 'Nancy Cunard: The Enigma of a Personality' in Ford, *Brave Poet, Indomitable Rebel*, p. 188.
91 Solita Solano in Ford, *Brave Poet, Indomitable Rebel*, p. 76.
92 For more details on the life of Nancy Cunard, including her work for the cause of racial equality, see Anne Chisolm, *Nancy Cunard* (Sidgewick and Jackson, London, 1979).
93 'The Question', *Authors Take Sides* (no page numbers).
94 Valentine Cunningham 'Neutral?: 1930s Writers and Taking Sides' in Frank Gloversmith (ed.), *Class, Culture and Social Change: A New View of the 1930s* (Harvester Press, Brighton, Sussex, 1980) p. 46. The 149th reply from George Bernard Shaw arrived late and remained as 'unclassified' inside the front cover.
95 *See Footnote opposite.*

Nancy Cunard's own contribution was, whilst unequivocally anti-Fascist, expressed in passionately humanitarian terms.

Spain is not 'politics' but life; its immediate future will affect every human who has a sense of what life and its facts mean, who has respect for himself and humanity.[96]

The Scottish writer, Naomi Mitchison, responded with similar conviction.

There is no question for any decent, kindly man or woman, let alone a poet or writer who *must* be more sensitive. We have to be against Franco and Fascism and for the people of Spain, and the future of gentleness and brotherhood which ordinary men and women want all over the world.[97]

Formerly a pacifist 'in the fullest sense', Rosamund Lehmann wrote that she had come to believe that 'non-resistance can be - in this case, is - a negative, sterile, even a destructive thing.' As a mother she felt 'convinced that upon the outcome of the struggle in Spain depends the future, the very life of my children.'[98] Vera Brittain, in contrast, was in the 'Neutral?' category, for although detesting 'Fascism and all that it stands for', she did not think it would be destroyed by fighting.

As an uncompromising Pacifist, I hold war to be a crime against humanity, whoever fights it and against whomever it is fought.[99]

It is perhaps interesting to note that Eleanor Smith, the only woman included in the 'Against the Government' category, also emphasised humanitarian concerns, albeit with irony.

---

95 In addition to those mentioned here, women contributors include Jenny Ballou, Pearl Binder, Kay Boyle, Margaret Cole, Carmel Haden Guest, Norah C. James, Storm Jameson, Rose Macaulay, Ethel Mannin, Elinor Mordaunt, Louise Morgan, Willa Muir, Sylvia Pankhurst, Naomi Royde Smith, Christina Stead, Helen Waddell, Rebecca West, Antonia White and Amabel Williams Ellis. Ruby M Ayres and Vita Sackville West were classed as 'Neutral?'
96 Nancy Cunard, *Authors Take Sides.*
97 Naomi Mitchison, op. cit.
98 Rosamund Lehmann, op. cit. Rosamund Lehmann also began a 'Books for Spain' appeal for the wounded, to be sent out by Spanish Medical Aid. *New Statesman & Nation*, 21 August, 1937. Re-printed in Cunningham, *Spanish Front*, pp. 230-231.
99 Vera Brittain, op. cit.

I was delighted to receive your unprejudiced brochure. Naturally, I am a warm adherent of General Franco's, being, like all of us, a humanitarian. The destruction of so many beautiful objects, and the massacre of so many innocent persons, makes one pity profoundly the ignorant red masses - subsidised by Russia - in Spain. Do you not agree?[100]

In contrast to the women quoted above, Ethel Mannin of the ILP adopted the more rigid form of party political discourse.

I am for the legal Government of Spain inasmuch as I am against Franco and Fascism, and that passionately, but with the defeat of Franco I hope for very much more than a mere Republican Spain (with the old bourgeois capitalist Government still in power) - for the establishment of a Workers' State, not on communist (USSR) lines, but CNT - FAI (Anarcho-Syndicalist).[101]

Nancy Cunard returned to Barcelona in the Autumn of 1938, finding 'everything could be summed up now by that terrible word "hunger".'[102] As the refugees began to stream into France 1939, she went to the border to report for the *Manchester Guardian*. She sent a report to them every two or three days for two weeks and everything she wrote appeared in print.[103] In recent years, it seems we have been inundated with filmed news reports showing refugees in identical conditions to those she was attempting to describe in her articles. The scale of the exodus must have been more difficult to imagine then.

It rained for two days, and the litter of rags and filth lies sodden on the ground. Fresher rags drape the rocks along the road. A dead ass lies on one side. A van has fallen into the ravine and has caught against a tree.... People are camping out everywhere in the open fields. You cannot try even to assess their thousands.[104]

---

100 Eleanor Smith, op. cit.
101 Ethel Mannin, op. cit. See also a longer article by Ethel Mannin, 'The Crime of the Arms Embargo' in the pamphlet *Spain and Us* published by the Holborn & West Central London Committee for Spanish Medical Aid. MML, Box 29, F/1.
102 Nancy Cunard, 'Spain' in Ford, *Brave Poet, Indomitable Rebel*, p. 168.
103 Letter from the news editor, W. P. Crozier to Nancy Cunard, 7 February 1939. Quoted by Ford, *Brave Poet, Indomitable Rebel*, p. 253.
104 Nancy Cunard, 'Contrasts on French Frontier: Clearing Up on the French Side: Misery Remains Over Border', *Manchester Guardian* Friday, 3 February 1939. Re-printed in *The Guardian Book of the Spanish Civil War* edited by R. H. Haigh, D. S. Morris, A. R. Peters (Wildwood House, Aldershot, 1987) pp. 298-99.

She sent an urgent telegram to the *Manchester Guardian* on 30 January. 'Beseech you open fund immediately in Guardian for possibly as much as half a million starving Spanish refugees pouring in stop situation catastrophic.'[105] Hundreds of pounds were raised in the appeal which ran in the *News Chronicle*, the *Daily Herald* and the *Manchester Guardian*.[106] As Anne Chisolm has observed, Nancy Cunard could not bring herself to write objective reports about the tragic last act being played out at the border.[107] 'Franco' wrote Nancy Cunard, 'stands condemned and judged for eternity.'[108]

One British woman journalist is known to have risked the consequences of being exposed as a spy. Sheila Grant Duff's own account of her short visit to Spain indicates that she lacked the detachment necessary to be a success as a secret agent, although she did manage to fulfil her mission on this particular occasion. The grand-daughter of British aristocrats, she had been influenced by the feminist and social reformer, Eva Hubbock.[109] At the age of twenty-one, she had become the first British woman to work as a foreign correspondent, covering Hitler's take over of the Saar in 1935 and then reporting from Prague. In 1937, the Spanish government wanted more information on the situation in Málaga, which by then had fallen to Franco. Ed Mowrer of the *Chicago Daily News* was willing to help but his paper was too well known for its anti-Franco line to send any of the staff correspondents. He asked Sheila Grant Duff to undertake the task, because, 'not altogether flatteringly' she wrote, he thought of her 'as someone who might slip in unnoticed.' She was to find out how Republican prisoners were being treated, whether Málaga harbour was being fortified, and gather information relating to the whereabouts of Arthur Koestler, who had been arrested as a spy whilst working for the *News Chronicle*. She made her way to Málaga from North Africa, where she contacted the American consul and was invited to dine. The other guests were Nationalist officers and conversation was 'exclusively

---

105 Quoted in Chisolm, *Nancy Cunard*, p. 251. Her estimate of half a million was close to figures calculated later.
106 Nancy Cunard, 'Spain' in Ford, *Brave Poet, Indomitable Rebel*, p. 170. See also 'S.O.S. - They are doomed to starve unless - An appeal by Nancy Cunard' in *Voice of Spain; Incorporating Spain at War* January 1939, pp. 19-25. MML Box 25.
107 Chisolm, *Nancy Cunard*, p. 253.
108 Quoted in Chisolm, *Nancy Cunard*, p. 251. For more on these articles by Nancy Cunard see Ockerstrom, 'The Other Narratives', pp. 151-161.
109 Sheila Grant Duff was born in 1913. Her grandfathers were Sir Mountstuart Grant Duff, the Liberal MP, and Sir John Lubbock, the first Lord Avebury. Her father died at the Battle of the Aisne in 1914.

about the horrors of Red rule.'[110] When her fellow guests conducted her back to the hotel, which turned out to be Franco's staff headquarters, they insisted on producing photographs to illustrate their stories. One of them became angry when she was unwilling to look at these pictures.

> Suddenly one of them looked at his watch. 'Good heavens!' he said, 'Twenty minutes to midnight! Do you want to come to the execution with us?' Silence fell and all three looked at me. I felt confronted, as I had never been confronted before, with a stark choice the consequences of which would stay with me for ever. For a young journalist it would be a sensational coup; for a spy it was precisely one of the things I had been sent to find out; for a human being, it would be to stand and watch people whom I regarded as friends and allies being put to death in cold blood. I knew I would never be able to live with this. I did not go.[111]

The following morning, her behaviour aroused even more suspicions. Thinking of Prague, the leaden skies and the snow piled in sodden heaps in the gutters, she let slip a few ill-chosen words to the same group of officers.

> How can you have a civil war when you have a country like this where the skies are blue and the sun is warm in February and the swallows are here already? 'You are talking like a Red,' said the angry one of the previous night, 'May I see your passport?'[112]

Her passport was only three days old, she had replaced the old one because it had a Soviet visa in it. The officers were due at the front, but would initiate a full investigation of the matter in Seville. She spent the day collecting the information she needed and caught the first bus to La Linea the next morning, walking across the border to arrive 'trembling but safe' in Gibraltar, perhaps not a woman cut out for a further career as a spy.[113]

Many women who were writing about Spain were also working to raise awareness of the war through membership of organisations from

---

110 Sheila Grant Duff, *The Parting of Ways: A Personal Account of the Thirties* (Peter Owen, London, 1982) pp. 149.
111 Ibid., pp. 149-50.
112 Ibid., p. 150.
113 Ibid., p. 151.

local to international level. There were numerous instances in which they held multiple memberships. Sylvia Townsend Warner and Elizabeth Wilkinson, for example, were both supporters of the Women's World Committee Against War and Fascism in addition to their activities in other groups.[114] Monica Whately, the LCC councillor for Limehouse, not only contributed to *Woman To-Day*, published by the British Section of the Women's World Committee Against War and Fascism, but was also the Honorary Secretary of the Six Point Group, which had contact both with the WWCAWF and with Spanish feminists. An entry in their annual report for 1936-37 explains how this was brought about.

> Miss Emma Goldman the famous American Anarchist who has suffered imprisonment and expatriation for her opinions gave an address at a Group Meeting on 31 May 1937 at the house of Miss Mary Grew the well-known actress. Miss Goldman has lived for some time in Spain, and her subject was 'The Emancipation of Spanish Women.' As a result the Group is in touch with a really heroic society of Spanish feminists, who have maintained the publication of their women's paper in Valencia in spite of the war around them and have done marvellous educational work among the peasants in the villages... They wished to establish contact with experienced feminists from other lands and learn methods from their advice and experience.[115]

A special appeal was later sent out to members to raise funds for Spanish feminists who were in a refugee camp in France, 'in order that they might live to carry on their work for equality for their sex.'[116] For this they were attacked by Fascist women through the pages of *Action* in an article entitled 'Feminists Duped by Reds'. They stated, 'We women of the British Union believe that the supporters of the feminist movement prefer dabbling in international politics to ventilating the legitimate grievances of their own countrywomen.'[117]

British readers of the anarchist publication, *Spain and the World* were also being informed about Spanish anarchist feminists. The aims

---

[114] Elizabeth Wilkinson was also the Secretary of the Spanish Women's Committee for Help to Spain, a grouping of women's organisations that brought together working parties of women, some of them unemployed, to make clothing for Spain. Jim Fyrth, *The Signal Was Spain: The Aid Spain Movement in Britain 1936-39* (Lawrence & Wishart, London, 1986) p. 200.
[115] Six Point Group Annual Reports, 1936-37, p. 4.
[116] Ibid., 1938-39, p. 6.
[117] Quoted by Martin Durham in 'Gender and the British Union of Fascists' *Journal of Contemporary History* vol.27, 1992, p.521.

and activities of 'Mujeres Libres' were featured in a full page spread, 'Women in the Revolution' in August 1937.[118] Optimism prevailed in the slogans of 'Mujeres Libres' reprinted in the article, including the unusually assertive 'Women: Your Efforts Will Decide Victory.' Ethel Mannin's contribution to the same paper the following year reflected the deterioration of the anarchist position in Spain, although she still continued to hope that the masses would find a path to freedom 'beyond the reach of governments and their hypocrisy and corruption.'

> We have seen how British and French 'democracy' have betrayed the Spanish people in their struggle for Freedom against Fascism. We have been warned. There is no spoon long enough to make it possible to eat with the devil with impunity.[119]

In contrast, members of the Women's International League for Peace and Freedom were attempting to apply pressure to bring peace through official government channels. The Quaker, Edith Pye, was a key link between the women of the League and Spain. Her work in Spain has been referred to in the previous chapter, but as an intermediary at international level, she was providing the eye-witness reports that stimulated League policies on Spain. Concerns regarding refugee relief and civilian evacuation were placed first on the list of proposals sent by the Women's League to the British Prime Minister and the Foreign Secretary. The League proposed that an offer of a Refugee Commissioner be made to the Spanish Government to 'use every opportunity to mitigate the suffering of the people. Further suggestions included the strengthening of the Non-intervention Agreement under an impartial and independent body, and the offer of mediation by League of Nations Commissioners in the negotiation of a peace settlement.[120] It is possible that a degree of cynicism amongst members due to the lack of success of these and other similar efforts may have affected their response to a proposal put forward by the independent MP, Eleanor Rathbone. In September 1937, she contacted the Women's League amongst other groups, appealing for signatories

---

118 *Spain and the World*, Freedom Press, 25 August 1937.
119 Ethel Mannin, *Spain and the World*, 30 September 1938, p. 3.
120 The letter from the Women's International League, 8 December 1936, (LSE Archive, WILPF 1/12) was issued following discussion of a letter from the Women's Peace Crusade to the Secretary of State for Foreign Affairs on 2 December 1936, in which similar ideas had been put forward but refugees were not mentioned. Minutes of WILPF, 8 December 1936, 292 (LSE Archive WILPF 1/12).

to a telegram which was to be sent to the leaders on both sides of the war, imploring the victors 'to show mercy in their hour of triumph.[121] The minutes of the Women's League meeting held the following month note that the telegram had not been sent as 'it had been found impossible to collect enough signatures to make it effective.'[122] The reasons for this are not recorded.

Women from established parliamentary and party political circles who had been to Spain were declaring their views in no uncertain terms through a variety of channels. Isabel Brown went to Spain as a member of a delegation from the British Anti-fascist Committee in August 1936, and as an ardent communist, was amused to find herself entitled 'Lady Brown' in the Catalan press.[123] Passing through the countryside between Barcelona and Madrid, she almost wept at the sight of the poverty stricken villages, where the defences consisted at times of a few sandbags and a boy of about 12 with a shotgun.[124] As evidence of foreign intervention, the group brought back Italian para- chutes and two German thermite bombs, only realising that the latter were still live after they had carried them back and delivered them to the War Office in Britain.[125] Her visit supplied fuel for the fire of her convictions about the need to campaign on behalf of the Republic.[126]

Women MPs of the all-party Parliamentary Spain Committee, the Duchess of Atholl, Eleanor Rathbone, and Ellen Wilkinson, visited Spain on various occasions. In the Spring of 1937, they went to Spain in an all-women delegation, together with Dame Rachel Crowdy, a representative of the League of Nations.[127] Helen Grant recorded meeting them in her diary. Collectively, they must have appeared a formidable force for she noted that the National Joint Committee representative, Geoffrey Garratt, referred to them as the 'monstrous

---

121 WILPF Minutes, September 1937, 403 (LSE Archive, WILPF 1/13).
122 WILPF Minutes, 12 October 1937, 410 (LSE Archive, WILPF 1/13).
123 Isabel Brown, IWM 844. Other members of the delegation included Viscount Hastings, Seymour Cocks MP and William Dobbie MP.
124 May Hill, *Red Roses for Isabel* (May Hill, London, 1982) p. 69.
125 Isabel Brown, IWM 13784. Also in Hill, *Red Roses for Isabel*, p. 70.
126 According to Ted Willis, at meetings Isabel Brown could make the audience weep, 'play- ing on their emotions like a piano.' IWM 13818. For more on Isabel Brown see Chapter 3. Not all those who went to Spain from within political circles were so well known, but nevertheless, they could contribute to the work of raising public awareness. Margaret Stewart, for example, secretary to the Liberal MP, Wilfred Roberts, wrote a pamphlet after visiting Barcelona, entitled *Reform Under Fire: Social Progress in Spain 1931-38* (Issued by New Fabian Research Bureau, published by Victor Gollancz, London, May 1938).
127 Dame Rachel Crowdy was the Head of Social Question Section, League of Nations. She was a trained nurse who had commanded VADs in France and Belgium during the First World War.

Regiment of Women.'[128] The group went to Barcelona, Valencia and Madrid, visiting hospitals and schools, and meeting prisoners of war. Kate Mangan, who was working in the press office in Valencia at the time, was given the task of looking after them during their visit to the city. Her impression was that they were 'determined to investigate facts and no nonsense about it.'

> The Duchess of Atholl was stout and wore a coat and skirt of some rough durable material like the upholstery of a railway carriage. Eleanor Rathbone was earnest and austere, interested in prison reform. Ellen Wilkinson was small, wore high heels, had red hair and was the only one who used face-powder.[129]

They also met many of the political leaders, and for the Duchess of Atholl, the most interesting of these encounters was with Dolores Ibárruri, widely known as 'La Pasionaria'. The Duchess had been a little hesitant about attending the meeting with the most famous female Communist MP '...as her nickname suggested to me a rather over-emotional young person.' Nevertheless, persuaded by Ellen Wilkinson, she agreed.

> I have never ceased to be glad that I did so, for the only person with whom I felt La Pasionaria could be compared was the woman I had always regarded as the greatest actress I had seen, Eleonora Duse. She swept into the room like a queen, yet she was a miner's daughter married to a miner - a woman who had had the sorrow of losing six out of eight children. I could understand nothing that she said, and she talked with great rapidity, but to look and listen was pleasure enough for me...[130]

This is indeed a remarkable statement from a 'true blue' Conservative about the most vividly 'red' icon of the Spanish war. As far apart as they could possibly be in both terms of image and experience, on the question of the war in Spain they could share at least some common ground.

Ellen Wilkinson believed that their visit had been appreciated in

---

128 Helen Grant, 'Spain, 25 March – 18 April 1937' p. 70. For more details of this visit see Sheila Hetherington, *Katharine Atholl 1874-1960: Against the Tide* (Aberdeen University Press, 1991, first published 1989) pp. 182-185.
129 Mangan, 'The Good Comrade', p. 414.
130 Quotations from Hetherington, *Katharine Atholl*, p. 185.

Spain, that 'It comforted the Spanish women that someone had come from the outside world... to witness the smouldering ruins of workers' areas where not one home is left standing.' The destruction she saw provoked her to write, 'my most personal memory of Madrid is the feeling of helpless choking rage as the shells fell, dealing death with their blind, stupid powers.'[131] In December of the same year she returned to Spain with Clement Attlee and Philip Noel-Baker.[132] She met many prominent leaders of the Republic and was photographed with them, standing out as a small, lone female figure amongst the large group of dignitaries.[133] The journey was not without hazards, but her reactions to these difficulties caused Philip Noel-Baker to regard her as 'a splendid spirit with a splendid soul.'[134] On the evening of her return to England she was on a platform appealing for funds to buy food and milk for Spanish children.

Do you really expect us to go to Spain and return impartial?
No longer is it a civil war, it is a fight between right and wrong.[135]

Just as Ellen Wilkinson was fired by her visits to Spain, the Duchess of Atholl, on her return from Spain with the women's delegation, set to work to write a book, *Searchlight on Spain*. In this carefully researched study she explored the issues that had led to the war, reviewed the current situation in Spain, and commented on the international aspects of the conflict.[136] Initially she had become involved with the war to help refugees, but as she learned more, she also came to see the dangers to British strategic interests should victory go to a dictator indebted to Hitler and Mussolini.[137] It was her conviction that the duty of an MP was to firstly 'try to get at the facts', and then 'to make them known.'[138] By publishing her book as a 'Penguin' paperback, she ensured that it reached a wide audience. The first edition of her book was published in the summer of 1938 and sold out

---

131 Ellen Wilkinson quoted by Betty D. Vernon, *Ellen Wilkinson,1891-1947* (Croom Helm, London, 1982) p. 164. Details of source not given.
132 The other member of the delegation was John Dugdale.
133 *Nuestro Combate: Our Fight, The Journal of the XV International Brigade* December 1937-January 1938, number 35, p. 5.
134 Interview with Philip Noel-Baker, *Daily Herald*, 10 December, 1937. Quoted in Vernon, *Ellen Wilkinson*, p. 165.
135 Ellen Wilkinson, quoted in Vernon, *Ellen Wilkinson*, p. 165. No further details of source given.
136 Duchess of Atholl, *Searchlight on Spain* (Penguin Books, Harmondsworth, England, 1938).
137 Ibid., pp. 316-337.
138 Ibid., p. xii.

within a week. After two further editions, over 300,000 copies had been sold and translations were published in German, French and Spanish.[139] Two contrasting reactions to her book are quoted in Sheila Hetherington's biography of the Duchess.[140] Both draw attention to her gender and social position, one to refute the claims that she had communist sympathies, and the other to vilify her as a traitor to the values of her class. The former was written by a Labour MP, Tom Johnston, who, whilst defending the sincerity of the Duchess, was seemingly also revelling in the discomfort to the Tories occasioned by such an apparently frail member of their own ranks.

> The 'Red Duchess' is a complete misnomer. She is a quiet, unobtru-
> sive, rather pale and tired-looking old lady. She possesses infinite
> courage of conviction. She is absolutely and fanatically sincere.
> What she believes she says. There is no facing both ways about Her
> Grace of Atholl. And now she has fallen foul of the Tory machine
> at Westminster. She has the powerful landed aristocracy in West
> Perthshire [her constituency] dancing with fury.[141]

In *The Patriot,* Franco's supporters viewed her book as 'a farrago of pernicious absurdity,' penned by a woman who should have known better.

> ...those who know the chivalry and noble nature of that great
> gentleman and patriot, Franco, must boil with indignation at this
> foul aspersion... and deplore that any woman of culture and
> position can repeat those infamous lies.[142]

Also published in 1938 was Eleanor Rathbone's book *War Can Be Averted.*[143] Apart from speaking in the House and giving much of her time and energy to various groups connected with Spain, she, like the Duchess, decided to publish her views on the policy of Non-intervention. As part of her defence of the notion of collective

---

139 Hetherington, *Katharine Atholl*, p. 197. A book written in response to *Searchlight on Spain*,
    entitled *Daylight on Spain*, written by C. Sarolea, had to be subsidised and distributed
    free. See Michael Alpert, 'Humanitarianism and Politics in the British Response to the
    Spanish Civil War, 1936-9' *European History Quarterly* 1984, vol.14, part 4, pp. 423-439, p. 437.
140 Hetherington, *Katharine Atholl*.
141 Quoted in Hetherington, *Katharine Atholl*, p. 197. No further details of source given.
142 Ibid.
143 Eleanor Rathbone, *War Can Be Averted: The Achievability of Collective Security* (Victor
    Gollancz, London, 1938).

security, she examined the practical application of the Non-intervention Agreement. She concluded that not only were suffering and injustice being ignored by inflicting this policy on a friendly Government,
but that the League of Nations was being further weakened by its lack
of support for Spain against foreign aggression. Her approach to the
subject was modest, but the result was a clear and concise analysis,
suitable for a wide readership. The reservations she felt about her
own abilities were expressed in the preface, along with her aim to
reach the 'ordinary citizen'.

> While writing this book, I have been beset by the conviction that it
> should have been written by someone else - someone with greater
> knowledge of armaments, international economics, international
> law and the history of the Empire and the League. I have tried to
> make up for this by a careful citing of authorities whenever these
> were not obvious. But a small compensation for not being an expert
> in these questions is that one can act, so to speak, as a foolometer
> to one's own book; can be sure one is answering - whether convinc-
> ingly or not - the difficulties which trouble intelligent and observant
> but non-expert enquirers, in language they can understand in a
> book they can afford to buy and find time to read.[144]

Amidst the dispassionately reasoned arguments in her book, her
feelings for the Spanish people suddenly erupt with volcanic force.

> Think of those men and women, with centuries of oppression behind
> them, bred in bitter poverty and ignorance, deserted by most of
> their natural leaders, delivered over defenceless to their enemies
> by the democracies which should have aided them. Think of them
> as I saw them last April in Madrid and Valencia, men and women,
> young and old, without a trace of fear or dejection in their faces
> though bombs were crashing a few yards away and taking their
> daily toll of victims, going about their daily business in cheerful
> serenity, building up a system of social services that would have
> been a credit to any nation at war, submitting to unaccustomed
> discipline, composing their party differences, going to the front or
> sending their men to the front as though to a fiesta, unstimulated -
> most of them - by hope of Heaven or fear of Hell, yet willing to leave

---

144 Eleanor Rathbone, *War Can Be Averted: The Achievability of Collective Security,* pp. vi-vii.

the golden Spanish sunshine and all the lovely sights and sounds of spring and go into the blackness of death or the greater blackness of cruel captivity without a thought of surrender.[145]

Mary Stocks, Eleanor Rathbone's biographer, viewed this passage as one in which Eleanor Rathbone had been 'a little carried away' by what she had seen in Spain.[146] Described as an old-fashioned Victorian and 'prudent revolutionary', Eleanor Rathbone has been regarded as a person who rarely deployed the emotional weapons in the reformer's armoury as 'emotionalism was not to her taste.'[147] In the writings of others, the degree of intensity in the passage quoted above was not unusual. If it had been penned by Sylvia Townsend Warner, or even by Ellen Wilkinson, well known for her passionate temperament, it would have caused little surprise. But Eleanor Rathbone too, like so many others, was deeply touched by what she had experienced in Spain. The 'spirit' of resistance engendered by prolonged bombardment was to become a familiar theme of the Second World War, but in Spain, this phenomenon of civilian fortitude was being seen on a grand scale for the first time. Few visitors remained unimpassioned when immersed in the rich ferment of a vividly contrasting culture, an emotively warm welcome, and the inspiring heroism of a people. Eleanor Rathbone's contact with Spanish people could certainly have been the inspiration for some of the conclusions she came to in her book.

It is only when people are 'all lit up' by the flame of great purpose and have 'forgotten themselves' that they are capable of the kind of effort that is going to be necessary to stop aggression and prevent Fascism from overrunning the world.[148]

Whilst in Madrid, both Eleanor Rathbone and the Duchess of Atholl made radio broadcasts on behalf of refugee children.[149] Foreign visitors were often asked to participate in this form of propaganda, and many were pleased to do so, although Ernest Hemingway

---

145 Ibid., p. 130. Quoted in Mary D. Stocks, *Eleanor Rathbone: A Biography* (Victor Gollancz, London, 1949) p. 243.
146 Stocks, *Eleanor Rathbone*, p. 243.
147 Brian Harrison, *Prudent Revolutionaries: Portraits of British Feminists Between the Wars* (Clarendon Press, Oxford, 1987) p. 124.
148 Rathbone, *War Can Be Averted*, p. 168.
149 Hetherington, *Katharine Atholl*, p. 185.

apparently declined.[150] Frida Stewart was only too pleased to stand in for several broadcasts when the British commentator was taken ill with jaundice. 'Aquí la voz de España' the broadcasts began, then she would start to speak from a dark little room high in the 'Telefónica' building in the city centre.[151] She wrote to her mother hoping that she would be able to hear the broadcasts.

> There are great things in the offing and we expect to get news of a big push this week. Everyone is keyed up and excited. Our late broadcast last night was cancelled owing to extra war news being put over... The 7pm one went all right we fondly hope. It is a peculiarly terrifying experience and one that won't get easier - there's something so remorseless and unresponsive about a mike! The wavelength is 30.45 short wave, in case you can borrow or steal a set for Monday.[152]

Broadcasts tended to take the rather rigid forms dictated by the demands of wartime propaganda. The fragile transcripts of some of Frida Stewart's speeches still survive, bearing the official censorship stamp for foreign press releases from the 'Oficina de Información y Prensa'. At times, however, she appealed to those at home on a more intimate level. Describing her impressions as a newcomer to Madrid, she tried to make people in England visualise the devastation that had been caused by the bombardment.

> It gave me an acute sense of depression, and of the futility of this method of war, which does not achieve anything - except to anger the people to further resistance when they see their precious city and their houses destroyed. I wonder how Londoners would feel if they saw Piccadilly in the state of the Puerta del Sol, which is the Madrid equivalent? I thought how if, instead of walking down the Gran Via, towards the University City of Madrid, I was walking down Shaftesbury Avenue towards the British Museum and it was the cinemas and theatres of west central London that were smashed by

---

150 Winifred Bates broadcast to America from Barcelona during the first months of the war, Tameside 232. In her autobiography, Leah Manning writes of broadcasting to Britain when she was in Bilbao, *A Life for Education* (Gollancz, London, 1970) p. 128. The comment on Hemingway is taken from the memoirs of the Scottish Communist MP, Willie Gallacher, and is quoted in Hetherington, *Katharine Atholl*, p. 185.
151 Frida Stewart, unpublished memoirs, p.167.
152 Frida Stewart, letter to Mother, 5 July 1937, papers of Frida Stewart.

shrapnel and spattered with bullets, instead of the cinemas of Western Madrid? And how if it were the new buildings of London University that had been bombed and ruined instead of Madrid's new University? I am sure if we could in England realise what it means to have your home town bombed and all the most precious things in it destroyed, we should have been roused to do more for Spain, especially for Madrid.[153]

In another broadcast, she talked about her visit to the trenches at the front which ran through the buildings of University City. The four or five impressive faculty buildings that had been completed before the outbreak of war now were largely in ruins, but one of the main themes of the broadcast was to emphasise that, despite all the difficulties, educational aspirations endured. Her report, 'University City', is worthy of inclusion here at some length because the immediacy of her description brings life in these trenches into sharp focus. Her words surely could not have failed to capture the attention of listeners, especially those with memories of the First World War and those, like the people she knew in Cambridge, who would have pricked up their ears at the mention of the word 'University'.

After passing down two streets leading to the University, we turn into a garden, where there is an entrance to the trenches. We pass through and walk along the trench, ducking at one or two places that are more exposed, hearing an odd bullet come and stab the wall with an angry little knock. Finally we come round the corner which brings us into full view of the 'Casa de Medicina'. How very fine it is! From here it seems hardly to be touched, its fine proportions and its golden yellow brick walls are not harmed, and even the windows are not all shattered. 'Wait till you see inside'... There are huge heaps of rubble lying around in one corner of the ceiling is a gaping hole, where a shell hit the building knocking down plaster and bricks everywhere...

From here we go out again and on towards the 'Clinico'. Shells are screaming overhead, soaring across and landing with a distant thunderous thud... We plunge into a trench which leads down into the bowels of the earth and for a bit we totter forward feeling our

---

153 Frida Stewart, transcript of a broadcast from Madrid, 'A Newcomer to Madrid' 1937, papers of Frida Stewart.

way along the walls in pitch darkness. At last a glimmer of light, and we come out into the front line of trenches proper. It is difficult to believe that these really are the 'primeras lineas'. We have heard so much about the trenches in other wars, in the Great War - about the horrors of mud, of wet, of cold; or of dust and dryness, and burning heat with lice and rats and conditions of indescribable misery. Here our ideas are completely changed. These trenches are little alleys of a miniature city, a trench city, of which the dugouts are the houses, miniature palaces cared for by their inmates with a pride that is touching when one thinks of the impermanent character of the buildings. And yet not so impermanent - some of the soldiers have been here five months without a break, several that we met, even longer... Some have planted flowers outside their door, which cheers the whole trench as well. Outside the doors the names of the palaces vaunt their pride. 'Casa Florida', 'Hotel Victoria', 'Hotel Rusia', 'Villa Pasionaria', and many others.

We go on along the trench. Strains of music can be heard. Guitars are brought into the trenches and nearly every one can sing and absolutely everyone can enjoy the Flamenco music. 'Casa Miaja' even has a gramophone. The Miajans invite us to sit down and hear a record, which we do. It is a 'fandanguilla' a very cheerful tune but alas, almost inaudible so husky and well-worn it is from much playing and trench wear and tear. It happens to be the only record they possess which explains its condition!

In the next 'palace' a soldier is sitting bent over a piece of wood which he is carving into a beautiful foliage pattern. It is to be the door of the dugout. The boy comes from Cordoba and was learning his profession when the war broke out... We are invited to look at the library - all sorts of books are there, ranging from arithmetic textbooks to economics, from thrillers of the peculiarly lurid Spanish variety, to serious novels and plays. Over the door someone has stuck a picture of Goethe. We feel more and more that this is really a University city after all, a trench university. They say that they have classes every day, for the illiterate soldiers, and more advanced ones for anyone who cares to join. Here at least war has been a breeding ground for culture and education.[154]

---

154 Friday Stewart, transcript of a broadcast from Madrid, 'University City' 1937, papers of Frida Stewart.

Penny Phelps also broadcast from Madrid, just before Christmas in 1937. She described her work as a nurse in a fever hospital, where she was responsible for controlling and treating an epidemic amongst the troops. The education of her patients was not overlooked. Amongst the medical details, she mentions how she has started a tiny library in the hospital,

> ...just a little room with a stove and a cupboard full of books. When I receive anything like a present for the hospital I write up on the wall who sent it, like, 'This came from the people of England.'[155]

She also spoke of the civilian injuries that she treated and the sick children who desperately needed milk. After making a general appeal on behalf of Spanish Medical Aid for funds, she then appealed to nurses directly.

> And if there are any nurses listening to me tonight, will you think about the need of trained nurses here? I know of a hospital where there are 500 wounded and only two trained British nurses. Can't you come and give us a hand? We are fighting here for the democratic rights of a brave and courageous people. Come and help us.[156]

In her memoirs she recalled that on the way to Madrid, she had been involved in a car crash. Uninjured, she luckily managed to catch a lift and arrive in the 'nick of time' to make her broadcast. Still a little out of breath, her appeal, 'as a consequence, sounded emotional and was judged very successful on that account.'[157]

Not all broadcasts made by British women were so distinctly personalised. Jane Patrick and Ethel MacDonald had gone to Barcelona from Glasgow where they were both very actively involved in anarchist politics.[158] Ethel MacDonald remained in Barcelona, working at the radio station as an English speaking broadcaster for the CNT-FAI.[159]

---

155 Penny Phelps, transcript of Radio Broadcast from Madrid, 20 December 1937, papers of Penny Phelps.
156 Ibid.
157 Penelope Fyvel (née Phelps) *English Penny* (Arthur H. Stockwell, Ilfracombe, Devon, 1992) p. 44
158 For more details of the Anti-Parliamentary Communist Federation and the formation of the United Socialist Movement see John Taylor Caldwell, *Come Dungeons Dark: The Life and Times of Guy Aldred, Glasgow Anarchist* (Luath Press, Barr, Scotland,1988).
159 Confederación Nacional de Trabajo/Federación Anarquista Ibérica: Anarcho-Syndicalist Trades Union and the Anarchist Doctrinal Vanguard.

Jane Patrick went on to Madrid where she worked in the Ministry of Information, also broadcasting whilst she was there.[160] They express their views in the rhetoric of the day, no hint of individual personality interrupts the flow of the political discourse. Jane Patrick begins by emphasising German and Italian intervention, then explores the nature of the war as 'an expression of the class struggle in its most extreme form,' in which the 'fascists hordes massacre the civilian population of any town that falls into their hands.'

> ...this is a war where the workers are fighting against their one-time masters, and there is no hatred like the vindictive hatred of the master when the slave has rebelled. There is no hatred like that of the property class who see their property and privileges threatened by the workers who want to do away with property and privileges for all time.[161]

She praises the stoicism of the people of Madrid in general, but they seem to lose their identity as individuals, merging together when she states, 'Madrid knows that this is a life and death struggle and Madrid is determined never to surrender.' She concludes by returning to the theme of Non-intervention, ending on a predictably revolutionary note.

> The governments of all the countries are equally guilty of this slaughter of Spain. Britain and France are not one whit better than Germany and Italy... We look to the workers in these countries to put an end to this pretence and to come to the help of Spain by forcing the hands of their governments immediately. No government will act unless forced to do so and the only pressure that can be put upon them is the threat of working-class revolt and the fear of an uprising in their own country.[162]

---

160 The speech was also published in Barcelona and in Britain. *Boletin de Información*, 24 March 1937. Reprinted as 'War in Spain: Radio Speech by Jane H. Patrick' in *News from Spain* (edited and published by the United Socialist Movement) Glasgow, 1 May 1937 (MML Box D2 File 0-2).

161 *Boletin de Información*, 24 March 1937. Reprinted as 'War in Spain: Radio Speech by Jane H. Patrick' in *News from Spain* (edited and published by the United Socialist Movement) Glasgow, 1 May 1937 (MML Box D2 File O-2).

162 Ibid. An outdated photograph of Jane Patrick was printed alongside one published version of this speech. But this inclusion does not reflect any desire on her part to encourage the intrusion of individuality on the political content of her words. According to the statement below the photograph, no recent picture was available because 'Comrade Patrick objects to portraits.'

Ethel MacDonald was also attempting to rouse the workers to action with revolutionary rhetoric.

English-speaking workers, why are you sleeping whilst your Spanish brothers and sisters are being murdered? Where are your traditions? Speak! Act! Answer with the word and answer with the deed... End class society now.[163]

Meanwhile, from the other side of the lines in the National Broadcasting Station of Salamanca, Florence Farmborough was also employing stylised propaganda to reassure the British public that they could sleep peacefully in the knowledge that Franco was fighting on their behalf. Awash with rhetoric, her speeches almost drown the listener in metaphor.

Though the majority of English people may not realise it, their night's rest is unbroken, their daily routine unhindered, their banking account holding good, their food continuing to be varied and abundant, their churches still open to public worship, only because Franco knows how to fight, and because he is standing at the helm of the Ship of European Civilisation, which he has successfully salvaged from the Red Rocks on which she was fast breaking to pieces, and is steering her through seas of heroic Spanish blood to that haven where Red doctrines shall be allowed no entrance and where Red tyranny shall be unknown.[164]

Her lengthy talks, broadcast on Sunday evenings to English speaking countries, were also published in book form as *Life and People in National Spain*. In the introduction, she takes pains to point out that although she writes from a foreign land, 'it is not a foreigner writing' but an Englishwoman, born and bred, with the welfare of England at heart. Having lived and worked in Valencia for ten years before the

163 Speeches of Ethel MacDonald from Barcelona published in the *Bellshill Speaker* from 12 March to 16 April 1937 inclusive, and in *Save Spain. Act*, Glasgow, 1 May 1937 (MML, Box B4, Q-14).
164 Florence Farmborough *Life and People in National Spain* (Sheed & Ward, London, 1938) p. 115. Another British woman, Dora Lennard Alonso, who was teaching English to Franco just before the war, also made propaganda broadcasts in English from Burgos and Vitoria. She is mentioned by Paul Preston in *Franco: A Biography* (Fontana Press, London, 1995, first published by Harper Collins, 1993) pp. 123 and 137, who is quoting from a newspaper article 'Franco - A Close-Up: Study of the Mind and the Nature of the Leader of the Junta Forces by His English Teacher', *The Morning Post*, 20 July 1937, p.10. Paul Preston has also written of references to her broadcasts in José Agusto Ventín Pereira, *La Guerra de la radio (1936-1939)* (Editorial Mitre, Barcelona, 1986).

5.5 Florence Farmborough in Valencia.

war, she felt it her duty to try to inform her countrymen about
National Spain. She was convinced that her experiences in Russia as a
nurse during the Revolution meant that she had been 'able to recognise, more clearly, perhaps, even than the Spaniards themselves, the
insidious treachery and rapidly-growing influence of the Red Agents of
Soviet Russia.' The justification for war to her was clear, and Franco
was the saviour of Spain.

On the 18th July, 1936, General Franco - born leader of men -
unsheathed his sword to right the many wrongs that hundreds of
thousands of his countrymen who were suffering at the hands of
their own kith and kin, who, pitifully misguided and ignorant, had
allowed themselves to be duped by the astute agents of Russia.[165]

The transportation of the Army of Africa to the Peninsula at the
start of the war was explained in one of Florence Farmborough's
broadcasts in quasi-biblical terms as an almost miraculous event. In
her version, Franco instructed his army to rely on their 'moral

---

165 Florence Farmborough *Life and People in National Spain* (Sheed & Ward, London, 1938),
    pp. 4-5.

courage, discipline and faith in victory' to help them cross over from Tetuán, whereupon 'his men crossed the Straits in their small craft, passing the battleships, cruisers, torpedo-boats and submarines of the Red Government,' safely reaching the Peninsular. 'Only history', she believed, 'will be able to pay just and adequate homage to this daring and mighty feat of military skill.' History, however, has recorded the occasion as one of the first significant examples of the air-lifting of troops, made possible by thirty German Junkers JU-52s and Italian bombers.[166]

Florence Farmborough has apparently left no other record of her experiences in Spain. Although on several occasions she was interviewed about Russia, she would not discuss Spain, despite being requested to do so.[167] However, both Jane Patrick and Ethel MacDonald wrote letters and reports from Spain which do reveal a little more of their characters as individuals. Readers of *News From Spain* would have learned of Jane Patrick's valiant attempts to maintain a vegetarian diet in Spain and of her joy on finding a man selling peanuts.[168] They may have glimpsed a resolute personality, who, when faced with an imminent downpour, still went out, 'to challenge' the weather.[169] The small insights that can be gained from her letters add a further dimension to the reasons she gave for being in Spain during her broadcasts. She wrote from Barcelona,

> There is exhilaration in danger. One can laugh and feel alive and joyous in the face of it, it is life. But poverty - the constant deadening effect of it - is death.[170]

Tension was building in Barcelona between those who wanted to implement further revolutionary changes quickly and those who believed that it was necessary to 'First Win the War' against

---

166 Paul Preston *A Concise History of the Spanish Civil War* (Fontana Press, London, 1996) p. 87.
167 Interviews with Florence Farmborough are held by the Sound Archive of the Imperial War Museum and in the Peter Liddle Collection, Leeds University. She also was the subject of a 'Yesterday's Witness' television production, 'Florence Farmborough: English Nurse with the Tsar's Army', 1974. The experiences she had as a nurse on the Russian front are discussed in Chapter 2.
168 Jane H. Patrick, letters from Madrid, 4 March 1937, and from Barcelona, 24 March 1937. Reprinted in 'From Madrid to Barcelona', *News from Spain* (edited and published by the United Socialist Movement) Glasgow, undated (MML Box D2 File O-1).
169 Ibid.
170 Jane H. Patrick, letter from Barcelona, 16 March 1937. Reprinted in 'From Madrid to Barcelona' *News from Spain* (edited and published by the United Socialist Movement) Glasgow, undated (MML Box D2 File O-1).

Fascism.[171] By the end of March 1937, Jane Patrick was fully aware of the fact that the Anarchist position was becoming weaker and that the 'Revolution' was in danger.

For my part, I see it slipping, slipping, and that has been the position for some time. However, perhaps, it will be possible for it to be saved. Let us hope so; but it seems to me that reaction is gaining a stronger hold each day.[172]

Reports from Jane Patrick and Ethel MacDonald on the events which took place in Barcelona at the beginning of May quickly appeared in print in Glasgow and were perhaps amongst the first to reach the outside world.[173] They witnessed some of the street fighting from their hotel, then on the following morning, joined their anarchist comrades, helping them by filling cartridge clips for the soldiers and preparing meals.

Next morning we decided that our places were with our comrades at headquarters, and at seven we set out. At that hour Spanish women go to market and, knowing this, both sides look out for them and cease fire to allow them to move about. We mingle with these women, some of whom carried little white flags in their hands. We would slink along a street, hugging a wall. At every corner where we knew there was a barricade, one of the women would poke her little flag round. At this signal firing would stop and we would scurry across. Sometimes though, firing went on over our heads (it was aimed at windows) and showers of plaster would fall about our ears. Behind every tree and every lamp post there was a soldier on one side or the other, and they would scowl at us or smile, waving us on.[174]

Jane Patrick returned home, but Ethel MacDonald remained in Barcelona. Throughout July and August, the story of her arrest, release and subsequent disappearance in Spain was reported in a

---

171 As expressed for example on many government posters 'Lo primero es ganar la Guerra.'
172 Jane H. Patrick, letter from Barcelona, 29 March 1937. Reprinted in 'From Madrid to Barcelona' (MML Box D2 File O-1).
173 Report from Jane H. Patrick Barcelona, 5 May, 1937, 'Showing that Anarchists Are Not to Blame', News From Spain, quoted by Hodgart, Ethel MacDonald, p. 12. She also quotes the claim, made in The Word in January 1942, that this was one of the first accounts of the 'May Days'.
174 Ethel MacDonald, Sunday Mail, 5 December 1937, quoted by Hodgart, Ethel MacDonald, pp. 13-14.

series of articles in the Glasgow press, where interest in the local girl from Bellshill was greatest.[175] After the May Days, she had attempted to help Anarchist and Trotskyist comrades who were in prison by smuggling in food and letters and carrying information. She was dubbed 'The Scots Scarlet Pimpernel' in the press through successfully helping several foreign Anarchists to escape. When arrested and imprisoned herself, she helped to organise simultaneous hunger strikes amongst the Anarchists in several prisons. Her case was taken up by Fenner Brockway, the Secretary of the ILP, and she was released in mid-July. However her difficulties were not over. A letter she wrote to Guy Aldred appeared in the press, in which she explained that she was unable to leave Spain as there were still outstanding charges against her. 'Even if these charges are withdrawn, I still could not leave the country because my passport is without a visa. If I apply I shall be arrested.'[176] Her plight worsened.

> My financial situation is bad... From the clothes aspect, if I am not home soon it will be too cold to come home at all... I am a terrible sight... All my documents and clothes have gone beyond recall. I have lost everything.'[177]

Concern for her spread as far afield as America and Canada according to another article, 'Bellshill Girl in Spain - American Radio Listeners Want To Hear Her.' It was claimed by a prominent news editor in Hollywood that hundreds of letters about her had been received from all parts of the USA and Canada. Seemingly, they had enjoyed her talks from Barcelona 'not because they agreed with what she said, but because they thought she had the finest radio speaking voice they had ever heard.'[178] Ill-health, due to lack of funds and the constant fear of re-arrest, eventually seems to have resulted in the involvement of the Foreign Office and arrangements were made for her to be taken to France for rest and treatment.[179] Her eventual return to Scotland in November 1937 was noted in the *Glasgow Herald*, with the restrained comment, typical of the paper's journalistic style, that she had arrived home the previous night after having 'undergone

175 For example, *Glasgow Herald*, 1937, 15 July, p. 2; 19 July, p. 9; 22 July, p. 7: 3 August, p. 8; 5 August, p. 10; 24 August, p. 16; 26 August, p. 17; 30 August, p. 9; 8 November, p. 3.
176 'Bellshill Girl's Plight', *Glasgow Herald*, 3 August, 1937, p. 8.
177 *Glasgow Evening Times*, 25 August 1937. Quoted in Hodgart, *Ethel MacDonald*, p. 16.
178 *Glasgow Herald*, 24 August 1937, p.16.
179 *Glasgow Herald*, 30 August 1937, p. 9.
180 *Glasgow Herald*, 8 November 1937, p. 3.

trying experiences' in Spain.[180] Her own feelings about what had happened to her, and her response to the welcome she received from a
crowd of about three hundred were reported in the *Evening Citizen*.

> There was sadness in Ethel MacDonald's face as she said, 'I went to
> Spain full of hopes and dreams. It promised to be a Utopia realised.
> I return full of sadness, dulled by the tragedy I have seen.' Then she
> whispered to her friends, 'I'm so thrilled by the welcome. But its ter-
> ribly embarrassing. Please take me away.'[181]

As difficult to imagine as it seems today, at the time of the Spanish
war, one of the most successful methods of reaching a wide audience
was by means of a public meeting. Halls were booked, speakers were
arranged, the audiences flocked in. Someone who had been to Spain
was always considered an added attraction amongst the more practised speakers. A member of the 'Friends', Norma Jacob, was a case in
point. Before she began working with refugees in Barcelona, she
joined her husband in Spain for a short visit in 1936, returning to
England to speak at fund-raising meetings.

> I know that the evening I had to do the public speaking was the
> night that Edward VIII resigned - abdicated - because we had this big
> meeting in Oxford Town Hall with a member of Parliament and
> Gilbert Murray, who was a very famous man, and me. I was by far
> the least important person there, but I had been there, I had the
> first-hand experience, and no one was going to stop me. I was going
> to tell them what I'd seen, and I've never minded public speaking
> since. I had something to say and I couldn't have been stopped.[182]

Nurses who had been in Spain were also able to give up-to-date
impressions of life at the front, increasing the receptivity of audiences
at public meetings. Some of the nurses who were home on leave spent
much of their time travelling round the country, speaking at as many
meetings as they could. Like Norma Jacob, unused to public speaking
and initially at times embarrassed and nervous to find themselves on
the platform, they nevertheless did their best to contribute to the

---

180 *Glasgow Herald*, 8 November 1937, p. 3.
181 Quoted in Hodgart, *Ethel MacDonald*, p. 19.
182 Norma Jacob, Oral History Interview #31, 31 March 1989, Archive of the American
　　Friends Service Committee, Philadelphia.

234 BRITISH WOMEN AND THE SPANISH CIVIL WAR

fund raising efforts, and were often singled out for special mention in the local and national press.[183]

Nurses were involved in the process of communication in both directions. Not only were they informing the British public about their work in Spain, they were also returning to the front to tell their colleagues in Spain about the work being done at home. Penny Phelps had been home on leave for three weeks to recover from typhoid. Her scrapbook contains a newspaper cutting of an article she wrote on her return to Spain. 'Trip to England by one of our Nurses' appeared in a paper distributed amongst the medical personnel. Although noting that there were those in England who 'stood aside' from the struggle in Spain, the overall impression she gives is one which emphasises the 'unceasing activity and propaganda work' being carried out at home.

> ...the demand for speakers from the Spanish Medical Aid Committee in London is very great and urgent. I addressed meetings practically every night in and around London. Wherever I went I saw and heard good work being done, by people who didn't only consist of young men, women and children, but old people as well. In my mind at the moment is an old lady of 70 years who came up to me as I was about to go home after a very successful meeting in Hornsey Town Hall. This old lady, placing her hand in mine said, 'My dear child, it is so good to know there are people like you out in Spain, who are keeping the flag of humanity - by which I mean humaneness - flying in those terrible regions. I can guess just what a comfort people like you are to everybody. For this is a sad world - there seems such confusion and such torturous thinking going on.' The old lady pressed something close in my hand, that she had been holding all the while. She made a hurried exit, and I was left standing in the hall holding a cheque for £100 for the Spanish Medical Aid.[184]

---

183 For example, Penny Phelps in 'Tottenham Nurse in Spain', *Tottenham and Edmonton Weekly Herald*, October 1937, private papers of Penny Phelps; Nurse Woodeford, *Daily Worker*, 24 September, 1936, p. 1, 29 September, 1936, p. 1; Nurse Margot Miller, 'They're in the News', *Woman To-Day* December 1936, p. 3: Enid Ramshaw in *Shields Weekly News*, 22 January, 1937, in Don Watson and John Corcoran, *The North East of England and the Spanish Civil War 1936-1939* (McGuffin Press, London, 1996) p. 43. After Lillian Urmston had spoken at meetings whilst on leave, a fund was started in her name in Stalybridge to send money for Spanish Medical Aid. Tameside 203.

184 In her scrapbook, Penny Phelps has labelled this cutting 'My trip to England, April 24th - May 13th 1937, taken from *La Voz de Sanitair*' [sic.].

Penny Phelps wrote in this article that she was 'more than glad to be back on Spanish soil again.' Susan Kingsley Kent has studied the disconnections that occur between those at home and those at the front during the First World War.[185] The response in Penny Phelps' case was similar. When asked how she felt when she was home on leave she replied, 'I couldn't bear it, because they were all talking about the Coronation.'[186] To her, the events taking place in England had seemed irrelevant and she was eager to return to Spain.[187] Images suggest that others shared her feelings. The smiles of four nurses photographed for the *Daily Worker*, setting off on the return trip to Spain together, could not be interpreted as anything other than genuine.[188]

The general public in Britain were also made aware of the situation in Spain through the work of British women artists. Felicity Ashbee had grown up with all the advantages of a privileged and artistic background as the daughter of Charles R. Ashbee, the founder of the Guild of Handicraft. She had studied art at the Byam Shaw Art School and, along with many intellectuals and artists of the period, became convinced by the arguments for 'popular front' politics, experiencing what she described as 'tantamount to a religious conversion'. She joined the Artists International Association in the early thirties and campaigned against fascism.[189] Amongst her posters for Spain were a series of three she produced for the National Joint Committee under the shared caption, 'They face famine in Spain.' The emaciated children in the poster appealing for milk are typical of what has been viewed as the 'unrelenting tragic realism of her images.'[190]

As members of the Artists International Association, other women such as Priscilla Thornycroft and Nan Youngman also designed posters and banners for Spanish Relief. When the Spanish war began, Priscilla Thornycroft was studying painting, drawing and commercial art at the Slade.

---

185 Susan Kingsley Kent, *Making Peace: The Reconstruction of Gender in Interwar Britain* (Princeton University Press, New Jersey, 1993) pp. 52-55.
186 Penny Phelps, AJ, 22-23 February 1996.
187 Certain nurses came home and did not return to Spain, for example, see Molly Murphy in Chapter 4. Sometimes nurses suffering from stress or injuries would remain in Spain for treatment and then return to duty, for example, Una Wilson after a breakdown in Fyrth, *The Signal Was Spain*, p. 77-78, and Patience Darton after being injured when the ambulance she was in went off the road, IWM 8398.
188 *Daily Worker*, 3 January 1938, p. 5 (Margaret Powell is second from the right.).
189 Felicity Ashbee, AJ, 2 March 2001. Her grandfather, H. S. Ashbee, a collector of pornographic material, is the subject of Ian Gibson's recent book, *The Erotomaniac: The Secret Life of Henry Spencer Ashbee* published by Faber and Faber in 2001.
190 Nigel Glendinning, 'Art and the Spanish Civil War' in Stephen M. Hart (ed.), *¡No Pasarán!': Art Literature and the Spanish Civil War* (Tamesis, London, 1988) p. 32. See also John Gorman, *Images of Labour* (Scorpion Press, 1985) p. 169.

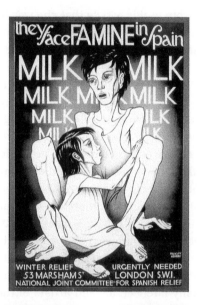

5.6 Felicity Ashbee: posters for the
National Joint Committee for Spanish Relief.

Campaigning 'day and night for Spain' entailed, amongst a variety of activities, crawling about on a studio floor to paint banners till her knees were damaged. But youthful enthusiasm did not always produce perfect results.

> And that was one of those typical things at those times - we all had good hearts but were fearfully inefficient. I was told to paint a banner for this ambulance for Spain and they gave me a bit of cloth, and I said, 'Well, how long is the ambulance?' And they said, 'Oh, it's the length of that banner,' the whole thing you see. So, true as I was, I painted on the whole banner which was very long, and when we were then meant to put it on the lorry, I think in front of the Houses of Parliament, the damn thing was at least 2 yards too long. [Laughter] So when it was photographed for the press, I had to hold one end [laughter], and when it went, I suppose they wrapped it round the back - typical - working all night on the banner which should have been for the whole journey on the side of the van.[191]

5.7 The Artists International Association lorry for Spain,
Priscilla Thornycroft on the left.

Her designs for posters were strongly influenced by those being used in Spain. Her intention was that 'people would understand what it was about', rather than striving for originality. Sometimes she even included photo-montage sections taken from other posters. For the 'All London Friends of Spain Week', her design of a peasant gathering corn was printed in the colours of the Republican flag and was similar

191 Priscilla Thornycroft (married Siebert) AJ, 28 April 2000.

5.8   Priscilla Thornycroft with Basque children in Trafalgar Square.

5.9 The poster for 'All London Friends of Spain Week'
designed by Priscilla Thornycroft.

in style to some of those being used as propaganda to increase agricultural production. On another occasion, her work was the subject of a newsreel film, although once again, things did not go according to plan. The Artists International Association had arranged for an enormous hoarding to be painted for the campaign for 'Food for Spain.' Priscilla Thornycroft had carefully prepared a design to be copied on to the hoarding with the help of Nan Youngman and Betty Rea. When she notified the newsreel cameramen that they would be working on the hoarding that day, the crew decided that rather than filming in the afternoon, they would come at once.

> The three of us, we painted frantically, 'Food for Spain', terribly badly, because we thought the message was more important than the art. [Laughter] Yes, it was one of those embarrassing things... I never saw the film but other people rang me up and said they'd taken a proper film and it really was in the Gaumont News, or Pathe perhaps.[192]

As this chapter has shown, the range of material about Spain circulating in Britain during the three years of the war was immense. To the numerous books, pamphlets, magazines, bulletins, and reports, must also be added the radio broadcasts, newsreels, newspaper articles, photographs and posters. It would be difficult to assess the impact of this deluge of images and text in general terms, although perhaps the continued production and sale of fund-raising pamphlets about Spain throughout the years of the war is an indication of a substantial degree of public interest in the subject. Mention has already been made of the response of individual women to items they saw in the press, Jessica Mitford to photographs of the *milicianas*, and of Nan Youngman to the news of the death of Felicia Browne. Nancy Cunard's booklet, *Authors Take Sides*, mentioned by several women during interviews for this study, paved the way two years later for an appeal from American writers to end the US arms embargo then in effect against Spain.[193] The impact of the broadcasts from Spain

---

192 Ibid. The newsreel was British Paramount News, Issue no. 833, 23 February 1939. 'Artists aid refugees by painting hoardings: London. Well known artists turn London streets into studios for vivid publicity scheme for Spanish refugee fund.' ITN Archive, London, tape V619 (1).

193 *American Neutrality* organised by Pearl Buck, Ernest Sutherland and Ernest Hemingway. Amongst those who signed were Edna Ferber, Dorothy Canfield Fisher and Lillian Hellman. See Ockerstrom, 'The Other Narratives', pp. 150-151.

made by the women in this chapter are particularly difficult to assess. Florence Farmborough's broadcasts on behalf of Franco were unforgettable for at least one of her listeners, the story being preserved in the annals of Farmborough history.

> Her manner of precise speech was developed over years of teaching English pronunciation, and the family tell the story of how one day she was coming down the steps of St. Paul's Cathedral in London talking to a friend when she passed a man who must have overheard her. He stopped and came back, and asked her if she had ever broadcast from Spain. There could be no other.[194]

Many people on the Left would have known about broadcasts from the Republic. In November 1936, for example, the *Left Review* notified readers of the establishment of a radio station in Madrid to broadcast twice a day in the principal European languages. Times of English broadcasts were given and a request was made for listeners to write to the Radio Station reporting on the quality of the reception, suitability of the hours chosen and in general making comments and suggestions.[195] Others would know through personal contacts. Frida Stewart's mother did indeed hear her daughter speaking from Madrid and sent a report of the broadcast to the local paper, which was published as 'Cambridge Lady in Madrid: Interesting Impressions Broadcast' with 'TRAGEDY OF UNIVERSITY', in bold capitals.[196] Nevertheless, in political terms, despite their efforts through writing and speaking about what they saw in Spain, those who wanted to change the policy of the British government on Non-intervention were unable achieve their aim.

A thread of empathy runs strongly through the words used by many of the women in this chapter. They were aware of its power, although perhaps less self-consciously than those who work in the media today. A foreign correspondent writing recently on this theme in an article entitled 'Thousands dead in India - not many interested', sadly observed that the news editor's first question on receiving a report of a disaster is always, 'Any Brits involved?'[197] We tend to

---

194 Family Profile no. 4 'Florence Farmborough 1887-1978, courtesy of the Farmborough family.
195 *Left Review* November 1936, p. 776.
196 Report from Jessie Stewart of broadcast by Frida Stewart, *Cambridge Daily News*, 29 July 1937.
197 Michael Nicholson, Chief Foreign Correspondent for ITN, *Independent*, 5 November 1999, p. 13.

identify more closely with those most like ourselves, and with the distress suffered by people who 'come crawling out of the wreckage of houses that once looked similar to the ones we live in.'[198] Such distress became the concern of many British women during the Spanish Civil War. The empathy in their voices made it impossible to completely ignore the essentially human dimension of the conflict.

---

198 Ibid.

CHAPTER SIX

Aftermath: Women and
the Memory of War

The stars are dead. The animals will not look.
We are left alone with our day, and the time is short, and
    History to the defeated
May say Alas but cannot help nor pardon.[1]

THESE WORDS BY W. H. AUDEN, taken from his poem about Spain, were
chosen by Frida Stewart to introduce the chapter of her memoirs
describing the fall of the Republic in 1939. The lines resonated with
her own sense of grief at what she could only view as a tragedy of
immense proportions, and with her remorse at the failure to prevent
it from happening. Studies of British women and the World Wars can
shed light on reactions to victory, but the Spanish war, although not
officially 'our' war, can help us to understand some of the responses
to defeat.[2] Not only were the many British women who had taken an
active role on Spanish soil forced to confront the overthrow of the
forces they had supported, but those in Britain too had to deal with
the failure of the cause they had espoused, and the return of defeated
husbands, fathers and friends. Women working here with Basque
refugee children had to face problems that Franco's victory brought
for their charges. This chapter therefore contains a range of events
and emotions, divided into two parts. The first examines the fall of the

---

1 W. H. Auden, 'Spain'. Two versions were published, the first in 1937, then a final revised
   version entitled 'Spain 1937' in 1940 in *Another Time* (Faber, London).
2 The themes in this chapter relate primarily to British women whose efforts had contributed towards support of the Republic in some way. Although a handful of women in
   this study had supported Franco's forces and were therefore on the winning side, the
   material from these sources is so limited that they are only included in this chapter for
   comparative purposes in certain instances.

Republic and its immediate aftermath from the perspective of the British women who had been involved with the war. The second addresses the process of coming to terms with defeat, a subject that entails the consideration of issues surrounding memory, reminiscence and remembrance. Through exploring how women in this study have used memories of the war within their narratives, and how they, themselves, are remembered or forgotten, a little more can be understood about their lives, and of the processes associated with remembering the past.

AFTERMATH OF WAR

No day, or even month, is usually specified by the women in this study as the moment which for them defined the end of the war. The period that became the 'aftermath' of the war began for some, not with Franco's declaration of victory on 1 April 1939, but earlier, either with the withdrawal of the International Brigades from the front in October 1938 or after the fall of Barcelona in January 1939.[3] Many of them felt the overthrow of the Republic as a devastating blow in the struggle against the forces of fascism. However, the themes that emerge from their narratives are largely practical, relating to the work of helping those that were suffering in the wake of defeat. Their overriding concerns are most commonly for people in the newly occupied territories in Spain, for the thousands of Spanish refugees in France, and for the refugees who were living in Britain.

Before the war was declared officially over, some of the women who had worked with the medical units in Spain and had been withdrawn with the International Brigades, had helped to form a group known simply as the 'British Medical Unit from Spain.' The members aimed to keep up support for people in what remained of the Republic and to raise money for medical supplies. In London, Patience Darton became part of this group, crossing paths for the first time with others who had also been working in Spain, such as Angela Guest.[4] She recalled this period of her life in interviews, seeming to find great pleasure in remembering the excitement of their activities

---

3 Franco's troops entered Madrid on 27 March 1939.
4 Angela Guest was the daughter of Carmel Haden Guest, a former suffragette and a leading campaigner in women's movements in the thirties, and Dr. Haden Guest, Labour MP and former Minister of Health. Her brother, David Guest, had joined the International Brigades and was killed on the Ebro. Angela Guest was not a trained nurse but worked in various medical units, undertaking a variety of tasks, including running a convalescent home.

at a time when there was still a slim hope for the Republic.[5]

Nan [Green] and Ena Vassey had a flat in Coram Street, they took me in because when I came back I had no idea what to do... I didn't want to be at home in the village in the country... You see, I'd always been in Nurses' Homes and living at home - I'd no idea about how you set about getting anywhere to live - not that I had any money. Nan Green and Ena Vassey took me in there and that was where we did all our speaking and things from. It was a little gang running round doing lots and lots of things. I mean we were busy all the time - lots of demos in those days - lovely demos - 'We demand arms for Spain', and we could often do things - women you see, particularly Nan Green and me because we spoke so nicely that the police didn't stop you in the same way that they did the others. We used to do a lot of popping round in and out of the undergrounds, in Trafalgar Square and Piccadilly Circus on the big demos - great big - really hundreds and thousands of people - up and down these undergrounds and the police pushing you around a great deal. And if I got pushed around I used to tick the police off and they used to take it you see, because I'd got a nice voice - the same with Angela [Guest]. We'd get up again and start another little 'We demand arms for Spain' somewhere round the top of the underground, particularly in Piccadilly Circus and Leicester Square - you can get quite a long way up and down - Ah me! It was quite different in those days.[6]

Nan Green spoke of two particular protests they organised.

Some of the nurses got up a little group, five or six of them I suppose and went to see Mrs Chamberlain to ask in a humanitarian way for help to Spain. When they got to Downing Street they were told that the family were at Chequers so they immediately took two taxis and went off there, but by the time they got to Chequers, [laugh] there were barricades up at the gates and they'd taken the precaution of taking the press with them, so we got a story but we didn't get anything out of Mrs Chamberlain. Many actions like this were taken. Angela Guest, who was always a person who liked taking explosive

---

5   Hopes at this point often centred around the possibility that the Republic could hold out until the outbreak of a wider conflict, and Spain would become an ally to be supported in a war with the axis powers.
6   Patience Darton, AJ, 8 March 1996.

actions got a bottle of red ink and splashed it on the doorstep of Downing Street, saying it was the blood of the Spanish people. But she was a great girl, she was always doing things like that.[7]

After several months, their group joined forces with the newly formed International Brigade Association (IBA), from which platform they continued to campaign on Spanish issues.[8]

Not all the women who had been in Spain were well enough to be active immediately on their return home. Joan Purser had been nursing in the cave hospital near the River Ebro as the last major battle of the war was being fought. She became ill and was sent home to England, taking several months to recover from typhoid fever. She was rather ashamed of having succumbed to this illness, saying in her interview, 'Don't put that down for goodness sake. Gracious, people were dying like flies of typhoid fever in Spain... I was very lucky to be back in London.'[9] A few nurses had returned earlier after being wounded, like Penny Phelps, but in certain instances, the exhaustion was as much mental as physical.[10] Molly Murphy was seemingly one of these.

It was splendid to be once more with my loved ones, and yet I was not happy. Time and again for hours on end I was living again with those I had left behind on the fluctuating front of the war in Spain. So many were dead who had been near to me... And I lived over and over again the dark nights when we picked our way between the beds and the mattresses on the floor, with covered flashlights and the bombs fell nearby and men groaned in pain. I saw again the girl in the street of Madrid with her face shot off and the corpses laid on the side of the street after a raid or heavy gunfire, waiting to be taken away. I was sinking into a nervous depression as the tiredness got the upper hand.[11]

7 Nan Green, IWM, 13799-4. Jim Fyrth names the five nurses who went to see Mrs Chamberlain with a letter protesting against the bombing of Barcelona, as Janet Robertson, Beryl Smithson, Louise Jones, Joan Purser, and Patience Darton. Aileen Palmer also helped to throw the red ink at the Prime Minister's door. Both she and Angela Guest were fined 10 shillings and bound over for six months. *The Signal Was Spain: The Aid Spain Movement in Britain 1936-39* (Lawrence & Wishart, London, 1986) pp. 137-8.
8 For more details see Bill Alexander, *No to Franco: The Struggle Never Stopped, 1939-1975* (Bill Alexander, London, 1992).
9 She had been told during her nursing training that if nurses got typhoid it was their own fault for being careless. Joan Purser, IWM, 14795. Only one British nurse, Ruth Ormesby, died in Spain. In April 1938, she fell to her death when trying to escape from a fire in the Spanish Medical Aid flat in Barcelona.
10 For Penny Phelps, see below.
11 Molly Murphy, unedited autobiography 'Nurse Molly', Museum of Labour History, p. 141 and also *Molly Murphy: Suffragette and Socialist* edited by Ralph Darlington (Institute of Social Research, University of Salford, 1998) p. 150.

When the Second World War began, she worked as a nurse with a mobile medical unit in London till 1942, once again dealing with death and injury on a grand scale. But the 'wretched nervous depression' returned and, as she puts it, she 'cracked up.'[12] It was never possible for her to fully resume her nursing career.

In Spain, relief work continued in the Republican zones as long as possible. Muriel McDiarmid was working in the canteens run by the Quakers in Barcelona. Her account of the city's fall, *Franco in Barcelona,* was published in 1939, claiming to be 'written by one of the few British people who remained in Barcelona after its occupation by Franco's troops.'[13] She describes life in the city just before it fell, the intensification of the bombing up to fourteen raids a day, and the shelling from battleships in the bay. However, the night of January 25th, with the exception of a terrible explosion at 11pm, was perfectly quiet. 'To me', she wrote, 'this was worse than the constant noise we had been hearing, it was so uncanny.' She goes on to describe the entry of Franco's troops the following day.

> About 3pm., from the roof of our house, I saw the first tanks enter down Bonanova. The men seated on them (Navarrese, with the red berets of the *Requetés*) pointed rifles at the pavement, but I did not see them fire. Later came the Moors and more Navarrese on foot... From personal observation, I can say that the Moors ran down Bonanova, one by one, very nervously, stopping to look cautiously down every side turning in case of ambushes. It was not in the least like a triumphal entry, and very different from the film version we saw later.[14]

Franco, she notes, had been in Burgos as his troops entered Barcelona, not at their head as the film had depicted. The next day she went out into the city to find that one of the main streets, the 'Diagonal', resembled a Moorish encampment, 'Such wretched, thin and saddle-sore animals as the mules I have never seen.'[15] She stayed long enough to witness the start of denunciations and reprisals and

12 Murphy, 'Nurse Molly', p. 150.
13 Muriel McDiarmid, *Franco in Barcelona* (United Editorial, London, April 1939). Muriel McDiarmid was not a Quaker. She had been an Assistant Secretary for the NJC and was a CP member.
14 Ibid., pp. 7-8. A similar account of these days is given by another woman also working with the Quakers in Barcelona, Kanty Cooper, *The Uprooted: Agony and Triumph Among the Debris of War* (Quartet Books, London, 1979).
15 Ibid., p. 8.

the closure of the schools. Before leaving in March, she was able to gather a great deal of information about conditions for the civilian population, the 'ghastly inadequacy of the food supply and the soaring prices of what is available.'

It was Franco's boast that he would immediately do away with the rationing system, but the queues for bread which followed this decision were literally miles in length. I have myself, seen soldiers jabbing women with bayonets and bringing the handles of their rifles down on women's feet, to keep them in order in the line.[16]

Rachael Dorothy Marshall, a district nurse from Norfolk, remained in Murcia working in the refugee children's hospital until April. Towards the end of her time there, food had been in desperately short supply for the first time. They had received a crate of toys at Christmas from Norwich children, and the beans in the beanbags were cooked and eaten when all else failed. 'They were appetising too,' she wrote, 'and we finished up by using the bags to patch the boys trousers!'[17] After Franco's victory, their unit was put under the control of 'Auxilio Social', the Nationalist relief agency, and the refugees were told to go home immediately.

We had to watch while parents came and took their sick children out of the hospital beds and carried them to the trains... We went to see one train leave. It was a pitiful sight... It was not a train as we know it, but a lot of cattle trucks. People were herded together in the trucks with their belongings. Many had no homes to go back to.[18]

The hospital staff were only given a few hours notice to prepare for closure. Children still in their care had to be moved to the over-crowded provincial hospital. The Friends' food store, which had supplied all the refugee colonies and canteens in the province, was commandeered and most of the contents given to the military.

Norma Jacob was possibly the only British woman who had worked in the Republic to return to Spain almost immediately after Franco's

---

16 Ibid., p.10.
17 Rachael Dorothy Marshall in an article by Whiffler, *Eastern Evening News*, Wednesday, May 17th 1939
18 Rachael Dorothy Marshall quoted in 'Last Days of Spanish War' *Eastern Evening News*, Monday, 5 June 1939.

victory, trying to carry on relief work she and her husband, Alfred Jacob, had been organising on behalf of the Quakers during the war.

It was in the early summer that we went back to Barcelona, this time taking the children with us. Everybody in London thought we were crazy. However, to us it seemed absolutely clear that war in the whole of Europe was about to begin (this was in June 1939). We had already seen enough of what war did to children to feel that our own must be spared that... The Franco authorities had taken over the large-scale operation, literally overnight... We now only served as agents for the transmission of the huge quantities of food still required, which the new authorities took over and distributed through their own institutions. From our own much more limited supplies we maintained a small number of individuals and families whom we knew to be in trouble because of the denial of ration cards.[19]

This work continued for about a year, despite threats to her husband who was told by the general in charge of the occupation that he would hanged in the main square as a punishment for feeding 'Red' children. In the summer of 1940, Alfred Jacob went out on one of his usual inspection tours, and did not return. After several days of anxiety, a very grubby postcard arrived from Zaragoza. His message, smuggled out by another prisoner who had been released, let them know his whereabouts. A frantic few days ensued for his wife, who was told at the prison that he had been moved to Madrid. She immediately followed and eventually secured his release with the help of the American Quaker, Howard Kershner.[20] Reunited, the family left for America soon afterwards.

According to their son, Piers Anthony, Alfred Jacob had been arrested for inadvertently being in an area near the border where preparations were being made for a visit from Hitler.[21] Piers Anthony's autobiographical writings bring into focus the problem of deleterious consequences for family relationships when parents give priority to a cause such as the war in Spain. Apart from brief periods with their

---

19 Norma Jacob, 'The Spanish Civil War', in Piers Anthony, *Bio of an Ogre* (Ace Books, New York, 1988) pp. 236-237.
20 Under pressure from Howard Kershner, the authorities eventually admitted that he was being held prisoner with others in cells under the Puerta del Sol. His release was only granted on condition that they left the country immediately. Norma Jacob returned to Barcelona to close down their office, and, with the help of friends, passage was arranged for the whole family from Portugal to America.
21 Anthony, *Bio of an Ogre*, p. 14.

mother and father in Spain during the war, he and his sister had lived with their grandparents and a nanny in England. Whilst recognising that the sacrifice of family unity was justifiable in his parents view because, as Quakers, they felt they must respond to the needs of the starving children, he points out that 'there was a cost, for all of us.'[22] His description of emotional difficulties he experienced as a child would doubtless serve as evidence of this in psychological terms.[23]

For the British women who were carrying out relief work in southern France after Franco's victory, particularly vivid memories remain of the internment camps where hundreds of thousands of Spaniards, and Brigaders who were unable to return to their own countries, were trying to survive. As Franco advanced, they had crossed the border, only to find themselves corralled, without adequate shelter, food or medical care. The Quakers, the National Joint Committee and Spanish Medical Aid were amongst the relief organisations helping to alleviate the distress of the exiles in these camps.[24] During the first weeks, Isabel Brown had been with a group from Britain that travelled in an NJC lorry, bringing food and clothing .[25]

> And I shall never forget for the rest of my life, which may not be too long as I'm eighty-three now, I'll never forget that experience because we'd made up parcels because the commandant of this interment camp had insisted there must be parcels. And then, when we got there, to our horror, he insisted the parcels must be addressed to a special person, an individual. Now, how could we know the names of individual soldiers? Finally we persuaded him that we would go back, because the soldiers had formed some committees, and get them to give us a list. We told them how many parcels we had, and they gave us a list and we wrote the names on. So we drove the lorry into the camp. It was a beautiful stretch

---

22 Ibid., p. 9.
23 Ibid., particularly references to his mother in the chapters on childhood in Part One. Martin Green, the son of Nan Green, was five years old when he went with his sister to A. S. Neill's school, Summerhill, whilst his parents were in Spain. In his introduction to his mother's memoirs, he mentions how this meant that the 'normal relationship a child has with his mother was broken', and how they only grew closer as she grew older.
24 Jim Fyrth lists some of those who were working in these groups. The British Quakers, led by Sir Richard Rees and William Brebner, included many of the women who had worked for them in Spain, Dr Audrey Russell, Edith Pye, Norma Jacob, Kanty Cooper, Mary Elmes and Dorothy Morris. The NJC office in Perpignan was run by Lady Hall, with the help of Donald Darling, Peter Rodd, Nancy Mitford and Frida Stewart. The SMAC team worked closely with them and included Nan Green, Ena Vassie, and Angela Guest. *The Signal Was Spain*, p. 296.
25 Angela Guest was also a member of this group.

of golden, golden, sands, two or three miles, just north on the coast near Perpignan, just above Port Bou on the blue beautiful Mediterranean, beautiful blue sky, sunshine. But the men were mostly in the water because they had not provided any shelter whatsoever for them. And they gathered flotsam, bits of wood that came in with the tiny tide of the Mediterranean, and they had dug undergrounds in the soft sand and tried to shore them up with whatever material they could get. They gathered up shells and little bits of rock. That was the only shelter they had from the blazing sun of the Mediterranean. But what hurt me most was we stood on this lorry and we had to pick up the parcels and call out a name and give it to whoever came and got it. and I watched one wounded soldier dragging almost half a leg through the sand to get away from the sun - that was their biggest enemy - and crawled under the lorry. I felt sorry for him. And his name wasn't on the list. And the look of disappointment - I'll never forget that picture.[26]

At Easter, Francesca Wilson went to help with the relief work at the camps, including some for women and children. She was taken to the camp on the beach at Argelès by someone already familiar with its horrors, Dr Audrey Russell, who had previously been working in Barcelona as a medical advisor in the refugee unit. Audrey Russell had joined in the retreat to France, being bombed and machine gunned on the way. She told Francesca Wilson how in the camps, 'Thousands of men have died who might have been saved, if they had had proper medical attention.'[27] Francesca Wilson found it difficult to describe her feelings on first sighting the camp.

It is impossible to imagine what eighty thousand men herded together behind barbed wire look like if one hasn't seen it. I wanted to cover my eyes - it was a sight so wounding to human dignity. Men penned into cages like wild animals; exposed to the stare of the passer-by, like cattle in the market place.[28]

Frida Stewart was a member of the NJC staff in France, helping to find suitable placements for the internees. She was also busily writing

---

26 Isabel Brown, IWM 844/8, reel 7.
27 Francesca M. Wilson, *In the Margins of Chaos: Recollections of Relief Work In and Between Three Wars* (John Murray, London, 1944) p. 223.
28 Ibid., p. 225.

numerous articles for appeals and letters to newspapers to publicise their desperate situation. When those in the camp at Argelès were eventually beginning to be moved elsewhere, she wrote a piece based on a conversation she had with an old Spanish soldier as they stood, divided by the wire fencing of the camp.

> 'Why do they evacuate the camp?' I asked.
>
> 'They hope the summer visitors will come back; it used to be a famous resort. But,' said he, looking round, and sniffing, significantly, 'it will never be the same Lido again. The shore is poisoned.'
>
> I was to agree that I personally would not choose the 'Plage d'Argelès' for a sea-side holiday this summer, but perhaps I have been too close to the camp to be unbiased. Perhaps the strand is not so much poisoned physically as morally and spiritually. It is not so much the typhoid germs, or the lice, the latrines or the smell of bad fish that poison the camp - the wind, that has harried the men all these weeks, will blow away smell and bugs and germs - but the knowledge of what the place has been, the ghost of the past of the 'plage', with its scenes of misery and ill-treatment of the finest people in the world, that would make it unbearable to stay in, ever again.[29]

As she worked, her frustration at the slow procedures for helping the refugees was poured out in letters to her mother. She wrote of how she was unable to think of anything other than the camp and the courage of the men.

> It's desperately depressing that we can only get out the tiniest frac-tion of them and I feel very ineffective fiddling around with our list of 500, and our card indexes. The Home Office is being unbelievably slow in giving permission for even our 60 names. By the way, Carmen's friend is on the list and I hope will be through in a very few days but it's in the lap of Whitehall and the Gods... It makes me wriggle with anger and shame to have all this dangling; and always having to say 'mañana' when one's asked 'When shall we go?'[30]

'Carmen's friend' was the refugee Silverio de la Torre, who, with his wife and little boy Fernando, were to be sponsored in England by Frida

---

29 Frida Stewart 'Evacuation from Argelès', papers of Frida Stewart.
30 Letter from Frida Stewart to her mother, Perpignan, 23 April 1939, papers of Frida Stewart.

Stewarts' parents and live in their home for over two years. During a brief respite, she found time to visit Pablo Casals who, at the time, was living about 20km away.

> We called on Casals yesterday...and found him installed in a gloomy commercial hotel, writing letters to the refugees who used to be in his orchestra, and are now in the camps. He said, rather dolefully, but quite resignedly, that he never has time to touch his cello, as he writes 6 or 7 hours every day - and writer's cramp is affecting his bow hand![31]

Preparations were soon underway to select almost 2000 refugees, some in family groups, to go to Mexico. She wrote light-heartedly to her father, 'I'm thinking of going to Mexico if there's any room on the boat - would you like to come?! Here's a card in case!'[32]

Another letter described her visit to Gurs to see the 'IB and Aviation Camps,' which she found 'as dismal as purgatory.'

> It is terrible to see how fascist the French army authorities are; the methods are exactly like the Hitler ones, and the Austrians and Germans in Gurs who have been in German camps say that this is as bad as anything there.[33]

Nevertheless, in Gurs as in the other camps, great efforts were made by the internees to keep up morale with cultural activities.[34] The importance of these activities to those in the camps should not be underestimated, although the efforts of relief workers to supply materials were gently mocked in a cartoon which Frida Stewart took care to preserve. However, as proof of the determination of those in the camps to produce something of value, albeit transient, from very little, she also treasured a small album that had been presented to her by 'los Internacionales' of Gurs. It contains tiny photographs of an exhibition they held of their paintings and sculpture at the end of 1939.[35] The cover has a soldier's head stencilled by hand

---

31 Letter from Frida Stewart to her sister, Katten, Perpignan, 1 May 1939, papers of Frida Stewart.
32 Letter from Frida Stewart to her father, Perpignan, 7 May 1939, papers of Frida Stewart.
33 Letter from Frida Stewart to her mother, Perpignan, 30 May 1939, papers of Frida Stewart.
34 Both Isabel Brown and Francesca Wilson remembered the urgency of the requests to supply materials for such projects. See Isabel Brown, IWM 844/8 BX, reel 7; Wilson, *In the Margins of Chaos* (1944) p. 226.
35 Album containing twelve pages of photographs dedicated to 'Frida Stewart y Molly Garrett: Un saludo de los Internacionales, 26.12.39,' papers of Frida Stewart.

6.1 Cartoon of the 'Palais des Expositions', France 1939.

in one corner. Inside, the roughly cut prints are glued to the small black pages, carefully covered by tissue paper. Photographs of model houses and sailing ships are intermingled with examples of political-montage and other artistic endeavours.

6.2 *Above and opposite*:
The exhibition in the camp at Gurs.

Even the precious supplies of soap could be put to artistic use. Both the Duchess of Atholl and Frida Stewart had been given sculptures carved from blocks of soap by Republican soldiers in the camps. Years later, the Duchess wrote a letter to Frida, recalling the soap sculpture she had been given, which she still carefully kept.[36] On several occasions, Frida spoke of her sadness when her own soap sculpture of a crucified soldier eventually disintegrated. For both women, the sculptures had come to represent the spirit of the people in the camps who, despite their defeat in Spain and an uncertain future, still struggled to keep morale high.

6.3 The Duchess of Atholl (right) with a Mexican diplomat
and his wife on board the refugee ship, the SS *Sinaia*, 1939.

The departure of the SS *Sinaia* for Mexico from Sète in southern France was another event recorded in Frida Stewart's letters home. The final preparations for the voyage had resulted in a 'hair-raising four days' for all concerned, as the refugees were collected together and transferred to the boat, a procedure she found 'more emotionally exhausting than anything I have ever experienced.' When the day of departure finally arrived the Duchess of Atholl and other dignitaries came to bid them farewell.

---

36 Letter to Frida Stewart from Katharine Atholl, London, 13 September 1955, MML, Box B7, D 17.

Frida Stewart tried to describe the occasion to her mother, writing that 'The scene on the quay-side needed Tolstoi at least to do it justice.'[37] Her article, 'The Sailing of the *Sinaia*' was most probably written with the aim of raising funds. She describes it as an event worthy of a place in modern history, brought about through the co-operation of English, French, Spanish and Mexicans, all working together, and culminating in the most moving experience of a lifetime.

> The time, the twenty third of May, 1939. The place, the little harbour town of Sète. The sun blazing down on a blue Mediterranean, and on the cobbles of the quayside, which radiate southern heat. The great steamer lying lazily alongside the dock, steaming gently, flags flying on her mast... On the decks, some seventeen hundred people standing, jammed in a solid mass, at silent attention. The band on the upper deck blows out music, gustily but ceremoniously - first the Marseillaise; then God Save the King; then the Himno de Riego, the hymn of the Spanish Republic. Speeches follow, in English and Spanish, and the crowds on the decks shout and wave, and cry 'Viva.' 'Viva Inglaterra,' 'Viva Mejico,' 'Viva la Libertad!' The squalling of the sirens, heaving up of the gangway steps, waving of hands, mopping of eyes - and the *Sinaia* slid away from the quayside, out into the open sea for her voyage to Vera Cruz.[38]

Nan Green sailed with the refugees as one of the few 'observers,' chosen because she could be useful in various ways.[39] Her Spanish was good, she could help with the care of the children on board, and on her return she planned to talk about her experience to raise funds for another ship. The voyage to Mexico lasted twenty three days. It was Nan Green's job to organise the feeding of the very young children. She worked with two Spanish girls, every three hours 'stirring great saucepans full of milk and various paps,' sterilising feeding bottles in between, and hardly ever getting up on deck.[40]

---

37 Her letter describes some of the small incidents of the day, the Duchess of Atholl tripping over the improvised coffee canteen on the quay and a hapless general who 'found himself with two family-less infants in his arms on the deck, and a choice of 1500 parents in the crowd!' Letter from Frida Stewart to her mother, Perpignan, 30 May 1939, papers of Frida Stewart.
38 Undated article by Frida Stewart, 'The Sailing of the *Sinaia*', papers of Frida Stewart.
39 Other observers included Sir Richard Rees and William Brebner.
40 Nan Green, unpublished memoirs, 'A Chronicle of Small Beer', p. 81.

We got to Puerto Rico and the democratic Puerto Ricanians had decided to welcome the Spanish refugees and they had hired coaches and a large hall to give them a banquet and a tour of the island. It was fantastic what they'd done. Unfortunately, you see, the American authorities who were in charge in Puerto Rico at that time refused to allow them to land. I was allowed to land because I had a passport, Sir Richard Rees, who'd come on behalf of the Quakers, I think, was allowed to land, and there was a French journalist - we had passports you see. So they took us round to show us what they had prepared. It was perfectly beautiful, a fleet of coaches, everything beautifully prepared and when we got back to the ship, the whole side of the ship was festooned with pieces of string and pieces of rope - they'd brought the whole thing down to the dockside and for the rest of that day, people were hauling up packets of cigars, boxes of chocolates, loaves of bread, anything they could give, bags of clothing, heaps of things, presents, presents - it didn't stop all the rest of the day. And they had two platforms, one down there and one up there, while people were addressing them, Puerto Ricanians were addressing their Spanish brothers through megaphones. It was - you could have stood there and wept all day with the beauty of it.[41]

She stayed for a while to see that refugees were settling in Mexico. She returned to England to raise more money but 'the entire scheme fell to the ground on the declaration of war.' No public meetings were allowed during the first weeks of the war, and no refugee ships would have been able to leave France.[42]

Nancy Cunard had also been to the camp in Argelès, determined to extricate a friend. In addition, she agreed to help four 'intellectuals' she had never met, allocated to her by the Intellectuals Committee in Paris. After endless bureaucratic delays, she secured the release of them all, accepting them as her personal responsibility. They stayed as Nancy Cunard's guests in Normandy until they had recuperated, eventually leaving for a new life in Mexico.[43] The 'nightmare' of the

41 Nan Green, Tameside 180, 7 August 1976.
42 Green, 'A Chronicle of Small Beer', p. 85.
43 Anne Chisolm, *Nancy Cunard* (Sidgwick & Jackson, GB, 1979) pp. 255-6. Chisolm records the difficulties of the journey across France during which they were all arrested and taken to police headquarters in Paris. The Spaniards, despite having the correct permits, were put on a train to be returned to the camp. With the help of the Intellectuals Committee, they were able to be reunited with Nancy Cunard in Paris a few days later. They leapt into a waiting taxi and drove to Normandy.

phoney war soon followed, and feeling 'sick at heart,' Nancy Cunard also went to Latin America to stay in Chile with her friend, Pablo Neruda. It was almost two years before she returned to Europe.[44]

Not all those who were in the camps in France were fortunate enough to leave before the start of the Second World War. Some internees were executed or sent to labour camps, others managed to escape and join the Resistance.[45] The fate of many remains unknown. One who was lost without trace was Roberto Vincenzi, a young Italian Lieutenant who had fought with the Garibaldis in the International Brigades. Whilst stationed at Quintanar he met Penny Phelps, the nurse who had been placed in charge of containing a fever outbreak in their unit.[46] They had fallen in love. Separated by new postings, they managed to keep in touch at first but then Penny Phelps was seriously wounded in an air raid on the medical unit where she was working near Castellón. She was sent home, still needing several operations for internal injuries. No news came of Roberto, and during her slow convalescence, she met and married a British doctor. Meanwhile, Roberto had crossed the border into France and was interned in Gurs, unable to return to Italy. His whereabouts were eventually discovered and Penny Phelps wrote to him of her difficult road to recovery, and of her marriage.

Then one day I found myself beginning to take an interest in life once more - I wanted to live - but somehow something had changed for me: I felt that life in Spain, what I had done there, the dear friends I had made (some of whom I should never see again), the way I had lived out there and my reactions to that life, had no connection at all with my life in England. I felt that living in Spain and living in England were two completely isolated experiences. During this period, Roberto, I had not forgotten you - far from it - but what I felt about the whole of my life in Spain I felt also about our relationship. I loved you in Spain - you stood for everything out there - you were part of it - you were a real fighter for the rights of mankind. I still do love you, Roberto, but in a different way: you were everything to me in Quintanar, and I loved our relationship - it was ideal, and I shall always remember it with great joy. But in England, while I was ill, Spain seemed so remote - almost another

---

44 Ibid., p. 257.
45 See for example, Louis Stein, *Beyond Death and Exile* (Harvard University Press, 1979).
46 See Chapter 4.

world. And now there is something I want to tell you, Roberto. While I was feeling like this, there was someone who helped me to get well again after I was so ill. He was a young doctor...[47]

She wrote of how she had grown to love this kind man, of how they had decided to marry, and of his understanding when she had told him about her feelings for Roberto in Spain. She asked him to write back and tell her if there was anything she and her husband could do to help. The reply, written in Spanish, is an eloquent expression of unselfish love in which he reviews their situation and admits that with the Republic defeated, he would have been unable to keep his promise to marry her in England.

> Dearest Penny, at last I have received news from you. Such a long time waiting... I thought that the wounds to your body caused by the fascist plane had taken your life... Penny, you have married - you have done the right thing! I do not reproach you for it at all... In my situation, how would I have been able to keep my promise? I find myself here surrounded by barbed wire, with no prospect of freeing myself, without knowing when we will leave here, and in the certainty that the bourgeoisie of whatever country we go to will make it difficult for us to find work, and besides, they will impose restrictions on our movements, seeing them as suspect. We are subject to imprisonment, persecution, unemployment etc., because we will continue with our fight, even when we must conduct it secretly, the only thing that matters to us is to arrive at the moment when all humanity is liberated from capitalist oppression... Don't think Penny, that I am writing these lines to you without feeling any pain. Penny, I love you still as much as at the beginning, more than at the beginning, but I realise with sorrow that you cannot be for me... In your letter you tell me not to feel bitterness towards your husband. What blame has he? How could I nurture mistrust for a man who would give you the happiness that I am unable to give you. He has given you his name, the pride of bearing it and bringing it honour. Be a worthy companion for him.[48]

They sent him cigarettes, he wrote with thanks on 23 August 1939.

---

47 Letter from Penny Phelps to Roberto Vincenzi, London, 24 June 1939, papers of Penny Phelps.
48 Letter from Roberto Vincezi to Penny Phelps, Gurs, 1 July 1939, papers of Penny Phelps.

Despite repeated attempts over the years, no more could ever be found out about what had happened to him after the German occupation of France.

Another Republican refugee was to change the life of a young Scotswoman in Oxford, just as the war was drawing to a close. Cora Blyth was helping in the local Basque children's colony at Aston where she had formed a firm friendship with Pili, one of the señoritas who had come to Britain with the children. There she met Luis Portillo who after the Ebro, like many others, had walked over the snow-covered Pyrenees into France. Sponsored by a British MP, he had been allowed entry to Britain and had been staying at the Basque colony on the estate of Lord Farringdon.

> He came with seven boys from this colony and joined mine and, I remember Pili taking me in to see him, she said, 'We've got this new man, Luis Portillo here.' [Laughter] And he was sitting by the fire reading and he looked up and he said, 'Oh, I've heard a lot about you,' - in Spanish, of course, and I immediately fell for him [laughter]. And that evening Pili and I had a long chat in bed, you know, 'Do you think he's married? He's got a ring on. Oh dear, do you think he's married?' And all this sort of thing. And next morning I had a chat with him and he said he wasn't married, but he had a fiancée in Vitoria, and the ring he wore was his grandmother's wedding ring, and so on, and he thought that his fiancée would expect him to come back. Of course, they all thought that as soon as we'd won the war, if we won, then they would all go back to Spain. However, gradually we got to know each other and I think the poor fiancée in Vitoria was perhaps written to, I don't know.[49]

When interviewed, she reflected on the reasons for the immediate attraction she had felt, saying with amusement, 'I've always been one for lame ducks, and I think that was why I was so attracted to Luis.' She believed that her upbringing was perhaps another factor.

> We weren't encouraged to think a lot of ourselves and I think I had really a tremendous lack of confidence. I'd never met the opposite sex before. So I think that meeting a refugee down on his luck was my big chance [laughter], though this was unconscious.[50]

---

49 Cora Blyth, AJ, 5 August 1996.
50 Ibid.

6.4 Cora Blyth (third from right) with Luis Portillo and some of the Basque girls, formerly from the Aston colony, pictured outside the Witney Council house where the girls lived for a while after the war.

Her parents, although recognising that he was an 'intellectual' still had strong reservations about her growing relationship with a Catholic who had no prospects.

Luis was invited to come and stay and it must have been a terrible ordeal for him. He had very few clothes, they were borrowed clothes, you know, they weren't a bit like what he would have worn in Spain where he always wore dark suits and white collars. He was dressed in sort of tweed jackets and grey flannel trousers... And we had a Sheltie dog which kept barking at Luis and father said to Luis, 'He knows you're trying to take Cora away.' And his idea was - he said to Luis, 'You ought to go to Latin America where you will be able to make a living.' And Mexico had offered double nationality to all the Spanish refugees and I think Luis was tempted but, the shipping was being sunk at a very terrifying rate at that time and he said cynically to me, 'He wants to get rid of me.'[Laughter] But I mean they were very polite and welcoming. It was a terrible cultural shock, both sides I think.[51]

51 Ibid.

They were married in March 1941, in the crypt of Westminster Cathedral because as a Protestant, she could not be married in front of the main altar. A Basque priest, Canon Onaindía, gave the address. Her parents did not attend the wedding.

So it was rather a strange little wedding and rather sad because it rained when we came out, no photos were taken or anything. And mother and father gave us a canteen of silver and some blankets and that was it... I think they just felt they couldn't really give their approval - so that was very sad. But once there were grandchildren, that was different.[52]

The children, four boys, were brought up as Catholics. The youngest, Michael, shared the keen interest of his parents in the labour movement, helping them in the running of the local Labour Party Committee rooms.

Some of the Basque children who were still in this country in 1939 were offered homes by people in Britain. Other children were still being repatriated. Frida Stewart was amongst those who shared the sad task of returning them to an uncertain future. Her postcard home on 20 December 1939 from Hendaye reads, 'Have just come from seeing the children off - a terribly moving thing, leaving them at the frontier - first time I ever heard them absolutely silent.'[53] Obtaining permission for new refugees to enter Britain was far from easy. Elizabeth Crump was working in the IBA offices in London and much of her secretarial work consisted of writing letters trying to help refugees wanting to come into Britain.[54] Several other women recalled how the refugees, often with professional qualifications in Spain, would have to struggle to find employment here.[55] Barbara Castle wrote of her parents' succession of refugees that included several Basque children and the former Under Secretary for Fine Arts in the Republican Government, who became a close family friend.[56]

52 Ibid.
53 Frida Stewart, postcard to mother, MML Box B-4:C/3j.
54 Elizabeth Crump (m. Thornycroft), AJ, 23 October 1996. Some of the limited numbers of 'respectable refugees' that were allowed entry were helped by a sub-committee of the National Joint Committee, entitled the 'British Committee for Refugees from Spain'. Lady Ruggles-Bryce and Miss Pollock arranged accommodation, Mrs Brinton and Chloe Vulliamy looked after their welfare. According to Jim Fyrth, by the autumn of 1939, there were 326 adult Spanish refugees in Britain, mainly professionals, office workers and skilled workers. The Signal was Spain, p. 297.
55 For example, Beryl Barker, IWM 13805-2, talking of the refugees in Sheffield, Fernando and Emilio. Fernando had been a dentist in Spain but was not allowed to practise here.

On the political front, women who had been outspoken in their support of the Republic had faced considerable challenges as the war dragged on. In the Conservative Party, the Duchess of Atholl was amongst a handful of MPs who did not support the policy of appeasement of the dictators. However, she was the only Conservative MP to vociferously oppose the unfair implementation of the Non-intervention policy in Spain. This brought her into conflict both with the Conservative Party leadership and with powerful members of her own constituency of Kinross and West Perth. Believing she could hold her seat as an independent candidate, she applied for the Chiltern Hundreds and a by-election was called for 21 December 1938. Frida Stewart was one of many NJC workers who volunteered to help during her campaign.

> Everyone who could drive or lend a car was welcome at Blair Atholl, and I drove the Austin Seven all over the grey-green country, bumping along hilly roads through Scotch mist and driving rain, visiting remote hamlets with election addresses, and piloting speakers to meetings. Her Grace was very calm and dignified under the strain, which must have been considerable; she had never been seriously opposed before in the feudal area, and the challenge was for her as much personal as political. In fact it was not. The challenge was one of principle against a whole party-political machine; and the Tories were determined that they were not going to be put in their place by one dissident individual, whatever her title. The Perthshire Conservatives rallied as never before to the true blue flag, and made sure their labourers and employers did the same. Their cars were everywhere, taking farm workers to the polls, with the hidden implication that they must vote the conformist ticket or else! The Duchess had relatively few cars, a slender purse compared to that of her opponents, and only her conscience to speak against the great myth, backed by wishful thinking, of Mr Chamberlain as the Saviour of Peace. 'To query the Munich settlement was to be a war-monger, and my opponents only too often claimed on their platforms that my policy meant war', wrote the Duchess in her post- mortem on the election: 'I believe I lost many women's votes on this account.'[57]

---

56 *See previous page]* Barbara Castle, *Fighting All the Way* (Pan Books, 1994, first published by Macmillan, London, 1993) pp. 93-94. Years later, one of the Basques, Aurelia, told Barbara Castle, 'I don't know how your mother managed. Your house was always full of refugees. You even brought home a bombed-out cat.'
57 Frida Stewart, unpublished memoirs, p. 188.

Frida's Stewart's assessment of the reasons for the loss of the seat by a fairly narrow margin have been substantiated by Sheila Hetherington in her biography of the Duchess, and in a study of the by-election by Stuart Ball.[58] Conservative voters and their leaders in the constituency were also, Stewart Ball believes, 'fed up with the Spanish wrangle' and desired a 'truly local MP, who would give priority to domestic issues.'[59] However, the many voters who had supported her were able to claim some satisfaction later. According to Sheila Hetherington, 'Elderly people on the estate still remember the election and say today: 'Aye, she was right, she was right. And there's a million dead that shouldn't be dead; and they knew she was right!'[60]

Several of the women in this study returned to Spain in the years following the defeat of the Republic, although this was not without hazards given Franco's policy towards those who had aided his enemies. One who crossed the border again, though not through choice, was Frida Stewart. She had been in Paris, still working to help refugees, when the Germans had occupied the city and was interned, firstly in Besançon, then in Vittel, for almost a year. She and a friend, Rosemary Say, managed to escape, and with the help of Republican exiles and the French resistance, eventually arrived home via Spain, Portugal and Ireland, having been entrusted with a secret message for General de Gaulle rolled inside a cigarette.[61] Frida Stewart began working for the Free French in London, but still went on writing articles in the hope that the people in Spain would not be forgotten. In 'Return to Spain' she describes her journey across the country, noting the general dislike amongst the Spaniards she encountered of 'the German officers who drive about in grand cars embellished with swastikas,'

---

58 Sheila Hetherington, *Katharine Atholl, 1874-1960: Against the Tide* (Aberdeen University Press, 1991, first edition 1989) Chapter 19; Stuart Ball, 'The Politics of Appeasement: the Fall of the Duchess of Atholl and the Kinross and West Perth By-election, December 1938', *The Scottish Historical Review* vol. LXIX, I: no.187: April 1990, pp. 49-83. The National Government candidate, William McNair Snadden, received 11, 808 votes, and the Duchess of Atholl, 10,495.
59 Ball, 'The Politics of Appeasement',*The Scottish Historical Review*, p. 83.
60 Hetherington, *Katharine Atholl*, pp. 216-7. The views of those who believed that the response of the Labour leadership had been inadequate have been well documented in other studies. See for example the attack by Sybil Wingate on the Labour Party's Spain Campaign Committee at the Labour Party Conference in May 1939, discussed in K. W. Watkins, *Britain Divided: the Effect of the Spanish Civil War on British Political Opinion* (Thomas Nelson & Sons Ltd., London, 1963) p. 194; C. Fleay and M. L. Sanders 'The Labour Spain Committee: Labour Party Policy and the Spanish Civil War' *The Historical Journal*, 28, 1, 1985, p. 194.
61 Frida Stewart's most detailed account of this episode is in *Dawn Escape* (Everybody's Books, London, undated, probably 1943).

and of 'the Italian commission who tour the country and requisition the olive harvest.' But her overriding impressions were of the widespread poverty she saw, and of the changed atmosphere in Madrid.

> We were struck by the very real distress that permeates the atmosphere of the town, especially in contrast to the Madrid of 1937. People were hungry enough then, but I never saw the haggard hopeless look that I noticed on the streets this year.[62]

The number of political prisoners in Franco's Spain was to remain high for many years, and thousands of women, sometimes with their children, were amongst them.[63] A leaflet, 'Mission to Spain', contains reports from Monica Whately, Leah Manning and Nan Green, written after their visit to Spain in 1947.[64] They went as a deputation from the International Women's Day Committee in response to a request from the Union of Spanish Women. Concern was growing about three particular Republican women who had been kept in prison for many months awaiting trial. Two faced sentences of thirty years, and the other, the death penalty, for having formed an illegal organisation to help prisoners. The effect on the sentences of the prisoners resulting from the presence of representatives from abroad cannot be judge with certainty, but the death sentence was avoided and thirty years imprisonment given instead, whilst the others received shorter terms.[65]

For those with a past history of helping the Republic, the risks of travelling to Spain were not to be taken lightly. Nan Green had only obtained a visa because her passport bore her new married name, Mrs Brake. Years later, Chloe Vulliamy, who had looked after Basque refugee children in Britain, was to find herself in difficulties because of her interest in the welfare of the families of political prisoners in

---

62 Frida Stewart, 'Return to Spain' undated, probably 1942, papers of Frida Stewart. The same article is partly recycled in 'Will Franco Fight', which discussed the valuable help Hitler was receiving from Franco and a 'neutral' Spain.

63 Michael Richards estimates that in 1940 there were 30,000 female political prisoners in Spain and that probably several thousand women were executed in the immediate post-war years. *A Time of Silence: Civil War and the Culture of Repression in Franco's Spain, 1936-1945.* For personal testimony of women who had been imprisoned see Shirley Mangini, *Memories of Resistance: Women's Voices from the Spanish Civil War* (Yale University Press, New Haven & London, 1995).

64 Leaflet, *Mission to Spain* by Leah Manning, also includes 'The Catholic Church' by Monica Whately and 'How do they live?' by Nan Green. (Emergency Committee for Democratic Spain, London, undated, probably 1947) Also reproduced as 'Mision en España' by the Union de Mujeres Españolas, Paris, in their bulletin, *Mujeres Antifascistas Españolas* no. 4, 15 January 1947.

65 See also Green, 'A Chronicle of Small Beer' p. 115.

Spain. Her local paper tells of how in 1963, Miss Vulliamy, aged 57, had taken a trip to Spain to escape the British winter weather. For eighteen months she had been sending gift parcels to families of political prisoners through the Appeal for Armistice in Spain Organisation. Whilst in Spain, she visited them, and seeing the poverty in which they were living, gave them money for food. In one family she visited, the husband had just been released after being so badly beaten that he was deaf in one ear. The article continued,

> Soon after leaving this house she was arrested and thrown into what she described later as a filthy cell. She was kept in custody for five days and was interrogated by as many as ten men at times. During the interrogation she was stripped twice and searched. She was accused of being a Communist spy distributing Moscow gold. She denied this and asked to see the British Consul but this was refused.[66]

After several days, she was put on a plane to London and warned, 'Do not come back.' Lillian Urmston was more fortunate on her return visits, made with her husband in 1949, 1953 and 1964 covering the different areas in which she had nursed.

> My husband was greatly impressed, that, on these three trips, someone always recognised me, called out 'Lilliana' and brought out groups of those who'd known me. Invariably, we ate, drank and reminisced, despite the interest shown by the Guardia Civil. As I'd become a writer/journalist, I was able to take money to help some of those in need.[67]

The IBA was very active in the work of helping political prisoners in Spain, but fellow Brigaders were also facing difficulties in some countries. For Patience Darton, the dream of being able to go everywhere and find former friends when the war was won was not to be realised.

> Some of the Poles had a very bad time, I mean, a lot of very stupid and horrid things happened to Brigaders in the countries, in the different countries - terrible things, undeserved things, because

---

66 'Five Days of Terror: Hempton Woman Gaoled as Spy in Spain,' *Banbury Adventurer* 30 January 1963, MML Box B-8: E/12, 57.
67 Letter from Lillian Buckoke (née Urmston) to Jim Fyrth, Sussex, 5 November 1985, MML Box D-1: B/1.

they'd been abroad they were not trusted... You don't always know
whether you should get in touch or not - still - terrible.[68]

After the Second World War, the majority of the women in this
study continued to participate in various causes. Their activities are
too numerous and diverse to cover here, but some are listed in the
individual profiles in Appendix I. It should be noted however, that a
significant proportion of them became involved in aspects of the
peace movement, working both at the level of International Peace
Conferences, and in the Campaign for Nuclear Disarmament in Britain.
The factors that had led them to become involved with the Spanish
war in so many different ways, continued to form a basis for their
concern with broad international issues.

MEMORY AND WAR

Along with those of many other nationalities, the British members of
the International Brigades have become part of the 'legend' of the Spanish
Civil War, 'volunteers for liberty', symbolising international solidarity
in the anti-fascist struggle.[69] Awareness of their own legendary qualities must surely have begun before they were withdrawn from Spain,
as Dolores Ibárruri, 'La Pasionaria', bid them farewell in Barcelona.

> You are history. You are legend. You are the heroic example of the
> solidarity and the universality of democracy.[70]

Reference has already been made in the Introduction to the legends
that have formed around the memory of the war in Spain. Here, the roles
played by British women in these legends will be considered, not only
as performers sharing the limelight, back-stage hands, and watchers in

---

68 Patience Edney (née Darton), IWM 8398, reel 7.
69 *Volunteer for Liberty* was the name of the paper produced by the International Brigade
   Association from 1939 to 1946, when the title was changed to *Spain Today*. *British
   Volunteers for Liberty* is the title of a book by Bill Alexander (Lawrence & Wishart, London,
   1986, first published 1982).
70 Dolores Ibárruri, (La Pasionaria) Barcelona, 29 October 1938. The speech is cited in many
   studies and continues, 'We will not forget you; and, when the olive tree of peace puts forth
   its leaves, entwined with the laurels of the Spanish Republic's victory, come back! Come
   back to us and here those of you who have no homeland will find a homeland, those who
   are forced to live without friends will find friends, and all of you will find the affection and
   the gratitude of the entire Spanish people who today and tomorrow will shout with enthusiasm: "Long live the heroes of the International Brigades." '

the wings, but also as agents who have contributed to the consolidation of the legends. As the years passed by, how did these women explore their own feelings about the war, and how did they attempt to come to terms with personal loss? How too did the women whose socialist beliefs had been intensified by Spanish issues respond to new challenges to their commitment? These are the questions that must be addressed in order to understand how the lives of the women in this study continued to be affected by the Spanish Civil War, long after it was over.

Recently there has been some shift towards public recognition of the role of women within the Brigades. La Pasionaria's farewell speech to the International Brigades did not make specific mention of women. She spoke of the 'men of the International Brigades', and of how 'these men reached our country as crusaders for freedom.'[71] However, in 1996, during the concert arranged to honour the Brigaders in Madrid, the same speech was read in Spanish, apparently updated from the original version and taking care to refer to the men and women of the Brigades.[72] British women do have a small but distinct role within the legend of the International Brigades, though because of their relatively small numbers and primarily non-combatant roles, their experiences are usually placed peripherally to those of the men.[73]

However, as Penny Summerfield notes in her book, *Reconstructing Women's Wartime Lives*, 'not all past experience, particularly women's, has been "legendised".'[74] The life histories of the majority of women in this study cannot therefore be easily examined within the context of a 'myth and reality' structure as have the memories of the veterans in Alistair Thomson's book, *Anzac Memories*.[75] Most of the British women involved with Spain were working at local level in the towns and

---

71 For the English translation, see for example Robert Low, *La Pasionaria: The Spanish Firebrand* (Hutchinson, London, 1992) p. 109.

72 Speech of Dolores Ibárruri, read by Esperanza Alonso, 'Homenaje a las Brigadas Internacionales', Palacio de los Deportes, Madrid, 5 November 1996, televised by TVE 2.

73 The exact numbers of British women in the Brigades has been impossible to establish with certainty. Many of the nurses who went out to Spain with Spanish Medical Aid were later incorporated into the Brigades and the Spanish Republican Army, but probably not all. The lists of Brigaders in the IBA archive only note a few of the medical staff (Marx Memorial Library Box D7, File A/1, A/2). Some of the minutes of the Spanish Medical Aid Committee are in the Modern Records Centre, but other records have still not been located. For more on the British male perception of the female role see Kris Rothstein ' "This Is Where War Is": British Masculinity and the Spanish Civil War', MA Dissertation, Department of Sociology, University of Essex, 1996.

74 Penny Summerfield, *Reconstructing Women's Wartime Lives* (Manchester University Press, 1998) p. 29.

75 Alistair Thomson, *Anzac Memories: Living with the Legend* (Oxford University Press, 1994).

villages of Britain, and committee work receives little public recognition. Even those working at national level are only remembered by
people who were themselves active in the campaigns, their families,
and a few historians. Legends seldom centre on those who work with
refugees. Quakers, for example, have a style of self-effacing, team
effort that does not lend itself to the creation of popular myths.[76]
Individual British women writers who went to Spain did not enhance
the 'mythological' qualities of their fame as did Ernest Hemingway, or
come to exemplify a particular political view of the war like George
Orwell.[77]

There are, however, a few exceptions, although the extent of their
impact as legends is felt only at local level, or amongst the others who
had been involved with the war, rather than within popular memory
in the broadest sense. Ethel MacDonald, the Glasgow anarchist who
had been broadcasting from Barcelona until she was arrested following the 'May Days', was awarded legendary status on her death by the
Glasgow Evening Citizen.

SCOTS "SCARLET PIMPERNEL" DIES: SHE BECAME LEGEND IN SPAIN.
The small dark-haired woman - once called Scotland's "Scarlet
Pimpernel" during the mid-1930s - is dead. And so ends the legend
of Ethel MacDonald.[78]

Death, in this instance, was seen as the ending of the legend, but
in anarchist circles at least, her legendary status surely persists.[79] In
the years since the war, the British women who had served with the
Brigades became what could be regarded as a small, 'legendary' elite
amongst the much wider group of women who had been involved with
the war in other ways. A recent publication, *Memorials of the Spanish
Civil War*, is dedicated to the subject of remembrance. This richly
illustrated book gives the histories leading up to the unveiling of
nearly forty memorials throughout Britain honouring the volunteers

---

76 With the advent of 'media hype' relief work has become more high-profile. Mother Teresa
   and Bob Geldorf are perhaps suitable examples.
77 The views put forward by George Orwell in *Homage to Catalonia* (Penguin Books,
   Harmondsworth, Middlesex, 1983, first published by Secker & Warburg, 1938) have more
   recently been aired in the film, *Land and Freedom* directed by Ken Loach.
78 *Glasgow Evening Citizen* on the death of Ethel MacDonald from multiple sclerosis,
   1 December 1960, quoted by Rhona M. Hodgart, *Ethel MacDonald: Glasgow Woman
   Anarchist* (Kate Sharpley Library, Pirate Press, Sheffield, undated) p. 20.
79 For more on women anarchists see the Kate Sharpley Library, B. M. Hurricane, London,
   WC1N 3XX.

who served in Spain.[80] Prominently labelled as 'The Official Publication of the International Brigade Association', it is helpful here as a
reflection of the 'official' face of the memory of the British volunteers.
Amongst those who were killed in the fighting, Felicia Browne, the
first to die, is assured of a place in the text amongst those who could
be regarded as 'warrior heroes'. Her story has all the ingredients
essential to heroic legend, the belief that she willingly sacrificed her
artistic career to take up arms for a greater cause, and the ultimate
sacrifice of her life to save that of a comrade.[81] The 'courageous
nurse' is represented by the inclusion of several individual examples.
Margaret Powell's name appears on the plaque in Southwark Town Hall.

6.5 Margaret Powell with Luis Portillo (left) and Jim Brewer,
after receiving an award from the Republican government in exile.

80 Colin Williams, Bill Alexander and John Gorman, *Memorials of the Spanish Civil War* (The Official
    Publication of the International Brigade Association, Alan Sutton Publishing, Stroud, Glouces-
    tershire, 1996) By the year 2000, there were 70 memorials, and more in the planning stages.
81 Ibid., p. 20. For more on Felicia Browne see Chapter 4 and Tom Buchanan's study of her
    life and legend based on newly-discovered letters written by her in 1936, 'The lost art of
    Felicia Browne' in *The Impact of the Spanish Civil War on Britain: War, Loss and Memory*
    (Sussex Academic Press, Brighton and Portland, 2007)

She is featured in the text as one of the last nurses to leave Spain and for having been created a Dame of the Order of Loyalty to the Spanish Republic in recognition of her 'valiant action as a nurse' and her 'self sacrifice and devotion to our wounded and to our war victims.'[82]

The words of Ann Murray are used to describe the suffering of the wounded men and several other nurses are briefly mentioned for their work under fire.[83] A photograph of Patience Darton nursing in Spain epitomises the notion of the nurse as a 'healing angel'. Gently bending over the wounded man to instruct a Spanish girl in the skills of nursing, she is bathed in a radiant light from a nearby window. At the ceremony in Camden Town Hall in 1995, as one of only a handful of surviving women who volunteered for Spain, she is shown standing before the newly unveiled plaque. Behind her stands a Brigader with the banner of the British Battalion, the image of 'lifetime commitment' as once again they see the words that have resounded through their lives, now etched boldly on the plaque, ¡NO PASARAN![84]

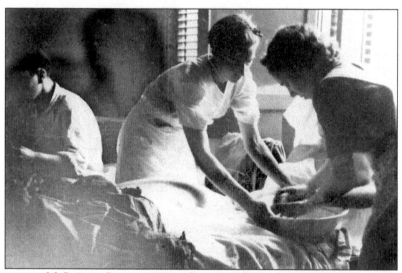

6.6 Patience Darton training a Spanish nurse in a hospital in Spain.

---

82 Ibid., p. 23. See report by Rosita Davson to the Spanish Medical Aid Committee, 15 February 1939 for an account of how Margaret Powell and Lillian Urmston were found amongst the refugees in the camps in France. Modern Records Centre, MSS 946/539.
83 Ibid., nurse Annie Knight (née Murray) pp. 42 & 44; nurses Winifred Wilson and Enid Ramshaw p. 70; Spanish Medical Aid worker Winifred Sandford (formerly, Bates) p. 114.
84 Ibid., Patience Edney (née Darton) in Spain p. 21; in Camden Town Hall on 25 April 1995, p. 19.

6.7 Patience Darton and Wally Togwell with the banner of the
British Battalion, Camden Town Hall, London, April 1995.

Several women are mentioned for their work in Britain, including
Isabel Brown, a legend amongst those involved with the war for her
stirring fund-raising speeches.[85] The book certainly achieves its objective, to be 'a tribute to all the
men and women who volunteered to fight for freedom in Spain', but
this aim leaves little room for the voices of those the Brigaders left
behind.[86] The International Brigade Association in Britain, unlike its
counterparts in other countries, consisted exclusively of Brigaders.
This rule had unfortunate repercussions, particularly for the wives of
Brigaders, who, after many years of unofficial activity in the group,
sometimes felt themselves marginalised on the death of their husbands.
Their general invisibility in the legends surrounding the Brigades also
emerges in this book. Only Win Albaya is quoted, remembering one of
the 'blackest' times when she had no news of her husband in Spain.[87]
The memories of how she, and many others, often had to struggle to
overcome daily financial hardships whilst their husbands were away
are not included. Their contribution has not been 'legendised'.

Many meetings have been held over the years that have reunited

---

85 Ibid., p. 68.
86 Ibid., inside front cover.
87 Ibid., p. 97. For more on Win Albaya (Albeye) and others, see Chapter 3.

IBA members, their families and friends. These meetings have offered a space for the consolidation of the stories of the past, for the transmission of narratives to others, and for the re-affirmation of a present purpose, namely, to continue the fight against fascism. The interactions of this group of 'witnesses' to the war in Spain can be considered in the light of the work of Jay Winter and Emmanuel Sivan on war and remembrance. They discuss the framework surrounding the term 'collective memory', taking particular interest in the intersection between private memories, family memories and collective memory.[88] Following the work of the anthropologist, Roger Bastide, they construct a helpful metaphor to illustrate the notion of collective memory, describing it as a 'sort of choir singing, or better still, a sing-along.'

This is a kind of event which is not very regimented, and in which each participant begins singing at a different time and using a somewhat different text or melody which he himself has composed or developed. But he does it according to norms - musical, linguistic, literary - accepted by other members of that informal choir. Moreover, when each sings, he hears himself in his inner ear, but he also hears the collective choir in his external ear. That is, he hears the product of the collective effort. Certainly, this collective product may modify or even slant his own singing, almost in spite of himself.[89]

However, when studying collective memory, their emphasis is on those who have agency within the social groups formed for the purposes of commemoration. They use the term 'collective remembrance' to denote this emphasis on activity as opposed to the more generalised idea of collective memory as 'some facet of the mental furniture of a population - what the French like to call their 'mentalités'.[90] Those who form bonds through their active participation in the work of remembrance form what Jay Winter terms 'fictive kinships', a type of association in which the bonds are social and experiential, as opposed to those based on blood ties or marriage.[91]

Although Winter and Sivan write of remembrance as being 'by its very nature vulnerable to decay', they also note how 'constant rehearsal, group action, ingenuity in mobilising resources are elements

88 Jay Winter and Emmanuel Sivan, Chapter 1, 'Setting the framework', in Jay Winter and Emmanuel Sivan (eds), *War and Remembrance in the Twentieth Century* (Cambridge University Press, 1999).
89 Ibid., p. 28.
90 Ibid., p. 9.
91 Jay Winter, Chapter 2, 'Forms of kinship and remembrance in the aftermath of the Great War,' in Winter & Sivan, *War and Remembrance*, p. 40.

6.8 Margaret Powell (centre) with Patience Darton (left)
and Lillian Urmston (right) at the unveiling of the International
Brigade Memorial, Jubilee Gardens, London, 5 October 1985.

which keep memory traces alive.'[92] This results in the creation of a
relatively more successful process of remembrance, as in the case of
the memory of the war in Spain. The memorials erected in the last few
years in commemoration of the volunteers who went to Spain show that
in this particular instance, the time has not yet come for forgetting.

The sense of 'fictive kinship' amongst those who had been
involved with Spain was powerful.[93] Nan Green, for many years the
Secretary of the IBA, in summing up the 1976 commemorative meeting

92 Jay Winter and Emmanual Sivan, Chapter 1, 'Setting the framework', in Winter & Sivan,
   War and Remembrance, p. 31.
93 The continuation of this 'fictive kinship' to the next generation is discussed in Chapter 7.

6.9 International Brigade Memorial,
Jubilee Gardens, London, 2000.

at Loughborough, spoke of her impressions of 'the warmth of people who fought in Spain and the people around them', and 'the kind of togetherness which many people haven't experienced since.'

> I think this link of Spain is something that we'll - well it will go on for good and all between us, and it will go on amongst the British people for ever and ever because nobody who was connected with those days will ever forget it.[94]

Nan Green had formed a friendship with the writer, Nancy Cunard. She wrote later that she had gradually become aware of Nancy Cunard's presence, 'as one becomes aware of a particular instrument in an orchestra, or a particular colour in a tapestry - and the tapestry was

---

94 Nan Green, Tameside 233.

Spain: the Spain of 1936-1939.'[95] They had exchanged many letters, and in one written shortly before she died in 1965, Nancy Cunard included a sequence from a long poem in the making that emphasised their common bond.

For Nan Especially

No war is ever the same as the one before
For all its Flanders muds, its bombs and guns;
Time sees to that - and yet, unerring, runs
One same, fast thread of continuity.
'Grapple it to thy heart with hooks of steel'
Wrote Shakespeare, naming friendship. Not strange that here
These words return to be loved and held most dear
By us who have one country most in mind,
Its steadfast pain in the blood, its nobility,
The force and vigour of its immortal kind

Ay, grapple it well.

We, Irish, Scots and Welsh,
We, English of many shires and many sires,
Some of us know - how soon and ah, how well-
What such-like friendship means, and so we went
To the dangerous, lovely land (some being new friends)
Who's set their hearts, however, on taking a hand
(And how!) in its battles...

Well grappled to the heart still is
By us that far music in all its tragedy,
Its sombre purple and violet with yellow shot-through,
Its scarlet and black...
On such there's no turning back...
How well these things are known to me and you.[96]

---

95 It is interesting to note the resonance between Nan Green's description of Nancy Cunard as an 'instrument in an orchestra' and the idea of collective memory as a 'choir' given above. Nan Green 'Nancy Cunard and Spain' in Hugh Ford (ed.), *Nancy Cunard: Brave Poet, Indomitable Rebel 1896-1965* (Chilton Book Co., Philadelphia & New York, 1968) p. 171.
96 Nancy Cunard, sequence from 'The Vision', February-March 1964, quoted by Nan Green, 'Nancy Cunard and Spain' in Ford, *Brave Poet, Indomitable Rebel*, pp. 175-76.

Nancy Cunard felt the pull of the group dynamic, although she was very much an individual player. The bond of Spain also linked her to Sylvia Townsend Warner, who wrote in her tribute to Nancy Cunard that 'Each of us sometimes found the other exasperating; but we saw eye to eye about Spain. It was that which cemented us.'[97] The hold that Spain exerted over her did not diminish. 'I've never seen a people who I admired more. I never again saw a country as much as I loved Spain,' she said many years afterwards.[98] For some, maintaining contact was more difficult for a variety of reasons, perhaps due to living abroad, or through the desire to put sad memories of the past behind them.[99] Unfortunately, it is now no longer possible to ask most of the women who did not keep in touch why this was so.

British women who were involved with the Spanish war have rarely presented what could be regarded as public 'institutionalised' narratives on the subject.[100] Women have however, frequently interacted with the 'collective memory' of the war through their autobiographical writings and in interviews.[101] Several examples will help to show the ways in which women have 'legendised' the past in their personal narratives, and the different methods by which their ideas have been transmitted to others.

Amongst women's writings on Spain are certain examples that illustrate perceptions of the 'mythic' qualities of those who fought in the International Brigades. Francesca Wilson worked with refugees in Spain and met Brigaders on various occasions. Her written impressions associate them with pagan and Christian heroes. The first example is

---

97   Sylvia Townsend Warner, 'Nancy Cunard', in Ford, *Brave Poet, Indomitable Rebel*, p. 327.
98   Val Warner and Michael Schmidt, 'Sylvia Townsend Warner in Conversation', *PN Review* 23, vol. 8, 1981, p.35, quoted by Maroula Joannou, 'Sylvia Townsend Warner in the 1930s', *A Weapon in the Struggle: The Cultural History of the Communist Party in Britain* edited by Andy Croft (Pluto Press, London, 1998) p. 97.
99   Those who lived abroad include for example, Rosaleen Smythe who went to live in Canada; Angela Guest who qualified as a doctor in America, and went to work in South Africa where she was killed in a car accident, her son becoming the ward of Patience Darton; Winifred Bates, who lived in America; Muriel McDiarmid, who lived for many years in France and Italy. Penny Phelps was amongst those who maintained only tenuous links with the group, moving into a new life with her husband, who became a Consultant Dermatologist. In her autobiography, the disjuncture between her life before and after the war is very marked. See Parts III, IV, and V, Penelope Fyvel (née Phelps, m. Feiwel) *English Penny* (Arthur H. Stockwell, Ilfracombe, 1992).
100 For more on different narrative modes see Elizabeth Tonkin, *Narrating Our Past: The Social Construction of Oral History* (Cambridge University Press, 1992) particularly p. 68, discussing the ideas of Alessandro Portelli. One 'institutionalised' narrative, *Britain in the Nineteen Thirties*, (Weidenfield and Nicholson, London, 1971) was written by Noreen Branson and Margot Heinemann, which devoted part of a chapter to the Spanish war and the British response.
101 For a discussion on the meanings of the term 'collective memory' see Winter & Sivan, *War and Remembrance*, pp. 16-29.

taken from an article that she probably wrote whilst the war was still in progress, and the second from her memoirs published in 1944.

> Listening to the tales told by soldiers of the International Brigade, I found myself saying very often, 'What a saga this will make one day! What a chapter in the annals of courage and adventure!' But will it be told or will it be buried in unknown graves in Spain?... Many of them are simple souls. I admire in them their simplicity, their single-mindedness, their lack of heroics, their earnestness. In the calm remoteness of England one and another of them come back into my mind - already half mythical. There is Sam, the first of the Brigade, whom I met in a restaurant in Valencia - bearded, black-spectacled, a bandage round his head: [his face like] a mask till he began to speak, then his loud cheerful voice was reassuring. He had lost an eye and got a bullet in his head, was going to Barcelona next day to have it out. He hoped it would be soon done - he wanted to get back to the front, he was in a hurry. 'Haven't you given enough?' I murmured, thinking vaguely of Odin. 'It isn't much is it?' he said embarrassed.[102]

> There was something fantastic about the International Brigade. Hundreds of years ago, I thought, there were the same incongruous bands from all over Europe struggling on the mountains and plains of Palestine, in a country not unlike this country of Spain, to save the tomb of Christ from the infidel. But it was easier to go on those crusades: there was glamour and prestige about them, public enthusiasm, the blessing of the church, the promise of life everlasting. These crusaders had come without arms or money or promises.[103]

The sacrifice of physical health and disregard for personal gain contributed to the creation of a mythic concept of the Brigaders as heroes in the public memory of those on the Left. This representation of their symbolic role was in marked contrast to the view of the authorities in Britain. Many Brigaders had been billed for their repatriation expenses, and were given little opportunity to make full use of their recent combat experience on the outbreak of the Second World War.[104]

---

102 Francesca Wilson, 'International Brigade', papers of Helen Grant, Cambridge University Library, Add. 8251, Box 1, II, p. 1.
103 Wilson, *In the Margins of Chaos*, p. 187.
104 There is no record of any of the Brigaders actually paying the £2. 4s. 11d. See Alexander, *British Volunteers for Liberty*, pp. 241, and 246-7 for their experiences when volunteering to serve during WW II.

It has been recognised that the public memory of Brigaders as 'heroes' of the Left in certain instances may compete, or on occasion even conflict, with the private memory of those who knew them best. The legacy of Brigaders' involvement with the Spanish war has produced a mixture of emotions amongst their relatives and friends, including transference of survivor guilt, jealousy and resentment.[105] However, writings about individual Brigaders by women seem more likely to take the form of tributes. Kathleen Gibbons epic poem, composed on the anniversary of the Battle of Jarama, records her husband's life of struggle from his impoverished childhood to his final days in a hospital bed. Her declamation of the poem during the interview was practised and confident, suggesting frequent recitals. The verses on Spain conclude with his return to the front after recovering from wounds, and his subsequent capture and imprisonment near Burgos, where despite the appalling conditions, the men attempted to maintain morale by running their own educational classes. Almost all twenty-two verses end with the words of the title, 'Like a Man', as an affirmation of heroic valour. The verses on his imprisonment and return to Britain were delivered with great emotion.

> Men clustered for warmth whilst enlightenment fought
> To fill in the gaps lack of learning had brought.
> When the day of the prisoners exchange arrived
> He was thrust forth, half naked, lice-ridden and shrived,
> But held his integrity high - like a man.
>
> Banners hung, many, at Victoria Station.
> His wife, with his boy-child waited in patience.
> He returned withered, greying and aged,
> My laughing, round-robin, from the fascist cage:
> My darling still breathed and thought - like a man.[106]

Describing his role in Spain, she has conflated notions of masculinity and heroism, contrasting these with the archetypal image of the patiently waiting wife and child.

---

105 Natalie Suart addresses these issues in her PhD thesis at De Montfort University on 'The Memory of the Spanish Civil War and the Family of the British International Brigaders'. Some examples of such cases were given in her paper, 'A Hero in the Family: the private memory of the relatives of the British International Brigaders', Cañada Blanch Centre for Contemporary Spanish Studies, London, 17 May 2000.
106 Kathleen Gibbons, verses 20 and 21, 'Like A Man', papers of Kathleen Gibbons.

A recent example of the continued transmission of such tributes occurred at a Summer School on the Spanish Civil War in 1999, when the Clarion Singers presented a programme of songs and readings associated with the war.[107] One of the singers, Elsie Marshall, had been very active in the Aid Spain campaigns. She remembered welcoming the Brigaders at the station on their return, and had composed a song in memory of one of them, affectionately known as 'Our Bert'. After his return from Spain, Bert was active in the National Union of Railworkers and as a Communist Councillor, until he was killed at work by a train. To a poignant melody, Elsie Marshall's 'Ballad to Bert Fletcher' was sung, unaccompanied and unfalteringly, by a young woman. The content and style combined to create a vivid portrayal of the ideal 'working-class hero.'

> We thought the train was the friendliest thing
> For on her back she bore
> Our heroes brave of the fine Brigade
> Who had fought in the Spanish war.
>
> They stepped out on the platform there
> Our hearts were filled with pride
> For we knew of the sacrifice they made
> To fight on freedom's side.
>
> One man amongst this little band
> Stood shyly on one side
> For he had been in Burgos jail
> Where many comrades died.
>
> The treatment which our friend received
> At his jailers' cruel hand
> Had left its mark, for he spoke to us
> With halting speech and shaking hand.
>
> But his words were inspiration to us
> To us who were standing there
> For his courage burned with a steadfast flame
> That warmed us in its flare.

---

107 The Clarion Choir was founded in 1940 by Colin Bradsworth, a Birmingham doctor and former Brigader, with the aim of promoting socialism through music.

He lived his life in the service of man
He listened to their woes
He fought their fight with reasons and might
Which baffled all their foes.

We thought the train was the cruellest thing
On that November day
When it dealt that treacherous, murderous blow
That took our Bert away.

Now we must work with all our strength
To see his life's work done
That men throughout the world shall live
In love, in peace, as one.[108]

The purpose of the tribute is not just to preserve the legend of the man, it is the continuation of commitment to the cause down through the generations. Heroes must not have died in vain, nor crusades halted for anything other than to regroup forces for the next battle, however distant the field.

Mention has already been made in Chapter 3 of widows' letters, written as formal expressions of grief and published at the time to inspire others. These letters can be seen as an early part of the process of trying to come to terms with the death of a loved one in the Spanish war. Many years after the war, Nan Green still viewed the death of her husband on the Ebro in terms of his role as a 'just warrior'.

He was killed almost in the last hour of the last day. But I've never felt able to be sorry for him because he was doing the right thing, he was doing his thing and it was the right thing, we all feel that. We had this privilege of being the - well,... you know, right straight down the high road of history in the right cause and there hasn't been anything like it since, so flawless and so black and white and so good and so wholesome, and he was doing that and he was sure that we would win, and he was sure that the French were going to send the things over and he was with the battalion and I think that that was his last - that's how he died, he died flying as it were, you know, like a bird dies.[109]

---

108 Elsie Marshall, 'Ballad to Bert Fletcher', Clarion Singers, performed at the Wedgwood Memorial College, 26 July 1999.
109 Nan Green, Tameside, 180, 7 August 1976.

6.10 Margot Heinemann after the war.

Death is sometimes expressed both in terms of personal loss, and of loss to the cause. Margot Heinemann, in an interview during her later years, recalled a poem she had written soon after the death of John Cornford.[110] Her poem conveys these twin losses with great intensity, and supports her belief that poetry 'reaches deep into the language we think in and the way we think' and 'keeps something alive from time past.'[111]

Grieve In A New Way For New Losses

And after the first sense 'He will not come again'
Fearing still the images of corruption,
To think he lies out there, and changes
In the process of the earth from what I knew,
Decays and even there in the grave, shut close
In the dark, away from me, speechless and cold,
Is in no way left the same that I have known.

And this is not more than we can deal with.

110 Margot Heinemann, IWM, 9239.
111 Margot Heinemann, 'English Poetry and the War in Spain: Some Records of a Generation', in Stephen M. Hart (ed.), *¡No Pasarán!': Art, Literature and the Spanish Civil War* (Tamesis Books, London, 1988).

In our long nights the honest tormentor speaks
And in our casual conversations:
'He was so live and young - need he have died,
Who had the wisest head, who worked so hard,
Led by his own sheer strength: whom I so loved?'
Yes, you'd like an army all of Sidney Cartons, -
The best world made conveniently by wasters,
    second rates,
Someone that we could spare,
And not the way it has to be made,
By the loss of our best and bravest everywhere.

And this is not more than we can deal with.[112]

Her choice of the plural pronoun in 'this is not more than we can deal with', underlines the importance of the notion of solidarity in facing such tragedies. Perhaps her acceptance in the last stanza of the fact that the best world 'has to be made' by such great sacrifices, brought her some comfort. Nevertheless, in the interview, when she is asked about John and the 'tragic losses of so many talented people', there are long pauses in the normally rapid flow of her responses. She regains her stride by changing to a more 'public' style of speech and summarising the various ways in which the Brigades played an important role in Spain.[113] Her reasons for doing so could be construed in different ways. She could be simply suppressing a painful memory, or she could be maintaining a denial of any personal doubts about the value of his sacrifice in retrospect. Given that the interview context itself was in this case rather formal and unsympathetic, she could perhaps have wished to avoid appearing vulnerable in any way. Two years after this interview, in an article on English poetry and the Spanish Civil War, she raised the subject herself.

---

112 First and last verses of 'Grieve in a New Way for New Losses' by Margot Heinemann, in Stephen Spender and John Lehmann (eds), *Poems for Spain* (Hogarth Press, London, 1939) p. 45-46. One of John Cornford's best known poems from Spain was *To Margot Heinemann* 'Heart of the heartless world', 1936, reproduced in, for example, Pat Sloan (ed.), *John Cornford: A Memoir* (Borderline Press, Fife, 1978, first published 1938) pp. 246-7.
113 Margot Heinemann, IWM 9239. She refers to 1) The military role of the Brigades in the defence of Madrid: 2) Their role as symbols of solidarity: 3) The fact that interest in the war was increased in Britain by having 'local boys' fighting there: 4) That by the time of the Second World War, people in Britain were conditioned to some extent to the idea of 'standing up to Fascism.'

When I read now about young British writers who were deluded by the myth of anti-fascism, or who took the easy road of action and commitment rather than the hard one of being a poet and objective, it is to [Sorley] Maclean's passionate lament that I turn to recall the feelings and conflicts of that generation.

> Cornford and Julian Bell
> and García Lorca
> Always going round in my head
> and sky black without an opening.
> Cornford and Julian Bell
> and García Lorca,
> The poets will not get over your death
> With the lie of the comfortable heart.[114]

Her comments would seem to imply that the question cannot be denied, that it continues to demand review, and that she still seeks reassurance from others that such a sacrifice was worthwhile.

Finally, in 1991, she wrote the poem 'Ringstead Mill', found amongst her papers after her death the following year. She and John Cornford had spent a short time together at Ringstead Mill, owned by the Cornfords, just before he left for Spain soon after the outbreak of war. Although the poem is intensely personal, the last stanza reveals her determination to claim a legacy for John and his comrades.

> Stranger whom I once knew well,
> Do not haunt this house.
> Sorrow's but a ravelled thread,
> To draw back the active dead,
> Nor is pleasure mutable
> Such as smiled on us.
> Stranger whom I once knew well,
> Do not haunt this house.
>
> Idle and low spirits can
> Take your name and face:

---

114 Sorley Maclean, *Spring Tide and Neap Tide: Selected Poems 1932-72* (Canongate, Edinburgh, 1977) p. 88. Quoted by Heinemann, 'English Poetry and the War in Spain', in Hart, *'¡No Pasarán!'* , pp. 59-60.

Old green sweater, battered coat,
Coal-black hair and sleeves too short.
Though I know the living man
Finished with this place,
Idle and low spirits can
Take you name and face.

Here we laid foundations where
never walls were built.
Faded in the fireside glow,
Things we knew or seemed to know
Blown around the empty air,
And the milk is spilt.
Here we laid foundations where
Never walls were built.

And the hard thing to believe
Still is what you said.
With a bullet in the brain,
How can matter think again?
All things that once live and move
Endlessly are dead.
And the hard thing to believe
Still is what you said.

So from these deserted rooms,
Even memory's past.
As your closely pencilled screed
Grows more faint and hard to read,
So our blueprints and our dreams,
Torn from time are lost.
So from these deserted rooms,
Even memory's passed.

Mountains that we saw far off,
Sleek with gentle snow,
To the climbers axe reveal
Ice that jars the swinging steel,
Armoured on a holdless cliff
With the clouds below -

Mountains that we saw far off,
Sleek with gentle snow.

Time bears down its heroes all
And the fronts they held.
Yet their charge of change survives
In the changed fight of our lives -
Poisoned fires they never dreamed of
Ring the unrented field.
Change is their memorial
Who have changed the world.[115]

Frida Stewart was also touched by the death of John Cornford in Spain, not only because he had been a family friend, but because she also was amongst those who viewed his death as a great misfortune for the socialist movement.

> Of course, he was everything because he was a romantic, good looking poet and writer and student, and from a good family, and just from that point of view it was a terrible shame that he was killed. He could have been very helpful - he could have been very useful today, because I'm sure he wouldn't have reneged on the things he believed in.[116]

In this passage, the death of someone so young has become a powerful symbol of the spirit of the dead as incorruptible. Ideological purity can be preserved undimmed across the years. Frida Stewart can propose that, unlike Stephen Spender for example, John Cornford would have continued to be committed to socialism if he had lived. This form of narrative, in which alternative possible histories are expressed, has been explored by Alessandro Portelli. In his study of Italian Communist Party activists he refers to their expressions of alternative realities as 'uchronic dreams'.[117] The 'dreams' may,

---

115 Margot Heinemann, 1991. My thanks to Jane Bernal for making me aware of her mother's poem, and for allowing me to include it in this book.
116 Frida Stewart, AJ, 30 March 1994.
117 *See nextpage]* Uchronia he defines in the words of Pierre Versins as 'that amazing theme in which the author imagines what would have happened if a certain historical event had not taken place'; the representation of 'an alternative present, a sort of parallel universe in which the different unfolding of an historical event had not taken place.' Alessandro Portelli, 'Uchronic Dreams', *The Myths We Live By* edited by Raphael Samuel and Paul Thompson (Routledge, London & New York, 1990) p. 150.

or may not, be based on a sound assessment of how events could have developed, but all have historical value as representations of how individuals construct their present identities. Amongst the retrospective discourses of women on the war in Spain are several examples of this type of firm belief that history could have unfolded very differently but for some significant factor. Celia Baker, for example, was amongst many in this study who sustained the belief that if it had not been for the British Government's support of the Non-intervention policy in Spain, the war would have been won by the Republic. 'I always felt in my heart that if they'd only listened about Spain, the Second World War would not have been necessary,' she said, but clearly recognised the insubstantial nature of all such speculation when she added, 'but that might have been wishful thinking.[118]

Those who work with oral testimony have paid great attention to the 'processes of composure' employed by each individual to develop a coherent narrative of their lives and 'a version of the self that can be lived with in relative psychic comfort.'[119] Two particular types of reminiscence have been identified, those that function as a 'life review' and those that are for the 'maintenance of self esteem.' During the course of an interview, a person may possibly move between the two forms, being alternately an 'explorer who in the face of death tests the validity of a life as it has been lived,' or 'the conserver who holds on to well established proofs of worth and value.'[120] In view of their strong beliefs and tendency to proactive engagement with issues, many of the women in this study had a great deal to reflect upon in their later years. Patience Darton recognised this when reviewing her experiences relating to Spain.

> But you know, when you go out when you're young to a thing like that, everything, one thing after the other, just happens, and in lots of things you feel, 'That's the way it is', and you don't draw conclusions until afterwards.[121]

---

118 Celia Baker, AJ, 20 May 1997.
119 This play on the meaning of the word 'composure' is attributed to Graham Dawson, and is discussed in Summerfield, *Reconstructing Women's Wartime Lives*, pp. 16-18.
120 Peter Coleman, 'Ageing and Life History: The Meaning of Reminiscence in Late Life', in S. Dex (ed.), *Life and Work History Analyses: Qualitative and Quantitative Developments* (Routledge, London, 1991) p. 140, also quoted in Summerfield, *Reconstructing Women's Wartime Lives*, pp. 18-19.
121 Patience Edney (née Darton), IWM, 8398.

Some of the women whose support of the Spanish Republic was bound up with their hopes for a socialist society were faced with the need to radically review their lives in view of events relating to the actions of the Soviet Union. The problems began for some, like Celia Baker, in August 1939 'that dreadful day when the Soviet Pact was signed.'

> I couldn't take the Soviet-German Pact, I could not accept it. I just thought it was the most terrible thing that had ever happened to me - that the Soviet Union, that we always held up as an ideal, which of course was fantasy, I suppose, ... I couldn't believe that they had to make a pact with fascism to protect themselves.[122]

Patience Darton was also uneasy about the arguments used in support of the Pact. Pragmatism, as usual, came to her aid.

> When you have one of these terribly elaborate things that you have to work out the theoretical things of it, they're nearly always wrong, I find, these highly worked out political things. Straight forward things are usually better.[123]

Charlotte Haldane followed a different path to a re-evaluation of her beliefs. After spending some time in Russia as a War Correspondent during 1941, she returned, disillusioned on finding things were not as she had believed, and immediately severed her connections with the Communist Party and then with her husband.[124] In the last chapter of her portentously entitled 1949 autobiography, *Truth Will Out*, she recounts the need she felt for self-analysis, as a 'Lone Female', 'mentally convalescent from the intellectual aberration' of the Stalinist Communism she felt had 'afflicted' her for the previous ten years.[125] This led directly to her investigation into the causes of 'the disorder', and the development of her personal theories on the nature of Communism and Communists. The analogy she draws between the Communist church and the Christian Church is discussed at some length. After commenting on the fact that as spiritual laxatives and opiates, both religion and Marxism fulfil similar

---

122 Celia Baker, AJ, 20 May 1997.
123 Patience Edney (née Darton), IWM 8398.
124 Charlotte Haldane, *Truth Will Out* (Weidenfeld & Nicolson, London, 1949) Chapter XI, 'Russian War Correspondent'.
125 Ibid., p. 275.

emotional criteria, she considers their irreconcilable differences. The key flaw in Marxism, she believes, is its lack of foundation on anything other than an expediency which 'can never be the basis of any religion, but only of spurious, bogus forms of anti-religion or pseudo-religion, such as Stalinism or Hitlerism.'[126]

Nevertheless, her great joy at the rediscovery of her 'moral integrity' was not unqualified.

> I had a deep and strong sense of guilt. I felt a traitor to the cause, especially to those comrades and of them particularly the dead, with whom I shared my previous loyalties, during the war in Spain. To feel disloyal, especially to the dead, to whom one cannot put one's case, nor explain one's impulsions or conclusions, is a peculiarly unpleasant experience.[127]

In order to regain her own sense of 'composure', she had entered the often painful process of 'life review' and could not emerge unscathed. She rejected further involvement in party politics.

> Politics, as my dear Papa had said, was a dirty business, even though in this country, fortunately, a less unsavoury one than in most others. But definitely a business, and not a vocation. Or if a vocation, not mine. Politics meant 'loyalty to my Party, right or wrong.' I had seen where that had led me.[128]

The analytical style she frequently adopts towards the examination of her past contrasts with the dark emotional imagery she employs in her poetry. The process of 'life review' led to her creation of an imagined, less vulnerable, self, a type of personal uchronic dream.

> Seeking
>
> Could I from myself escape
> And shape my destiny to other ends
> I should no longer be the torn leaf from the holly tree
> Swept along dead streets by deaf men.
> I should have a mind to be unkind next time

---

126 Ibid., p. 306.
127 Ibid., p. 239.
128 Ibid., p. 269.

To those fates that await for their becoming
An open welcoming soul
In which to hollow a warm home
For their cold black breeding.

There would be no more for them greedy feeding
On my soul's fruit.
I should not for them make willing music,
Piping tunes better left unsung;
My heart nevermore passion's playground
For the meeting and beating upon one another
Of fierce loves and hates.

No, I should have a heart steeled
And for mind a sure shield
Impregnable to imagination's onslaught.
None but the purest, clearest thought
Would be allowed to penetrate
Such unscalable barriers as would stand
To guard my peace, my sleep and my sweet dreams.[129]

Nan Green also went through 'the painful process of real thinking.'[130] Her growing disquiet throughout the fifties with aspects of Soviet and Chinese Communism is expressed in religious terms as 'unlearning blind faith.'[131] She began to question the idolatry surrounding their leaders, seeing at first hand the mass hysteria of the mourners in Peking when Stalin died in 1953, and then later, gradually starting to wonder why there were quite so many portraits of the supposedly humble Mao.[132] For her, the difficulties she experienced in changing such long-standing habits of thought were comparable to those faced by members of the Church of England on hearing of Darwin's discoveries.[133]

For many people, the definitive moment for re-evaluation came in 1956. Marjorie Jacobs left the Communist Party after events in Hungary led her to believe something was 'very, very, wrong.' Her husband, a Brigader, thought differently.

---

129 Ibid., 'Seeking', facing page 1.
130 Gordon Childe quoted by Nan Green, 'A Chronicle of Small Beer', p. 119.
131 Green, 'A Chronicle of Small Beer', p. 119 & 133.
132 Ibid., pp. 132-3.
133 Ibid., p. 147.

He said there must be an explanation for it, and he took a dim view of me, and he carried on and stayed in the Communist Party... And of course, we [those who resigned] were left bereft. We'd had the Communist Party for all those years, the backing, the comradeship, the education and so on, and suddenly we'd got nothing. And Lionel carried on with his trade union work and his political work and it just - that was the end of the marriage really, as such.[134]

Marjorie Jacobs choice of the powerful word 'bereft' to describe her sense of loss after leaving the Party, is perhaps interesting in view of her almost immediate reclamation of the religious belief she had held as a child.[135] 'The Communist Party' she said, 'had convinced me that the religious part of life was wrong, and that religion had been used to control the people.' After Hungary, she re-affirmed her belief that the 'socialist part of it [Communism] was correct - the Christian part of it,' but regretted her former rejection of the spiritual dimension, believing that things would have been much better 'if we'd only understood what Christ was teaching.'[136] Her return to religious beliefs supports the assertion, made by Charlotte Haldane amongst others, that the attractions of communism and religion have much in common.

The efforts of Margot Heinemann to come to terms with the need to review her socialist beliefs after the events of 1956 can be followed through her novel, *The Adventurers*, published in 1960.[137] The book is a portrayal of the pressures faced by Welsh miners in the labour movement at various levels. She began writing in 1954 or 1955 in a confident 'socialist realist' style, but, as Andy Croft has pointed out, the second half of the novel 'is a record of the loss of that confidence' as the narrative adopts a guarded uncertainty about the future.[138] Later interviews show that her perspective on the Spanish Civil War remained unchanged, continuing to be, in the terminology of oral historians, composed in a narrative style that would ensure 'the maintenance of self esteem.'[139] However, her general political beliefs had been reviewed and qualified through the challenges of the fifties.

---

134 Marjorie Jacobs, AJ, 2 August 1996.
135 See Chapter 2.
136 Marjorie Jacobs, AJ, 2 August 1996.
137 Margot Heinemann, *The Adventurers* (Lawrence & Wishart, London, 1960).
138 Andy Croft 'The End of Socialist Realism: Margot Heinemann's *The Adventurers*', in David Margolies and Maroula Joannou (eds) *Heart of the Heartless World: Essays in Cultural Resistance in Memory of Margot Heinemann* (Pluto Press, London, 1995) p. 205.
139 Apart from the interview IWM 9239, see 'Remembering 1936: Women and the War in Spain', *Women's Review* Number 12, October 1986, pp. 14-15.

What was new about that period for many of us was that for the first
time, one didn't in one sense, get over it at all: some kinds of easy
confidence one will never have again, and I think rightly not.[140]

Sylvia Townsend Warner allowed her membership of the Party
to lapse during the fifties. Along with other writers on the Left, she
became a literary casualty of the Cold War. Asked why she had
written no more novels after 1954, she replied 'We had fought, we had
retreated, we were betrayed and now we were misrepresented.'[141]

Noreen Branson, aged 85 at the time of being interviewed in 1996,
was a member of the Democratic Left, still maintaining her socialist
beliefs, but handing on the torch to others.

But I think with the collapse of the Soviet Union everybody's got to
start re-thinking the way forward, because I think it is perfectly
obvious still, to me at any rate, that capitalism is not the solution
to people's problems. And I think that we need a socialist society,
but obviously not run in the way that it was in Russia. That's my
opinion - but I don't think it's for people my age to decide, it's the
young ones who've got to move forward, isn't it?[142]

This passage could perhaps be read in the light of Alessandro
Portelli's discussion of instances in which 'uchronia' has occurred
amongst those who were forced to face the deferral of their aims.

The function of the uchronic motif is to keep up hope: if our past
leaders missed their chance to 'shoot when the thrush was flying
by', better leaders in the future will not. The world of our desires is
possible: we needn't even change the magic, but only work it more
correctly, and perhaps replace a few people at the top.[143]

Noreen Branson viewed the fundamental problem of the collapse
of the Soviet Union as one of defective leadership. Frida Stewart had
developed arguments along similar lines that successfully resolved
many of the issues to her own satisfaction.

---

140 Margot Heinemann, undated letter to Arnold Kettle, quoted by Croft, 'The End of
   Socialist Realism', in Margolies & Joannou, *Heart of the Heartless World*, p. 212.
141 See Maroula Joannou, 'Sylvia Townsend Warner in the 1930s' in Croft, *A Weapon in the
   Struggle*, p. 103.
142 Noreen Branson, AJ, 26 January 1996.
143 Portelli, 'Uchronic Dreams', in Samuel & Thompson, *The Myths We Live By*, p. 156.

We should not blame Communism for the evils of Ceaucescu or Stalin any more than we blame Christianity for the Inquisition, or for Cromwell's crimes, or the Crusades... Can you imagine turning your back on the Ninth symphony just because it has been badly performed? Well I can't! What is great and good and beautiful does not turn out to be paltry and rotten just because the wrong people got hold of it and mis-interpreted it! Communism has not yet had an adequate performance, and we'll have to work for it long and hard before this can happen.[144]

It could no longer be denied that the Soviet Union had failed in practical terms to match ideals with reality. Cuba, however, could still be a possible source of hope.

My visit to Cuba made a great impression on me, and re-kindled I think, my belief that socialism is the answer in the end. It wasn't the same as seeing people fighting for their - well, they are fighting there of course - but there was something about the Spanish people and the way they built up their own culture and belief round their cause which was very inspiring. And I don't - I can't think of any other experience I've had which gives you that feeling of something really worth fighting for.[145]

In the midst of disillusion, the Spanish Republic becomes a beacon of what might have been. There had been little chance to build a new Spain before the outbreak of war, when Republican ideals, although besieged from many quarters, were still viable. Hopes for implementation of these ideals were ended by war, but the ideals themselves had not failed.

The symbolism of issues surrounding the war in Spain may help to explain the strong emotions expressed on the subject by many of the women in this study. Overwhelmingly, their feelings about the experience were positive, unless, like Elizabeth Monkhouse, they wished they had done more.

I felt agonised about it - in fact, looking back over my life I can't forgive myself for never having gone to Spain - to have stayed put... It's something I shall always regret because it was cheering on the sidelines instead of going in to it.[146]

---

144 Frida Knight (née Stewart), quoted in Molly Andrews, *Lifetimes of Commitment: Ageing, Politics, Psychology* (Cambridge University Press, 1991) p. 186.
145 Frida Stewart, AJ, 11 December 1995.
146 Elizabeth Monkhouse had worked for the Spanish Medical Aid Committee in Dundee, and with the Basque children. IWM, 13813-1.

When interviewed in 1983, Dr Janet Vaughan still regretted that she had not gone there.

I felt it my duty to go, I think. You see I'm always one who likes to do things rather than to theorise about them, and sitting in a committee trying to run affairs from afar wasn't the sort of thing I cared for doing really. I was making arrangements to go out to Barcelona when the war came to an end.[147]

The words of Ann Murray who had been a nurse in Spain, typify the feelings expressed by many others who had no regrets about having gone.

The Spanish War had a terrific impact on me personally, a terrific impact. It was the most important thing in my life. It was a terrific experience I would never like to have missed. I have certainly no regrets at having gone there at all. I know what a struggle the Spanish people had and how cheerful and good they were to us. The spirit of the people was terrific. I've never known anything like it. I would never expect to see anything like it again.[148]

Her repeated use of the word 'terrific', may be more than a superficial repetitive limitation. She seemed haunted by the 'gruesomeness' of the suffering she had seen in Spain, the children mutilated by grenades, the young men 'with their bodies torn and their limbs smashed.'[149] Her experiences were both of terrific importance to her, and terrifyingly disturbing. In a short memoir, another nurse, Margaret Powell, uses a similar word, a choice which reflects the problems she had with frequent nightmares about the patients she was unable to save.

Though I am now nearer 70 than 60 and have led a busy and fairly interesting life living and working in other countries, and I am a mother and grandmother, my time in and experience of the Spanish Civil War is the most vivid and the most terrible.[150]

---

147 Dr (later Dame) Janet Vaughan, IWM, 13796-1. Janet Vaughan, a member of the Spanish Medical Aid Committee, was very interested in the advances made in Spain relating to blood transfusion. She became involved in the preparations for blood donor centres before the start of the Second World War.
148 Annie Knight (née Murray), Ian MacDougall (ed.) *Voices from the Spanish Civil War: Personal Recollections of Scottish Volunteers in Republican Spain 1936-39* (Polygon, Edinburgh, 1986) p. 74.
149 See also Chapter 4. Quote taken from Williams, Alexander and Gorman, *Memorials of the Spanish Civil War* p. 42.
150 Margaret Powell, short memoir dated 13 July 1980, papers of her daughter, Ruth Muller.

This enduringly 'vivid' nature of the memory of Spain is mentioned by many of the women who had spent some time there. Margaret Stewart, for example, began a speech by saying, 'Fifty years is a very long time, yet the Spanish war remains as vividly in my memory as if it were only yesterday.'[151]

Oral testimony excels as a medium for the communication of such strongly emotive memories. The spoken word can at times, convey greater conviction, wider associations, deeper meanings, than the simple words on a page. Tone, pace, accent, all transmit messages to the listener that are lost to the reader. Margaret Stewart's simple comments, that Spain was, after all, 'the thing' - that 'there's been nothing like Spain' can be seen as a case in point.[152] The recording was made by Jim Fyrth in the course of his research, both Margaret Stewart and Helen Grant being present together.[153] It is clearly not a formal interview, rather a meeting of three like-minded spirits, chatting over tea. To achieve their full impact, Margaret Stewart's words require an awareness of the emphasis in 'the thing', the recognition of the defining class-based cadences in which she speaks, and the sounds of the background chorus of collective approval. 'Oral' testimony is alas, rarely presented in 'aural' form. In many instances, even more could be conveyed by the inclusion of a visual record. We can only imagine Joan Purser's home as she remembers Spain and tells us, 'I say I feel cold now, and I say to myself, "It isn't like Teruel." I look on it as the best part of my life - I had no personal possessions - look at all this clobber.'[154]

The women who gave frequent interviews and were accustomed to public speaking developed effective strategies to communicate the points they wished to make. Their interviews contrast markedly with those carried out with 'first-timers' who are often inclined to doubt that anyone could really be interested in what they might say. Isabel Brown, perhaps the most experienced speaker of all, would adopt her platform style in an interview whenever the chance arose. When asked how she felt when the Fascists won the war, her response was typically oratorical.

---

151 Margaret Stewart, notes for a speech on the fiftieth anniversary of the war, papers of Margaret Stewart.
152 Margaret Stewart (m. Wilson), IWM, 13807-1.
153 For more on Helen Grant, see Chapters 2 and 4.
154 Joan Purser, IWM, 13795. The battles for Teruel were often fought in deep snow, sometimes temperatures reached -20°C.

Oh, obviously we felt terribly sad. I was really sad. I hadn't the sense of defeat, I had the sense of terrible concern, because when I'd said in my speeches, 'It's Guernica today, it'll be Paris and London tomorrow,' I really believed that to be true. And it was only weeks before the war started. And we did get bombs on London. We did get bombs on Paris. We did get them on Coventry and so on. And it is my firm conviction that all the anti-Fascist work we did was a victory because it united the whole of the British people, except a tiny reactionary fraction which never counted... but it certainly united miners and Lords, girls working in the factory and duchesses. We were certainly united - it would have happened anyway, but it happened immediately because the solidarity of the British people during that war was fantastic.[155]

She has successfully created a rhetoric that turned defeat in Spain into the basis for a greater victory against Hitler.

In some cases, women who spoke frequently on the subject of Spain would tell particular narratives of their war experiences as parables.[156] Defined as a short story that illustrates a religious or ethical point, a parable is easily accessible to an audience through the use of familiar things in the telling. In this instance, such simple stories could become a highly effective form for the communication of beliefs and ideas about the war in Spain and were often repeated many times. Nan Green, for example, told the parable of the pencils in her memoirs but had given a fuller and livelier version of the same story during an interview in 1976.

It was at the hospital in Huete in a village where half the houses were caves. They were hollowed out of the hillside, very nice dry sort of sandy stuff with a chimney put up through the ground that was the only ventilation they had - and perhaps a door, perhaps a curtain, very poor, very poor village indeed. We went out to look for some women who'd promised to come and help in the hospital, and we went into this particular cave where there was nobody but an old woman. The woman we were looking for was out... We started to look round and she showed us on the wall some sheets of paper with children's drawings on them in coloured chalks. She said, 'Yes,

---

155 Isabel Brown, IWM, 844/8, reel 8.
156 Some of those in this study, in addition to speaking at meetings on Spain, gave many interviews over the years and spoke in schools and institutions on the subject.

that was done by my grandchild. Before we had the Republic we never had a pencil in this village and now they not only go to school and learn but they have coloured pencils. I'll come and work in your hospital if you like.' You see, it meant so much to them, this idea of education, that this old girl was prepared to come as well as the young one because the Republic meant that their children would get educated.

In her memoirs, written just before her death in 1984, the heavily emphasised and more formulaic structure given to the old lady's reply has perhaps less impact than the oral, more spontaneous, version.

Before the Republic there wasn't a pencil in this village, and now all the children go to school. YES, my daughter will come and help! Those wounded men are fighting so that our children can learn.[157]

One of the most moving parables was told by Patience Darton to illustrate her own, almost religious experience, of being raised from the depths of despair by the words of a Spanish peasant. She was working in the cave hospital near the Ebro, conditions were grim and the war was not going well for the Republic. Patience Darton often appeared to re-live her experiences as she recounted them. The transcript pales in comparison with the original oral version, but merits printing in its entirety as an outstanding example of the telling of a story that, like a parable, has the purpose of illuminating a specific point, in this case, the moral justification for fighting the war. The children she hears are the young boys who had been called up to fight in the Ebro offensive, singing as they marched to the front.

There was a very nice English man there, badly wounded in the liver, again who we couldn't save [sigh] and it was very wretched because they were so bad, they went on so, and we had so many. And I was on nights, well we worked most of the time, but I was always on at night, and this darkness and the discomfort and the seriousness of it I got really - I thought it wasn't worth it, I thought no war is worth all this, this misery and this horror. And a chap had come in, I saw him come in, long before, from outside with bundles of stuff - was let in properly. And he was sitting on the side of a bed

---

157 Green, 'A Chronicle of Small Beer,' p. 57.

smoking cigarettes which he'd rolled, talking to a chap - one of those deserting to the front who was only lightly wounded, an officer who had his arm strapped up and was going to go back. And they were talking and laughing and smoking and I was in this terrible state, running round, people dying and very wretched and these children singing in the road.

So in a break - there's always a pause in these things - I went over and said, 'How can you be talking and laughing, can't you see what's going on? Can't you hear those children singing?' And the chap was very serious, very nice man, a marvellous man, and he said he was just a Spaniard from the locality and he'd brought up fruit for us, he'd been taking it to the front but he heard about the hospital and he'd brought up... I said, 'Well, is it worth it, all this? Can you not hear those children singing?' And he said he was an analphabetic peasant in the locality there, they hadn't even got a road only a track to their village. They were terribly poor and they didn't know much that was going on, they were used to being voted for, they were voted as so many souls belonging to the owner of the land - he just put in their votes, so many numbered. But they'd heard, a couple of years before, that there was going to be an election in which they could vote. And they went and voted, it was the first time they'd known they'd voted, they went over the tracks and voted.

They heard nothing more about it, until they heard that the village next to them was measuring out the land. So they went over to see what this measuring out the land was, and the Popular Front had got in and this was a little land reform thing, only it hadn't got to them. And they didn't know how to measure, they hadn't got anything to measure with, so they went and found out how to do these things, what was going on. The landlord had flown, and they measured out their land. He became - he was elected the local mayor. Every village had a mayor, it would be a village council in England, but there they all had a mayor. He was the mayor, he learnt to read and write.

They organised everything, and then he, oh, five or six weeks before this battle, the Ebro, he was sent for to Barcelona, he had a letter, it was the first letter he'd ever had - and of course, he could read it - he had a letter to go to Barcelona, and he went down to the particular place on the road where he was picked up, and he went in a car - the first time he'd been in a car, with leather seats. And he sat in this car with leather seats and he went to Barcelona where they were told that there was going to be this battle and the roads

were going to be built and that the local authorities had got to be able
to provide for both the people coming over, the refugees coming our
way which happened when we had an attack, when we attacked the
people came over to us - got to pass them through so they didn't get
in the way of the soldiers and the hospital nor anything else - they
were to see that that was their job to do, and he was to supply so
much food for the army and for anything else that was going on - he
had to have these stores ready and it had to be organised to do it.

And he did all those things, and they did very well at them, they
managed an awful lot of food, they were ready to pass the refugees
back but they didn't get any there. But he said, 'I became a man, and
that's what we're fighting for.' [Pause] And he just said this all
quite simply, quite straight forward, he summed up what was the
matter with me, and he told me what was going on. Marvellous, the
Spaniards are. I mean they really have enormous insight. And they
fought you see, they stood up and fought, fought for two and a bit
years against Hitler which nobody else did.[158]

The writings of British women that relate to the war in Spain
have sometimes taken the form of novels. Like Margot Heinemann's
Adventurers, these novels may have significant autobiographical
content. This can be another form of remembrance, allowing greater
freedom of expression, to use the words of Gerald Brenan, 'You can't
get at the truth by history; you can only get at it through novels.'[159]
Margaret Higonnet pointed out that the many forms taken by women's
writing during the First World War require the development of a more
inclusive and sophisticated response which would take into consideration 'the interplay of historical record and crafted memorial.'[160]
The same should be said of women's writings on Spain. Ethel Mannin's
descriptions of left-wing meetings about Spain in *Comrade O Comrade
or Low Down on the Left*, have a particular pithy quality as she plays
on their divisions with heavy irony.[161] In *The Pursuit of Love: A Novel*,
Nancy Mitford gives us parodies of the relief workers she met in her

---

158 Patience Edney (née Darton) IWM, 8398, reel 9.
159 Gerald Brenan to Raymond Carr, on being asked to write a volume on Spain for the *Oxford
   History of Europe*, quoted by James K. Hopkins in *Into the Heart of the Fire: The British in
   the Spanish Civil War* (Stanford University Press, 1998) p. xiii.
160 Higonnet goes on to suggest that 'an anthology of mixed forms, which includes poetry and
   journalism, letters and snapshot fictional sketches, may be the most appropriate way to
   begin to reassess women's record of the Great War.' Margaret R. Higonnet, 'Another Record:
   A Different War' *Women's Studies Quarterly* 1995, vol. 23, parts 3 & 4, pp. 85-96, p. 94.
161 Ethel Mannin, *Comrade O Comrade or Low Down on the Left* (Jarrolds, London, 1945).

description of the Republican refugee camp near Perpignan.[162] The allocation of cabins on the ship taking the exiles to Mexico is given light-hearted treatment.

> Linda looked at the list of families. It took the form of a card index, the head of each family having a card on which was written the number and names of his dependants.
> 'It doesn't give their ages,' said Linda. 'How am I to know if there are young babies?'...
> 'Quite easy', said Christian. 'With the Spaniards you can always tell. Before the war they were called either after saints or after episodes in the life of the Virgin - Anunciata, Asuncion, Purificacion, Concepcion, Consalacion, etc. Since the Civil War they are all called Carlos after Charlie Marx, Federigo after Freddie Engels, or Estalina (very popular until the Russians let them down with a wallop), or else nice slogans like Solidaridad-Obreara, Libertad, and so on. Then you know the children are under three. Couldn't be simpler, really.[163]

The flippant style manages to convey, in a striking manner, the huge changes that have been wrought by the civil war, even in the simple matter of naming babies.

One lesser known novel relating to the war in Spain is *Spanish Portrait*.[164] The author, known by the pen name of Elizabeth Lake, was Inez Pearn, who for a short time was the wife of Stephen Spender. They married in December 1936 after knowing each other for less than a month. Tiring of the 'sordid round of affairs', Spender had decided to take 'an absolute final step.'[165] Marie Agnes Pearn, always known as Inez, had been in Spain working as a governess but had returned to Britain after the summer to study the Spanish poet, Góngora, at Oxford. As a member of the local Spanish Aid Committee, she had met Spender when he came to speak at one of their meetings. They separated in the Summer of 1939 and despite Spender's protests, were divorced soon afterwards.

162 Nancy Mitford, *The Pursuit of Love: A Novel* (Hamish Hamilton, London, 1945). Frida Stewart was working in the camp and remembered meeting Nancy Mitford. She didn't see herself as one of the characters described in the book, but thought the descriptions of others she recognised were rather 'cruel'.
163 Mitford, *The Pursuit of Love*, p. 118. Spellings of names are as in the original.
164 Elizabeth Lake, *Spanish Portrait* (Pilot Press, London, 1945).
165 Quoted by Hugh David, *Stephen Spender: A Portrait with Background* (Heinemann, London, 1992) p. 190.

302   BRITISH WOMEN AND THE SPANISH CIVIL WAR

Spanish Portrait covers a period from Autumn 1934 to the Autumn of 1937. It is primarily a love story, set against a background of the tensions brewing before the war. Maria, the English heroine who had been working as a governess, meets Alonso, a Spanish upper-class painter. The story is presented as a series of long dialogues, records of conversational details, which whilst seeming trivial to the reader, also impart the feeling that to the author, in the guise of the heroine, each word is saturated with significance. When war breaks out, Maria is back in England, and is unable to return to Spain. Alonso, unlike his friends, doesn't fight on the 'right side'. As a 'geographical', he takes the line of least resistance when the town he was in falls to Franco. Maria tries to verify if he is alive or dead but the book ends with the question left unanswered. Inez Pearn died aged 63. Her daughter regrets not having asked her mother more about the book, although she knew it to be an autobiographical narrative of memories that retained the power to upset her mother greatly when she returned to Spain during the seventies.[166]

Another little known novel, *Red Candles in Spain* by Thora Stowell, was published in London in 1938.[167] The Foreword states clearly that this will be a tale of ordinary people living in a country at war.

> The events in Spain out of which this story is made were of so little importance in the history of the war that they have never been chronicled in any newspaper. The crushing of Arila, first by one army and then by the other, was of no military consequence, merely an apparently cruel twist of the wheel of Fate. But to those who lived in Arila, and who were swept away by that tide, it seemed the Flood itself. Many of the events are true and I am grateful to friends in Spain who have allowed me to use their tragic experiences for my purpose. All the characters are fictional. Arila is not the name of a real place.[168]

The story which unfolds is that of a young British woman, determined to rescue her orphaned six year-old nephew from the clutches of wicked Spanish communist relatives in war-torn Spain.

---

166 Conversations with Dr Vicky Randall, Department of Government, University of Essex (daughter of Inez Pearn) who also kindly allowed me to borrow her mother's book.
167 *Red Candles in Spain* (John Gifford, London, 1938). Thora Stowell was apparently a pseudonym used by Alice Mary Dicken. Other books by Thora Stowell are cited in the above edition. Titles include *Strange Wheat, The Crooked Plough, The Black Camel, The Book of Animal Life* and *The Ways of Birds*.
168 Stowell, *Red Candles in Spain*, 'Foreword'.

The novel, although evidently not written for children, is constructed in the 'bogey-man' tradition. The man falsely claiming to be the boy's uncle, and holding him prisoner in squalid conditions, is the head of the local Communist Party. He is known as 'El Lobo', the Wolf, and is portrayed as the villain in a fairy story, 'hatchet faced, with a loose, cruel mouth, and close-set piercing black eyes under bushy eyebrows that meet in the middle.'[169] Dirty and drunken, he gives the heroine 'a look so piercing, so malevolent, that her blood seemed to freeze in her veins.'[170] The book has a happy ending, with the heroine, her gallant suitor, and the boy all finally reaching safety. Nevertheless, they now know that once the red candles of revolution are lit, all hopes of happiness 'may vanish like a puff of smoke on a summer day.'[171] From her safe haven, these final words spoken by the heroine place the desire for peace within the comforting security of her traditional religious beliefs.

> Across the starry silence came the sound of Christmas bells ringing out for Midnight Mass. If only that message of peace and goodwill could be understood by the listening world![172]

Although not included here for its literary merit, the book is evidence of how powerful the fear of disorder can be, and that above all else, some women may wish for nothing more than a return to their former well-ordered lives.

Unfortunately, some of the memoirs and diaries written by women about Spain remain unpublished. In other instances they have been published posthumously, edited by others. Two relatively recent examples are worthy of brief note to illustrate the issues that can arise in such circumstances relating to the inevitable manipulation of the authors' identity through the process of editing. The autobiography of Molly Murphy, a nurse in Spain during the war, was entitled 'Nurse Molly' in its unpublished form. There are long detailed chapters on her nursing training and work. The depth of her own sense of identity as a nurse is re-affirmed in the closing chapter of her book, when, despite no longer being well enough to work, she writes, 'Perhaps for as long as may be, I'll nurse flowers, for nurse something

---

169 Ibid., p. 52.
170 Ibid., p. 52.
171 Ibid., p. 287.
172 Ibid., p. 287.

I must.'[173] Her book has now been published under the title of *Molly Murphy: Suffragette and Socialist*.[174] Although these political aspects of her life were also important to her, it seems unjust to shift the focus of her life so dramatically by changing the title of her book, and then in the introduction, state that 'the principal problem with Molly's autobiography is its failure to deal with the rise of Stalinism inside the USSR and its baneful impact of the British Communist Party's politics.'[175]

The diaries of Priscilla Scott-Ellis, who nursed Franco's troops during the war, have recently been edited and published as *The Chances of Death: A Diary of the Spanish Civil War*.[176] Her original diaries were free-flowing and detailed daily accounts, embellished with introspective observations and her personal opinions of others. Both in style and content, therefore, the diaries differ significantly from the narratives produced by women in the years following the war. The several volumes of her diaries were subjected to substantial editing before publication, and it is interesting to read the original diaries and note the pattern of selected cuts. On her return from Spain in 1939, Priscilla Scott-Ellis had prepared the diaries for publication but this idea was abandoned with the outbreak of the Second World War. Her sister, Gaenor Heathcoat Amory, explains in the foreword to the *Chances of Death* that this first editing was done merely to ensure that nothing was said about their friends, Prince Alfonso d'Orleans Bourbon, his wife, Princess Beatrice and their family, 'that could in any way embarrass them.'[177] The original diaries have a rough pencil line drawn through the sections to be taken out, but the words are still clearly legible. These same passages are missing in the version finally published in 1997. Unfortunately, without them, it is impossible to understand the expressions of emotion which colour many of the daily entries. Priscilla Scott-Ellis was deeply affected by her feelings for the son of the Prince and Princess, Ataúlfo, whom she had known since childhood. All references to these feelings have been expunged. For example, on 21 January 1938 she wrote that she was in the depths of depression and so nervous that she did not know what to do with

173 Murphy, 'Nurse Molly', p. 153.
174 Darlington, *Molly Murphy*.
175 Darlington, *Molly Murphy*, Introduction, p. v.
176 Priscilla Scott-Ellis, *The Chances of Death: A Diary of the Spanish Civil War* edited by Raymond Carr (Michael Russell, Wilby, Norwich, 1995).
177 Ibid., p. x. Alfonso was a first cousin of the King of Spain, Alfonso XIII. In the diaries, he is usually referred to as Prince Ali, and his wife as Princess Bee. They were close family friends often visited by 'Pip' when she was in Spain. See Chapter 4.

herself. No explanation for this is given in the published version of her diary. Her state of mind becomes more understandable after reading the sentences which follow in her original text.

> I can't sleep and have not done so for 3 nights which is really not surprising when I have to spend my whole day keeping a firm grip on myself not to appear to be in love with Ataúlfo. I don't know whether I am getting less controlled, more frustrated or more in love but it is pure hell whatever it is and leaves me in a state of being unable to sleep, unable to eat and feeling miserable. God how I hate life sometimes and I can't get away from it. Oh hell.[178]

Her reaction to the theft of her 'poor dear radio' as a 'great tragedy' becomes understandable after reading her unedited words, explaining that it had been a birthday present from Ataúlfo and would therefore be irreplaceable. She adds furiously, '...if only they had taken anything but Ataúlfo's radio! Swine.'[179] Occasionally she refers to sexual flirtations with other men using suggestive, rather than explicit comments. A brief note on 'hot technique', and observations such as 'one must admit that doctors know their way about', were adequate personal reminders. On an emotional level, however, the diary is her confidant. 'God I wish I could just go to sleep and never wake up again' she writes when she realises she has no hope of marrying Ataúlfo. After the death of his elder brother, his duty was made clear. Whilst motoring to Málaga he tells her, 'After Alonso died, I promised Mama that I would only marry a Princess.'

> I shall never know how I came through that. Such a simple sentence and it just sent all my hopes and the foundations of my life crashing. I had not realised until he said that, just how much I had been building on the chance of my marrying him one day for the last four years.[180]

Over the next few days, the pages of her diary are full of the desolation of unrequited love, the desperate fight to keep from breaking down in public, and finally, her decision to reject the discovery that even without the promise to his mother, he would not have married her.

---

178 Diaries of Priscilla Scott-Ellis, 21 January 1938, University of Cardiff Library.
179 Scott-Ellis, *The Chances of Death*, p. 53; Diaries of Priscilla Scott-Ellis, 12 March 1938.
180 Diaries of Priscilla Scott-Ellis, 2 September 1938.

I don't know whether it is perseverance, fake optimism or vanity, but I still live in a land of dreams as to how one day I shall marry Ataúlfo just as if I did not know it was quite impossible.[181]

This material may at first seem to have little to offer other than providing a story line for a trite romantic novel. But these feelings should be valued as contributions to our understanding of the past. Readers of the published version of these diaries are left with an impression of a young woman inclined to frequent irrational over-reaction. Emerging from the hand-written original pages is a girl for whom war is a backdrop for being in love.[182] Perhaps her feelings were edited out as irrelevant, not part of her work in the medical units, which the editor had decided was the 'main interest of her diaries.' But her experience of the war cannot be understood when the emotion that coloured her days is washed out of the landscape. To those who are interested in the individual's emotional responses to events, her passions and her 'flirtations' are an essential part of history.[183]

Priscilla Scott-Ellis returned to Spain after the war to work in the Consulate in Barcelona. There she met and married the reputedly 'dazzlingly good-looking' son of the Marques de Castellvell, José Luis de Vilallonga.[184] However, many of the women in this study who had sympathised with the cause of the Republic decided not to go to Spain whilst Franco was still in power.[185] Although Leah Manning had gone to Spain to attend the trials of political prisoners in the forties, she had no wish to return during the remainder of dictatorship.[186] Nevertheless, writing in her 1970 autobiography, she hoped that the part she had played in the lives of four thousand Basque children would not be forgotten in Spain.

---

181 Ibid., 4 September 1938.
182 For male attitudes to love during the war see Rothstein, '"This is Where War Is": British Masculinity and the Spanish Civil War', Chapter 4, Comradeship, Sexuality and Gender.
183 See for example, diaries of Priscilla Scott-Ellis, 9 December 1938.
184 They lived for several years in Argentina then in France. After their divorce, she married again and lived in America till her death in 1983. Foreword by Gaenor Heathcoat Amory in Scott-Ellis, The Chances of Death, p. x. For the perspective of Vilallonga on their relationship and his disclosures regarding other reasons preventing a marriage between Priscilla Scott-Ellis and Ataúlfo, see José Luis Vilallonga, La Cruda y Tierna Verdad: Memorias no Autorizadas (Plaza & Janés, Barcelona, 2000). Many of his assertions are analysed and contested by Paul Preston in an excellent chapter on Priscilla Scott-Ellis, in Palomas de Guerra: Cinco mujeres marcadas por la guerra civil (Plaza y Janés, Barcelona, 2001) and in English as Doves of War: Four Women of Spain, (HarperCollins, London, 2002).
185 Franco died in 1975.
186 Leah Manning died in 1977.

Perhaps, many years hence, in happier times, they will erect a statue of me, with children, in the Park in Bilbao... Except for poignant memories the Spanish chapter is closed for me.[187]

Patience Darton was reluctant to return to Spain and face ghosts from her past, but was also loath to steal any of the limelight she felt was due to those who had fought in the Brigades. She therefore decided not to visit Spain with the group of Brigaders who returned soon after the death of Franco.

I knew the Spaniards would be marvellous to them - to us, but that if there was a nurse, they make a terrible fuss of us and this wouldn't be fair, the chaps were so looking forward to this enormous 'do'... Mind you, I'm very proud of having been an International Brigader and having a pay book and so on, but one does get much more attention, and it was they who did all the fighting - the chaps - much worse for them.[188]

Her words illustrate not only her concern for the feelings of her comrades, but also the relatively low value she places on her own part in the war, with its not inconsiderable adversities. Apart from the difficulties experienced by all those living and working so near the front, she had been thrown through the windscreen of a lorry when she was travelling between units, receiving serious facial injuries.[189]

For those who actually experienced the events of the war, commemorative meetings are not only about the past, they are also about continuing to live with the memories. Their importance as an occasion for public declarations is matched by their value as a space for private interactions. The international 'Homage to the Brigaders' in Spain on the sixtieth anniversary of the war was an opportunity for Patience Darton to return and meet her ghosts, and also the scene for the fortuitous reunion of many old friends, including Rosaleen Smythe and Dr. Reggie Saxton, who had worked together in the medical units.[190] As the war reached its final stages, their close relationship

---

187 Leah Manning, *A Life for Education: An Autobiography* (Victor Gollancz, London, 1970) p. 140.
188 Patience Edney (née Darton) IWM 8398, reel 8.
189 She recounts with great amusement how when she was in hospital with a broken jaw and nose, the mayor came to visit her and made a marvellous speech to the staff about how she had given her 'all' to Spain. In a terrible temper, but unable to speak properly because of her injuries, she related how she had tried to say, ' I hadn't given my all, my face was nothing like my all - there was lots of me left.' IWM 8398, reel 13.
190 Patience Darton's return to Spain is referred to in Chapters 1 and 4.

had ended. She married a Canadian and went to live there, enduring difficult years during the height of anti-Communist attitudes. Dr Saxton eventually married too. The decades passed with no contact between them. But the 'Homage' brought them together again. Both by that time alone, they speak of meeting again as 'quite something' for both of them.[191] This is, without doubt, an understatement of noteworthy proportions. After several shorter visits, aged almost ninety, Dr. Saxton moved to Canada and they were together again.

Many women in this study considered the war in Spain to have been of tremendous importance in their lives. Amongst Frida Stewart's papers are a few tattered sheets on which she had written a summary of her life in the rather shaky handwriting of her later years. It begins, 'The most significant moment in my life was the day the ambulance took me across the border into Spain.'[192] As this chapter has shown, lives were irrevocably altered both in personal and political terms. At the time of the war, the majority of these women were young, and perhaps consequently more impressionable. Moreover, sharing this experience with others strengthened both the commitment they felt whilst the war was in progress, and their memory of the war in later years. As the years after the war passed by, many people in Britain could continue to think of Spain as a symbol for their unfulfilled, but not extinguished, hopes for the future.

---

191 Rosaleen Smythe AJ, 10 April 1999.
192 Frida Stewart, undated memoir, papers of Frida Stewart.

CHAPTER SEVEN

Conclusion

IT HAS BEEN SAID THAT 'The Spanish Civil War was as a mirror into which men gazed and had cast back at them not a picture of reality, but the image of the hopes and fears of their generation.'[1] However, although the 'reality' of the issues at stake in Spain may have been more complex than many people in other countries imagined, nevertheless, the hopes they cherished and the fears they saw for the future were very real. As this study has shown, women too could see in the mirror of the Spanish war, not only a horrifying magnification of their anxieties for the fate of their families in the maelstrom of modern warfare, but also the clearly discernible image of an emergent, more egalitarian, social order being brutally stifled at birth.

The majority of women in this study believed that the support of the British government for the policy of Non-intervention was a crucial factor in Franco's eventual victory. Gerald Howson's study, *Arms for Spain*, strongly endorses their views.[2] The policy forced the Republicans to search far and wide in the attempt to buy arms 'illegally', whilst Franco received a plentiful supply of materials and men from Germany and Italy. If it were indeed the case, as has been claimed, that Britain needed to keep all the arms she could get for her own re-armament programme, Howson believes 'one is entitled to ask why British arms exports to everywhere except Spain not only continued but actually increased from 1936 until shortly after the Second World War.'[3] His research has revealed a catalogue of arms-racketeering and political chicanery in the dealings of many

1 K. W. Watkins, *Britain Divided: The Effect of the Spanish Civil War on British Political Opinion* (Thomas Nelson, London 1963) p. 13.
2 Gerald Howson, *Arms for Spain: The Untold Story of the Spanish Civil War* (John Murray, London, 1998).
3 Ibid., pp. 247-8.

countries with a Republic desperate to buy weapons to defend itself against a well-armed enemy. The inability to obtain more than a fraction of what they needed tipped the balance strongly against them. It has also often been argued that partly due to the efforts of the International Brigades in prolonging the war, Britain had longer to rearm before confronting Hitler.[4] Any advantage gained in this way must however be balanced against that given to the Axis. As a German general pointed out to National Socialist leaders, 'Two years of real war experience' had been of more use to the efficiency of the new army than 'a whole ten years of peace-time training could have been.'[5]

The campaigns relating to the war in Spain were seen by some of the women studied here as instrumental in raising British public awareness of vital issues. Noreen Branson and Margot Heinemann put forward this view in their jointly written book on Britain in the thirties.

> Now far-reaching political questions - such as racialism, militarism, national independence and fascism - became mass issues on which millions of people were involved in some kind of protest action and the subject of intense discussion within the labour movement.'[6]

This mass mobilisation over several years was seen by many, including Isabel Brown, as a defining experience for the nation when faced with unfavourable odds for victory in the Second World War.

> I feel enormously proud of the reaction of the British nation to the Spanish war. And I think we were heartened by the courage of the Spanish people that in the face of defeat they still went on fighting. That was a tremendous thing. And when Churchill's speech - 'We'll go on fighting on the beaches' and what have you - it really represented what we could do.[7]

But this study has taken as its focus the women themselves rather than the historical significance of the war. By using a wide variety of

---

4   Paul Preston is amongst those who present this view, for example in his introduction to *Memorials of the Spanish Civil War* edited by Colin Williams, Bill Alexander and John Gorman (Alan Sutton, Stroud, Gloucestershire,1996).
5   Lecture given by General von Reichenau, Commander of the Fourth Army Group to the National Socialist leaders at Leipzig on 'The German Attitude towards events in Spain', *News Chronicle*, 12 July 1938, quoted by Watkins, *Britain Divided*, p. 7.
6   Noreen Branson and Margot Heinemann, *Britain in the Nineteen Thirties* (Weidenfield & Nicholson, London, 1971) p. 324.
7   Isabel Brown, IWM, 844/8, reel 8.

sources and different methodological approaches to look at their lives and their narratives, it has been possible to add a little to the jigsaw of women's history before yet more pieces are lost. Some of the complexities surrounding the motivational forces affecting these women have been explored, from character traits to ideological concerns. It has become clear that their experiences frequently followed a similar pattern. Many showed early manifestations of an awareness of the sufferings of others, great independence of spirit and a strong desire to learn. As their awareness of the wider world grew, they felt compelled to respond to the problems and perils they saw around them.

The study of women's work in Britain for Spanish causes has revealed much about women's patterns of mobilisation. Within the committee culture that prevailed in the Aid Spain campaigns, women had the opportunity to contribute on a significant scale, through co-operation rather than competition. In contrast with women during both World Wars, those whose husbands and sons were fighting in Spain had to endure hardship, anxiety and bereavement as a minority group. British women's narratives of work in Spain gave insight into women's work in war time. The challenges they encountered, the experiences that affected them most deeply, and their reactions to tensions, whether working near the front-lines or with the vast numbers of refugees in the rear-guard, have all given a further perspective on the interactions between women and war.

Another aspect of the distinctive engagement with war amongst these women was their determination to communicate to others the empathy they felt towards those who were suffering in Spain. When those British women who had supported the Republic were finally faced with defeat, these losses had to be placed within their narratives of the war. Their responses, personal and public, formed a pathway into a discussion of memory and remembrance.

One of the themes that has recurred continually throughout this study is that of women's approach to political involvement and, in particular, their enthusiasm for practical action on the issues they believed were most crucial. These women cared about people, and these concerns tended to take priority over those of a party political nature. It has been claimed that one of the most thoroughly substantiated findings in social science is that men are more likely to participate in politics than women.[8] This can, in part, still be attributed to exclusion.

8   Lester W. Milbrath and M. L. Goel, *Political Participation: How and Why Do People Get Involved with Politics* (Rand McNally College Publishing, Chicago, 1977, first edition 1965) p. 116.

Despite increases in the numbers of women MPs, a masculine approach still prevails in parliament. Wales, at the time of writing, is the only democratic country in the west with a majority of women ministers in the cabinet. Recent articles continue to point out that a 'boozer' sub-culture still exists in the trade union movement, and that 'Men still rule the union roost.'[9] As one northern activist put it to a prospective female union member, 'Don't you worry yourself, there's no sexism in this union, pet.'[10] However, as has been pointed out in this study, the definition of the 'political' should be broadened to include more than just these traditional hierarchical, largely male-dominated, political structures. Such a shift has implications not only for historians, but also for the politicians of today. As long ago as 1984, social scientists were writing that 'women's concerns cannot simply be appended to trade union demands or to the politics of labour movements and political parties. Instead, the conception both of political struggle and of political objectives must be transformed.'[11] This lesson has still to be learned. Before the last elections in 1997, a relatively high proportion of women joined 'New Labour' and helped to vote Tony Blair into power. But already, less than three years later, they are drifting away, 13% less satisfied with government performance than men. Their needs apparently have not been met, despite the influx of Labour women MPs.

Urgent questions are being asked, but it is of little help to wonder 'How can women be made to emulate the credulity and loyalty of the normal - i.e. male - voter?'[12] Groups such as Opinion Leader Research advise the government on women's attitudes to the current political situation. Through views expressed by women voters, their research shows how women's view of politics differs from their male counterparts. Having 'less tribal instincts than men, they are not into the game of politics so they see no particular reason to be loyal to a party and are more likely to switch.'[13] Women, their research suggests, are

9 Barrie Clement, 'Men rule the union roost: Few women are allowed access to the top jobs', *The Independent on Sunday*, 18 July 1999, p.12. The same article points out that 'apart from Christine Hancock at the Royal College of Nursing - which is not part of the "official" union movement because it is not affiliated to the TUC, there are no female general secretaries of large or influential unions.'
10 Ibid.
11 Janet Siltanen and Michelle Stanworth, *Women and the Public Sphere* (Hutchinson, London, 1984) pp. 201-2.
12 Catherine Bennett, 'Why Tony's no ladies' man', *The Guardian*, 13 April 2000, p. 5.
13 Deborah Mattinson, quoted by Jo Dillon, 'Parties have women on their mind', *The Independent on Sunday*, 26 March 2000, p. 9.

'not interested in large "p" politics'.[14] On the emergence of 'New
Labour', women began to believe that the Labour Party had changed
and 'broken free from its unattractive, male dominated past.' They
hoped that 'they were witnessing the start of a new approach to
politics; one that differed from what had gone before, and was, essentially less 'male' in both its agenda and its approach.'[15] The report
stresses that women saw Labour's electoral victory only as a
beginning, 'a first step that will change politics for the good and for
the better, a new approach to politics that is practical, 'can do' and
focused on the things that matter.' Now however, they fear that
the government has reverted to form, and the report advises that
immediate action is required if women's votes are not to be lost.

Outside the traditional regimented political structure there is,
however, a long tradition of women taking action of a different type.
The underestimated 'power of the matriarch' can be seen in the mothers
of the Disappeared in Latin America, still asking questions today, and
in the recent 'Million Mom March' in Washington in favour of stricter
gun control.[16] But if there is to be any change to reverse the ever-
growing apathy towards issues on the British political agenda that will
encompass the greater inclusion of women, then consideration must
be given to feelings of 'political efficacy'. The belief in one's own ability
to influence the course of events is an essential ingredient of political
participation.[17] This study has shown that the enthusiasm and commitment of women can be a powerful force, if certain criteria are met.
Of course, the nature of the cause is important, as is an increased
degree of organisational flexibility, but they must also have a clear
perception of the efficacy of their actions, no matter how modest.
Political leaders should look to history for inspiration on this subject.
Perhaps no better example of the sustained voluntary mobilisation of
huge numbers of women in peace-time Britain can be seen than that

14 Deborah Mattinson, Opinion Leader Research, London, WC1 8HR, report entitled 'Keeping
   Women's Votes', January, 2000. Similar quotations and arguments are used in the pamphlet *Winning for Women* by Harriet Harman and Deborah Mattinson (Fabian Society,
   pamphlet 596, London, 2000).
15 Ibid. It has been noted by others that women should not be regarded as having the unique
   responsibility of bringing the 'humanistic principles derived from nurturing and caring in
   the private world of personal relationships and family to bear on the public sphere.' This
   'skirts perilously close to recommending that women shoulder responsibility for human-
   ising a public arena brutalised by men's neglect' thereby institutionalising the artificial
   divisions between the public (male) and private (female) within the heart of the public
   sphere itself. Siltanen and Stanworth, *Women and the Public Sphere*, p. 199.
16 Yvonne Roberts, 'Mother Courage: There's more power in female protest', *The
   Independent on Sunday*, 21 May 2000, p. 19.
17 See also Milbrath and Goel, *Political Participation*, p. 57.

of the campaigns to support those in Republican Spain, in which all these essential ingredients were operating to an exceptional degree.

Finally, this study has raised issues about these women and the remembrance of their lives in the future. Many of the women in this study wanted to tell their stories to others, especially to those of the next generation. Those like Nan Green hoped that their narratives would help to preserve and convey their beliefs.

> Well, we're getting older, we're getting less active, people are dying, people are retiring, we haven't got an office, we've just got a relatively small organisation and it becomes more difficult for us. We are hoping that the - we are hoping and expecting that the torch will be taken up, and it is being taken up by the younger generation.[18]

To some extent, these hopes have indeed been fulfilled. The group recently formed by the descendants of British Brigaders, the International Brigade Memorial Trust, has a growing membership who share an interest in the Brigades for a variety of reasons. Together they have become an 'audience', all of whom, in one way or another, contribute to the process of transmitting the 'message' of the Brigaders to resist fascism.

Through historical research, I too have become the 'audience' for the women in this group of narrators, interacting with them not only as a historian but also on a personal level. Traditionally, the 'personal' reaction of the historian is written out of the record, its relevance disregarded. However, my personal response is a means by which to evaluate the impact these women have had on their 'audience', and is therefore a small part of the study. What follows can therefore be considered as evidence of their success at engaging my personal commitment to their narratives.

During the five years spent in this research, it seemed that amongst the women who were in Spain, memories of the days spent in the cave hospital during the battle of the Ebro were especially vivid.[19] Somehow, these memories were strangely fascinating, perhaps, in part, as a result of the powerful image of the cave itself. A few black and white photographs taken at that time show the massive overhanging

---

18 Nan Green, Tameside, 180, 7 August 1976.
19 Patience Darton, Nan Green, Leah Manning and Winifred Bates all had vivid memories of their days in the cave hospital, see Chapters 4 & 6 of this study, and also Jim Fyrth *The Signal was Spain: The Aid Spain Movement in Britain 1936-39* (Lawrence & Wishart, London, 1986) pp. 127-131. Lillian Urmston was also there, see photograph MML A-2: File C/35.

rock, and the dark long slit of the cave mouth, with the barely discernible shapes of a row of camp bed ends. The gloomy interior shots reveal the wounded lying in these beds, swathed in bandages. Some showed patients being given blood transfusions against a background of the rocky walls and stony cave floor, others showed a wounded woman and child from the nearby village of La Bisbal de Falset. New and insistent questions were evoked by this combination of memories and images. How was this experience, so intense for these British women, remembered by the people who lived there still? Were the villagers passing on the memory of the hospital to the next generation or was all forgotten? Would it not be helpful for a historian interested in the processes of remembering and remembrance to visit such a focal point of memory?

Although still remote in geographical terms, the web page of La Bisbal de Falset brings information about the village and its inhabitants to your home computer in seconds. From these pages you can learn that the village was probably founded during the Moorish occupation of Spain and that the economy today is based on the co-operative farming of olives and fruit. The pictures show the truth of the local rhyme, describing, 'La Bisbal in a rock', for the village blends harmoniously with the surrounding mountains. A photograph of the cave is included, mainly because of its importance as the site for the fiesta of Santa Lucía in August each year, when a mass is held, followed by the dancing of traditional Catalan 'sardanas' and an 'almuerzo de fraternidad', a sort of community luncheon.[20] One sentence notes the role of the cave as a military hospital during the civil war. I decided to go there in person, already wondering to what extent the research trip would be, in some respects, a pilgrimage.

The road to La Bisbal de Falset winds high above the Ebro river in the Sierra del Montsant. The rock formations seem to be oozing from the mountains, petrified in mid-flow like gelatinous darkly golden syrup. Beneath these immense rounded slabs are the caves that since prehistoric times, have offered shelter to human beings. The cave of Santa Lucía was not easy to find. Eventually, as the warm spring afternoon unfolded, I found myself standing outside the locked door of the town hall in the village. At first there was no sign of any of the three hundred remaining inhabitants in the narrow streets. Perhaps, I

---

20 It is also known as the cave of Santa Llúcia. Both names for the cave are in current usage. The earlier name of 'Llúcia', probably dating from Roman times, has been catholicised by moving the accent to become 'Lucía', the name of a female saint.

thought, the tortuous drive along the mountain roads may prove fruitless after all. But I was fortunate, as I stood uncertain what to do, the mayor's assistant passed by. On inquiring if I needed help and hearing of my interest in the cave, he took me to meet the mayor who quickly changed roles from that of 'farmer straight from the fields' to that of 'local dignitary'. He opened up the town hall and rang a man who knew the history of the cave well, a local artist, Francesc Masip i Masip. A few minutes later, we set off together, driving over what looked like a cliff edge to find the track below and to see across the valley, the cave itself.

7.1 'The Cave of Sant Lucia, 2000' by local artist, Francesc Masip.

As we drew closer I could see a small metal cage suspended on a chain from the roof. Inside was a small statue of Santa Lucía, and another similar figure was behind glass in the shrine within the cave, adorned with floral tributes. Francesc knew a great deal about the cave hospital although he was born after the war had ended, during the 'Hungry Years'. His grandfather had helped to carry away the bodies of those who had died there, and to bury them in a communal grave at the other side of the village. He knew where the operating theatre had been, and showed me where the only two electric lights had been fixed to the roof, worked from a small dynamo across the valley.

The incoming wounded, if they survived the difficult journey back across the river Ebro and along the mountain tracks, were off-loaded into tents in the valley below where 'triage' sorted them out. They were then carried on stretchers up the steep hill to the operating theatre and to the relative comfort of a hospital camp bed. He said that the water from the spring was renowned for its healing properties and helped to prevent the wounds becoming infected, but many died as their wounds were so severe. A list had been kept of the names of the dead by the villagers. He would let me have a copy. As we walked slowly back along the track, he told me the names of all the plants that grew around the cave, rosemary and thyme and many others I didn't recognise.

In his house he brought out the fragments of a china cup that he had unearthed, decorated with a Republican flag and three bands in the same colours, violet, yellow and red. It had been broken and buried after the war when it was not wise to possess such things. Those had been difficult days and a blanket of silence would have lain over the memory of the cave as a hospital. But now, things are changing. Books are being published in Catalan about the Battle of the Ebro.[21] The villagers of La Bisbal de Falset have decided to put up a sign on the road so that people can find the cave. It may become almost as busy as it was in the war, with coach loads of visitors on battlefield tours around the Ebro, an ideal place to stop for refreshments and a quick look at a reconstructed civil war hospital.

But when I went back to the cave early the following morning, peace prevailed. I tried to imagine what it must have been like for Leah Manning sitting up all night with the dying Welsh Brigader when she made a brief visit to the cave, and for Patience Darton, exhausted and down-hearted, listening to the Spaniard explaining why he fought to defend the Republic.[22] However, I'm not much good at that sort of thing. I saw no ghosts, heard no voices. The presence of the religious icons that represent so much to others, had little resonance for me. Not withstanding my lack of spirituality, I did begin to have the feeling that this was a 'site of remembrance'. Those I had met in the village welcomed outside interest in the cave and its history. Together we could write something about this episode in the war, combining their memories with those of the foreigners who found themselves briefly sharing a common cause.

---

21 Edmon Castell et al, *La Batalla de l'Ebre: Història, paisatge, patrimoni* (ECSA, Barcelona, 1999).
22 Leah Manning knew the dying Brigader, Harry Dobson, as he had volunteered for Spain after hearing her speak on the subject at a meeting in Wales. Leah Manning, *A Life for Education* (Gollancz, London, 1970) p. 136; Patience Darton, IWM 8398 and Chapter 6.

So the visit to the village and the cave is not only one of closure for this particular research, but also one of new beginnings into the study of remembrance. A historian, especially one working with oral sources, becomes a conductor in more than one sense. As metal conducts electricity, the historian acts as a medium of transmission carrying voices to a wider audience. My own case illustrates clearly how those of the next generation, through contact with survivors of a particular experience, can be drawn into a network that will help to ensure the survival of the narratives.[23] But historians also become conductors orchestrating memories, giving their own interpretation of the collective voice. The interactions that occur during such a process may have unforeseen results. Years have passed since I wrote the first few lines of the Introduction that tell of the return of the Brigaders to Spain in 1996. Like the women in this study looking back on the war in Spain, some of the details have faded from my memory, but I have found, as they did, that the emotions remain. I arrived just in time to catch the last waves in the wake of their lives, and I can say, as they have said about Spain, it was a truly memorable experience.

---

23 For a discussion of this subject see Jay Winter and Emmanuel Sivan (eds), *War and Remembrance in the Twentieth Century* (Cambridge University Press, 1999) p. 18.

Profiles*

VALENTINE ACKLAND

Born:	May 1906, London.
Family Background:	Father a dentist in the West-end of London. Mother a High Anglo-Catholic, with 'malade imaginaire'. One elder sister.
Education:	Expensive but poor.
Pre-war:	Considered entering the Catholic Church as a young woman. No early background of political involvement. Joined the Communist Party around 1935, was a founder member of a writers and readers group of the Left Book Club and worked in the Peace Movement. Her relationship with Sylvia Townsend Warner dated from 1930 onwards.
Spanish Civil War:	Attempted to form a group of first-aid volunteers to go to Spain. Spent a few weeks in Barcelona early in the war then in 1937 attended the Writers Congress in Madrid. Wrote about Spanish issues and organised film shows, book sales etc., to raise funds.
Post-war:	Writing and translating. Died November 1969.

---

* It has not been possible to include profiles of all the women in this study due to lack of information.

KATHARINE ATHOLL (née Ramsay)

Born: November 1874, Scotland.

Family Background: Father Sir James Ramsay, Mother was his
                         second wife, Charlotte Stewart. Three older
                         sisters from Father's first marriage, two
                         younger brothers and two younger sisters.
                         Brought up as members of the Scottish
                         Episcopal Church.
                         Katharine joined the Church of Scotland, 1910.

Education: Schooled by elder sisters at first then, from
                         13 years of age, at Wimbledon High School
                         for Girls. Studied piano at the Royal College
                         of Music in 1892.

Pre-War: Married Bardie, the Marquis of Tullibardine,
                         (later the Duke of Atholl) in 1899. Elected MP
                         for West Perthshire 1923 (entered Parliament,
                         January 1924). Junior Education minister
                         1924-9. Campaigned strongly against female
                         circumcision in Africa, and for the delay of
                         Indian Independence.

Spanish Civil War: Extensive committee work, particularly as the
                         Chairman of the National Joint Committee for
                         Spanish Relief and the Basque Children's
                         Committee. She visited Spain, wrote about
                         Spanish issues, and raised questions in the
                         House. She lost her parliamentary seat in
                         December 1938 partly as a result of her
                         stance on Spain.

Post War: During the Second World War she worked on
                         behalf of the Red Cross and to help refugees.
                         Died 1960

CELIA BAKER (née Block)

Born:	1916, Hackney.
Family Background:	Father a furrier. Two elder brothers, three younger brothers and a sister. Father chairman of the local Labour Party. Mother opened their house for use as Committee Rooms. Both parents were progressive Jews and Celia became very religious aged 12-14 years, though it had 'ceased to matter' by the time she married a Catholic.
Education:	Good education at Buxton Street School, Whitechapel, but left at 14 years of age.
Pre-war:	Worked as an office junior, then in book-keeping. Joined Toynbee Hall, Rebel Players, later Unity Theatre. Attended political Summer Schools and went to anti-fascist demonstrations.
Spanish Civil War:	Performed in theatre productions to raise funds for Spain and to increase awareness of Spanish issues. Collected with mother for Spanish Relief.
Post-war:	Married a member of Unity Theatre, worked as a school secretary when her children were young, then in a medical college. Continued to work for various causes, particularly in campaigns for peace. Died 1998.

WINIFRED BATES (later m. Sandford)

Born:	1898, London.
Family Background:	Both parents were Labour Party supporters and former Baptists.
Pre-war:	Taught in the East End of London in the 1920s. Both she and her husband, the writer, Ralph Bates, were Communist Party members.

From 1930 onwards, they made lengthy stays in the mountainous regions of Spain, during which she learned the language.

Spanish Civil War: From November 1936, she worked in Barcelona as a journalist and broadcaster for the United Socialist Party of Catalonia, then in July 1937 she began working for the Spanish Medical Aid Committee as a personnel officer for their staff in Spain. Many of her reports and photographs were used for publicity work. In late 1938 and in 1939 she made fund-raising tours of Britain and the USA for Spanish refugees.

Post-war: Worked in China as a translator, and on her return to England, taught Esperanto. Lived in the USA during the McCarthy period.

CORA BLYTH (m. Portillo)

Born: 1919, Kirkcaldy, Fife.

Family Background: Father a linen manufacturer with a strong interest in music. Mother came from a musical family and played the violin. Two elder sisters both studied music. Parents were 'Conservatives by habit'. Father nominally a Presbyterian and mother Church of England.

Education: Governess at home, then boarding school when 10 years of age, in St. Andrews. Studied French and Spanish at Oxford.

Spanish Civil War: Helped to teach Basque children in her local colony at Aston, where she met the Republican refugee, Luis Portillo.

Post-war: Married Luis in 1941. During the Second World War, she worked for postal censorship, then prepared broadcasts for Latin America. Has four sons. Worked as a London Tourist

Guide, and as a teacher of Spanish.
Campaigned for the Labour Party, then
later for the Liberal Democrats.
Worked for Amnesty International until 2000
and continues to do voluntary work locally.

ELSIE BOOTH

Born: March 1914, Miles Platting, Ardwick.

Family Background: Father a crane driver, mother worked in
                             munitions during World War I, then did
                             cleaning jobs and took in washing.
                             Elsie was the youngest in the family,
                             having one elder brother and two sisters.
                             Parents not very political, mother voted
                             Conservative. Father died when she was
                             15 years old, mother died the following year,
                             after which she lived with her brother, then
                             with the sisters.

Education: Attended the local church school, left aged 14.

Pre-war: Worked in a cotton mill where she joined the
                             union. Married Sid Booth in 1932 when aged
                             18. Sid had worked on the railway and was
                             interested in the Unions although he was
                             unemployed when they married. She joined
                             the Friends of the Soviet Union, then the
                             Communist Party in 1934. She was active in
                             the Workers' Birth Control Clinic and the
                             Maternal Mortality Group. She also went to
                             Paris as a delegate to a conference organised
                             by Women Against War and Fascism.

Spanish Civil War: Whilst her husband was in the International
                             Brigade, she was unable to find work so she
                             and her small boy aged about 18 months old
                             mainly relied on money from Dependants Aid.
                             Attended Aid Spain meetings when she could.
                             Her husband returned from Spain wounded.

| Post-war: | She began working again when the Second World War began, firstly as a shop assistant in the Co-op, and then in the Manchester Corporation Electric Works. Her second child, a daughter, was born in 1941. She remained a member of the Communist Party, and was very active in campaigns for workers' rights and family allowances. Died in 1996. |

NOREEN BRANSON (née Browne)

Born:	16 May 1910, London.
Family Background:	Father was an officer in the army, killed in the First World War. Mother also died during the war so she was brought up by very strict grandparents. She had an older twin brother and sister. Her upbringing was very religious but she became atheist when she was 16 years of age.
Education:	Taught by governesses till about 12 years of age, then at Queensgate Girls Day School. She then studied piano at the Tobias Maté School of Music.
Pre-war:	Met Clive Branson in 1931 at a drama group, and married him four weeks later. She joined the Communist Party in 1932, becoming the Battersea Branch Secretary. She was also active in the Co-op Women's Guild. One daughter.
Spanish Civil War:	Whilst her husband was in Spain in the International Brigades, she was the representative of the Co-operative Women's Guild on the Battersea Aid Spain Committee.
Post-war:	Wrote several books, including *Britain in the Nineteen Thirties* with Margot Heinemann. Worked in the Labour Research Department.

ISABEL BROWN

Born: 6 December 1894, Tyneside.

Family Background: Working-class family, two older sisters, no
                         history of political militancy. She became
                         deeply involved with the local church in her
                         adolescence, till reading undermined her faith.

Education: She was awarded a scholarship at High
                         School, then went to teacher training college
                         in Sunderland.

Pre-war: Joined the Labour Party in 1918 and became
                         the NUT representative on the county
                         committee. Married Ernest Brown in 1921, a
                         son was born the following year. She became
                         the Secretary of the Communist Party branch
                         in her area. Went to Moscow in 1924.
                         During the 1926 General Strike, she was
                         imprisoned for a speeches she made at a
                         public meetings. Worked with various groups,
                         including the Committee for the Relief of
                         Victims of Fascism.

Spanish Civil War: Famous as a speaker at fund-raising meetings
                         for Spanish causes and was particularly active
                         in the formation and running of Spanish
                         Medical Aid. Visited Spain during the war
                         and later went to help refugees in the camps
                         in France.

Post-war: During the Second World War she spoke at
                         meetings for Soviet Aid. For several years
                         after 1940 she was the Communist Party
                         National Women's Organiser. When the war
                         ended she continued to work in a variety of
                         ways in a voluntary capacity for the
                         Communist Party, speaking at meetings and
                         attending international conferences.

FELICIA BROWNE

Born: 1904.

Family Background: Middle class family. Father had progressive
                     views. Mother died when she was a child.

Education: Father encouraged her artistic talents.
                     Attended Slade School of Art 1924-6. In 1928
                     she went to Berlin to study metal-work at
                     Charlottenburg Technische Stadtschule, then
                     became an apprentice to a stone mason from
                     1929-31. She won a scholarship to Goldsmith's
                     College to study metal-work and also worked
                     at the Central School of Arts and Crafts.
                     Spoke several languages.

Pre-war: In Berlin she had taken part in anti-Fascist
                     street fighting and when Hitler came to power,
                     she gave almost all her money to refugees.
                     Visited the Soviet Union in 1931, and lectured
                     on her return to England. Joined the
                     Communist Party in 1933 and became a mem-
                     ber of the Artists International Association.

Spanish Civil War: She was touring in Spain at outbreak of war and
                     immediately enrolled in a People's Militia. She
                     was killed whilst taking part in a reconnaissance
                     mission in Aragón on 22 August 1936.

ELIZABETH CRUMP (M. Thornycroft)

Born: August 1918, Cheltenham.

Family Background: Father a teacher, who after being invalided
                     out of the First World War, taught at Bedales
                     as Senior English Master. Mother ran the
                     library there. Father subsequently taught
                     Speech and Drama at the Royal Academy of
                     Music and helped to found New College.
                     He had come from a religious background but
                     became an agnostic 'free thinker.' No particular

family involvement with party politics.
One brother.

Education: At Bedales till 17 years of age, then secretarial
                        training in London.

Pre-war: Studied in Germany and became anti-Nazi.

Spanish Civil War: Helped to form a Committee at Bedales to
                        raise money for an ambulance and did office
                        work for the International Brigade in London
                        to help refugees and political prisoners.
                        Through Bedales, in 1938 she came into con-
                        tact with her future husband, Chris Thorny-
                        croft, who had been in the International
                        Brigades in Spain.

Post-war   Worked for the Czech Trust Fund and in an
                        aircraft production factory during the Second
                        World War. Three children. She had joined
                        the Communist Party during the war but left
                        around 1956. Became a member of CND and
                        Amnesty International.

NANCY CUNARD

Born: 10 March 1896, Leicestershire.

Family Background: Father an English baronet, mother American.
                        Great grandfather founded the Cunard line of
                        steamships. Irish ancestors. Only child.

Education: Was taught by a governess whose previous pupil
                        was Vita Sackville West. School at Miss Woolf's
                        in London in 1910. Went to Munich in 1912 to
                        study music. Finishing school in Paris in 1913.

Pre-war: Married Sydney Fairbairn 1916 but the marriage
                        only lasted twenty months. Moved in literary
                        circles in Paris during the 20s, writing and
                        publishing, founding the Hours Press in
                        Réanville in 1928, moving it to Paris in 1929,
                        mainly for the publication of contemporary

poetry. Her campaigns for racial equality and
her relationship with the Negro musician,
Henry Crowder, resulted in a deep public rift
with her mother.

Spanish Civil War: Instigated the pamphlet, *Authors Take Sides*,
worked as a journalist in Spain, and with
Spanish refugees.

Post-war: During the Second World War, she was at first
in Chile and Mexico then worked with the
Free French in London. Continued to write
until her death in 1965.

PATIENCE DARTON (m. Edney)

Born: 1911, Orpington.

Family Background: Father a book publisher who went 'broke'
when Patience was a small child. Mother
came from a comfortable background with no
experience of managing without money.
Three brothers and a sister.
High Church background, but as a young
woman attended Christian Socialist churches.

Education: Private school in St. Albans, left aged 14.

Pre-war: Taught children privately and in a private
school. Worked in a tea shop before doing
training as a nurse and midwife in London.
Began to vote for the Labour Party.

Spanish Civil War: Went to Spain in February 1937, initially
nursed Tom Wintringham in hospital in
Valencia, then worked in medical units in
Aragon, Brunete, Teruel and in the cave
hospital near the Ebro. Joined the Communist
Party when she came back to London.

Post-war: On her return she instructed nurses in the
work of war nursing for the London County
Council. In the fifties she was in China,

working as an interpreter and at the Foreign
Languages Press. She was active in the
International Brigade Association until her
death in Madrid in 1996.

MARY DOCHERTY

Born:	27 April 1908, Cowdenbeath.
Family Background:	Father a miner and foundry worker. When unemployed as a result of his union activities he sold firewood. One elder sister and one younger. Attended the ILP Sunday School, and the Proletarian Sunday School.
Education:	Did well at school, and passed the exam for 'Higher Grade' but left in 1922.
Pre-war:	Shop work and in service. Joined the Communist Party in 1926 and started work as a servant to a doctor and his wife. Often in poor health and developed TB. Went to Russia with the Young Communist League where she spent time in a sanatorium. When cured she returned home but was unable to get a reference. Worked as a cleaner in hospital, then had various jobs in service.
Spanish Civil War:	Worked in the Aid Spain group in Cowdenbeath, organising meetings and chalking slogans. She was the treasurer of a women's fund which collected money for the local wives of Brigaders.
Post-war:	During the Second World War, she worked in a munitions factory, then looked after children in a hostel in Rosyth. Eventually started working for the Co-op Bakery, where she was employed for fifteen years. Continued to do general party work and was in charge of the Cowdenbeath Women's Section for many years.

FLORENCE FARMBOROUGH

Born:	15 April 1887, Steeple Claydon, Buckinghamshire.
Family Background:	Father had no children from his first marriage, but then in his fifties, married a woman twenty years his junior. Florence was the fourth of six children and felt she did not belong either to the older group or the younger. She was named after Florence Nightingale, who lived nearby. Father had land but gave up work when Florence was a child. Church of England upbringing.
Education:	Educated at home with a governess, then when a teenager attended St. Thorolds School in London, which she describes as select and strict.
Pre-war:	Became a governess to a family in Russia in 1906, and was working for a Russian doctor as a companion for his daughters when the First World War began. With them, she trained as a Red Cross nurse in Princess Galitsin's Hospital. From there she went as a nurse to the Polish front line where she worked in Red Cross Surgical Field unit, keeping a diary and taking photographs. After leaving Russia in 1918 she returned to England, but in the 1920s began to work as a lecturer in English at the University of Luis Vives in Valencia.
Spanish Civil War:	When war broke out she joined Franco's translation and radio staff, making propaganda broadcasts which were published as *Life and People in Nationalist Spain*.
Post-war:	She returned to England at the start of the Second World War. During the Battle of Britain she worked with Women's Voluntary Service. From 1941 till the end of the war, she was in

Jamaica, working as a censor on the mail to
South America. She lived in England after the
war, publishing two books on her Russian
experiences. She died on 18 August 1978.

KATHLEEN GIBBONS (Née Dooley)

Born:	June 1911, Hemsworth, Yorkshire.
Family Background:	Father a miner who died a year after she was born. Mother married the lodger, who had a drink problem. Moved to Doncaster area where mother ran small business for some years. Seven older siblings, plus another who died. Catholic upbringing with an interest in Irish politics and a brother, Pat, who was an ardent socialist.
Education:	Catholic school, where the nuns were very severe, then council school till 13 years old.
Pre-war:	In service from age 13 until 16, then worked as a bus conductress in Doncaster. Married her first husband when she was 19 years old and moved to Kentish Town. Worked in the Palace Cinema, then selling encyclopaedias, and had a variety of office jobs. After the birth of her first child her marriage began to fail and she left the Catholic Church. She met Danny Gibbons and joined the Communist Party soon afterwards, attending anti-Fascist demonstrations in London. She supported the family on her earnings whilst Danny was unemployed.
Spanish Civil War:	Whilst Danny was in Spain with the International Brigades she campaigned on Spanish issues. After spending a period at home recovering from wounds, Danny returned to Spain and was taken prisoner. Their child was born whilst he was in prison.

When he came back he was ill and never fully recovered, but managed to work as an odd job man for a trade union.

Post-war: During the Second World War the children were evacuated and she had several jobs, including making jettison tanks for aircraft. After the war she worked for London Transport and was active in the Railway Women's Union. She continued to campaign for many issues, at local and national level, and for the last few years has been fund-raising for the homeless.

HELEN GRANT (née Newsome)

Born: 26 December 1903, Clifton, Bristol.

Education: Private schools in Bristol and Lausanne followed by Mrs Hoster's Secretarial College. Secretarial work in Brussels and for Walter de la Mare before going to Somerville College, Oxford, to study Spanish and French from 1927-30. During this period she also spent time in Spain, forming friendships within literary circles.

Pre-war: She was a strong supporter of the Republican government as a result of her contact with the Spanish Liberals of the Residencia de Estudiantes in Madrid. She also stayed in Granada with the family of Fernando de los Rios, who became the Minister of Education. She taught Spanish at Birmingham University from 1934-39. Married the economist, A. T. K. Grant.

Spanish Civil War: Went to Spain to act as interpreter for a group sent out by the Society of Friends, from March to April 1937, and kept a diary of her experiences. On her return she spoke at many meetings to raise funds for Spanish

relief and for the Basque children in Britain.
In November 1938 she was the Labour Party
candidate in a by-election.

Post-war: During the Second World War she worked for
the Foreign Office, the BBC European Service,
and the US Office of War Information.
She was a lecturer in Spanish at Cambridge
University from 1945 to 1966 and became a
Fellow of Girton College. She wrote and
translated books on Spanish literature.
She died in June 1992.

NAN GREEN (née Farrow)

Born: 1904, Beeston, near Nottingham

Family Background: Father had been a manager of a factory,
but after 1916 they lived in 'reduced circumstances'. Mother became ill. Three older
siblings, one died, two younger. Parents were
High Anglican and voted Conservative.

Education: Small private schools.

Pre-war: Began office work when 15 years old and became
a Fabian as a result of dealing with workmen's
compensation claims in an insurance office.
Met George Green, a musician, through a
rambling association. They married and had
two children. They joined the Communist
Party in the early 30s and moved to London.
She became a branch secretary in 1934.

Spanish Civil War: After George went to Spain with the Brigades,
she was asked to go there to carry out
administration work in the medical units.
Wogan Phillips offered to pay for the children
to go to boarding school, and, after much
thought, she decided to send them to
Summerhill. George Green was killed in 1938
during the Battle of the Ebro. In 1939 she

went to the refugee camps in France and
sailed with 2,000 Spanish refugees to Mexico,
helping to care for the infants on the journey.

Post-war: During the Second World War she worked in
Poplar Town Hall as Invasion Defence Officer.
She continued to work for Spanish refugees and
for political prisoners in Spain. In the 1950s she
also worked in the Peace Movement, interpreting
at conferences. She spent some years in China
working for the Foreign Languages Publishing
House in Peking, returning to England just
before the Cultural Revolution. She then held
the post of Secretary of the International
Brigade Association until she died in 1984.

CHARLOTTE HALDANE

Born: 1894, London.

Family Background: Father a 'self-made man', 'financially prosperous'
from the Rhineland. Mother born in America.
Charlotte born and brought up in England with a
younger sister. Deeply religious as a child and influenced to a great extent by her English nanny.

Education: Taught by a German governess, who she
disliked intensely, followed by attendance at
an English school where she admired the
headmistress, a feminist and leader in women's
education. She then went to school in Antwerp
till 16 years of age. When the family returned
to London, she went to a business school.

Pre-war: Worked as a secretary/receptionist for a concert agent. She began to write and managed
to get a job with the *Express*. She married
J. B. S. Haldane after her divorce from her first
husband, by whom she had a son. She visited
Spain twice in 1933 and learned Spanish.

Spanish Civil War:	Already a member of the Labour Party, she joined the Communist Party in 1937 and worked for the Comintern in Paris helping to organise the volunteers who were on their way to join the International Brigades in Spain. She acted as guide and interpreter to Paul Robeson when he toured Spain towards the end of 1937. In Britain, she worked as the Honorary Secretary of the Dependants Aid Committee. Her son joined the International Brigades.
Post-war:	During the Second World War she worked on the St. Pancras Borough Council Air Raid Precautions Emergency Committee, then as a war correspondent in Russia. She subsequently broke with the Communist Party and her husband, writing of her reasons in *Truth Will Out* which was published in 1948.

MARGOT HEINEMANN

Born:	1913, West London
Family Background:	Parents were German Jews, father a 'reluctant' banker in the City and mother a pacifist and 'drawing room socialist.' Both voted Labour and had attended ILP meetings. She had an elder sister and a brother.
Education:	South Hampstead High School, followed by Roedean and a Scholarship to Newnham to read English.
Pre-war:	She taught in the Cambridge Socialist Society at Cambridge, joining the Communist Party and meeting John Cornford in 1934. She then taught factory workers at Cadbury's Bournville in Birmingham.
Spanish Civil War:	Various activities for Spanish relief, selling pamphlets, propaganda work and solidarity meetings etc. After John Cornford was killed

she began working in the Labour Research
Department.

Post-war: She taught English Literature first at Camden
High School for Girls, later at Goldsmiths
College, and finally at New Hall, Cambridge,
also writing and publishing several books.
She had one daughter from her partnership
with J. D. Bernal. She died on 10 June 1992.

MARJORIE JACOBS

Born: 1915, Nottingham.

Family Background: Father was a wholesale potato merchant but
business declined and he eventually went
bankrupt when he became ill around the time
of the General Strike. Mother had been a
teacher. Two older siblings and one younger,
plus a brother who died of diphtheria. Strong
religious background as members of a Chapel
where her great-uncle was an Elder. Mother a
Conservative, Father had socialist leanings,
though not a member of a political party.

Education: Left school aged 14.

Pre-war: Worked as a salesgirl, and in office work.
She began reading Left Book Club books and
when aged about 17 years old, she became
the only member of her family to join the
Communist Party.

Spanish Civil War: Door to door collections of money and milk
for Spanish relief.

Post-war: Married a Brigader, Lionel Jacobs and had
two children. Left the Communist Party in
1956 and returned to religious beliefs.

ROSE KERRIGAN

Born:	1903, Ireland.
Family Background:	Father a Jewish tailor from Glasgow who worked in Ireland till fired for being too outspoken, then lived hand to mouth in Glasgow. Bankrupt when Rose aged eleven. As the second of four surviving children, and the only girl, she had heavy domestic duties. Parents not members of any party, but anti-war. Rose attended a socialist Sunday School. When 12 years old, she played an active part in the Glasgow rent strike.
Education:	Left school aged 14.
Pre-war:	Worked in a department store and was fired for defending a conscientious objector. Had various jobs in which she tried to organise women to join unions. Joined the Communist Party when it was first formed. Met her husband, Peter Kerrigan, through a socialist group organised ramble. Married at 23 years of age. Accompanied him to Russia in 1935 when he was sent there as a Comintern representative.
Spanish Civil War:	Husband went to Spain as a Political Commissar in the International Brigades and later as a Daily Worker correspondent. Rose had one child already, and the second of their three children was born shortly after he left. She collected for Spanish relief, though with young children it was sometimes difficult.
Post-war:	During the Second World War, she worked as a collector for an insurance company, where she organised the first women's branch of the staff union. She then had a variety of jobs, including working for several years in a clothing factory where she began the first union for the female workforce. She supported CND and after retirement, worked for her local pensioners' rights group. Died in 1995.

MICKY LEWIS

Born:	1917, Manchester.
Family Background:	Father a cabinet maker from Eastern Europe, a member of the Jewish Workers' Circle. Mother from Manchester. Eight children in the family, Micky the second youngest.
Education:	Left school aged 14.
Pre-war:	Worked in a dress factory where she became involved with the Trade Union. Joined the Labour League of Youth, then the Young Communist League.
Spanish Civil War:	Collecting door to door, leafleting, meetings, whitewashing slogans.
Post-war:	Worked in munitions during the Second World War, moving to London and marrying Nat Lewis in 1943. Had two children, then worked in the school meals service. Continues to be very active in various groups at local and national level, including Age Concern, Hackney Pensioners Press and Dial a Ride transport. She is on the management committee of the Senior Citizens Club and continues her political involvement as a member of the Communist Party and on a Better Government committee.

MURIEL MCDIARMID (M. Nicholas)

Born:	1900, South London.
Family Background:	Father a civil servant.
Education:	City of London School for Girls, followed by evening classes and a scholarship to Kings College, London, to study French. Graduated 1924.
Pre-war:	Various jobs before 1922. In 1926 began work in France for Ciro Pearls.

Spanish Civil War: In 1936, she applied for work with the National
                      Joint Committee for Spanish Relief and was
                      taken on as the Assistant Secretary. She also
                      helped with Basque Children's Committee
                      work. Became a member of the Communist
                      Party. In October 1938, she went to Barcelona
                      to help in the canteens run by the Quakers,
                      although not a Quaker herself. Kept a diary
                      of the fall of the city which was published as
                      Franco in Barcelona. After leaving Spain, she
                      helped in the refugee camps in France.

Post-war: During the Second World War she was business
                      manager of the Journal *Labour Monthly*, work-
                      ing with R. Palme Dutt. She later worked for the
                      US Army. After the war, she and her husband
                      lived in France and Italy for many years.

ETHEL MACDONALD

Born: 24 February 1909, Bellshill, Lanarkshire.

Family Background: One of a family of nine children. Left home
                      aged 16.

Education: Motherwell High School.

Pre-war: Worked as waitress in Glasgow. Joined the
                      Independent Labour Party aged 16. Came into
                      contact with Guy Aldred, leader of the United
                      Socialist Movement, an anarchist group in
                      Glasgow, when she asked him to fight a case
                      for her against the Labour Exchange. Worked
                      as secretary for Aldred then for his group.

Spanish Civil War: Broadcast from Barcelona for the anarcho-
                      syndicalists from November 1936 to September
                      1937, becoming known as the 'Scots Scarlet
                      Pimpernel' for helping anarchists to escape.
                      She was arrested herself, then disappeared,
                      eventually returning to Glasgow in
                      November 1937.

Post-war: After Spain she worked with French
                         Anarchists in Paris then with Strickland
                         Press, printing *The Word*. Died 1 December
                         1960, in Glasgow.

INEZ ISABEL MACDONALD

Born: 27 May 1902, London.

Education: St. Margaret's School, Bushey, then the
                         Institute St. Jacques, Pau. Newnham College
                         1922-29. Studied French and Spanish.

Pre-war: After her PhD in 1929 she was Secretary at
                         Cheltenham Ladies College. She returned to
                         Cambridge, becoming a Resident Fellow at
                         Newnham College in 1937.

Spanish Civil War: During the summer of 1937 she worked in
                         Murcia as the Superintendent of the children's
                         hospital founded by Francesca Wilson.

Post-war: She continued to work in the interests of Spanish
                         refugees in Cambridge, organising weekly
                         meetings at Newnham where many friendships
                         were formed between her students and the
                         refugees. She held various university posts as
                         a tutor and lecturer, and was highly regarded
                         for her teaching abilities, and as a Hispanist.
                         Her wide range of publications on Spanish
                         literature and history included some on the
                         works of Lope de Vega. She was writing a study
                         of his life and work when she died in 1955.

LEAH MANNING (née Perrett)

Born: 14 April 1886, Droitwich, Worcestershire.

Family Background: Father a Captain in the Salvation Army, formerly
                         a baker, mother a former teacher, the daughter
                         of a timber merchant in London. Leah lived

with maternal grandparents in Stoke Newington when her parents went to Canada with the surviving five of twelve children. Grandfather a Liberal and radical thinker.

Education: Educated at home by grandmother at first, then after school went to Homerton Teacher Training College, Cambridge, where she joined the University Fabian Society.

Pre-war: Worked as a teacher in Cambridge. She married Will Manning around 1913 or 1914. Became a member firstly of the Independent Labour Party, then the Labour Party. Between 1929 and 1931 she was the Labour MP for Islington East. She was also president of the National Union of Teachers and Joint Secretary of the Co-ordinating Committee Against War and Fascism. In 1934, she went to Spain as part of a delegation to investigate the suppression of the Asturian miners' uprising, publishing a book, *What I Saw In Spain* in the following year.

Spanish Civil War: She played a leading role on national committees for Spain, making several trips there. She was particularly involved with the arrangements for the evacuation of the Basque children to Britain, and with their subsequent care.

Post-war: She was the MP for Epping from 1945 to 1950, after which she returned to work as a teacher. She established a family planning clinic in Harlow. In 1966 she was made a Dame Commander of the Order of the British Empire. Her autobiography was published in 1970 and she died in 1977.

JESSICA MITFORD

Born: 11 September 1917, Gloucestershire.

Family Background: Father the 2nd Lord Redesdale. Mother cam-
                             paigned for the Conservatives during elections.
                             She had one brother and six sisters, of whom
                             Jessica was the fifth. Pam enjoyed the country
                             life, Nancy became a novelist, Diana married
                             Oswald Mosley, Unity became a camp-follower
                             of Hitler, Deborah married the 11th Duke of
                             Devonshire.

Education: Taught at home by mother and governesses,
                             attended a private day school for girls for a
                             few months. Read her way through the family
                             library, then socialist literature. Sent to Paris
                             to study French at the Sorbonne.

Spanish Civil War: Ran away to Spain with her second cousin,
                             Esmond Romilly, who had been in the Inter-
                             national Brigades. She helped him in his work
                             as a journalist in Bilbao for the *News Chronicle*.
                             They had to leave Spain due to family pressure
                             and were married in France in 1937.

Post-war: They returned to London, but in 1939 they
                             went to the USA where they worked in a
                             variety of jobs. Esmond was killed in the
                             Canadian Airforce in 1941. Their daughter
                             was born after his death. Jessica later
                             married a lawyer, Robert Teuhaft and joined
                             the American Communist Party in 1943,
                             resigning after the invasion of Hungary in
                             1956. They had two children. Further books
                             followed the success of the first part of her
                             autobiography, *Hons and Rebels* in 1960.
                             She died in California on 23 July 1996.

MOLLY MURPHY (née Morris)

Born:	8 March 1890, Leyland, Lancashire.
Family Background:	Mother was of Anglo-Irish stock, and had been a pupil teacher. Father was departmental manager in a rubber goods factory until his radicalism led to him leaving over wage claim when Molly was 10 years old. They moved to the Salford slums and lived there until mother became a manager in a dairy shop. Seven children in the family.
Education:	Evening classes after having left school.
Pre-war:	Joined the Manchester Committee of the Women's Social and Political Union with her mother. In 1912, she began work as the full time organiser in the Sheffield branch of Women's Social and Political Union. She trained as a nurse in Hammersmith, then in 1921 married Jack Murphy, who had been proposing to her for several years. They went to Moscow together where she met Lenin. Their son was born after her return to England. They left the Communist Party in the early thirties and joined the Labour Party.
Spanish Civil War:	She volunteered to serve as a nurse in Spain and left in January 1937, returning in poor health at the end of July.
Post-war:	During the Second World War she worked for a mobile medical unit in St. Pancras. Ill health prevented her return to full time nursing after the war.

ANNIE MURRAY (m. Knight)

Born:	April 1906, Aberdeenshire, Scotland.
Family Background:	Father had a small farm but poor eyesight hindered his work. He was a member of the

United Free Church of Scotland and a Liberal.
Mother used to read and recite Burns. Seven
brothers and sisters.

Pre-war: After working for several years on the farm,
                        she trained as a nurse in Edinburgh Royal
                        Infirmary, and led a protest against conditions
                        there. She joined the Communist Party in the
                        mid-thirties.

Spanish Civil War: In 1936 she went to Spain as a nurse, where
                        for part of the time she worked on a hospital
                        train in Catalonia. Her brothers both joined
                        the International Brigades and she nursed
                        one of them when he was wounded.

Post-war: During and after the Second World War she was
                        in charge of an air-raid station in London and
                        later became matron of a children's nursery
                        in Stepney. Married Frank Knight in 1948.
                        Died in 1997.

PENNY PHELPS (m. Feiwel, pen-name Fyvel)

Born: 24 April 1909, Tottenham.

Family Background: Father a casual worker often unemployed,
                        the 'black sheep' of his Quaker family.
                        Mother was a coal merchant's daughter.
                        Nine brothers and sisters, plus one 'adopted.'

Education: Poor education due to responsibilities of
                        looking after younger members of the family.
                        Left school aged 13.

Pre-war: Worked in factories, in service, and in dress-
                        making. Joined the Plymouth Brethren and
                        began to go to evening classes. In 1927 began
                        nursing training in the Eastern Fever Hospital
                        in Homerton. Later trained at Charing Cross
                        Hospital to become a State Registered Nurse,
                        then spent a year at Hillcroft College in 1934.

Spanish Civil War: Nursing in Hertfordshire when the war began.
                       Volunteered for Spain in 1937. Worked in
                       various units, and was in charge of containing
                       an outbreak of scarlet fever and typhoid in
                       the Garibaldi Battalion, where she was given
                       the rank of Honorary Medical Officer. In 1938
                       she was severely wounded by a bomb blast
                       and was taken back to England for surgery.

Post-war: During her convalescence, she met Dr Michael
                       Feiwel, marrying him in late 1938. In the
                       Second World War she worked at a First Aid
                       Post, then later became a social worker for
                       Physically Handicapped Youth. For many years
                       she helped her husband in the running of his
                       private medical practice in Harley Street. She
                       published her memoirs, *English Penny*, in 1992.

MARGARET POWELL (m. Lesser)

Born: 26 March 1913, near Llangenny, Wales.

Family Background: Parents were hill farmers. Father Welsh,
                       mother Irish. Nine children altogether,
                       Margaret around midway. Father died when
                       she was quite young. Mother married again
                       but unhappily. Older brothers were sent to
                       Canada through Dr Barnardo's organisation.
                       Four sisters trained as nurses.

Education: Basic education in village school, then
                       nursing training when aged 18 in St. Giles
                       Hospital, Camberwell.

Pre-war: Worked in a TB hospital in Black Notley, join-
                       ing the CommunistParty in the early thirties.

Spanish Civil War: In 1936 she was training as a midwife, but
                       volunteered to serve in Spain. Leah Manning
                       persuaded her to finish her training. She left
                       for Spain early in 1937 and nursed on the
                       Aragón front, in Teruel and on the Ebro,

working mainly with a Spanish medical unit. She was with them in the camps in France until found by the Quakers. She was later created a Dame of the Order of Loyalty to the Spanish Republic by the government in exile.

Post-war: She was a founder member of the nurses union, which later became part of the National Union of Public Employees, During the Second World War, she worked as an ARP as a nurse, then in postal censorship because of her knowledge of Catalan. She volunteered for the British Army United Nations Relief and Administration and worked with Yugoslav refugees in Egypt, then in a Displaced Persons camp in West Germany where she was in charge of maternity and child welfare. She married Sam Lesser, a former Brigader, in 1950, and they had one daughter. She became a Health Visitor, but her career was interrupted by a period of several years spent living in Moscow with her husband, a *Daily Worker* correspondent. When they came back she returned to work and was active in CND, but her health deteriorated in the 1970s. She died in 1990.

EDITH PYE

Born: 20 October 1876, London.

Family Background: Father, William Arthur Pye JP, was a wine merchant. She was the eldest of eight children.

Education: Trained as an SRN and midwife.

Pre-war: By 1907 she was Superintendent of District Nurses in London. Joined the Society of Friends in 1908. In December 1914 she set up a maternity hospital for women refugees near the front lines in France, staying there until 1919.

From 1921 to 1922 she worked in Vienna trying to feed severely undernourished children. She became active in the Women's International League and in 1934 was elected president of the British Institute of Midwives. She was also vice-chairman of the Friends German Emergency Committee, dealing with refugees.

Spanish Civil War: She worked on the Friends Spain Committee and with other committees carrying out relief work for Spain. She instigated the formation of an international commission in Geneva for child refugees in Spain. Visited Spain in December 1937. From January 1939 till 1940 she worked with Spanish refugees near the border.

Post-war: During the Second World War she was honorary secretary to the Famine Relief Committee, working with the Red Cross to help children in parts of Europe occupied by Germany. Died on 16 December 1965, in Street.

ELEANOR RATHBONE

Born: 12 May 1872, London.

Family Background: Father was William Rathbone VI, Liberal MP. She grew up in Liverpool. There were five siblings from her father's first marriage, and four others from his second marriage. Her father was a Unitarian, and mother an Anglican. There was also a strong influence from earlier Rathbones who had been Quakers, though Eleanor had no particular religious creed as adult.

Education: A succession of governesses as they moved between houses. Kensington High School followed by Somerville College, Oxford in 1893.

Pre-war: Whilst at Oxford she became a suffragist and continued to be active in the movement,

	being president of the National Union of Societies for Equal Citizenship from 1919 to 1928. In 1909 she had become the first woman member of Liverpool City Council as an Independent. She worked for the League of Nations Union on the General Council and later on Executive Committee. In 1929, she became an Independent University MP, and remained in parliament for 16 years.
Spanish Civil War:	She visited Spain with Ellen Wilkinson, the Duchess of Atholl and Dame Rachel Crowdie in the spring of 1937 to see the situation at first hand. She was vice-chairman of the National Joint Committee for Spanish Relief, a member of the Parliamentary Committee for Spain and later also on the Spanish Medical Aid Committee. She spoke against non-intervention, publishing her book, *War Can Be Averted* in 1938, which gave her views on the war in Spain.
Post-war:	During the Second World War she continued to work in various ways to help displaced people. Died in 1946.

PRISCILLA SCOTT-ELLIS

Born:	15 November 1916.
Family Background:	Father was the 8th Lord Howard de Walden. Mother was a Van Raalte whose family were close friends with the Infante Alfonso d'Orleans Bourbon (a first cousin of the King of Spain), his wife, Princess Beatrice, and their children. Priscilla was one of six children brought up in Belgrave Square and at Chirk Castle in North Wales.
Education:	Day school in London till aged 9, followed by governesses at Chirk, then boarding school

when 15 years of age. Finishing school in
Paris, and Munich to study German.

Spanish Civil War: After a short First Aid course and some lessons
in Spanish, she left for Spain in October 1937.
After a brief period of nursing training in Jerez,
she began work as a nurse for Franco's forces,
often in medical units near the front lines.

Post-war: During the Second World War she joined an
ambulance unit and went To France. After
the fall of France she ran a hospital for Polish
soldiers in Scotland. Suffering from Raynaud's
disease, she needed a warmer climate so went
to work in Consulate in Barcelona where she
met José Luis de Vilallonga. They married in
1945 and lived in Argentina with their two
children, then in Paris. When they separated,
Priscilla returned to England and had a variety
of jobs before marrying Ian Hanson, the singer.
She lived in the USA until her death in 1983.

THORA SILVERTHORNE (m. Sinclair-Loutit, m. Craig)

Born: 1910, South Wales.

Family Background: Father a miner, a trade union activist and Communist Party member. Mother died when Thora was
about 15 years old. Seven brothers and sisters.

Education: Nursing training at the Radcliffe Infirmary in
Oxford and London.

Pre-war: Known as 'Red Silverthorne' when training as
a nurse. Was always involved in political
groups, the Young Communist League, the
Labour Party, and the Communist Party.

Spanish Civil War: Went to Spain as a nurse with the first medical
unit to leave Britain in August 1936. Worked
as a theatre nurse, often with the Catalan
surgeon, Dr. Broggi.

Post-war: On her return, she continued her nursing
                             work and founded the first union for nurses in
                             Britain. As Secretary of the Socialist Medical
                             Association, she was among the delegates who
                             met with Clement Attlee in 1945 to discuss
                             the creation of the National Health Service.
                             She had two daughters. After retiring from
                             her work as a Civil Service Union official, she
                             lived with her second husband in Wales, later
                             returning to London where she died in 1998.

ROSALEEN SMYTHE (m. Ross)

Born: 12 May 1909, Bedfordshire.

Family Background: Father was an engineer and mother a former
                             teacher. They came from Catholic families
                             but were no longer practising. Her father was
                             chairman of the local Independent Labour
                             Party branch, mother had utopian socialist
                             beliefs. She had two older sisters and a
                             younger brother.

Education: Being considered a 'delicate' child, she went
                             first to a Dame school, then to a small private
                             school, the fees being paid from the Co-op
                             dividend. When she was 15 years old, to help
                             pay for her own lessons, she began to work
                             there as a part-time assistant teacher.

Pre-war: Office work and evening classes locally until
                             aged 17, then to London to work where she
                             met Winifred and Ralph Bates who encour-
                             aged her interest in politics. She joined the
                             Communist Party and joined in anti-Mosley
                             demonstrations.

Spanish Civil War: She was with Ralph and Winifred in the
                             Pyrenees when the war began. She was soon
                             able to begin work for a newspaper in
                             Barcelona with Winifred, then joined the

medical unit in Grañen as an administrator.
As the war progressed, she worked in various
places, including a hospital in El Escorial,
keeping records of the casualties and helping
out with nursing duties when needed.

Post-war: She married a Canadian Brigader and went to
live in Canada. Their son was born in 1940.
Her husband found it difficult to find work
after having fought in the Brigades. She had
office jobs whilst continuing to be active on
Spanish issues in the 'Friends of Free Spain'.
She continued to support the Canadian
Communist Party but her main area of work
was in the Peace Movement.

FRIDA STEWART (m. Knight)

Born: 11 November 1910, Cambridge.

Family Background: Father was Dean of Chapel at Trinity College.
Mother an early student at Newnham. Three
sisters and one brother.

Education: Dame School and then the Perse School.
Ill health led to an extended period of convalescence away from school. Studied violin at
the Royal College of Music and in Germany.

Pre-war: Worked with the unemployed at Manchester
University Settlement organising theatre
productions, then for Hull University College,
teaching evening classes in rural areas. She
joined the Communist Party around the time
of the outbreak of war in Spain.

Spanish Civil War: Founded Aid Spain Committees in Hull and
York, then was asked to drive an ambulance
to Spain in 1937. She worked with Francesca
Wilson in a children's hospital for refugees in
Murcia, then spent some time in Madrid,
helping journalists and making broadcasts.

On her return, she was responsible for visiting Basque children's colonies to write reports for the Committee and organising concert tours to raise funds. She then went to France to help refugees from Spain in the camps.

Post-war: At the start of the Second World War, she was in Paris helping refugees. She was interned by the Germans, but after nearly a year, she escaped with the help of the French Resistance and eventually arrived back in Britain with a secret message for General de Gaulle. She worked with the Free French in London, and in 1944 married the microbiologist, B. C. J. G. Knight. By 1951 they had four children. She campaigned for many causes throughout the remainder of her life, being particularly active in the Peace Movement. After visiting Cuba in 1992, she founded the Cambridge Cuba Solidarity Campaign. Several of her books on historical subjects and music were published, and she was working on her memoirs, mainly written in the post-war period, when she died in 1996.

PRISCILLA THORNYCROFT (m. Siebert)

Born: 21 April 1917, Golders Green.

Family Background: Mother from a theatrical Fabian family whose parents were friends with George Bernard Shaw and Eleanor Marx. Father, from a Liberal family, famous as sculptors, was manager at an engineering works, developing experimental diesel engines. Mother very active 'doing good works'. Priscilla was born midway between four brothers and sisters.

Education: Kindergarten (expelled for misbehaviour which included organising the other children to hide when they were called in to the lessons), followed by Worthing High School, then to Bedales to join her sister and brother, where her father had been one of the first pupils. Studied art at the Slade in London.

Pre-war:

Whilst at the Slade she became the student representative in the Artists International Association, and was very much involved in the campaigns for peace. The first major demonstration she attended was when Haile Selassie arrived in London, during which the demonstrators were charged by mounted police and 'batonned.' She joined the Communist Party after attending a holiday camp for the unemployed, run by the students of Oxford University where her brother, Chris, was studying.

Spanish Civil War:

As a member of the AIA, she prepared banners and placards for demonstrations, and painted posters and hoardings as publicity for various campaigns for the Republic. Organised painting classes for the children in the Basque colony in Worthing, which her mother and sister helped to run.

Post-war:

She met a German refugee, Hans Siebert, a teacher who had escaped from a Nazi concentration camp. He was interned at the start of the Second World War, but Eleanor Rathbone helped to arrange his release. Priscilla married him in 1942. They had two children. After the war, they lived in the Soviet sector of Berlin, then in Dresden, where Hans was head of a teacher training college. Priscilla worked as a freelance illustrator of children's books and magazines and was a member of the Democratic Women's League, on the committee of the Artists' Union, and in an Artists' co-operative. She continues to paint and exhibit her work.

SYLVIA TOWNSEND WARNER

Born:	6 December 1893, Harrow-on-the-Hill.
Family Background:	Father, a Cambridge graduate, followed in the family tradition to teach at Harrow. Mother, Nora Hudleston, had been brought up in India until the family fortunes changed and they returned to England. Sylvia was an only child, influenced by her father who was an admirer of Voltaire and the Enlightenment, and a convinced atheist.
Education:	Went to local kindergarten aged 6 but was withdrawn after a term. She was then taught at home by mother and had governesses for languages, but mainly learned from father, a teacher of high repute.
Pre-war:	She worked for the Carnegie United Kingdom Trust on a Tudor Church Music Research Project as a member of editorial committee. Several of her novels became well known during the twenties. She joined the Communist Party in 1935 and became Secretary of the Dorset Peace Council in 1936. She was a founder member of her local Left Book Club writers and readers group.
Spanish Civil War:	She went to Barcelona in September 1936 with Valentine Ackland and to the Writers Congress in Madrid in 1937. She wrote many articles and poems about Spain, and spoke at fund-raising meetings. Her historical novel, *After the Death of Don Juan* (Chatto & Windus, London, 1938), was a reflection of contemporary Spanish issues.
Post-war:	She continued writing and was a supporter of the Communist Party until the 1950s. Died in 1973.

LILLIAN URMSTON (m. Buckoke)

Born:	7 June 1915, near Stalybridge.
Family Background:	Father had worked with horses but then went into the steel industry and worked as under-manager in the stores. Parents brought their four children up in the Church of England. Lillian was a keen member of the congregation and taught at the Sunday School.
Education:	Local primary school and St. Paul's Elementary School. She won scholarships from her local secondary school but the family could not afford to take them up.
Pre-war:	She was unhappy working in an office so began nursing training at a local hospital. After becoming an SRN she took a course on tropical fevers. Midwifery training followed, during which she saw conditions of extreme poverty. She joined the Territorial Army Nursing Service at the time of the invasion of Abyssinia. She worked as a Staff Nurse in a nursing home in the Lake District for six months whilst repeatedly applying to nurse in Spain.
Spanish Civil War:	She arrived in Spain in June 1937 and worked on the Aragón front, in Teruel and in the railway tunnel near Flix. She was held in the camps in France with a group of Spanish medical staff until Rosita Davson arranged for her release.
Post-war:	She continued to try to raise funds to help Spanish refugees and lectured and wrote articles on nursing in war-time. During the Second World War she was an army nursing officer. She was badly hurt by shell fire in Anzio, Italy, suffering spinal injuries from which she never fully recovered. She met her future husband whilst in hospital and they married in 1945. After the war she worked as

356 BRITISH WOMEN AND THE SPANISH CIVIL WAR

356 BRITISH WOMEN AND THE SPANISH CIVIL WAR

a journalist for several newspapers. She and
her husband went to Kuala Lumpur to help the
Chinese Indian survivors from the railways.
They also helped prostitutes in Singapore to
form a union. She returned to Spain several
times to visit the areas where she had worked
as a nurse. She was often recognised by people
she had known during the war. Died in 1990.

ELLEN WILKINSON

Born: 8 October 1891.

Family Background: Father was a cotton operative who later
                      became an insurance clerk. Mother came from
                      Lancashire. Ellen was one of four children,
                      brought up in Ardwick, near Manchester.
                      Both parents were Methodists. Father voted
                      Conservative. Her mother became ill with
                      cancer and died in 1916.

Education: Began elementary school but became ill so
                      did not return till 8 years of age, when she
                      attended Ardwick Higher Elementary Grade
                      in 1902. Always won scholarships after
                      11 years old. In 1906 she began teacher
                      training and won a scholarship to Manchester
                      University in 1910.

Pre-war: After graduating from university, she became
                      an organiser for the National Union of Women's
                      Suffrage Societies in Manchester. In 1915, she
                      became a Trade Union Organiser and in 1923,
                      a City Councillor. She was a member of the
                      Communist Party from 1920 to 1924, before
                      being elected as the Labour MP for Middles-
                      borough East in 1924, and for Jarrow in 1935.
                      She visited Spain in 1934 to report on the
                      suppression of the Asturian miners uprising.

Spanish Civil War: Visited Spain on several occasions. Apart from
                     her visit with the Duchess of Atholl and other
                     women MPs, she also went with Clement Attlee
                     in late 1937, meeting leaders of the Republic
                     and visiting the International Brigades. She
                     was a member of the Parliamentary Commit-
                     tee for Spain and of committees for Spanish
                     relief, often speaking at public meetings on
                     their behalf.

Post-war: During the Second World War, she became
                     Parliamentary Secretary to the Home Secretary,
                     Herbert Morrison. She was responsible for
                     air-raid shelter matters and policy. After the
                     war she became Minister of Education, but
                     died in 1947, aged only 55, following an
                     attack of bronchitis.

FRANCESCA MARY WILSON

Born: 1 January 1881, Newcastle on Tyne

Family Background: Father had a factory supplying furs for an
                     American hat manufacturer. Both parents
                     were in the Society of Friends but mother
                     joined the Plymouth Brethren when Francesca
                     was 4 years of age. With her two older sisters
                     and younger brother, she was taken to their
                     meetings, but, unlike her sister, she did not
                     feel herself to be 'saved'.

Education: Educated at home until aged 13, when Father
                     overruled her mother and insisted that she
                     should be 'properly educated' at Newcastle
                     High School. Newnham College, Cambridge,
                     reading History from 1906-1909. Trained as a
                     teacher in Cambridge in 1912.

Pre-war: Although some sources state that she was
                     not actually a Friend despite working closely
                     with them, she does apparently appear on

the lists of the Newcastle Friends Monthly Meeting until 1925, after which she transferred her membership to Warwickshire. She held various teaching posts from 1911 onwards, at Bedales, in Bath and in Gravesend. She began working with Belgian refugees in 1914. Between 1916 and 1923, she served with the Friends War Victims Relief Committee in Holland, France, north Africa (with Serbian refugees), Austria and Russia. From 1925 to 1939 she was Senior History Mistress at the Church High School in Birmingham, taking time off for refugee work.

Spanish Civil War: She worked with refugees in Spain, particularly with Malagan refugees in Murcia where she founded a children's hospital. She also set up workshops where the refugees could make clothing for themselves, and a farm colony for orphaned Spanish boys. In 1939, she went to southern France to help with the relief work for the Spanish refugees in the camps.

Post-war: Worked with Polish refugees in Hungary and wrote two books about her refugee work, *In the Margins of Chaos* (1944), and *Aftermath* (1945). In 1945, she became chief welfare officer in UNRRA, initially in Dachau. She finally resigned from the Friends in the early 1950s. For many years, a series of refugees stayed in her home in London. She continued to lecture and to write books.
Died 4 March 1981.

APPENDIX II

Interviews:
Theory and Methodology

IN VIEW OF THE EXTENSIVE USE of oral sources in this study, a brief discussion of the theoretical background that has informed their use is included here, together with an outline of the methodological approach employed in the interviews carried out during this research.[1]

The subjectivity of oral testimony has frequently been cited as problematical, although it is now widely acknowledged that written sources are also largely based on subjective opinions, traditionally those that have reflected the narrow perspective of white, upper-class males. Furthermore, the validity of any historical source can be challenged, archival records are only as good as the data collected, statistics reflect the preconceptions of the analyst, autobiographies distort the past to display a positive public face, photographs and film can be faked. Such problems can to some extent be overcome by analysing sources in conjunction with other primary material. Criticisms centred on the lack of objective reliability of oral testimony can therefore be countered by testing their validity against other traditional sources. Those who favour the use of oral testimony can point to the many benefits its use can bring, justifiably arguing that it gives voice to many of those who would be unlikely to leave a written record behind them. Disadvantages can be countered by advantages. For example, the deterioration of memory that may have occurred with the passage of time can be offset to some extent by the possibility that a retrospective view of the distant past may reveal more of the 'truth' than an immediate testimony influenced by the need to consider political and personal repercussions.

---

1 The interviews carried out during the course of this research are listed in the Bibliography.

However, this traditional approach to historical sources differs markedly from the more recent work of those using written or oral narratives in which a fundamental shift has taken place in the nature of the historical questions under examination. These sources are particularly rich in material which can be explored to discover 'not just what people did, but what they wanted to do, what they believed they were doing, what they now think they did.'[2] The debates which have centred around this change of emphasis have included a significant contribution from feminist scholarship. Rather than accepting the limitations imposed by the production of objective, generalised accounts, historians can now adopt an approach which recognises the value of heterogeneity and contextuality.[3] There is now a greater awareness that objectivity, if defined as inter-subjective agreement, is in itself a subjective concept.[4] Conversely, it has also been argued that if the subjective impressions of a personal narrative are regarded as windows through which the individual and their relationships can be explored, by precise analysis of the language used they can become sources of objective knowledge of the social world.[5] Variations between narratives, rather than acting as an obstacle to generalised conclusions, can therefore become a resource for understanding the way in which individuals relate both to a group and to the discourses within society that are relevant to their lives.

Oral historians have discussed at length the subjective nature of memory and theories relating to what has been termed 'composure'. This term encompasses both the process of creating a narrative of personal experiences, and also that of achieving 'composure' by producing a version of the self which can be lived with in relative psychic comfort.[6] Increasing historical interest in areas such as

---

2 Alessandro Portelli, 'The Peculiarities of Oral History', *History Workshop Journal* 12, 1981, pp. 99-100.
3 For a discussion of the feminist contribution to the use of personal testimony see Penny Summerfield, *Reconstructing Women's Wartime Lives* (Manchester University Press, 1998) pp. 9-16.
4 Selma Leydesdorff, Luisa Passerini and Paul Thompson, *International Yearbook of Oral History and Life Stories: Gender and Memory* vol. IV, (Oxford University Press, 1996) p. 6.
5 Steinar Kvale, *InterViews: An Introduction to Qualitative Research Interviewing* (Sage, London, 1996) Ch. 4, 'Objectivity in Qualitative Research' argues this case. Criticisms of the approaches taken by oral historians can be found in 'Oral Narratives: Secondary Revision and the Memory of the Vietnam War' by Patrick Hagopian, *History Workshop Journal* no. 32, Autumn 1991, pp. 134-50.
6 Graham Dawson was instrumental in the formulation of these theories, see *Soldier Heroes, British Adventure, Empire and the Imagining of Masculinities* (Routledge, London, 1994). See also Alistair Thomson, *Anzac Memories: :Living with the Legend* (Oxford University Press, Australia, 1994).

composure and motivation has led to the growth of a new inter-disciplinary field, 'Psychohistory'. There are many problems inherent in the combination of historical methodology with that of the thera-peutically orientated discipline of psychoanalysis. Practical and methodological problems have been identified, such as the difficulty of gathering data on childhood, and the 'danger of circular reasoning in hypothesising antecedents from adult words and actions,' together with questions of a more theoretical nature, such as 'whether psycho-analytic theory is valid for other times and places (and, indeed, whether the application of any contemporary model can illuminate the special 'mentalities' of earlier periods).'[7]

An awareness of these debates associated with the use of oral sources has raised challenging issues during the course of this research which, in certain instances, have been referred to in the preceding chapters. However, to have a fully integrated psycho-historical approach, extensive knowledge in both the field of psychology and in the relevant historical subject would be required. As so little research had been carried out on the British women involved with the Spanish Civil War, it seemed that a broad study should be the first step, on which future work, per-haps drawing more deeply on psychoanalytical theory, could be based.

During the course of this research, one of the issues encountered that had far-reaching implications, including those of a psychological nature, was that of the relationship between interviewer and inter-viewee. The interaction between a historian and his or her subject is usually a complex one, and the historian may experience a wide range of emotional responses related to the research process. When a biog-rapher touches the unpublished documents and journals of a deceased subject, 'the poignancy of that moment when you first trace your finger over your subject's handwriting' has been referred to as 'almost overwhelming.'[8] If the subject of research is another living individual, a two-way interaction can occur, one that both may find rewarding. Those being interviewed have a new and potentially wider audience for their narratives. The historian may find answers in the narratives to questions as yet un-formulated, or even discover treasures amongst the letters, documents and diaries that are often brought out to be shared during interviews.

---

7 Geoffrey Cocks and Travis L. Crosby, *Psycho/History: Readings in the Method of Psychology, Psychoanalysis and History* (Yale University Press, New Haven & London, 1987) p. x.
8 Dea Birkett and Julie Wheelwright, ' "How Could She?" Unpalatable Facts and Feminists' Heroines', *Gender and History* vol. 2, No.1, Spring 1990, pp. 49-57, p. 54.

However, though rewards may increase over several such meetings, so too does the potential for unforeseen difficulties. The dangers of the historian unwittingly fulfilling a role as therapist may lead an interviewee to feel deserted when the historian moves on to a new subject. Historians, on the other hand, may find that their 'heroines' present them with 'unpalatable facts', that the narratives may reveal attitudes that do not conform to our expectations today.[9] It then becomes a challenge to overcome the reluctance to confront our own disillusion and restore such attitudes to their historical context. The oral historian may also have to confront personal distress, rarely anticipated at the outset of the research, on the death of someone with whom a close relationship has been established through the detailed discussion of a life history. It has been noted in guides to qualitative research that a lone researcher will be particularly vulnerable in this way, a comment that can be fully endorsed from personal experience.[10]

Legal and ethical matters relating to the obligations of the historian have often been raised by those working in the field of oral history. As guidelines recommend, all those who were interviewed specifically for this study signed a release form to allow me to use the recorded material. Ethical considerations are rather complex. Whilst endorsing the right of the historian to analyse material gained from oral testimony as thoroughly as information gained from more traditional sources, a clear responsibility exists towards interviewees, who have also contributed time and effort to the study, whatever their reasons for participating. The balance of power in the relationship between interviewee and historian tends to favour the latter, who usually has the last word, although more co-operative studies have been attempted.[11] Anonymity is one way in which historians try to limit the vulnerability of their interviewees, but this reduces their agency in the act of contribution to the historical record. Whether or not pseudonyms are employed, the responsibilities of the historian include a duty to explain the general purpose and form of the research to the interviewee. To give one example, if the intention is to use a psychoanalytical approach to the material gained from an in-depth interview, then the

9   Ibid. This theme is explored through the authors' research on women who rebelled against the restrictions of their gender, becoming, for example, soldiers or explorers.
10 Raymond M. Lee, *Doing Research on Sensitive Topics* (Sage, London, 1993).
11 Portelli is amongst those who have pointed out that in the production of oral history studies, organisation is not technical, it is political. See 'The Peculiarities of Oral History', pp. 104-5.

full implications of this should be made very clear on initial contact.
The methodological approach adopted for the interviews carried
out for this study did not include attempts to adhere to any method of
systematic sampling. After meeting several of these women during an
earlier research project in 1994, other contacts were made largely
through the process of 'snowballing'. The women interviewed were
happy to make a recorded interview and to be named in the study.
Two requests for interviews were unsuccessful, one because the
woman concerned had just published her memoirs and felt she did
not want to add anything further, and the other because of poor
health. The choice of subjects as interviewees was severely limited
by the number of women who had died before research began. By
using other sources, such as previously recorded interviews, diaries
and biographies, it was possible to increase the breadth of source
material to give a wider range of perspectives. As was pointed out
in the Introduction, the study has this selection of women and their
narratives as its focus, that is to say, a wide group drawn from those
actively involved, rather than claiming to present an overview of
British women in general and the war in Spain.

The interviews were carried out in the homes of the interviewees,
usually with no one else present. The few exceptions to this occurred
when interviewees felt they would need support in remembering
factual details. Micky Lewis, for example, wanted her husband to be
there because he 'takes on the political stuff, he remembers the parts,
I don't remember that so much, I remember the feelings.' Penny
Phelps frequently turned to her husband for the names of places
where she had worked in Spain, even though he had not been there
during the civil war. Interviews were recorded on video wherever
possible. There were no objections to this, and the interviewees did
not seem to be distracted by the presence of the camera. The addition
of a visual record has proved worthwhile in several ways, not only has
it ensured clarity in certain instances in the narratives where body
language and facial expressions were used, but it has also preserved
a more complete historical record of the interview for future study
and teaching. Although the women interviewed knew of my interest in
the Spanish Civil War, I took care to explain that I was also interested
in their lives as a whole, from childhood to the present day. The aim
was to achieve a narrative that was as free flowing as possible in order
to allow each interviewee the freedom to select what they considered
important in their lives. I learned to make as few interruptions as

possible, regretting earlier ill-timed questions that seemed in retrospect to have prevented an interviewee continuing along a particularly interesting line of thought. Although I was aware of the general areas to be covered in the interview, questions were only asked in significant pauses, or later on in the interview when it seemed appropriate to return to points that could be clarified or expanded. If an interviewee became upset, I found it difficult to continue on that theme, and perhaps I failed in my role as historian by changing the subject to something less distressing. When I first began to carry out the interviews, I was not sufficiently aware of how tiring talking for several hours might be for the interviewees. Shared enjoyment of the interview prevented me from recognising it at the time, but when I rang the next day I soon realised that recalling the past and the emotions this process evoked could be an exhausting process. Where possible, interviews therefore took place in two sessions, preferably on separate occasions, but at least with a break in the middle of the day.

Implicit in the approach taken in carrying out interviews during this research was the recognition that, in my role as audience, I was to some extent influencing the narratives produced. Some of the interviews carried out in the 1970s and 80s were very different, having a much more structured approach and often a question/answer formula concerned primarily with the recovery of factual information. The power imbalance in the relationship between interviewer and interviewee was often marked, there being only rare instances in which women interviewees maintained control of the agenda.[12] In the case of the interviews I recorded, there were several factors that contributed to the establishment of a degree of rapport. Gender was one such factor, as was the tendency to enjoy a good chat over cups of tea. There was also a rather interesting parallel between their attitudes in the thirties and those of my own generation in the sixties. We had shared a belief that we could change the world for the better, although they had placed their faith in a new socio-political order, whereas in the sixties some of us had been less practical and had trusted in love and 'flower power'. In this, we had all been somewhat disappointed.

I found it helpful to transcribe the interviews myself, thereby having the opportunity to listen again in detail, and to make note of pauses, tone of voice, laughter etc. In the early stages, I also made use

---

12 Compare, for example, the interview with the indomitable Isabel Brown (IWM 844), with that of Annie Knight (IWM 11318) in which she is constantly under pressure to provide specific dates and place names.

of NUD*IST (Non-numerical Unstructured Data * Indexing Searching and Theorising), a software programme for qualitative research. As the developers of the programme claim, the programme functions well as a 'container for thinking'. The process of coding involves the construction of an analytical framework for the chapters. The text is coded at different 'nodes', which can be viewed as a hierarchical tree or as a list. Free nodes can be used as a holding place for tentative ideas or apparently unconnected concepts. Text which could be useful in several ways can be duplicated as many times as required, and a record is retained of all other placements. The structure can be quickly re-shaped when necessary by moving or merging nodes. The text can be searched in a variety of ways which help to locate specific words and ideas, therefore material relating to themes which emerge later on in the research process can be quickly retrieved and explored.

During the long process of research and writing for this study, I have found it very helpful to maintain contact with the interviewees when possible. I send cards to inform them of my progress and several interviewees have been helpful in answering questions that have arisen later. All have agreed that their interviews can be placed in a public sound archive for future researchers. The ethical treatment of interviewees, and the acknowledgement of the significant contribution they make to a study such as this, will hopefully ensure that in the future, historians will continue to be able to count on the support of all those who can help them in their research.

Organisations and Groups

The groups and organisations listed below are some of those that were encountered during the course of this research, other than those run from within the political parties. The names of leading committee members and supporters, especially women, have been included in certain instances, together with a few examples of the campaigns organised by each group.

ALL LONDON SPANISH AID SPAIN COUNCIL

Chairman: Harry Adams   Hon. Treasurer: Miss Eva Reckitt

Forty-three patrons listed, including the following twenty-two women:-
The Duchess of Atholl; Countess of Antrim; Mrs E. Corbett Ashby; Lady Ruggles-Brice; Lady Noel Buxton; Dr. Stella Churchill; Lady Colefax; Dr. Margaret Deas; Marchioness of Donegall; Margery Fry; Megan Lloyd George, MP; Viscountess Gladstone; Mrs Charlotte Haldane; Dame Adelaide Livingstone; Lady Marley; Naomi Mitchison; Mrs Pethwick-Lawrence; Eleanor Rathbone, MP; Hon. Mrs Gilbert Rollo; Dame Marie Tempest DBE; Monica Whately, LCC; Ellen Wilkinson, MP.

Campaigns included:-
London to adopt 50,000 Spanish Children
London Goodwill Foodship to Spain, Christmas 1938
Send a Spanish Refugee Ship to the New World
Food and Freedom for Spain: Spain Fiestas, 7 January and 10 March 1939,

ARTISTS INTERNATIONAL ASSOCIATION

Women members included:-
Felicia Browne, Betty Rea, Priscilla Thornycroft, Nan Youngman

Fund-raising efforts included:-
'Artists Help Spain' exhibition, December 1936
'Felicia Browne' commemorative exhibition, 1936
'Portraits for Spain' scheme
Albert Hall meeting, June 1937, with Paul Robeson
Cabaret, March 1938

BASQUE CHILDREN'S COMMITTEE

Chairman: the Duchess of Atholl
Vice-chairs: Eleanor Rathbone MP, Vincent Tewson of the TUC
Treasurer: Viscount Cecil
Organising Secretary: Betty Arne, later succeeded by
Dr Betty Morgan

Women attending main committee meetings included:-
Miss Anderson, Dame Janet Campbell, Lady Layton,
Muriel McDiarmid, Leah Manning, Edith Pye, Eleanor Rathbone MP,
Hon. Mrs Wilfred Roberts, Mrs Gilbert Rollo, Dr Audrey Russell,
Frida Stewart, Mary Sutherland, Ellen Wilkinson

Local committees throughout Britain supported by a wide range
of groups within the community. For example, the Worthing
Committee for Refugee Children (Chairman Mrs Barber, Hon.
Secretary Mrs O. Thornycroft, later Miss K. Thornycroft), listed
the following supporters:-

Convent of Sion, Congregational Church, Broadwater Working
Men's Conservative Club, Worthing Labour Party, Lancing
Women's Institute, 8th Worthing Brownies, Lancing College,
Worthing Liberal Association, and the staff of Worthing banks,
shops, and other business houses, Court Lily of West Sussex AOF,
the Odeon Cinema, many Churches in Worthing, Co-operative
Guilds, Sunday School and Worthing High School for Girls.

BISHOPS' COMMITTEE FOR THE RELIEF
OF SPANISH DISTRESS

President: Cardinal Hinsley   Chairman: Lord Howard of Penrith

Members included:-
Marqués del Moral
Gabriel Herbert

Fund-raising to support a field hospital and mobile dressing station behind the Nationalist lines.

FOODSHIP COMMITTEES

Examples include:-

British Youth Foodship Committee
Established by groups belonging to the British Youth Peace Assembly, representing nearly forty political, religious and social organisations of young people. Local groups collected money and tinned food which was sent to Republican Spain.

Christian Foodship Committe
Treasurer: Dean of Canterbury

Maintained a colony for Basque refugee children in Eastern Spain with resident priest.

Eastern Counties Foodship for Spain
Hon. Treasurer: Mrs. Hardman

Supporters included:- Mrs. Rackham JP, Lady Hopkins, Miss E. M. Ramsay, Mrs. A. S. Eddington, Lady Noel Buxton, The Mistress of Girton College, The Principal of Newnham College, Lady Thomson

Manchester Foodship for Spain
Hon. Secretary: Winifred Horrocks

Organised an exhibition of Picasso's 'Guernica' and 67 preparatory studies in a Manchester Motor Showroom, entrance fee 6d, all proceeds to the foodship.

Appealed for gifts of food, 'Housewives Day', 21 - 28 January 1939, receptacles placed in local grocery stores.

FRIENDS OF NATIONAL SPAIN

Chairman: the Rt. Hon. Lord Phillimore

Committee members: Capt. Victor Cazalet, Douglas Jerrold, Arthur Loveday, Sir Henry Lunn, the Marquis del Moral, the Rt. Hon. Lord Newton, Sir N. Stewart-Sandeman, Lawrence Venn

Annual subscriptions and donations in return for publications and invitations to join in the activities of the group in support of Franco.

FRIENDS SERVICE COUNCIL

Members especially involved with the war in Spain included Edith Pye, who instigated the formation in Geneva of the international commission for the assistance of child refugees in Spain. Other members and associates carried out relief work, especially in Barcelona and Murcia, running canteens for food distribution, and helping to organise refugee centres, colonies and hospitals for refugee children.

INTERNATIONAL BRIGADE DEPENDANTS AND WOUNDED AID COMMITTEE

Hon. Secretary: Charlotte Haldane

Patrons included:-
Harry Adams, the Duchess of Atholl, H. N. Brailsford, Seymour Cocks MP, Prof. J. B. S. Haldane, Will Lawther, Olver Harris, Sir Walter Layton, Earl of Listowel, Sir Peter Chalmers Mitchell, J. B. Priestly, Eleanor Rathbone MP, Wilfred Roberts MP, Ald. J. Reeves. E. Shinwell MP, G. R. Strauss MP, Ellen Wilkinson MP.

INTERNATIONAL COMMITTEE FOR RELIEF OF VICTIMISED TEACHERS

Hon. Secretary: Miss J. M. Thomas

Money raised by the Spanish Teachers' Emergency Fund given to the Save the Children Fund to support them in their work in Spain.

NATIONAL JOINT COMMITTEE FOR SPANISH RELIEF

Chairman: Duchess of Atholl
Vice-chairmen: The Earl of Listowel, Eleanor Rathbone MP.

Working as an umbrella group to co-ordinate the efforts of a
variety of other organisations, including the Service Council of
the Society of Friends, the Save the Children Fund, the Spanish
Medical Aid Committee, the Spanish Youth Foodship Committee,
the Spanish Women's Committee for Help to Spain, the Women's
Committee Against War and Fascism, the Basque Children's
Committee and many others. Branches throughout Britain holding
meetings, events and appeals to fund relief work in Spain and to
support refugees in Britain. Appeals were sometimes made particularly to women, as in the case of the Milk Fund Appeal, supported
by women such as Vera Brittain, Elizabeth M. Cadbury, Stella
Churchill, Dorothy Gladstone, Storm Jameson, Naomi Mitchson,
Flora Robson, Virginia Woolf, Margery Fry, Eva M. Hubback.

PARLIAMENTARY COMMITTEE FOR SPAIN

Secretaries: Wilfred Roberts (Liberal) and John Jagger (Labour)

Twelve other MPs as members, including the Duchess of Atholl
(Conservative), Megan Lloyd George (Labour), Eleanor Rathbone
(Independent) and Ellen Wilkinson (Labour).

THE SCOTTISH AMBULANCE UNIT IN SPAIN

Chairman: D. M. Stevenson
Organiser and Treasurer: Miss A. C. Webster

The committee included: -
Ishbel, Marchioness of Aberdeen and Temair, GBE, the Countess of
Oxford and Asquith, the Hon. Mrs. Forrester-Paton, Prof. and Mrs.
Glaister, Sir Thomas and Lady Glen-Coats, Mrs. John M. Hogg Lenzie,
Miss Fernanda Jacobsen, Lady Swan, Lady Wilson of Uddingston.

Personnel, ambulances and supplies of food sent to Spain with
Fernanda Jacobsen as Commandant.

SIX POINT GROUP

National President: Mrs Pethwick Lawrence
Hon. Secretary: Monica Whately

Contact was established with Spanish feminists in Valencia during the war through Emma Goldman, the American Anarchist. An appeal was launched to help those who were later in the camps in France.

THE SPANISH MEDICAL AID COMMITTEE

President: Dr Christopher Addison MP
Chairman: Dr Hyacinth Morgan
Vice-Chairman: Dr Somerville-Hastings
Secretary: Dr Charles Brook
Treasurer: Lady Hastings

Women Committee members included:-
Isabel Brown, Leah Manning, Ellen Wilkinson, Megan Lloyd George MP, Dr Janet Vaughan, Eleanor Rathbone MP, Rebecca West.

Approximately 200 branches throughout Britain including for example:-
Holborn and West Central London Committee for Spanish Medical Aid. Chairmen: Janet Vaughan then Eva C. Reckitt; Hon. Secretary: Portia Holman.

Fund-raising on a wide scale to send medical personnel, ambulances and equipment to Spain. publication of booklets, such as *Spain and Us* with contributions from J. B. Priestly, Rebecca West, Stephen Spender, Ethel Mannin, and *Spain: the Child and the War*, written by an English woman journalist who had been working in Spain since the beginning of the war.

THE SPANISH WOMEN'S COMMITTEE
FOR HELP TO SPAIN

Secretary: Elizabeth Wilkinson

A collection of women's organisations bringing together working parties to make clothing, as for example, those made by unemployed women in a disused factory in Harwick.

WOMEN'S CO-OPERATIVE GUILD

President: Mrs. E. Williams   Vice-president: Mrs C. Dodsworth

The Annual Report for May 1938 - May 1939 states that 898 branches had sent money, food and clothing to Spain, 127 branches had also contributed through local aid committees, and that milk tokens had been on sale regularly in 124 branches in addition to those bought direct from Co-operative Societies. Knitted garments had been contributed by 124 branches, and 144 Basque children were being either wholly or partially maintained by Guild members.

WOMEN'S INTERNATIONAL LEAGUE FOR PEACE AND FREEDOM

President: Mrs Duncan Harris

Members attending meetings included :-
Miss Pye, Dr. Hilda Clark, Miss Marshall, Mrs Thornycroft, Miss Sheepshanks, Miss Rinder, Miss White, Mrs Ross, Mrs Sturge, Mrs Lankester, Mrs Vipont Brown, Miss Anderson, Miss Dickinson, Mrs Innes Mrs Hunter, Mrs Thoday, Miss Chick.

Letters to the Prime Minister, the Foreign Secretary, the Spanish Ambassador, President of the League of Nations, urging, for example, the cessation of civilian bombing, the dissolution of the Non-intervention Committee and its replacement by a more effective international control commission in Spain.

THE WOMEN'S WORLD COMMITTEE AGAINST WAR AND FASCISM

Chairman: Enid Rosser   Secretary: Hilda Vernon

Supporters included:-
Vera Brittain, Storm Jameson, Jennie Lee, Ethel Mannin, Dame Sybil Thorndyke, Sylvia Townsend Warner, Ellen Wilkinson.

Articles and appeals for funds in their journal, *Woman To-Day*, and appeals in pamphlets, such as *Are Women and Children Guilty - Help us to fill this lorry each month!*, supported by Edith Summerskill.

Sources and Bibliography

ARCHIVES AND COLLECTIONS

American Friends Service Committee, Philadelphia, USA
British Library, Newspaper Library, Colindale, London
Cambridge University Archives
Fawcett Library, London Guildhall University (now the Women's Library)
Friends House Library, London
Girton College Archive, Cambridge
The International Brigade Memorial Archive, Marx Memorial Library,
    London (MML)
Imperial War Museum Sound Archive, London (IWM)
Imperial War Museum Photographic Archive, London
Kate Sharpley Library, BM Hurricane, London
The Liddle Collection, Leeds University Library
Archive Division of the British Library of Political and Economic Science,
    London School of Economics (LSE)
Modern Records Centre, University of Warwick (MRC)
National Museum of Labour History, Manchester
National Sound Archive, London
Newnham College Archive, Cambridge
South Wales Miners' Library, Swansea
Frida Stewart, private collection, Cambridge
Tameside Local Studies Library, Stalybridge
Working Class Movement Library, Salford

PRIMARY SOURCES: TAPED INTERVIEWS

Angela Jackson

Felicity Ashbee, 2 March 2001
Celia Baker, 20 May 1997
Cora Blyth (m. Portillo), 5 August 1996
Noreen Branson, 26 January 1996

Elizabeth Crump (m. Thornycroft) 23 October 1996
Patience Darton, (m. Edney) 18 March 1994, 18 March 1996
Kathleen Gibbons, 6 August 1998
Marjorie Jacobs, 2 August 1996
Micky Lewis, 9 July 1996
Earl of Listowel, 27 November 1995
Penny Phelps (m. Feiwel), 22 - 23 February 1996
Sam Lesser, 10 April 1996, 24 August 1999
Thora Silverthorne (m. Craig), 3 January 1996
Rosaleen Smythe (m. Ross), 10 April 1999
Frida Stewart (m. Knight), 30 March 1994, 11 December 1995
Margaret Stewart (m. Wilson), 17 December 1995
Priscilla Thornycroft (m. Siebert), 28 April 2000

American Friends Service Committee, Philadelphia, USA

Norma Jacob, # 31

Sue Bruley, Private Collection

Isabel Brown, 3 September 1976
Betty Harrison, 31 August 1976
Rose Kerrigan, 25 October 1976
Bessie Wild, 8 September 1977

Maria Delgado, Private Collection

Win Albeye, 1986
Doris Wood, 1986

Imperial War Museum Sound Archive, London

Wyn Albeye, 13821
Beryl Barker, 13805
Noreen Branson, 9212
Isabel Brown, 844 and 13784
Lillian Buckoke, (née Urmston) 845
Catherine Collins, 11297
Thora Craig (née Silverthorne), 13770

Patience Edney (née Darton), 8398
Mary Freeman, 842
Helen Grant, 13808
Nan Green, 815, 10361, 13782, 13799
Marion Hague and Win Hawkins, 13832
Margot Heinemann, 9239
Portia Holman, 13971
Kathleen Holmes, 13817
Marie Jacobs, 13819
Rose Kerrigan, 796
Annie Knight (née Murray), 11318, 13787
Frida Knight (née Stewart), 13801
Tony McLean, 838
Elizabeth Monkhouse, 13813
Dora Pointer, 13826
Joan Purser, 13795
Wilfred Roberts, 13785
Winifred Sandford, (m. Bates) 816
Mary Slater, 814
Diana Smythies, 7371
Marie Stephenson, 13802
Janet Vaughan, 13796
Margaret Wilson (née Stewart), 13807

Liddle Collection, Brotherton Library, Leeds University

Florence Farmborough, 1975

National Sound Archive:
Labour Oral History Project, London

Helen Cameron C609/43/01-02
Martha Feeney C609/44/01-02
Isa Paton C609/43/01-02
Aileen Plant C609/25/01-02
Dot Welsh C609/23/01 F4343
Naomi Wolff C609/03/01 F4083

Mike Squires, Private Collection

Yvonne Kapp, 1 March 1994

South Wales Coalfield Collection, Swansea

Lilian May Price, AUD/385

Tameside Local Studies Library, Stalybridge

Elsie Booth, 756
Isabel Brown, 176
Nan Green, 180
Mary Slater, 181
Winifred Sandford (m. Bates), 192
Rose Kerrigan, 197
Lillian Buckoke (née Urmston), 203
Mary Whitehead, 211
Elsie Booth/Mary Freeman/Lillian Walker, 215
Ivy Edwards, 237
Margaret Brooks/Harold Fraser, 241
Loughborough Conference on the Spanish Civil War in 1976, 232 and 233

PRIMARY SOURCES: MEMOIRS AND AUTOBIOGRAPHIES

Ackland, Valentine *For Sylvia: An Honest Account* (Methuen, London, 1986, first published by Chatto & Windus, 1985)

Atholl, Katharine *Working Partnership: Being the Lives of John George, 8th. Duke of Atholl KT, GCVO, CB, DSO, and of his Wife, Katharine Marjory Ramsay, DBE., Hon LLD, FRCM* (Arthur Barker, London, 1958)

Bates, Winifred 'A Woman's Work in War Time' (MML, Box 29/D/7)

Berg, Leila *Flickerbook* (Granta Books, London, 1997)

Bingham de Urquidi Mary, *Mercy in Madrid: Nursing and Humanitarian Protection during the Spanish Civil War, 1936-7,* Edicions del Sur, Argentina, 2004 (First published as *Misericordia en Madrid* by B. Costa Amic Editores, México, 1975)

Castle, Barbara *Fighting All the Way* (Pan Books 1994, first published by Macmillan, London 1993)

Cooper, Kanty *The Uprooted: Agony and Triumph Among the Debris of War* (Quartet Books, London 1979)

Davies, Dorothy 'Six Months in Southern Spain' (MML, Box D-2: AC/1)

Docherty, Mary *A Miner's Lass* (Lancashire Community Press, Preston, 1992)

Duff, Sheila Grant *The Parting of Ways: A Personal Account of the Thirties* (Peter Owen, London, 1982)

Farmborough, Florence *Nurse at the Russian Front: A Diary 1914-18* (Constable, London, 1974)

Fernandez, Aurora (m. Edenhofer), 'Memoir', 1983 (MML, Box 29, File D/9)

Fyvel, Penelope *English Penny* (Arthur Stockwell, Ilfracombe, Devon, 1992)

Gellhorn, Martha 'The Third Winter', an extract from *The Face of War* in Murray A. Sperber, (ed.), *And I Remember Spain: A Spanish Civil War Anthology* (Hart-Davis, MacGibbon, London, 1974)

Grant, Helen 'Spain, March 25th - April 18th 1937' (Papers of Helen Grant, Cambridge University Library)

Green, Nan 'A Chronicle of Small Beer' (Papers of Nan Green, Martin Green), published as *A Chronicle of Small Beer: The Memoirs of Nan Green* (Trent Editions, Nottingham, 2005).

Haldane, Charlotte *Truth Will Out* (Weidenfeld & Nicholson, London 1949)

Heinemann, Margot 'Remembering 1936', *Women's Review*, October 1986

Herbert, Gabriel (m. Alexander Dru), 'Memoir' 1982 (Papers of Michael Alpert)

Jacob, Norma 'The Spanish Civil War' in Piers Anthony, *Bio of an Ogre* (Ace Books, New York, 1988) pp. 229-243

McDiarmid, Muriel *Franco in Barcelona* (United Editorial Ltd., Speedoe Press Services, London, 1939)

McNair, John *Spanish Diary* (Greater Manchester ILP Publications, a collection of articles and pamphlets first published in the *Socialist Leader*, 1974)

Mangan, Kate and Jan Kurzke 'The Good Comrade' (Jan Kurzke Papers, Archives of the International Institute for Social History, Amsterdam.)

Manning, Leah *A Life for Education* (Victor Gollancz, London, 1970)

Mitford, Jessica *Hons and Rebels* (Victor Gollancz, London, 1961)

Murphy, Molly 'Nurse Molly' (National Museum of Labour History), published as *Molly Murphy: Suffragette and Socialist* edited by Ralph Darlington (Institute of Social Research, University of Salford, 1998)

Powell, Margaret 'Memoir', 1970 (Papers of Margaret Lesser, Ruth Muller)

Scott-Ellis, Priscilla 'Diaries 1937-1939' (University of Cardiff), published as *The Chances of Death: A Diary of the Spanish Civil War* edited by Raymond Carr (Michael Russell Ltd., Norwich, 1995)

Stewart, Frida 'Memoirs' (Papers of Frida Stewart). Now published as *Firing a Shot for Freedom: The Memoirs of Frida Stewart* with a Foreword and Afterword by Angela Jackson (The Clapton Press, London, 2020)

Stewart, Frida *Dawn Escape* (Everybody's Books, London, undated, probably 1943)

Stratton, Harry *To Anti-Fascism by Taxi* (Alun Books, Port Talbot, West Glamorgan, 1984)

Townsend Warner, Sylvia 'Barcelona', *Left Review* October 1936; Soldiers and Sickles in Spain', *The Countryman* October 1937

Urmston, Lillian 'English Nurse in Spain', *Nursing Mirror*, series of seven articles, 13 May - 24 June 1939

Wilkinson, Ellen in *Myself When Young by Famous Women of Today* edited by Margot, Countess of Oxford and Asquith (Frederick Muller, London, 1938)

Wilson, Francesca M. *In the Margins of Chaos: Recollections of Relief Work in and Between Three Wars* (John Murray, London, 1944)

Wilson, Francesca M. *Francesca Wilson: A Life of Service and Adventure* edited by June Horder and published privately in 1993, Part I 'Autobiographical Fragments'

Zagier, David 'Seven Days Among the Loyalists: A Tale of Civil War Time' (Family papers, Don Zagier)

OTHER PRINTED PRIMARY SOURCES

Atholl, Katharine *Women and Politics* (Philip Allan, London, 1931)

Atholl, Katharine *Searchlight on Spain* (Penguin Books, Harmondsworth, Middlesex, 1938)

British Medical Aid for Spain (The *News Chronicle*, undated)

Cloud, Yvonne *The Basque Children in England* (Victor Gollancz, London, 1937)

Farmborough, Florence *Life and People in National Spain* (Sheed & Ward, London 1938)

Fascists at Olympia (Publisher unknown, 1934). Includes contributions from Vera Brittain, Pearl Binder, Storm Jameson and Naomi Mitchison.

Grant, Helen *Rebellion in Spain* (Birmingham Council for Peace and Liberty, c.1937)

Heinemann, Margot *The Adventurers* (Lawrence & Wishart, London, 1960)

Heinemann, Margot 'English Poetry and the War in Spain: Some Records of a Generation' in Stephen M Hart (ed.), *'¡No Pasarán!' Art, Literature and the Spanish Civil War* (Tamesis Books, London, 1988)

Lake, Elizabeth *Spanish Portrait* (Pilot Press, London, 1945)

Lehmann, John (ed.) *Authors Take Sides On The Spanish War* (Lawrence and Wishart, London, 1937)

Mannin, Ethel *Comrade O Comrade or Low Down on the Left* (Jarrolds, London, 1945)

Medical Aid for Spain (Spanish Medical Aid Committee, 1937)

Mission to Spain (Emergency Committee for Democratic Spain). Includes articles by Leah Manning, Monica Whately and Nan Green.

Mitford, Nancy *The Pursuit of Love: A Novel* (Hamish Hamilton, London, 1945)

A Nation in Retreat (British Committee for Refugees from Spain, 1939). Includes contributions from Nancy Cunard, Edith Pye and Lillian Urmston.

Rathbone, Eleanor F. *War Can Be Averted: the Achievability of Collective Security* (Victor Gollancz, London, 1938)

Spain: The Child and The War (Holburn and West Central Committee for Spanish Medical Aid 1937), introduction by Leah Manning.

Stewart, Jessie (ed.) *Recuerdos: The Basque Hostel at Cambridge* (Cambridge Daily News, c.1938)

Stewart, Margaret *Reform Under Fire: Social Progress in Spain 1931-1938* (New Fabian Research Bureau and Victor Gollancz, London, 1938)

Stowell, Thora *Red Candles in Spain* (John Gifford, London, 1938)

Townsend Warner, Sylvia 'The Drought Breaks', Life and Letters Today, Summer 1937; 'Benicasim', Left Review, March 1938

SECONDARY SOURCES: PUBLISHED BOOKS AND ARTICLES

Ackelsberg, Martha A. *Free Women of Spain: Anarchism and the Struggle for the Emancipation of Women* (Indiana University Press, 1991)

Alberti, Johanna 'British Feminists and Anti-Fascism in the 1930s' in Sybil Oldfield, (ed.), *This Working Day World: Women's Lives and Culture(s) in Britain 1914-1945* (Taylor and Francis, London, 1994)

Alasuntari, Pertti *Researching Culture: Qualitative Method and Cultural Studies* (Sage, London, 1995)

Aldgate, Anthony *British Newsreels and the Spanish Civil War* (Scolar Press, London, 1979)

Alexander, Bill *British Volunteers for Liberty: Spain 1936-39* (Lawrence & Wishart, London 1986, first published 1982)

Alexander, Bill *No to Franco: The Struggle Never Stopped, 1939-1975* (Bill Alexander, London, 1992)

Alpert, Michael 'Humanitarianism and Politics in the British Response to the Spanish Civil War 1936-1939', *European History Quarterly*, vol. 14, no. 4, Oct. 1984

Andrews, Molly *Lifetimes of Commitment: Ageing, Politics, Psychology* (Cambridge University Press, 1991)

Anthony, Piers *Bio of an Ogre* (Ace Books, New York, 1988)

Arrien, Gregorio *Niños Vascos Evacuados A Gran Bretaña 1937-1940* (Asociación de Niños Evacuados, 1991)

Ball, Stuart 'The Politics of Appeasement: The Fall of the Duchess of Atholl and the Kinross and West Perth By-election Dec. 1938', *Scottish Historical Review*, 187, April 1990

Baxell, Richard *British Volunteers in the Spanish Civil War: The British Battalion in the International Brigades, 1936-39* (Warren & Pell Publishing, Pontypool, 2007. First published by Routledge/Cañada Blanch Studies on Contemporary Spain, London, 2004)

Beddoe, Deidre *Back to Home and Duty: Women Between the Wars 1918-1939* (Pandora, London, 1989)

Bell, Adrian *Only for Three Months: The Basque Children in Exile* (Mousehold Press, Norwich, 1996)

Berry, David *The Sociology of Grass Roots Politics: A Study of Party Membership* (Macmillan, London, 1970)

Bill, Ron, and Stan Newens *Leah Manning* (Leah Manning Trust in association with Square One Books, Harlow, 1991)

Birkett, D., and J. Wheelwright ' "How Could She?" Unpalatable facts and feminists' Heroines' *Gender and History* vol. 2, no. 1, Spring 1990

Bourke, Joanna *Dismembering the Male: Men's Bodies, Britain, and the Great War* (Reaktion Books, London & Chicago, 1996)

Bourke, Joanna *An Intimate History of Killing: Face-to-face Combat in Twentieth-Century Warfare* (Granta, London, 2000, first edition 1999)

Branson, Noreen, and Margot Heinemann *Britain in the Nineteen Thirties* (Weidenfield & Nicholson, London, 1971)

Brenan, Gerald *The Spanish Labyrinth* (Cambridge University Press, 1990, first published 1943)

Brock Griggs, Anne *Women and Fascism; 10 Important Points; You Have the Vote Yet Are Still Powerless* (BUF Publications Ltd., London, c. 1935)

Broe, Mary Lynn, and Angela Ingram (eds) *'Writing Against the Grain': Women's Writing in Exile* (University of North Carolina Press, Chapel Hill, 1989)

Brothers, Caroline *War and Photography* (Routledge, London, 1997)

Bruley, Sue *Leninism, Stalinism and the Women's Movement in Britain, 1920-1939* (Garland, London, 1986)

Bruley, Sue 'A Woman's Right to Work? The Role of Women in the Unemployed Movement Between the Wars', in Oldfield (ed.), *This Working Day World: Women's Lives and Culture(s) in Britain 1914-1945* (Taylor and Francis, London, 1994)

Buchanan, Tom 'The Role of the British Labour Movement in the Origins and Work of the Basque Children's Committee, 1937-39', *European History Quarterly* vol. 18 (1988), 155-174

Buchanan, Tom *The Spanish Civil War and the British Labour Movement* (Cambridge University Press, 1991)

Buchanan, Tom 'Britain's Popular Front?: Aid Spain and the British Labour Movement' *History Workshop Journal*, 31, 1991, 60-72

Buchanan, Tom 'Divided Loyalties: The Impact of the Spanish Civil War on Britain's Civil Service Trade Unions, 1936-39' *Historical Research GB*, 1992 65 (156) 90-107

Buchanan, Tom '"A Far Away Country of Which We Know Nothing"?: Perceptions of Spain and its Civil War in Britain 1931-1939' *Twentieth Century British History*, vol. 4, no. 1, 1993, pp.1-24

Buchanan, Tom *Britain and the Spanish Civil War* (Cambridge University Press, 1997)

Buchanan, Tom *The Impact of the Spanish Civil War on Britain: War, Loss and Memory* (Sussex Academic Press, Brighton & Portland, 2007)

Caldwell, John Taylor *Come Dungeons Dark: The Life and Times of Guy Aldred, Glasgow Anarchist* (Luath Press, Barr, Scotland, 1988)

Castell, Edmon, et al *La Batalla de l'Ebre: Història, paisatge, patrimoni* (ECSA, Barcelona, 1999)

Chambers, Colin *The Story of Unity Theatre* (Lawrence & Wishart, London, 1989)

Chisolm, Anne *Nancy Cunard* (Sidgwick & Jackson, London, 1979)

Cocks, Geoffrey, and Travis L. Crosby *Psycho/History: Readings in the Method of Psychology, Psychoanalysis, and History* (Yale University Press, New Haven & London, 1987)

Coni, Nick *Medicine and Warfare: Spain 1936-1939*, (Routledge/Cañada Blanch Studies on Contemporary Spain, London, 2007)

Corkill, D., and S. Rawnsley (eds) *The Road to Spain: Anti-Fascists at War, 1936-39* (Borderline Press, Scotland 1981)

Croft, Andy (ed.) *A Weapon in the Struggle: The Cultural History of the Communist Party in Britain* (Pluto Press, London, 1998)

Cullen, Stephen M. 'The Development of the Ideas and Policy of the British Union of Fascists, 1932-40', *Journal of Contemporary History*, vol. 22, 1987, p. 115-136

Cullen, Stephen M. 'Four Women for Mosley: Women in the British Union of Fascists, 1932-1940', *Oral History*, Spring 1996, Political Lives, p.49-59

Cunningham, Valentine. (ed.) *Spanish Front: Writers on the Civil War* (Oxford University Press, 1986)

Cunningham, Valentine 'Neutral?: 1930s Writers and Taking Sides', in Frank Gloversmith, (ed.), *Class, Culture and Social Change: A New View of the 1930s* (Harvester Press, Brighton, Sussex, 1980)

David, Hugh *Stephen Spender: A Portrait with Background* (Heinemann, London, 1992)

Davison, Peter (ed.) *Orwell in Spain* (Penguin Books, London, 2001)

Davison, Peter (ed.) *The Lost Orwell* (Timewell Press, London, 2006)

Dawson, Graham *Soldier Heroes, British Adventure, Empire and the Imagining of Masculinities* (Routledge, London, 1994)

Dex, S. (ed.) *Life and Work History Analyses: Qualitative and Quantitative Developments* (Routledge, London, 1991)

Durham, Martin 'Women and the British Union of Fascists 1932-1940', *Immigrants and Minorities*, vol. 8, March 1989, nos 1 & 2

Durham, Martin 'Gender and the British Union of Fascists', *Journal of Contemporary History* vol. 27, 1992, p. 513-529

Durham, Martin 'Women in the British Union of Fascists, 1932-1940' in Sybil Oldfield, (ed.), *This Working Day World: Women's Lives and Culture(s) in Britain 1914-1945* (Taylor and Francis, London, 1994)

Elshtain, Jean Bethke *Women and War* (Harvester Press, Brighton, Sussex, 1987)

Fielding, Daphne *Emerald and Nancy: Lady Cunard and her Daughter* (Eyre & Spottiswoode, London, 1968)

Fleay, C., and M. L. Sanders 'Communications: The Labour Spain Committee; Labour Party Policy and the Spanish Civil War', *Historical Journal*, 27, 4. 1985, 187-197

Ford, Hugh (ed.) *Nancy Cunard: Brave Poet, Indomitable Rebel 1896-1965* (Chilton Book Co., Philadelphia, New York & London, 1968)

Francis, Hywel *Wales and the Spanish Civil War* (Lawrence & Wishart, London, 1984. Re-published by Warren & Pell Publishing, Pontypool, UK, 2004)

Francis, Hywel 'Say Nothing and Leave in the Middle of the Night': The Spanish Civil War Revisited', *History Workshop Journal*, 1991; 32: 69-76

Fraser, Ronald *In Search of a Past* (Verso, London, 1984)

Fraser, Ronald *Blood of Spain: The Experience of Civil War 1936-1939* (Penguin, Harmondsworth, England, 1981, first published by Allen Lane, 1979)

Frisch, Michael *A Shared Authority: Essays on the Craft and Meaning of Oral and Public History* (State University of New York Press, Albany, 1990)

Fyrth, Jim *The Signal Was Spain: The Aid Spain Movement in Britain 1936-39* (Lawrence & Wishart, London, 1986)

Fyrth, Jim, and Sally Alexander (eds) *Women's Voices from the Spanish Civil War* (Lawrence & Wishart, London, 1991)

Fyrth, Jim 'The Aid Spain Movement in Britain, 1936-39', *History Workshop Journal*, Issue 35, 1993, pp. 153-164

Geiser, Carl *Prisoners of the Good Fight* (Lawrence Hill, Connecticut, 1986)

Gibson, Ian *The Erotomaniac: The Secret Life of Henry Spencer Ashbee* (Faber & Faber, London, 2001.

Gloversmith, Frank (ed.) *Class, Culture and Social Change: A New View of the 1930s* (Harvester Press, Brighton, Sussex, 1980)

González Martínez, Carmen *Guerra Civil en Murcia: Un análisis sobre el poder y los comportamientos colectivos* (Universidad de Murcia, Spain, 1999)

Gorman, John *Images of Labour* (Scorpion Press, Great Britain, 1985)

Graham, Helen *Spanish Cultural Studies Reader: The Struggle for Modernity* (Oxford University Press, 1995)

Graves, Pamela M. *Labour Women: Women in British Working-Class Politics 1918-1939* (Cambridge University Press, 1994)

Griffiths, Richard *Fellow Travellers of the Right: British Enthusiasts for Nazi Germany 1933-1939* (Constable, London, 1980)

Haigh, R. H., D. S. Morris and A. R. Peters (eds) *The Guardian Book of the Spanish Civil War* (Wildwood House, Aldershot, 1987)

Patrick Hagopian 'Oral Narratives: Secondary Revision and the Memory of the Vietnam War', *History Workshop* no. 32, 1991

Harman, Claire *Sylvia Townsend Warner: A Biography* (Chatto & Windus, London, 1989)

Hallahmi, B. Beit, and Michael Argyle *The Psychology of Religious Behaviour, Belief and Experience* (Routledge, London & New York, 1997)

Harrison, Brian *Prudent Revolutionaries: Portraits of British Feminists Between the Wars* (Clarendon Press, Oxford 1987)

Hart, Stephen M. (ed.) *'¡No Pasarán!' Art, Literature and the Spanish Civil War* (Tamesis Books, London, 1988)

Heaton, P. M. *Welsh Blockade Runners in the Spanish Civil War* (Starling Press, Pontypool, Gwent, 1985)

Hess, Robert D., and Judith V. Torney *The Development of Political Attitudes in Children* (Aldine Publishing, Chicago, 1967)

Hetherington, S. *Katharine Atholl 1876-1960: Against the Tide* (Aberdeen University Press, 1989)

Higonnet, Margaret R., and Jane Jenson (eds) *Behind the Lines: Gender and the Two World Wars* (Yale University Press, New Haven, 1987)

Higonnet, Margaret 'Another Record: A Different War', *Women's Studies Quarterly*, 1995, vol. 23, part 3/4, pp. 85-96

Hill, May *Red Roses for Isabel: Highlights in the Life of Isabel Brown* (May Hill, London, 1982)

Hodgart, Rhona M. *Ethel MacDonald: Glasgow Woman Anarchist* (Kate Sharpley Library, London, undated)

Hollis, Patricia *Ladies Elect: Women in English Local Government 1865-1914* (Oxford University Press, 1987)

Hopkins, James K. *Into the Heart of the Fire: The British in the Spanish Civil War* (Stanford University Press, 1998)

Howkins, Alun 'Class Against Class: The Political Culture of the Communist Party of Great Britain, 1930-35', in Frank Gloversmith, *Class Culture and Social Change: A New View of the 1930s* (Harvester Press, Brighton, Sussex, 1980)

Howson, Gerald *Arms for Spain: The Untold Story of the Spanish Civil War* (John Murray, London, 1998)

Ingram, Kevin *Rebel: The Short Life of Esmond Romilly* (Weidenfeld & Nicolson, London 1985)

Jenkins, Hugh *Rank and File* (Croom Helm, London, 1980)

Joannou, Maroula 'Sylvia Townsend Warner in the 1930s', in Andy Croft, (ed.), *A Weapon in the Struggle: The Cultural History of the Communist Party in Britain* (Pluto Press, London, 1998)

Keene, Judith *The Last Mile to Huesca: An Australian Nurse in the Spanish Civil War* (New South Wales University Press, 1988)

Kent, Susan Kingsley *Making Peace: The Reconstruction of Gender in Interwar Britain* (Princeton University Press, New Jersey, 1993)

Klehr, Harvey, John Earl Haynes, Fridrikh Igorevich Firsov *The Secret World of American Communism* (Yale University Press, New Haven & London, 1995)

Knight Frida *The Strange Case of Thomas Walker: Ten Years in the Life of a Manchester Radical* (Lawrence & Wishart, London, 1957)

Knight, Frida *University Rebel: The Life of William Frend 1757-1841* (Gollancz, London, 1971)

Knight, Frida *The French Resistance 1940-1944* (Lawrence & Wishart, London, 1975)

Kvale, Steinar *Inter-Views: An Introduction to Qualitative Research Interviewing* (Sage, London, 1996)

Lannon, Frances *Privilege, Persecution and Prophecy: The Catholic Church in Spain 1875-1975* (Clarendon Press, Oxford, 1987)

Lannon, Frances 'Women and Images of Women in the Spanish Civil War', *Transactions of the Royal Historical Society*, 1991 pp. 213-228

Lee, Raymond M. *Doing Research on Sensitive Topics* (Sage, London, 1993)

Legarreta, Dorothy *The Guernica Generation: The Basque Refugee Children of the Spanish Civil War* (University of Nevada Press, 1984)

Lerner, Gerda *The Majority Finds its Past* (Oxford University Press, 1979)

Levine, Philippa *Victorian Feminism 1850-1900* (Hutchinson, London, 1987)

Leydesdorff, Selma, Luisa Passerini and Paul Thompson *International Yearbook of Oral History and Life Stories: Gender and Memory* vol. IV, (Oxford University Press, 1996)

Light, Alison *Forever England: Femininity, Literature and Conservatism Between the Wars* (Routledge, London, 1991)

Linehan, Thomas P. 'The British Union of Fascists in Hackney and Stoke Newington, 1933-40', in Geoffrey Alderman and Colin Holmes, (eds), *Outsiders and Outcasts: Essays in Honour of William J. Fishman* (Duckworth, London 1993)

Loftus, Elizabeth F., Mahzarin R. Banaji, Jonathan W. Schooler and Rachel A. Foster 'Who Remembers What?: Gender Differences in Memory,' *Michigan Quarterly Review*, 1987, vol. 26, part 1, pp. 64-85

Lovenduski, Joni, and Pippa Norris (eds) *Gender and Party Politics* (Sage Publications, London, 1993)

Low, Robert *La Pasionaria: The Spanish Firebrand* (Hutchinson, London, 1992)

Lummis, Trevor *Listening to History* (Hutchinson, London, 1984)

MacDougall, Ian (ed.) *Voices from the Spanish Civil War: Personal Recollections of Scottish Volunteers in Republican Spain 1936-39* (Polygon, Edinburgh, 1986)

McKibbin, Ross *Ideologies of Class* (Clarendon Press, Oxford, 1990)

Maclean, Sorley *Spring Tide and Neap Tide: Selected Poems 1932-72* (Canongate, Edinburgh, 1977)

McWilliam, Rohan *Popular Politics in Nineteenth Century England* (Routledge, London, 1998)

Mangini, Shirley *Memories of Resistance: Women's Voices from the Spanish Civil War* (Yale University Press, New Haven & London, 1995)

Margolies, David, and Maroula Joannou (eds) *Heart of the Heartless World: Essays in Cultural Resistance in Memory of Margot Heinemann* (Pluto Press, London, 1995)

Maxwell, William (ed.) *The Letters of Sylvia Townsend Warner* (Chatto & Windus, London, 1982)

Mendlesohn, Farah *Quaker Relief Work in the Spanish Civil War* (Edwin Mellen Press, New York, 2002)

Midgley, Clare *Women Against Slavery: The British Campaigns 1780-1870* (Routledge, London, 1992)

Milbrath, Lester W., and M. L. Goel *How and Why do People Get Involved with Politics* (Rand MacNally College Publishing Co., Chicago, 1977, first edition 1965)

Mitchell, David *The Spanish Civil War* (Granada, London, 1982)

Mitchell, Juliet, and Ann Oakley (eds) *The Rights and Wrongs of Women* (Penguin, London, 1976)

Mitchell, Margaret 'The Effects of Unemployment on the Social Condition of Women and Children in the 1930s' *History Workshop Journal*, Issue 19, Spring 1985

Montseny, Federica 'La Sanidad y La Asistencia Social Durante La Guerra Civil', in *Los Medicos y La Medicina en La Guerra Civil Española* (Beecham, Madrid, 1986) pp. 95-101

Moradiellos, Enrique *La Perfidia de Albión: El Gobierno británico y la guerra civil española* (siglo veintiuno editores, sa., Madrid, 1996)

Morris, Lynda, and Robert Radford *The Story of the Artists International Association, 1933-1953* (Museum of Modern Art, Oxford, 1983)

Mowat, Charles Loch *Britain Between the Wars 1918-1940* (Methuen & Co. Ltd., London 1955)

Mulford, Wendy *This Narrow Place: Sylvia Townsend Warner and Valentine Ackland, Life, Letters and Politics 1930-1951* (Pandora, London, 1988)

Nash, Mary ' "Milicianas" and Homefront Heroines: Images of Women in Revolutionary Spain' *History of European Ideas*, 1989 vol. ll, pp. 235-244

Nash, Mary *Defying Male Civilization: Women in the Spanish Civil War* (Arden Press, Colorado, 1995)

Nicholls, C. S. (ed.) *Dictionary of National Biography: Missing Persons* (Oxford University Press, 1993)

Oldfield, Sybil (ed.) *This Working Day World: Women's Lives and Culture(s) in Britain 1914-1945* (Taylor and Francis, London, 1994)

Orwell, George *Homage to Catalonia* (Penguin Books, Harmondsworth, Middlesex, 1983, first published by Secker & Warburg, 1938)

Osuna, Rafael *Pablo Neruda y Nancy Cunard* (Editorial Origenes: Tratados de Crítica Literaria, Madrid, 1987)

Pettifer, James *Cockburn in Spain: Despatches from the Spanish Civil War* (Lawrence & Wishart, London 1986)

Pimlott, Ben *Labour and the Left in the 1930s* (Cambridge University Press, 1977)

Portelli, Alessandro 'The Peculiarities of Oral History', *History Workshop Journal*, no. 12, 1981, pp. 96-107

Portelli, Alessandro 'Uchronic Dreams: Working-class Memory and Possible Worlds', in Raphael Samuel and Paul Thompson, (eds), *The Myths We Live By* (Routledge, London, 1990)

Preston, Paul *Franco: A Biography* (Fontana Press, London, 1995, first published by Harper Collins, 1993)

Preston, Paul *A Concise History of the Spanish Civil War* (Fontana Press, London, 1996)

Preston, Paul *Palomas de Guerra: Cinco mujeres marcadas por la guerra civil* (Plaza y Janés, Barcelona, 2001). Published in English as *Doves of War: Four Women of Spain* (HarperCollins, London, 2002)

Preston, Paul *We Saw Spain Die. Foreign Correspondents in the Spanish Civil War.* (Constable, London, 2008), published in Spanish as *Idealistas bajo las balas. Corresponsales extranjeros en la guerra de España*, (Debate, Barcelona, 2007), and in Catalan as *Idealistes sota les bales. Històries de la guerra civil* (Proa/PPM Editorial, Barcelona, 2007).

Prochaska, F. K. *Women and Philanthropy in 19th Century England* (Clarendon Press, Oxford 1980)

Pryce-Jones, David *Unity Mitford: A Quest* (Weidenfeld & Nicolson, London, 1976)

Randall, Vicky *Women and Politics* (Macmillan, London, 1982)

Richards, Michael *A Time of Silence: Civil War and the Culture of Repression in Franco's Spain, 1936-1945* (Cambridge University Press, 1998)

Rowbotham, Sheila *Hidden from History: 300 Years of Women's Oppression and the Fight Against It* (Pluto Press, London, 1973)

Rust, William *Britons in Spain: The History of the British Battalion of the XVth International Brigade* (Warren & Pell Publishing, Pontypool, 2003. First published by Lawrence & Wishart, London, 1939)

Rust, William (edited and completed by Allen Hutt) *The Story of the Daily Worker* (People's Press Printing Society, London, 1949)

Salt, Chrys, Pam Schweitzer and Mervyn Wilson *Of Whole Heart Cometh Hope: Centenary Memories of the Co-operative Women's Guild* (Age Exchange Theatre Company, 1983)

Samuel, Raphael, and Paul Thompson (eds) *The Myths We Live By* (Routledge, London, 1990)

Schwarzkopf, Jutta 'The Sexual Division of the Chartist Family', *BSSLH*, vol. 54, no. 1, Spring 1989

Scott, Joan W. *Gender and the Politics of History* (Columbia University Press, 1988)

Scott, Joan W. 'Rewriting History', in Margaret R Higonnet and Jane Jenson (eds) *Behind the Lines: Gender and the Two World Wars* (Yale University Press, New Haven, 1987)

Sheridan, Dorothy 'Ambivalent Memories: Women and the 1939-45 War in Britain', *Oral History*, Spring 1990, pp. 32-40

Siltanen, Janet, and Michelle Stanworth (eds) *Women and the Public Sphere* (Hutchinson, London, 1984)

Sloan, Pat (ed.) *John Cornford: A Memoir* (Borderline Press, Fife, 1978, first published 1938)

Spender, Stephen, and John Lehmann (eds) *Poems for Spain* (Hogarth Press, London, 1939)

Squires, Mike *The Aid to Spain Movement in Battersea 1936-1939* (Elmfield Publications, London, 1994)

Stewart, Louis, H. *Changemakers: A Jungian Perspective on Sibling Position and the Family Atmosphere* (Routledge, London, 1992)

Stocks, Mary *Eleanor Rathbone: A Biography* (Victor Gollancz, London 1949)

Stradling, Robert *Cardiff and the Spanish Civil War* (Butetown History and Arts Centre, 1996)

Strong, Tracy B., and Helene Keyssar *Right in Her Soul: The Life of Anna Louise Strong* (Random House, New York, 1983)

Sulloway, Frank J. *Born to Rebel: Birth Order, Family Dynamics and Creative Lives* (Abacus, London, 1998. First published in Britain by Little, Brown and Co., 1996)

Summerfield, Penny *Reconstructing Women's Wartime Lives* (Manchester University Press, 1998)

Symonds, Julian *The 30s* (The Cresset Press, London, 1960)

Taylor, Barbara *Eve and the New Jerusalem: Socialism and Feminism in the Nineteenth Century* (Virago, London, 1983)

Taylor, R., and N. Young (eds) *British Peace Movements in the Twentieth Century* (Manchester University Press, 1987)

Thompson, Dorothy *The Chartists* (Temple Smith, London, 1984)

Thompson, Paul *The Voice of the Past* (Oxford University Press, 1988, first edition 1978)

Thomson, Alistair *Anzac Memories: Living with the Legend* (Oxford University Press, 1994)

Thwaites, Peter 'The Independent Labour Party Contingent in the Spanish Civil War', *Imperial War Museum Review*, no. 2. pp. 50-61

Todd, Nigel *In Excited Times: The People Against the Blackshirts* (Bewick Press, Newcastle upon Tyne, 1995)

Tonkin, Elizabeth *Narrating Our Past: The Social Construction of Oral History* (Cambridge University Press, 1992)

Usandizaga, Aránzazu (ed.) *Ve y cuenta lo que pasó en España: Mujeres extranjeras en la guerra civil: una antología* (Planeta, Barcelona, 2000)

Ventín Pereira, José Agusto *La Guerra de la radio (1936-1939)* (Editorial Mitre, Barcelona, 1986)

Vernon, Betty *Ellen Wilkinson* (Croom Helm, London, 1982)

Vicinus, Martha *Independent Women: Work and Community for Single Women 1850-1920* (University of Chicago Press, 1985)

Vilallonga, José Luis *La Cruda y Tierna Verdad: Memorias no Autorizadas* (Plaza & Janés, Barcelona, 2000)

Watkins, K. W. *Britain Divided: The Effect of the Spanish Civil War on British Political Opinion* (Thomas Nelson, London, 1963)

Watson, Don, and John Corcoran *The North East of England and the Spanish Civil War 1936-1939* (McGuffin Press, London, 1996)

Weinbren, Daniel *Generating Socialism: Recollections of Life in the Labour Party* (Sutton Publishing, Stroud, Gloucestershire, 1997)

Williams, Colin, Bill Alexander and John Gorman *Memorials of the Spanish Civil War* (Alan Sutton, Stroud, Gloucestershire, 1996)

Willis, Liz *Women in the Spanish Revolution* (Solidarity Pamphlet no. 40, October, 1975)

Winter, Jay *Sites of Memory, Sites of Mourning* (Cambridge University Press, 1995)

Winter, Jay, and Emmanuel Sivan (eds) *War and Remembrance in the Twentieth Century* (Cambridge University Press, 1999)

SECONDARY SOURCES: UNPUBLISHED

Graham, Helen 'The Spanish Civil War in Perspective 60 Years On' (Transcript of lecture at Staffordshire University, July 1996)

Herbert, Michael 'Anti-Fascism in Manchester 1932-1940' MA Thesis, Department of Economic History, Manchester Metropolitan University, 1996

Linehan, Thomas P. 'The British Union of Fascists in East London and SW Essex, 1932-1940', PhD Thesis, University of London, 1992

Mendlesohn, Farah 'Practising Peace: American and British Quaker Relief in the Spanish Civil War' (PhD Thesis, University of York, 1997)

Ockerstrom, Lolly 'The Other Narratives: British and American Women Writers and the Spanish Civil War', PhD Thesis, Department of English, Northeastern University, Boston, Massachusetts, June 1997

Rothstein, Kris ' "This is Where War Is", British Masculinity and the Spanish Civil War', (MA Dissertation, University of Essex, Department of Sociology, 1996)

Index

BOOKS BY ANGELA JACKSON

BRITISH WOMEN AND THE SPANISH CIVIL WAR
(Routledge/Cañada Blanch Centre for Contemporary Spanish Studies, London, 2002. Revised edition, Warren & Pell, Barcelona, 2009) Published in Spanish as *Las mujeres británicas y la Guerra Civil española* (University of Valencia, 2010).

BEYOND THE BATTLEFIELD: Testimony, Memory and Remembrance of a Cave Hospital in the Spanish Civil War
(Warren & Pell, Abersychan, 2005). Published in Catalan as *Més enllà del camp de batalla: Testimoni, memòria i record d'una cova hospital en la Guerra Civil espanyola* (Cossetània Edicions, Valls, 2004).

WARM EARTH (Pegasus, Cambridge, 2007)

AT THE MARGINS OF MAYHEM: Prologue and Epilogue to the Last Great Battle of the Spanish Civil War
(Warren & Pell, Abersychan, 2008). Published in Catalan as *Els brigadistes entre nosaltres: Pròleg i epíleg a l'última gran batalla de la Guerra Civil espanyola* (Cossetània Edicions, Valls, 2004).

PRELUDE TO THE LAST BATTLE: The International Brigades in the Priorat 1938/Preludi de l'última batalla 1938
(Bilingual edition, Cossetània Edicions, Valls, 2004).

ANTIFASCISTAS: British and Irish Volunteers in the Spanish Civil War
(with Richard Baxell and Jim Jump, Lawrence & Wishart, London, 2010). Published in Spanish as *Voluntarios Británicas e Irlandeses en la Guerra Civil Española* (Pamiela, Arre, and Editorial Piedra de Rayo S.L., Logroño, 2016).

'FOR US IT WAS HEAVEN': The Passion Grief and Fortitude of Patience Darton from the Spanish Civil War to Mao's China
(Sussex Academic Press, Brighton/Cañada Blanch Centre for Contemporary Spanish Studies, London, 2012). Published in Spanish as *Para nosotros era el cielo. Pasión, dolor y fortaleza de Patience Darton: de la guerra civil española a la China de Mao* (Ediciones San Juan de Dios, Barcelona, 2012).

Foreword and Afterword to *FIRING A SHOT FOR FREEDOM: The Memoirs of Frida Stewart* (The Clapton Press, London, 2020).

ALSO FROM THE CLAPTON PRESS

**FIRING A SHOT FOR FREEDOM: The Memoirs of Frida Stewart
with a foreword and afterword by Angela Jackson**
Frida Stewart was a graduate of the Royal College of Music who
became involved with Aid for Spain during the Civil War and ended
up driving an ambulance out to Murcia. She went on to Madrid
where she worked for the Republican Press Office, visiting the front
and "firing a shot for freedom". She was later in France when the
Nazis invaded and was imprisoned in an internment camp, from
which she escaped with a friend. This is her story, described by Paul
Preston as "an utterly riveting and deeply moving memoir . . ."

BOADILLA by Esmond Romilly
The nephew that Winston Churchill disowned describes his experi-
ences fighting with the International Brigade in the Battle of Madrid.
Written on his honeymoon in St. Jean de Luz after he eloped with
Jessica Mitford.

MY HOUSE IN MALAGA by Sir Peter Chalmers Mitchell
While most ex-pats fled to Gibraltar in 1936, Sir Peter stayed on to
protect his house and servants from the fascists. He ended up in
prison for sheltering Arthur Koestler from Franco's rabid head of
propaganda, who had threatened to "shoot him like a dog".

SPANISH PORTRAIT by Elizabeth Lake
A brutally honest, semi-autobiographical novel set in San Sebastian
and Madrid between 1934 and 1936, portraying a frantic love affair
against a background of apprehension and confusion as Spain drift-
ed inexorably towards civil war.

SOME STILL LIVE by F.G. Tinker Jr.
Frank G. Tinker was a US pilot who signed up with the Republican
forces because he didn't like Mussolini. He was also attracted by the
prospect of adventure and a generous pay cheque. This is an account
of his experiences in Spain.

The Clapton Press

Lightning Source UK Ltd.
Milton Keynes UK
UKHW020852100821
388622UK00013B/917